The Praeger Handbook of Education and Psychology

Volume 4

Edited by JOE L. KINCHELOE AND
RAYMOND A. HORN Jr.

Shirley R. Steinberg, *Associate Editor*

Westport, Connecticut
London

Library of Congress Cataloging-in-Publication Data

The Praeger handbook of education and psychology / edited by Joe L. Kincheloe and
Raymond A. Horn Jr.
    v. cm.
    Includes bibliographical references and index.
    ISBN 0–313–33122–7 (set : alk. paper)—ISBN 0–313–33123–5 (vol 1 : alk. paper)—
    ISBN 0–313–33124–3 (vol 2 : alk. paper)—ISBN 0–313–34056–0 (vol 3 : alk. paper)—
    ISBN 0–313–34057–9 (vol 4 : alk. paper)   1. Educational psychology—Handbooks, manuals, etc.
    I. Kincheloe, Joe L. II. Horn, R. A. (Raymond A.)
  LB1051.P635   2007
  371.4–dc22   2006031061

British Library Cataloguing in Publication Data is available.

Library of Congress Catalog Card Number: 2006031061
ISBN: 0–313–33122–7 (set)
      0–313–33123–5 (vol. 1)
      0–313–33124–3 (vol. 2)
      0–313–34056–0 (vol. 3)
      0–313–34057–9 (vol. 4)

First published in 2007

Praeger Publishers, 88 Post Road West, Westport, CT 06881
An imprint of Greenwood Publishing Group, Inc.
www.praeger.com

Printed in the United States of America

The paper used in this book complies with the
Permanent Paper Standard issued by the National
Information Standards Organization (Z39.48–1984).

10 9 8 7 6 5 4 3 2 1

Contents

VOLUME 2

PART III   ISSUES IN EDUCATION AND PSYCHOLOGY

Constructivism

Creativity

Criticality

Culture/Cultural Studies

Developmentalism

VOLUME 4

Situated Cognition

Teaching

CHAPTER 83

Situated Cognition and Beyond: Martin Heidegger on Transformations in Being and Identity

DAVID HUNG, JEANETTE BOPRY, CHEE-KIT LOOI,
AND THIAM SENG KOH

With growing attention being paid to situated cognition—where context and cognition are deemed inseparable and interwoven—there has also been increased interest in Martin Heidegger's work, even if only on a small scale. It is the intent of this manuscript to reconsider Heidegger's *Being and Time*, in particular the concepts of *Dasein*, *worldhood*, and *understanding* in relationship to situated views on learning, cognition, and identity. Recent works in situated cognition point toward learning as an appropriation of "ways of seeing meaning"—related to identity formation of the individual within a social community. In terms of learning, researchers are now distinguishing between learning *about* and learning *to be*. Learning *to be* (or just being) forms the essence of identity formation. Whereas most learning in schools relates to learning *about* subject-knowledge domains such as Mathematics, Science, Literature, and other disciplines, in learning *to be*—such as in becoming a member of a community of practice—an individual develops a social identity. The identity under development shapes what that person comes to know. Fundamentally, educational psychology is understood as an account of change in learning and behavior, and our aim in this chapter is to bring consistency of such a change in relation to situated cognition.

Identity creation is a transformation process, a metamorphosis. Identities are shaped through local interactions in which individuals confirm or disconfirm each others' state of identity. In this sense, identity is always mutually constitutive, and reconstituted through local interactions within the community. Knowledge cannot be detached from the knower, it has no independent existence; it is part and parcel of the identity of the individual.

SITUATED COGNITION

Martin Heidegger's work provides a theoretical foundation for recent formulations in situated cognition. According to William Clancey, there are three aspects of situatedness: social function which regulates behavior (meaning of action), the structural mechanism which is concerned with the physical coordination of perception, conception and action (the internal mechanism), and the behavioral content which relates cognition to spatial-temporal settings (local feedback and time-sensitve nature of action in place). These aspects of situated cognition emphasize the contextual dimensions of knowing where meanings are inseparable from relations among situations and actions. In other words, meanings are perceived as inseparable from interpretation, and knowledge is linked to the relations of which it is a product. Knowledge is fundamentally co-specified by the mind and world which, like a woof and warp, need each other to complete an otherwise incoherent pattern. It is impossible to capture the densely interwoven nature of conceptual knowledge completely in explicit, abstract accounts, which Clancey calls descriptions. The situated cognition perspective as advocated does not deal primarily with the relationship between entities as distinct and separate, instead, it considers the system—context, persons, culture, language, intersubjectivity—as a whole coexisting and jointly defining the construction of meanings. The whole is not composed as separate entities but is a confluence of inseparable factors that depend on one another for their very definition and meaning. John Dewey expressed the view that knowledge is not just a mental state; rather, it is an experienced relation of things where no meaning exist outside of such relations. According to such a perspective, the mind incorporates person-environment interaction, where activity involves a transaction between person and environment that changes both. In this sense, learning means being woven into the perceived fabric of life as authentic activity. For Martin Heidegger (elaborated in the next section), existence and interpretation are the same thing, thus making interpretation key to all three aspects of situatedness. Existence and interpretation are essentially the same thing because human-kind cannot be divorced from interpretation. From a post-modern perspective, all "realities" are interpretations.

Situated cognition research signals a shift from the study of how we process representations to how representations are created and given meaning. An essential idea is that this process is perceptual and inherently dialectic. As representations emerge from the interaction of mental processes with the environment, they are not the stuff of mental processing. Each time we create these representations, we are engaged in an act of perceiving and reconstructing; we are interpreting. Categorizations of things in the world are not retrieved descriptions, but created anew each time. Mental organizations do not merely create activity like stored programs (as in AI research), but are created in the course of the activity, always as new, living structures. In other words, situated cognition researchers hypothesize that we do not have an internal memory of representations, but a process memory, that is, a memory for reconstructing events and words. As a product of interaction with the environment (sensory, gestural, and interpersonal) and not a fixed substrate from which behavior is generated, representations cannot correspond to an external, objective reality. In addition, representations may themselves be interpreted interactively, in successive cycles of perceiving and acting Instead of an objectivist worldview where the aim is to arrive at the one singular "truth," the situated view is a relational perspective where knowing is a social process of continually seeking for explanations of holistic phenomena and yet preserving an awareness of the inadequacy of any unified conclusion.

Theoretical foundations for situated cognition can be provided by the writings of Martin Heidegger, in particular, his emphasis on the nondualistic nature of mind and body, or the unity of mind and external reality. Situated cognition emphasizes the relativist in situ emergence of meanings arising from persons-and-context as a unity rather than as a duality—person and context. In the sections below, we discuss the writings of Martin Heidegger with emphasis on his masterwork, Being and Time and how his views ground a relativist stance by focusing on the transformations in individual identity or Being as a basis for educational psychology.

DASEIN, WORLDHOOD, AND UNDERSTANDING

A great deal of dispute has focused on the person and thought of the philosophy of Martin Heidegger. There is considerable debate about the extent of difference between the thought of the early and the late Heidegger. We do know that Heidegger's major work, *Being and Time*, was dedicated to Husserl who is associated with phenomenology. Heidegger's thought is complex, and any attempt to convey it in brief fashion must necessarily produce distortion. In this paper, we confine our discussion to the notion of *Dasein* and the more general concept of *Being*.

Heidegger begins *Being and Time* with the question of Being, or of what it is to Be (*Sein*). "To Be" here is similar to the notion of learning *to be*. More specifically, it is an inquiry into the meaning of Being (*Sinn von Sein*). From Heidegger's perspective, Being cannot be defined because Being is not an *entity*. Various translators and commentators have translated this term *Being* as "being-there" (the literal meaning), "being-here," or some variation thereof. In one sense, we could almost render *Dasein* as "human being," since it is a way of understanding our human existence, and thus derivatively, of understanding being in general. Here Heidegger reverses the common tendency to understand Being, or even the being of humans, from an understanding of the being of specific objects. In fact, *Dasein* rejects the distinction of object and subject, even in the Kierkegaardian form that stresses subjectivity. Heidegger says, *Dasein* is not only close to us, we *are* it, each of us, we ourselves.

Dasein and Worldhood

Dasein is important because it is through it that we know the world. As our knowing of the world is mediated by it, its presence must be acknowledged. *Dasein* must be understood in light of Heidegger's conception of the world, for it is very wrapped up with the human relationship to the world. We cannot conceive of *Dasein* apart from the world. He says that modes of *Dasein* or Being "must be seen and understood *a priori* as grounded upon that state of *Being* which we have called '*Being-in-the-world*'." By being in the world, however, Heidegger does not mean *in* as a spatial location, the way knowledge is in the mind (as a container) or water is in a cup. Rather, it means something like "being associated with" or "being familiar with." *Dasein* and the world are not two entities that could be conceived of as existing side by side: "Being-in is not a "property" which *Dasein* sometimes has and sometimes does not have. The relationship toward the world is possible only because *Dasein*, as Being-in-the-world, is as it is." *Being* can only be understood in context and in relation with the world. This relationship between *Being* and *World* is intertwined, and although Being can be phenomenologically perceived separately from World, being exists or takes meaning only in relation to the world. Although Being is here interposed with context-world, Being is recognized as an individual distinctive identity as transformed in the process of Being-in-the-world. Being can also be understood in the context of educational psychology as the individual learning-in-the-world.

In other words, *Dasein* is a relationship, a quality of the way we are related to the world. The world here is being understood as our environment, that in which we are found. The German *Umwelt* (world) carries the idea of the "the world around." [Umwelt is more like a species-specific niche] *Dasein* then is a way of being so related to the world that its contents are not merely objects, separate from us with their own independent identities, but objects only in relation to us. Objects may be regarded either as *vorhanden* or as *zuhanden*, perhaps best rendered as "present at hand" and "ready to hand." In seeing objects as present at hand, we are thinking of them in terms of their discernible qualities or attributes, which may be examined, analyzed, classified, and the like. This, however, says Heidegger, is not the primordial way of relating to them, which would be ready to hand. "Present at hand" is a derived or secondary way of reflecting on them. We thus cannot conceive of *Dasein* apart from World, because it is prior to any separation of self from world in the objective or cognitive sense. World is *given* along with *Dasein* prior to any act of conceptualizing. Indeed, all conceptualizing takes place in terms of World, which is prior to it.

The primordial way of treating an object such as a hammer as "ready to hand," is in terms of using it to drive nails or pound on other objects. This ready-to-hand character cannot be grasped theoretically. It demands that account be taken of what Heidegger calls the *towards-which* (*das*

Wozu) of equipment. For example, the shoe that is to be produced is for wearing, the clock is for telling the time, and so on. Heidegger is quite clear about this priority: "The kind of dealing which is closest to us is . . . not a bare perceptual cognition, but rather that kind of concern which manipulates things and puts them to use." As this pragmatic orientation is so immediate, we may tend to overlook it. If, however, the hammer were to break, we would become very conscious of the importance of the "ready to hand" dimension.

In a way that almost seems to recall parallel observations in Wittgenstein, Heidegger admits that our relationship of practical concern toward a thing may escape our awareness or notice because of its very familiarity and everyday character. For example, we may take for granted the significance of a hammer as a piece of practical equipment that is "ready-to-hand," that when we consciously consider it we look at it "objectively." But as soon as the hammer becomes broken, we see all too clearly what "hammer" really means to us as something ready-to-hand. More especially, "when something ready-to-hand is found missing, though its everyday presence (*Zugegensein*) has been so obvious that we have never taken any notice of it, this makes a *break* in those referential emptiness, and now sees for the first time *what* the missing article was ready-to-hand *with*, and what it was ready-to-hand *for*."

Dasein is thrown into the world in that Dasein is "always ready" in a specific situation that determines the possibilities that are available to it, with the mood or "state of mind" that reveals its throwness. Dasein is "thrown possibility, through and through." Such a notion of *Being* and the situated-ness of being thrown-into-the-world are central to situated cognition. In this sense, learning translates into Being (that is, the whole person as a character or identity) and Being is thrown into actions in the world until "breakdowns" occur of which reflection is then interposed. In this sense, the world that is before us is the current world authentically ready-to-hand (soon to be realized) or present-at-hand (already realized as current). In Heidegger's view the world is an environment (*Umwelt*) to which man has a practical relationship of concern.

If Dasein is our way of being in the world, then our understanding of the world is through and constrained by Daisen. Thus, to be situated means to be situated within Daisen or our within our experience of the world. Situated cognition must be considered as experiential. When we say cognition is situated, we mean that it is situated in the flow of experience that comprises Being.

Understanding and Interpretation

As understanding is *a priori*, Heidegger views it as prior to cognition. This is because understanding is rooted in possibility, in Dasein's ability-to-be or "potentially-for-Being" (*Seinkonnen*). Dasein *has* possibilities before it *knows* possibilities. Understanding projects Dasein's Being both upon its "for-the-sake- of-which" and upon significance, as the worldhood of its current world. At the deepest level, understanding involves not seeing actual objects or situations so much as seeing the possible use, possible contexts, and possible ways of service. We return to the notion of "potentially-for-Being" (*Seinkonnen*). Congruent to Wittgenstein's thought in his later writings, it is forms of life and "life" which determines meaning and potentials for subsequent understanding. It is life which determines logical grammar, and not the other way around.

Interpretation, to Heidegger, is working out the possibilities *projected* in understanding. The interpretative function of understanding is not some "additional something" which is different from understanding itself, but rather an explication or elucidation of it. Understanding operates through a projection of possibilities; interpretation constitutes a working out of this projection, which makes explicit what was already given through human awareness. What is explicitly understood "has the structure of *something as something*." We "see" something as a table, a door, or a bridge. This relates closely to what has been said earlier about "in order to" (*Um-zu*) or "for the sake of what" (*Worumwillen*). We see a pen for the purpose of writing and communicating; or see a key for the purpose of locking and unlocking. This is connected with the fact that meaning is not just a property attached to objects, but is grounded in human life and attitudes. The situation provides the context and richness for projecting possibilities and understanding the world.

We are also reminded of Wittgenstein's thoughts that only in the stream of thought and life do words have meaning, and that each use of language occurs within a separate and apparently self-contained system complete with its own rules. In this sense our use of language is similar to playing a game. We require an awareness of the operative rules and significance of the terms within the context of the purpose for which we are using language. Each use of language constitutes a separate "language game," and the various games have little to do with one another. Interpretation, in other words, is projected in the everyday contexts through which understanding arises. The characterization of language as a "game" presumes that language is not a private phenomenon, arising when an individual mind grasps a truth or fact about the world and then expresses it, but rather that language is a social phenomenon, acquiring its meaning in social interaction.

SITUATED COGNITION AND BEYOND

From the writings of Martin Heidegger we discuss its relevance and contributions for situated cognition, but more importantly, we highlight dimensions which perhaps can be further explored in the field of situated cognition and beyond. As a precursor, we highlight that the original conceptions of situated cognition are very much aligned to Heidegger's works but we recognized that subsequent poliferations began to misunderstand the epistemologies underpinning situated cognition. The two fundamental epistemologies of situated cognition are: (1) the nondualistic and relativist stance between mind and the world; and (2) the in situ or emerging nature of cognition. The fundamental nondualistic stance is strongly mooted in Heidegger's integration of existence and interpretation as essentially being the same. Furthermore, Heidegger stresses the dimension of "throwness" and "being in the world" as in situ emerging phenomena from Dasein's point of view until breakdowns occur. Dasein is simply thrown into actions and mind and worldhood is a unity. In this sense, context and cognition are interwoven as depicted by purposeful activities. Within purposeful activities, signs are "ready-to-hand" in "our everyday dealings;" they are produced for "various purposes," which relate to human purposes. The "indicating" of a sign is not the "property" of an "entity;" but occurs as the "toward-which" (*das Wozu*) of a serviceability and the "for-which" (*das Wofur*) of a usability. This issue of "purposefulness" can be further elaborated within situated cognition as the role of descriptions and reflections of actions are not well articulated within literature in situated cognition. Descriptions and reflections arise out of possible breakdowns in cognition and activity and these are brought into the open through language and representations. Dasein works with these articulated or explicit descriptions as signs to further in situ phenomena from his or her perspective. In the notion of "purpose" in practical-meaning usage, meaning is that *from* which something is understandable as the thing that it is. Meaning is the "upon-which" of a projection in terms of which something becomes intelligible as something, it gets its structure from a foresight and a fore-conception. The use of metaphors in order to explain, interpret, or understand a phenomena is along the same vein of thinking, where one metaphorical idea is used as an "upon which" projection onto another. To reiterate, situated cognition does not adequately account for this projection of meaning in situated and emerging actions.

The concept of "purposiveness" also emphasizes meaning, intention, and experiential processes, and an active organism that exhibits thought, emotion, volition (agency, and control) over its functioning. Purposive behavior consists of integrated acts associated with physical and social environments, with change and process being central features of the whole—a spatial and temporal confluence of people, settings, and activities that constitutes a complex organized unity.

However, the organism is the one that undergoes emerging change in identity, Being, or Dasein. There are no separate actors in an event; instead, there are acting relationships, such that the actions of one person can only be described and understood in relation to the actions of other persons, and in relation to the situational and temporal circumstances in which the actors are involved. The situated cognition perspective as advocated does not deal primarily with the relationship between entities as distinct, instead, it considers the system—context, persons, culture, language, intersubjectivity—as a whole coexisting and jointly defining the construction of meanings. The whole is not composed as separate entities but is a confluence of inseparable factors that depend on one another for their very definition and meaning. In other words, situated cognition points toward defining things which emerge from within the processes of acting and inquiry. However, where situated cognition needs to continue to define is how the human organism restructures or reorganizes itself in purposive behavior with regards to agency, self-regulatory behaviors, and control. In other words, how would an organism or organisms within the social context undergo continuous transformations in embodied thinking, emotion, and volition. In contrast with the distributed view of situated cognition, cognition is embodied *only* in the operation of the living systems interacting with the artifacts around them.

The notions of Heidegger and situated cognition compel us to consider the life-community as the meaningful contexts for learning and thinking. Similar to Heidegger's thought of "being-in-the-world," Polanyi observes that the primitive sentiments of sharing values, experiences, and joint activities in the community are *prior* to formal articulation—that is, reflection. By fully participating in a "ritual," the members of a group affirm the community of their existence, and at the same time identify the life of their group with that of antecedent groups, from whom the ritual has descended to them. The assimilation of great systems of articulate lore by novices of various grades is made possible by a *previous act of affiliation*. Hence, identity is formed within the individual but co-constructed with other members of a community. This implies that each community has a set of beliefs, values, and "way of seeing" which characterize the members.

The view of situated cognition has yet to account for an intricate balance between the social and contextual dimensions of cognition and the individual *transformations* in knowing, understanding, and identity. Such a basis for individual transformation forms the premise for educational psychology and theories of situated cognition in relation to learning. Clancey refers to this as using a "both/and" logic rather than an "either/or" logic. Besides transformations at the cognitive level, we need to recognize transformations at the personal-emotive level and also at the level through which actions and decisions are meted out. Being or identity is complex and it involves the entire psyche of the individual in relation to the social-cultural and environmental levels. The identity perspective from Heidegger helps us to move away from behaviorist critiques of situated cognition as doing and responding without reflection.

On the aspect of situatedness concerning the structural mechanism for coordination, the interpretation of meanings is based on the authenticity of purpose. Congruent with recent notions of how learning ought to be authentic in meaning interpretation, Heidegger's work reminds us to project meanings for purposefulness and to challenge them to see potentials for applications and contexts. Not only is meaning personal for *Dasein* or Being, meaning should also be negotiated with others in the community. Who we are (our identity) at a particular instance of our history and the medium (situated context in the world) we are in mutually specify each other, contributing to creating the world of the next instant, and so on, creating the world by living in it. It means that learning is a reciprocal dynamic process in which structural changes occurring in one (that is living system or environment) trigger changes in the other. In other words, we are always learning as we experience being-in-the-world. Problems which stimulate the intelligence of the learner grow out of conditions of the present experiences; but these problems should be catalysts which arouses the interests for an active quest for yet unanswered questions of the future. According to John Dewey, new facts and ideas become the ground for further experiences in which new problems are presented. The process is a continuous spiral. In this regard, all of the central concepts of learning, thinking, and identity are to be conceived in active and relational terms rather than in terms of static objectivist matching and representations. Meaning constructions are purpose-driven according to relational contexts and thus constantly fluid, albeit relatively fixed patterns of phenomena observed across similar situations. Mind and body are perceived as an aspect of person-environment interaction, where activity involves a transaction or interaction between person and environment that changes both.

On the aspect of situatedness relating cognition to spatial-temporal settings, human beings are thrust into the world with tools and material objects as "ready-at-hand" until breakdown occurs. A hammer is used for the purpose of hammering until it fails to achieve its purpose. At such a stage, reflection as a process to reconsider the purposes for which an object is to us is usually necessary. Current work in situated cognition can emphasize the role of reflection, abstraction of meanings, and how as humans we are able to engage in metacognitive thought where language and thinking are central. Identity can be modified through reflection in the context of prior situated understanding. However, the field of situated cognition needs a balance between meanings as always situated and when interpretations have value for transfer across contexts resultant from reflection. Meanings are implicit and embedded into the forms of life, as Wittgenstein explains, and usually made explicit only through reflection and secondary orders of perception. Meaning is personal at the phenomenal level when one is engaged and absorbed in the situation. It can become more explicit when one starts to move away from the situatedness, and can be shared as one articulates at the description level.

Situated cognition implies learning "to be" as contextualized. For example, one learns to be a scientist in the context of the scientific practice and in the process appropriates the "ways of seeing" meanings within that practice. In this sense, identity is context dependent such as the community of practice being an important instance of a rich situated context. From Heidegger's view point, identity as *Being* is thrown into the real world and not necessarily constrained to a limited community. In other words, *Being* should be cast from the perspective of Being *in general* rather than Being within a *situated context*. In other words, Being can transcend a situated context into a generalized Worldhood. Although Being is purpose-driven, Being or identity can be cast from the perspective of identity as a "process-journey" unfolding in situ (as Being is continually being transformed through each experience) according to broad rather than narrow prescriptive conceptions of purpose. Here purpose is generalized to actions in the world rather than specific situations. In other words, when identity is formed within individuals, such a state is contextless rather than bound to specific contexts. From a situated cognition perspective, knowledge and information is contextually bound, whereas we argue from Heidegger's viewpoint that identity is presented as context-free, or more accurately, identity is bound to Worldhood as the largest possible context. In other words, within Worldhood, identity is transferable across contexts. If we think of situatedness as a continuum, then Worldhood lies at one end of the extremes—the unsituated end. This provides us with a framework for rephrasing the problem of transfer of learning across different contexts as one that is less relevant. Instead, learning involves the ability to generate appropriate states of the living organisms on demand. These states form part of our identity, and it is identity that we carry with us from one context to another.

CONCLUSION

A consistent framework in needed in situated cognition and beyond to account for embodied cognition within the individual Dasein or Being since the organism emerges in situ through personal experience in the context of worldhood. On the other hand, situated cognition needs to account for purposeiveness and breakdowns with regards to reflections and descriptions of these interpretations. The organism needs to also observe phenomena and "metacogite" on reflections and descriptions made by Dasein at the social level. A consistent framework needs to be developed at the social to individual levels.

Summing up the process of learning and identity, we conclude by emphasizing that learners (or *Dasein*) commonly begin with certain naïve, "romantic" conceptions (and beliefs) of the situated world and move through an incredible deconstruction and transformation of their identities and arrive at more accurate and mature worldviews through an ongoing, dialectic cycle—knowing that theories and principles are the product of human construction, imagination, insight, and experience. This understanding begins at the phenomenal level and provides the basis for human knowing at a tacit level which may transform into more explicit understanding at the description level. Such a transformation in identity implies a metamorphosis in different levels of Being—thought, emotion, and volition. Such a transformation is dialectical in that social levels of *Dasein* are also metamorphosized.

The problem posed by situated cognition for educational psychology is that field needs to move toward a transactional worldview; away from "what is stored in the brain" to "what forms of interactions are possible." Intelligence can not be seen as a trait as much as an ability to join and create worlds of understanding. Clancey, for example, supports a move toward ecological psychology (beyond situated cognition) to accomplish this goal. The important question stops being "what is happening in the brain?" and becomes "what are the transactional functions of the capabilities of an organism (with a brain) in its everyday life within a specific niche (both cultural and physical)?" Ecolgical psychology requires us to understand systems of which we are a part: systems upon which we have an impact even as it has an impact upon us. Important contributors to ecological psychology include Gregory Bateson, Heinz Von Foerster, Humberto Maturana, and James J. Gibson, although the work of the last requires some reformulation to work well with situated cognition as explicated by Clancey. Situated cognition demands that we take a total-system view, that we consider mental processes as constructors of order rather than containers of information.

Situated cognition and ecological psychology are proposed as alternatives for reconceptualizing educational psychology—a relational stance between persons-and-context where the emphasis may not be only in persons or context but in the dialectical interactions between both entities. Heidegger's views provide a theory of learning which does not deal simply with descriptive theories of knowledge acquisition, but provides insights into how learning occurs as situated within the individual in dynamic interrelationships to the context.

FURTHER READING

Clancey, W. (1997). *Situated Cognition*. Cambridge: Cambridge University Press.
Heidegger, M. (1962). *Being and Time*. Oxford: Blackwell.
Polanyi, M. (1964). *Personal Knowledge: Towards a Post-Critical Philosophy*. New York: Harper & Row.
Wittgenstein, L. (1958). *Philosophical Investigations*. Cambridge: Basil Blackwell.

CHAPTER 84

Situating Situated Cognition

WOLFF-MICHAEL ROTH

During the 1990s, it has become fashionable to talk about knowing and learning in terms of distributed cognition, embodied cognition, and situated cognition. All of these terms imply that knowing (etymologically, knowing and cognition have the same origins) exceeds what can be found in the head. Like many others the reader may ask, "What do you mean, isn't all we know in our heads?" In this contribution, I articulate how and why we understand knowing as situated (which implies embodied and distributed) and what implications this has for education and psychology. Let me begin with the following two examples from my own experience.

Over the past fifteen years, I have become very familiar with my word processor. Many people in my surrounding know this and ask me questions about how to do this or that with the software. Sometimes I can provide them with an answer, but more often than not, I cannot articulate in so many words how I do it. However, as soon as I am sitting in front of a computer, I can show how to implement what the person wants to do, or walk him or her through over the telephone, both of us sitting in front of our machines. As another example, consider this. Several years ago, I wanted to call an old friend. At first, I tried to remember her number, but as hard as I tried, it did not come back. Then I was looking for it in different places, but could not find it. Eventually I gave up searching and trying to remember. For some reason, I picked up the phone: my hands began to move over the dial composing a number without looking at it. Through the receiver, I heard a combination of sounds that rang familiar. When I had finished dialing, I knew I had the right number even before I heard my old friend's voice on the other end.

In both of these instances, I failed remembering something and articulating it in words. In the first instance, it was a practice, a patterned way of doing something. In the second instance, it was a fact, something one can state in so many words. If I had taken a written test, such as those that are used in formal schooling, I would have failed, utterly so, in both instances. That is, my test responses would have been interpreted to mean that I did not know. Fortunately, I did not have to take a test; in fact, virtually all circumstances in which I operate on a daily basis and which show what "I" know have little to do with testing situations.

In both situations, I knew as soon as I was interacting with the computer and telephone, respectively. It was not that these items were just there but my knowing was in the interaction and anyone watching me would have observed it as such. More so, "my" knowing was in the interaction with the two devices. That is, whereas isolating me from my normal environments would have made me look dumb in both situations, operating the devices exhibited patterned ways of doing relevant activities and therefore exhibited knowing. This is what all three terms, embodied, distributed, and situated cognition are about. To understand the patterned actions that you could have seen observing me in the two situations cannot be explained by looking at my brain alone. My knowing cannot be understood by looking at my brain and the computer or telephone. Rather, to understand my patterned actions, you need to look at the interaction (or rather transaction) of Michael and computer (telephone), and at the structure characterizing the two entities involved (device, me). In fact, what is relevant is not the structure these devices have for everyone, but the objective way that they appeared to me in those situations.

I remembered the telephone number but it was not through my conscious thoughts. Rather, I knew the number with my body, or rather, the knowing was exhibited in the patterned actions of my hands and fingers and in the apparently correct outcome of my dialing. Perhaps less evident but equally so, my knowing of how to do some formatting with my word processor is embodied. To articulate how to do something, I have to sit down, take the mouse and keyboard, whisk the cursor across pull-down windows, and select from the options that appear. I know that I know when I am there, and I do not have to memorize any of it. Memorizing is prohibitive, and does not guarantee success to some beginner with the software.

The terms embodied, distributed, and situated cognition do not mean that there is nothing or little in the brain, or, as some critics facetiously said to me, a brain scattered across the environment. All three terms are intended to highlight that to understand knowing (and learning), we need to take into account more than some stuff that might be located in our minds, which we carry around, and which someone else can test us for at any moment. We need to look at a person in the setting. More so, we need to look at the person acting in the setting. But it is well known (e.g., just think of divergent testimonials of the "same" event in courts of law) that a setting does not appear to all persons in the same way. That is, to understand *why* a person is doing something, we need to understand "the person acting in the setting as it appears to him or her." Talk about situated cognition therefore means talk about the interactions of people with objects and tools rather than talk about what is in their brains. It is a choice that we make about how we look, and, therefore, we situate situated cognition.

What is being considered in analyzing some phenomenon is called a unit of analysis. Scholars who think about knowing and learning in terms of embodied, distributed, and situated cognition articulate their unit of analysis "the person acting in the setting as it appears to him or her" in different ways. Some prefer to speak of transacting, which implies that person and setting mutually constitute one another or, alternatively, that person and setting stand in a dialectical relationship. To express this in yet another way, dialectical means a chicken-and-egg type situation, where one automatically implies the other. That is, the setting always exists for the person, but there is no person without setting. Other scholars prefer to speak of a person acting in his or her lifeworld, where the latter term denotes the setting as it appears to the acting person.

AGENCY AND STRUCTURE

Situated cognition can be understood within a framework of agency and structure when these terms are thought dialectically, as two sides of the same coin. First, agency denotes the capacity to act. It is immediately clear that there is no agency without structure: Humans, like all beings, need a material body to act and thereby to display knowing. Structure is everywhere. It is self-evident to most that our bodies are structured and so is the world in which we live. Most people attend less to the fact that our ways of seeing, hearing, feeling, moving, and doing things are structured, too. When we speak to someone, we hear words not inchoate sounds; furthermore, when we hear barking rather than a noise, we hear a dog barking rather than another animal. We see trucks as trucks, cars as cars, and wheelchairs as wheelchairs. We do not confuse one type of thing for another.

Second, there is no structure without agency. We cannot experience space, time, dogs, trucks, cars, or wheelchairs without having acted in a world of things and people. How do we come to see the world in a structured way?

A number of classical studies exemplify the inseparability of knowing and action. In one study, kittens were initially raised in the dark and experienced light only under controlled conditions. Each kitten from one experimental group was allowed to move around normally, but was harnessed to a carriage that contained a second, matched kitten from the second group. Both groups of animals therefore shared the same visual experience. However, the first group of animals was active, the second group was physically passive. After a few weeks, the kittens were released. Members of the first group behaved normally. Members of the second group behaved as if they were blind: they bumped into objects and fell over edges. The scientists then sacrificed the animals and looked at the brain and found that there was ten times the development in the active kittens than it was in the passive kittens. We can conclude that experiences cause brain growth, but one must actively participate in the experiences for growth to take place. That is, agency leads to structure, both in the world (a kittens recognizes a *material edge* as an edge) and in brains (kittens recognize a material edge as *edge*). The first in each couplet is the material part of the dialectic, the second is an aspect of the brain—researchers have come to talk about these patterns as schemas.

In a similar vein, the philosopher Maurice Merleau-Ponty suggested many years ago—something recent neuroscientific research verified—that everything we know about the world is the result of our moving around in and interacting with it. Thus, we do not see the roundness of a ball, but in seeing a ball partially, that is, from one side, we know what we will see when we walk around it, turn our head, or move our eyes from left to right. We also know what we would feel if we were to touch it, and how this feeling would change if we were to move our hands over the ball. Remember my knowledge of the word processor? It is not my knowledge per se that counts but my knowing what will happen if I move about within it, constrained and enabled by its structures as these are given to me.

The example with the kittens shows us something else. Structures are not only nonidentical partners with agency, but also are dialectical themselves in the sense that they always exist simultaneously as objectively experienced structures in the world and as (mental) schemas. The structures in the world are not only material, but also social. These structures in the world are resources for actions. We therefore speak of them as sociomaterial resources. These resources both enable and constrain what humans want to do.

To see how all of this plays out when we observe real human beings while going about their business, I provide the following example from a seventh-grade science course that I had taught many years ago. In analyzing the episode, I exemplify the situated (embodied, distributed) nature of cognition by showing (a) how hand gestures, body movement, pitch, and orientation are used to coordinate conversations and (b) how hand gestures present ideas not concurrently expressed in words and animate static structures perceptually available to other participants.

DESIGNING THE "ELEVATOR THING"

In this science course, students learned about the physics of simple machines largely by designing machines themselves, including the entire process from initial conception to the completion of a prototype. The following episode was recorded while the students designed something like a Rube Goldberg machine, a device that consists of several interacting elements and brings about

Figure 84.1
The three girls are focusing on this sketch of a Rube Goldberg machine, deliberating how to implement the "elevator thing" on the left side of the drawing, which they intend to move a ball to the top of the tower, from where it begins its journey to launch a few processes

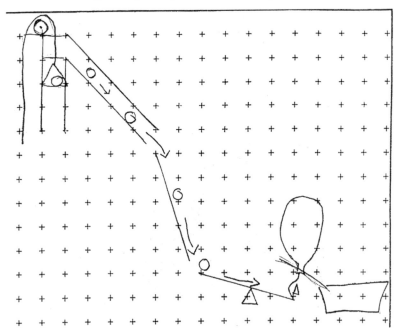

a desired event only after having completed a number of intervening processes. The three girls (Amanda, Bella, and Leanne) in the episode had decided to make a food dispenser, in which a ball is moved in an elevator up to the top of a tower, then first rolls down a chute onto an inclined plane, and then falls onto and tips a balance. The nail on the other side of the balance pokes a balloon, which, upon exploding, releases the food for the cat that was stored inside it (Figure 84.1). I begin by providing a gloss of the conversation and then move on to show different aspects of situated cognition in action.

The episode was recorded just when the three girls were deliberating how to go about building what they called the "elevator thing" on the far left of their design sketch (Figure 84.1). Leanne was just finishing to articulate their next steps by pointing to the elevator and saying that they had to build this part for which she had brought wood (line 01). She finished by uttering a little drawn out "So:?," which ended in a rising pitch as if she was asking, "Do we start?" or "How do we start?" There was a pause, which in fact constituted an opportunity (resource) for another person to take a turn at talking. Here, Bella began to articulate, which turned out to become an alternative to Leanne's proposal of building the elevator from scratch.[1]

01 Leanne:	I have wood over there to build it. So:?
02	(0.79)
03 Bella:	*[Figure 84.2a] Or (0.40)]
	((her hand moves forward to Figure 84.2b))
04	*[Figure 84.2b] [my brother *[Figure 84.2c] (0.22)
05 Amanda:	°Uh um°.

Figure 84.2
Moving her right hand forward toward the design, Bella (left) indicates intention to take the turn at talk; by withdrawing her left hand from the design, Leanne (right) indicates willingness to relinquish her turn at talk. Amanda (center) exhibits attention to the current speaker, which she makes visible to the others by adjusting her gaze direction

```
                ((Erects body, orients gaze))
06              [(1.55)
                ((rH moves to scratch herself ))
07 Bella:       he [has a parking lot
                ((rH returns to drawing, stops at tower part))
08              (0.90)
09              um: (0.20) you can take this part out (0.32)]
                ((repeatedly moves up and down along tower
                ((Amanda turns gaze to diagram))
10              then you pull like *[Figure 84.3a] this [*[Figure 84.3b)
                ((hand moves to top, then toward the bottom of tower part))
11              (0.45)
12              ((Bella's hand retracts to Figure 84.4a, up to Figure 84.4b))
                and then put some batteries in it]] and it works.
                ((hand rocks back and forth))
13 Leanne:      ((nods repeatedly))
```

Bella began to speak, and over the next 11.7 seconds, produced the idea that they could take a part out of her brother's parking lot (lines 04, 07). She did not specify which part, she wanted to take out, but pointed to what Leanne elsewhere called "the elevator part," allowing us to infer that she meant the lift. Bella then said that they would pull on it in some way (line 10), while moving her hand along the tower part (Figure 84.3). Finally, she proposed to put some batteries in it (presumably the lift), while making a repeated gesture with her right hand as if she was putting a battery in a horizontal battery receptacle (Figure 84.4).

With the "Or" (line 03) Bella announced an alternative to what Leanne had just proposed. It was a contrast to what has been proposed before, when Leanne had asked for the materials. Bella was responsible for bringing a pulley, and this responsibility was inscribed into the diagram, at the bottom, where they noted the materials needed and who was supposed to bring them. Subsequently, Bella admitted that she did not bring a pulley or even have one. The two other girls talked about the chute, the pipe-shaped part leading away from the top of the tower. The "or" sets up a difference, a contradiction with what they had done or were presently doing. In this episode, Bella then develops a different idea, it takes shape in her talk and action, but at the same time retains its ephemeral nature, for talk and gestures "vanish" as soon as they have been

Figure 84.3
Bella's iconic gesture animates the elevator, which expresses knowing in action that her speech does not make available to her peers

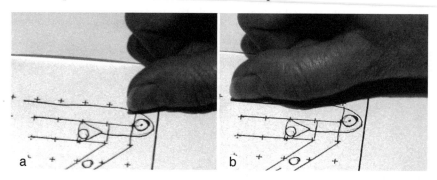

produced, they recede into the past, increasingly so, unless it is reproduced in subsequent actions and talk.

Although this episode may appear straightforward, it is rife with complexity and shows just how much human beings need to know to communicate about something, to take turns at talk, to understand what someone else is talking about even if they do not say it. Situated cognition researchers therefore might ask questions such as, "How did the girls know when to talk?," "How did they gain and maintain a turn at talk?," or "How did a speaker know that others were listening and being attentive?" Researchers may also ask, "How did participants know what a speaker was talking about?" The answers to all questions will involve the relation between the girls and their situation, both in its material and social aspects.

GAINING AND MAINTAINING TURNS AT TALK

When we talk, others normally listen. Changeovers occur when the current speaker has stopped, when there is a pause, so that someone else can begin speaking. Thus, the pause after Leanne had stopped speaking (line 02) allowed Bella to begin (line 03). Bella not only uttered "Or," but also moved her hand forward placing her finger on the tower part of the design. She thereby indicated in two ways that it was her turn: by beginning to speak and by moving her hand forward

Figure 84.4
After Bella stopped to point to the paper, Leanne raised her gaze, acknowledging listening (a–b). It also allowed her to see the gesture showing how the batteries were oriented (b–c). She acknowledged understanding by nodding (b–c)

toward the design (Figures 84.2a–b). Leanne acknowledged the change of turn by retracting her own hand, which had thus far rested on the tower part (Figures 84.2b–c). That is, even without having to think and say, "Oh, I am giving up my turn at talk," Leanne's change in body position articulates this situation.

By uttering "Or," Bella had announced an alternative design possibility, which means that others would normally wait until she had completed describing the possibility. But whenever there is a longer pause, others can take it as an opportunity (resource) for taking a turn and for talking themselves. Making some noise or producing a gesture, which most often occurs unconsciously, indicates to others that the speaker wants to continue. The noise or gestures are resources that may have the outcome of constraining the listeners to continue listening. One such occasion was apparent when, after a conversationally long 0.90-second pause (line 08), Bella produced an "um:" that was drawn out, before she continued talking (line 09). In one sense, her hand was still on the drawing, an indication that she had not yet abandoned her turn at talk, so that the "um:" constituted an added resource for indicating (likely without being consciously aware of it) that she was intending to continue.

A striking example how gestures are used to maintain a turn occurred after Bella had apparently completed the description of her design alternative (line 10). That she had completed articulating the idea was also visually apparent when Bella was pulling her hand back from the drawing that was the focus of the three girls' attention. If we look ahead, we see in fact that the battery idea (line 12) was almost like an afterthought. Therefore, the lengthening pause (line 11) became a resource for others to start talking. When Bella moved her hand forward again (line 12), it became a gesture that can be experienced in the same way as if she had said, "Don't start, I am not yet finished." Neither Amanda nor Leanne began, thereby providing Bella with the opportunity to propose an addition to the lift idea, namely operating it by using the batteries rather than the hand operation that she had earlier described (line 10, Figure 84.2).

EXHIBITING ATTENTION

Under normal (most) circumstances, participants in a conversation do not tell one another explicitly that they are listening and paying attention. Saying so would in fact interrupt the current speaker and take the turn at talk away from him or her. However, there are other ways to exhibit attention, some of which can be seen in this episode. For example, Amanda had oriented her upper body and her gaze toward Leanne (Figure 84.2a). When Bella began to speak, Amanda moved her body upward and turned her head, so that she was now facing the speaker (Figure 84.2b). However, when Bella returned her hand to the diagram (line 04), Amanda shifted her gaze, watching where Bella pointed and moved her hand that enacted pulling. When Bella was done with this part of her explanation, Amanda reoriented herself to face Bella. In both cases, Amanda made her attentive listening available to Bella: she looked at the speaker and then followed the hand that pointed and moved about. If Bella had had not been present, or if the girls had been in a telephone conference call, Amanda could not have shown attention in this way. Making some noise at a volume lower than the current speaker, often "Uh um" (line 05), is another way of exhibiting attention. Listeners also nod their heads in the way Leanne had done (line 13), visible in the difference between Figures 84.4b and 84.4c. This nodding could also have meant agreement, which might even have been the case. But immediately after this episode, Leanne critiqued Bella's idea, and thereby exhibited that she was not in agreement. All of these ways usually are unconscious, but they are structures in the setting that allow speakers to know that others are listening even without thinking about it. Attention is exhibited with and through the body (cognition as embodied), and it is available to others there in the setting (cognition as situated and distributed).

WHAT DID BELLA TALK ABOUT?

Our (Western) culture is almost obsessively preoccupied with language—which has led the philosopher Jacques Derrida to call it logocentric, centered on language. However, in much of everyday life, words are only a small part of what it takes to experience a situation as meaningful. To understand others, we need to be attuned to not only the words others say but to their gestures, body positions, voice inflections, current activity, objects and events, and so on. Gestures play an important role in our knowledgeable everyday behavior, in part because they articulate explicit links between the current speaker, talk, and the surrounding world. Thus, a speaker may be pointing at something or in some direction, and thereby establish a link between what is concurrently said and some thing out there. In the present situation, Bella pointed to the diagram (line 03, Figure 84.2b), and, more specifically, to the tower part of the diagram. This gesture therefore is a resource for the listeners to make a link between what she was going to say and the tower part. That is, although Bella continued by saying "my brother" (line 04), one knows that she was talking about the tower. She then moved her hand away from the drawing to scratch herself (line 06), but then pointed to the tower again while saying that he had a parking lot. Because of her pointing, the audience is attuned again to the tower part rather than to the brother or his garage, though the relevance of the latter is implied. This became clear from the next part of her presentation.

Bella said that her brother had a parking garage and that one "can take this part out" (line 09). This statement is contradictory. She was pointing to the drawing not to her brother's parking garage. But she said that one could take some part out of the parking garage, although she pointed to the drawing when she said "this." Yet taken as a whole, her communication can be understood. She literally made a connection between the two, the tower in their design (which she pointed to) and an equivalent part in her brother's parking garage (which she described verbally) are to become one and the same thing.

Bella actually did not just point but moved her hand up and down right next to the tower, similar to a subsequent gesture that accompanied the end of the utterance, "you pull like this" (line 10, Figure 84.3). Moving gestures trace out a path, and this path resembles some entity or event. Such gestures are called iconic (from the Greek for "to be like"), because they depict some object, for example, in the setting. Thus, to know which object the gesture is intended to make salient, listeners need to be attuned to the setting.

The iconic gesture accompanying the utterance "this part" served to make the tower figure; this movement actually turned out to be better than simple pointing, which is inherently underspecified in terms of its aim, and could be a general or specific pointing. The moving gesture, however, paralleled the tower and therefore made its shape more salient. It made it more apparent that she wanted others to attend to the vertical aspect of the tower rather than to the triangular elevator or the pulley on top (Figure 84.1). In line 10, Bella said that the parking lot part would allow them "to pull like this." However, neither her peers nor we would understand what she was saying, unless we attended to her gesture, formed when the thumb followed the line from the top toward the bottom of the tower configuration (Figure 84.3a–b). The gesture made the situation a dynamic one, as we can literally see the movement of a hand pulling down on the string, which, mediated by the pulley, would bring the triangular elevator and ball up to the beginning of the chute.

In this situation, it is quite evident that we need to attend to sound (words), the movement of the hand (gesture), and the diagram, which are in the setting. I don't have to think, "I am seeing Bella's hand pulling on the string," but the pulling is out there, immediately apparent to everyone who is attentive. For speaker and audience, cognition therefore becomes situated, because it is not just something happening in their heads, but also something involving their bodies and things in the world that matter. All of these are resources in the setting for making sense, therefore need to be included in the analysis of knowing—so that it makes sense of speaking of cognition as situated.

INTERACTION IS A COORDINATED ACTION IN SITUATION

Social interaction involves several people. Like a dance involving two or more individuals, interaction requires coordination. Both interaction and coordination imply a phenomenon that goes beyond the individual human being, and especially beyond the human mind. To understand what is being communicated (in words, gesture, body position, and setting) and how it is communicated, we need to attend to the situation as a whole. We cannot understand an action by itself, but have to see it as both a response to a previous action and the antecedent of a subsequent action. This is why cognition is situated not only in a material but also in a social sense. Take the following example.

While Bella was developing the alternative design, or rather, the particular implementation of the "elevator" part, Amanda and Leanne provided her with evidence that they were attuned to the unfolding design. In fact, when there was evidence that Bella did not continue while attention was focused elsewhere, alignment was signaled. After Bella had uttered "my brother" (line 04), Amanda had turned her gaze from the previous speaker Leanne to face Bella; Leanne was still looking down toward the drawing. Her gaze moved up to meet that of Bella only 0.97 seconds after Bella had completed; the pause was produced long enough until alignment had occurred and was signaled to have occurred. By the time Bella had uttered "lot" (line 07), Leanne was gazing at the diagram as if following the pointing finger, but Amanda was still gazing at Bella. The latter's continuation fell precisely together with the point in time when Amanda, too, had directed her gaze at the diagram. At "this part" (line 09) both listeners were looking at the diagram until Bella had finished the description of what to do with the part from her brother's garage. Both simultaneously moved their gaze to look Bella squarely into the face. Amanda continued to gaze at Bella, whereas Leanne nodded repeatedly (line 13). After the episode presented here, Leanne, still facing Bella, began to talk and Amanda shifted her gaze to the next speaker after having briefly dropped it downward in the direction of the design.

DIALECTIC OF SITUATED ACTION

In the forgoing section, we have seen a brief episode from a design activity, which took the three girls from initially sketchy ideas and possibilities via several drawings and many gesturally enacted visions to a completed prototype (Figure 84.5). We can envision the complexity of human activity if we just think about the fact that the three girls worked for nearly ten hours, amounting to more than 3,000 episodes such as the one discussed here, one following the other. However, without the overall activity of designing the Rube Goldberg device, the individual actions make no sense. Bella's talk about her brother's garage, a part of which they could use here made sense, because all participants were attuned to the motive of the activity, the production of Rube Goldberg machines. This motive existed at a collective level, others in the class were doing it too; Amanda, Bella, and Leanne concretely realized the motive in their own project, the cat feeder. Being in this classroom, therefore, contextualized each action in the collective motive. In this way, each action was further situated in a social way. This is what gives an action its sense, the connection it has to previous and subsequent actions, for reasons others can understand, and for whom actors produce resources to help others understand.

Actions are not only socially situated in the group and materially situated in the world: they are also situated in the body of the person who acts. That is, when the students uttered words and sentence fragments, they just produced them without doing much planning ahead of time;

Figure 84.5
Each action during the process of designing a Rube Goldberg machine, made sense because it was situated in the collectively motivated activity, which included an exposition in the library, available for everybody in the school to visit

when they used gestures and oriented their bodies, they, as any other individual, did not plan such movements but unconsciously moved. Actions are situated in our bodies of which we are, most of the time, not even conscious, but without which there would not be an action at all. Yet although components of actions are produced unconsciously, they are properly sequenced and coordinated with the actions of others and the surrounding material structures.

This way of understanding actions as situated allows us to understand meaning in a new way. Meaning is not something that is attached to things, or put down in writing during a test, but is something happening as people act, each action being grounded simultaneously in the social and material setting and in the body.

KNOWING IS SITUATED ACTION

People continuously act. Each action produces an outcome, which can be a word, sentence, gesture, artifact, and even a pause. Each outcome is a resource for subsequent actions by the same person or by others in the setting. From this perspective, situations continuously unfold, operated upon by the human beings present. They use these resources not only to produce a design, or to make available to one another some idea, but also to manage the conversation itself. Cognition is situated because people are always oriented toward their setting, and without the setting and motive of the activity in which they participate, there is no way of understanding what is going on. It is the situation as a whole that allows us to understand, and it is the situation as a whole that we draw on to make our own understanding available to others.

If, however, we attend to many things other than words while attending to others, communicating, and speaking, then cognition is inherently situated. It is situated not like an object that is placed somewhere, but in that all action is transaction in an irreducible unit. This unit cannot be broken down into a person, on the one hand, and his or her lifeworld, on the other. Person and lifeworld presuppose one another, they are, in other words, dialectically related. All knowing is inferred from action, even by everyday folk as they attempt to understand others; and because all action is situated, all knowing is situated. Acknowledging this fact is an instance of situating cognition in the situation, which has led me to the title of this contribution—situating situated cognition.

Cognition is not just situated, a phenomenon out there. To be consistent with the approach advocated here, my own work is situated, taking cognition as its object. My writing, my analysis therefore actively situates cognition in situation, but is itself a form of situated cognition that cannot be understood unless we take into account the entire setting that includes me, computer, camera, VCR, Internet, word processor, library, and so on. My concrete analyses of one episode exemplify how situated cognition itself becomes situated.

TERMS FOR READERS

Agency—A term that denotes the fundamental capacity to act. Agency stands in a dialectical relation with structures, with which it forms a unit. Without agency, there would not be structures recognized by and acted toward by human beings.

Dialectical relation—A relation is dialectical when it is based on the identity of nonidentical things, two things that are prerequisites of one another, like a chicken and the egg. A chicken comes from the egg but the egg comes from the chicken. In theories of situated cognition, the object of a person's attention is both material and mental. It is therefore *one* object that simultaneously appears twice, as material out there and as perception inside body.

Gesture—Gestures come in many forms and have many functions. Gestures that are used for pointing are called deictic gestures; an example was found in Figure 84.2b. A gesture that depicts something is an iconic gesture, because it resembles something else in an image-like fashion, something else it is said to stand for. Thus, in Figure 84.3, the thumb moved up and down the drawing, thereby standing for the pulling motion required to get the elevator with the ball moving up in the tower. Although they do not say in the way words do (to linguists, body language is an oxymoron, because there is no grammar for body movements), gestures are a central aspect of human communication.

Resources—Resources are the structures in the world surrounding a human being. Resources can be social, as in the patterned ways that we greet other people, or material, such as the characteristic shapes of the things surrounding us in everyday life.

Schema—Structured aspects of the human body that make us perceive and act in the world in the patterned ways we do. These structures are experience-dependent and therefore are different for different individuals, though they are more similar within a culture than between cultures. Seeing the left part of Figure 84.1 as an elevator is possible because of the schemas that the girls and we have developed through experience. Schemas are part of a dialectical unit together with social and material structures that characterize the world in which we find ourselves.

Structure—A term that denotes the second part of the agency | structure dialectic. Although structures constitute a unit, we can associate them with the world surrounding the person (resources) or with the body (schema).

NOTE

1. The following transcription conventions have been used: (0.41) – time in seconds; [] – bridging consecutive lines indicate beginning and ending of overlapping speech; °Yea° – degree signs enclose speech with lower than normal volume; *ten* – italicized utterances were stressed; u:m – each colon indicates an extension of a phoneme by 0.1 seconds; *[Fig. 84.2c] – the asterisk aligns speech and video offprints in a figure, here Figure 84.2c; ((rH moves)) – double parentheses enclose descriptions of actions, here the movement of the right hand; and.,?! – punctuation is used to indicate speech features, such as rising intonation heard as a question, or falling intonation to indicate the end of an idea unit (sentence).

FURTHER READING

Lave, J. (1988). *Cognition in Practice: Mind, Mathematics and Culture in Everyday Life*. Cambridge: Cambridge University Press.

Roth, W.-M. (2001). Situating Cognition. *Journal of the Learning Sciences*, 10, 27–61.

Suchman, L. A. (1987). *Plans and Situated Actions: The Problem of Human-Machine Communication*. Cambridge: Cambridge University Press.

CHAPTER 85

Stakeholder-Driven Educational Systems Design: At the Intersection of Educational Psychology and Systems

DIANA RYAN AND JEANETTE BOPRY

The current interest in communities of practice within educational psychology brings up the question of how the concept of design relates to such communities and how that view intersects with current theories and practices in educational system design. Etienne Wenger (1998), one of the originators of this theory, claims it is not possible to design communities of practice, however, according to Bela H. Banathy (1996) and others who study educational systems design (ESD), the design process part is of the emergent practice of the community members themselves. We find an intersection between the constraints to design suggested by the notions of situated cognition, communities of practice, and enaction theory and the ongoing developments in systems design theory and practice.

SYSTEMS DESIGN

Current developments in educational systems design reveal that attention to cognitive engagement and action by a community of learners is an essential part of systems design practice. This is a relatively recent development in systems design.

Systems design is a practice that originated in the early twentieth century and gained prominence during World War II because of its positive impact on the war effort. Applications to training in the United States during that era were particularly remarkable and the practice of systems design became a foundational pillar of the field of Educational Technology. From this perspective, trained and educated experts from outside educational systems diagnose problems and prescribe solutions to improve systems. They also draw up plans for potential new systems. It is the job of experts to decide what individual educational systems should look like and how the members of the systems should go about achieving these expert visions. This view of systems supports the idea that an educational system can be designed exclusive of stakeholder interaction and that a template of that system can be applied to any educational system.

The form of systems design that interests us, social systems design, has its roots squarely in instructional design as its major proponent, Bela H. Banathy (1919–2003), was a practitioner in that field. One of his primary interests was the development of social systems design for educational change. Others associated with the theories and practices of educational systems design include Charles M. Reigeluth and Patrick M. Jenlink. All three claim that the traditional assembly-line view of creating educational systems is consistent with the industrial-age model of education and not appropriate for the information age. They each express an eagerness to see the approach change for educational systems as it has for other social systems. What Banathy, Reigeluth, and Jenlink offer has much in common with the thinking of proponents of situated cognition, communities of practice, and enaction theory.

EDUCATIONAL SYSTEMS DESIGN

From a systems view, expert knowledge is only one of the many dimensions of the design process. The educational system is seen as nested within and interconnected with other social systems in which an individual may have many overlapping memberships. Local interactions create meaning and action by stakeholders in each of those systems. In this view, the design of the educational systems is the result of the interaction of the stakeholders in that system grappling with their respective needs, values and desires. Those with professional experience in designing educational systems are a subset of the broader system of stakeholders, contributing to the process, but not controlling or dictating it.

While there has been a great press for reform of education systems since the late 1980s, most agree there has been little fundamental change. For at least two decades educational systems researchers and practioners have called for educational systems to make adjustments, improve, or restructure. Instructional design has traditionally focused on well-designed, efficient, and effective instruction as the source of learning and change. Banathy's work drew the attention of education theorists and practioners to the comparison of school-based practices with practices in the broader social system. He compares the idea of focusing on teaching with focusing on learning. When teaching is in focus, you enhance teaching: the key performer is the teacher. When learning is in focus, the key performer is the learner. Energy is brought to bear on the learner interacting with the problem or issue. Banathy uses this as an analogy for the system: focus must be placed on the stakeholders that define the system. Banathy says that stakeholders must design the system rather than outside experts. He claims we have reached the end of the era of social engineering by outside experts. Instead, we have entered an age of *user- designers*: people designing their own systems.

For Banathy the fact of self-reflective consciousness makes it the responsibilty of humans to guide their own social evolution. He calls for communities to develop this evolutionary competency by envisioning and working toward an ideal image of themselves. He considers it a basic right of people to guide their own destinies by taking part in decisions that have an impact on their lives, to take responsibility for the creation of communites that are caring, nurturing and healthy. To design one's own future is a fundamental human right. He further holds that it is only once these rights are ceded to stakeholders in communities that a truly democratic civil society will emerge. This democratic civil society will continually reproduce within its practices the same rights that brought it about.

THE INTERSECTION WITH EDUCATIONAL PSYCHOLOGY

The idea of stakeholder design is key to understanding how educational psychology's current views of learning, cognition and development intersect with educational systems theories and practices. The theories of situated cognition, communities of practice, and enaction place the learner and task in the context of social practices. Theorists propose that learning is situated in the social experience of learners and continuously emerges from this activity. It is not the end result of knowledge transmitted by an outside expert. Those who are working for fundamental change in educational systems design propose that the traditional top-down, expert-driven design approach to change be made into an intimate social process of idealized design by user-designers. This "way of seeing" the design of educational systems as a process embedded in communities of practice is a relatively recent development. Advocates of this approach assume that successful educational systems design is an interactive, dynamic social process in a unique context. From this point of view, the community of stakeholders must be involved in the design process. The educational community is only one part of a complex and interrelated world that must be taken into consideration if the design is to succeed. Advocates believe that the community stakeholders themselves must envision "what should be" in order to design a system that is open to purposeful development. One can trigger change in a system by changing the environment in which it operates (as is attempted by lawmakers, for example); what the change will be, however, is determined inside the system through the practices generated by its membership.

Enaction and Social Systems Design

Current developments influencing educational psychology (situated cognition, communities of practice, enaction) recognize that learner interaction with and/or within an environment is the source of learning. The principle tenet of enaction is that we relate to the world through action rather than through representations. Viability in the various spheres through which we move requires *effective action*. Social systems scaffold effective action. So, within the enactive framework social systems provide the milieu for the survival of their members. Social systems are constituted in social practices; a social system is both the medium and outcome of the reproduction of these practices. It is both the creation of its constituent members and the milieu that supports their survival. Changes in membership or member interaction affect the entity as a whole. The individual member is not a dispensable component of the system. A social system is a unit only by virtue of the members that comprise it. As a consensual domain, societies are what we, as participants in their realization, make them to be. They are our responsibility.

Social system design offers an opportunity for members of a community to engage in conscious, goal-oriented design. Design, here, is grounded in the context of the affected community rather than in theoretical prescription and all members of a social system can be expected to have an impact on proposed changes. Design must be an instantiation of effective action.

Enaction supports a proscriptive rather than prescriptive approach to design. Within the enactive framework prescription is viewed with suspicion. To tell someone else what to do is to use them as an extension of one's own cognition and to remove them from the center of their own cognitive activity. To be allowed to be at the center of one's own cognition seems a basic human right. To tell someone how to do something makes alternatives not chosen invisible. Learners are deprived of meaningful acts of creativity. *Proscription,* or telling someone what *not* to do, immediately brings to mind the question *"Why not?"* What is hidden by prescription is made visible by proscription. Proscription demands creativity on the part of learners because the problem of *what to do* is theirs to solve. At one and the same time, proscription creates an environment conducive to creativity and a critical stance.

For those interested in the connection of educational systems design and enaction, the question becomes "Does prescription have any place in the design of educational activity, or by extension in the design of social systems?" At the heart of the enactive suspicion of prescription is a rejection of oppressive activity. To the extent that prescription is not oppressive and does not remove the stakeholder from the center of his or her own cognitive experience, it may be considered a tool of design. In other words, to make prescriptions for oneself cannot be considered an oppressive activity. To the extent that, in stakeholder-based design, prescriptions are a consensus of the community, they cannot be considered oppressive to members of that community. The key here seems to be true consensus rather than majority rule.

In Banathy's ESD approach, the prescriptions that will affect the community involved in the design process come from within the community rather than from without (i.e., from theory or from outside experts). The process of design within his model is understood to be evolutionary. Changes are made in cycles; those that are made early on help determine those that can be made at a later time. This approach to social systems design has built-in protection against oppressive activity. Here stakeholder design uses short-term prescriptions in the service of a community-determined goal. Because the community can revisit these prescriptions at short intervals and even the goal can be renegotiated, the potential for oppressive activity is mitigated.

Situated Cognition, Communities of Practice, and Social Systems Design

Situated cognition and communities of practice are also concepts that intersect with this approach to social systems design. Theorists in the 1990s, in relating thinking, learning and development, changed the view of these as separate elements to seeing them as dynamic parts of a whole relationship. The idea of mindful interaction between the individual and the environment that dated from Dewey decades earlier was coming to the forefront of thinking in educational psychology. Full-blown situated cognition, as Clancey (1997) defines it, is enactive and encompasses both the social and the cognitive. A narrower form that ignores internal cognitive structure in favor of an in-depth discussion of the social environment is assumed in Lave and Wenger's (1991) discussions of communities of practice.

Until recently it has been assumed that learning is an individual activity and that it is the result of teaching. What Lave and Wenger propose in their concept of communities of practice is that learning is a social experience that results from engagement in everyday social practices. They focus on how social relationships rather than cognitive structures shape learning. They argue that communities of practice exist everywhere and that members of these communities are involved in activities and relationships that develop over time. Community members develop ways of doing things that are mutually valued and in so doing, they learn from each other. Learning is situated in the community where a given skill is relevant.

Wenger discusses communities of practice as subgroups of larger social systems that contribute both to the viability of the members of the subgroup and to the viability of the larger system within which the subgroup resides. So, a group of engineers at Ford Motor Company who come together to contribute to solving one another's problems may also affect the viability of the company within the economic environment. They do this by affecting a change in the practice of members of the larger system in such a way that there is an effect upon that system's economic viability in its interactions with its environment. These communities then, may have a design impact on the larger system by effecting change from within.

Wenger argues that communities of practice cannot be designed into existence. While it is the case that these types of systems are immune to creation from the outside, they do emerge as a response to a perceived need on the part of those who will comprise the community. If once a community exists members choose to organize or be organized for the purpose of change then Banathy's approach comes into play. Banathy and proponents of his approach would say that if participants themselves deliberately and mindfully envision and take responsible social action for change relevant to the system, then it is social systems design.

SOCIAL SYSTEMS DESIGN AS PROCESS AND CONTEXT FOR SOCIAL PRACTICE

Banathy's user-designer approach acknowledges the complexity of the educational system and considers change from multiple perspectives, but always puts primary decision-making power in the hand of stakeholders. He stresses that the challenge of designing self-governing and self-organizing societies is not to create and impose coercive societal-level design from the top down or project the outcome. Banathy focuses on an evolutionary change process; change can be expected to take time to accomplish. Thus, he only broadly describes the complex task that is set for individuals in communities in larger social systems rather than prescibing specific procedures.

He concludes his book, *Designing Social Systems in a Changing World*, with several generalizations for designers of a new society. They have to (1) transcend the system boundaries that exist now and learn to think anew about the world, rather than extrapolate from it, (2) create ideal visions of future society based on shared ideas and values, (3) engage in disciplined inquiry of design to bring those images to life. In addition, he stresses these caveates: (4) Authentic and sustainable design must be genuinely participative by individuals at all levels of society; (5) The design of the design inquiry itself and all the various design processes must be established at the various societal levels; (6) A prerequisite to design is that a design culture and evolutional competence must be developed across the society; 7) Design inquiry should ethically; reflectively, and never-endingly pursue the ideal from multiple perspectives; and 8) Take advantage of existing and emerging technologies for communicating at all levels of the design inquiry.

Banathy's educational systems design perspective has influenced a number of systemic change efforts in education and has lead to efforts to create contexts for stakeholder-based changes. As the study of systemic change in education has matured, there have been theoretical and practical efforts to clarify and develop this area of research and practice. Reigeluth's work has included clarifying what Banathy and those working with ESD mean by systemic change and how stakeholder roles at various nested levels of the system are differentiated in the ESD approach. Distinctions are made between state-wide, district-wide, school-wide and ecological approaches to systemic change. Banthy's three "lenses" are used to describe educational systems from this perspective: a birds-eye lens, a functions/structure lens, and a process lens. The bird's eye lens provides an overall view of the relationships in the system environment and context. The functions/structure lens looks at the purposes and components of any system and their relationships to each other, and the process lens looks at how the systems' purposes are attained and how the system behaves over time. Ecological systemic thinkers view systems as complex, multidimensional organizations. Systemic change from this view considers change as comprehensive and evolving from a continuing process of dialogue and self-examination by all who are impacted by the system—the user-designers.

Reigeluth, Jenlink, Carr, and Nelson have done extensive work over the past several years to develop specific process guidelines for facilitating change in school districts based on the ESD approach. They propose some process maps developed from their experiences and that of others engaged in educational change at the district level. Their guidance system reflects skills and knowledge essential for process facilitators who are assisting a school district and community in developing its own changes.

Like Banathy, they define the approach as one that recognizes the interrelationships and interdependencies among the parts of the educational system. As a consequence desired changes in one part of the system must be accompanied by changes in any other parts that affect those desired changes. They recognize the interrelationships and interdependencies between the educational system and its community: parents, employers, social service agencies, religious organizations, etc. All these stakeholders are recognized as having ownership of the change effort.

The guidance system describes specific activities that the process facilitator and the community stakeholders would use in creating the envisioned community. The list of prerequisite beliefs they propose for the faciltator include, systemic thinking (similar to Banathy's), inclusivity (all stakeholders in the educational system are included), stakeholder ownership (all stakeholders are empowered rather than represented), coevolution (mutal change in concert with interrelated parts or persons of a system), collaboration (the process of creating safe and trusting purposeful relationship), community (a state of being and becoming a whole toward action for change) and wholeness (participants ability to see relationships which connect them to their educational system and community). Reigeluth, Jenlink, Carr, and Nelson (1998) lay out a series of discreet events or transition points that occur in the systemic change process. Phase I assures the faciltiator and the district are in a state of readiness for the systemic change effort and it is sealed with a formal agreement. Phase II of the system is to develop a core team. That team would then expand into a decisioning team and a design support team. The community enters Phase III with the facilitator helping the expanded teams to prepare themselves for the redesign process. In addition to these discrete events, Reigeluth et al., propose that there are many continuous events integral to the process. Among these events are: Engaging in self-disclosure where particpants contuiously engage in self-disclosure as it applies to dialogue and design conversation, guiding and evolving community as opposed to groups and teams, and organizational learning. Organizational learning is another of the key events for its relationship to educational psychology. This event entails the continuous development of skills and knowledge about forms of organizational learning and how they relate to systemic change. Their guidelines calls for continuous redesign of the process as it unfolds. Rather than expert, top-down leadership, the idea is to empower and support a flatter, more democratice environment.

APPLYING THESE IDEAS TO THE CLASSROOM

If one applies this idea to education one begins to see, in the classroom, a set or series of communities that contribute to the viability of their members in the classroom setting. Some of these communities may contribute to the instructional prerogatives of the teacher, others to the place of individual students in the larger social hierarchy that is part of the lived experience of students within the school setting. The teachers' lounge will provide insight into other communities. The school itself may be seen as a subgroup within a larger community that includes parents, professionals, service providers, etc.

Design choices should emerge from the local community (or communities) that the design affects. Banathy's social system design model grounds design decisions in the stakeholder community. The implications of educational systems design and the user-designer approach as they relate to the classroom level of the system have given rise to new challenges in educational systems design and highlight the way in which the area intersects with educational psychology. Reigeluth and Squire say that an ecological systems thinker examines a student/ teacher relationship just as an ecologist would examine the relationships of forest denizens in their forest as part of a nested system. The stakeholders in the classroom system are seen within the context of the classroom as it is nested within the context of the school, within the district, within a state educational system and so on. Banathy calls for using a variety of modes: self-directed learning, team learning, technology-assisted learning, and social and organizational learning. Reigeluth calls for information-age instructional design that utilizes self-regulated learning and shared decision-making, focusing on real world problems and building cooperative relationships through learning teams. He challenges practitioners and researchers in the field to consider the implications of shared decision making which might incorporate the notion of "user-designers."

TERMS FOR READERS

Communities of Practice—Wenger uses this term to describe systems that organize attempts by members to improve their own practice.

Educational Systems Design—ESD is defined as the process of educational communities, at whatever level of the system, collectively designing their own educational systems.

Enaction—Fundamentally, enaction is the position that the primary way that we relate to the world is by interacting with it rather than by processing representations of it. Enaction is a framework, in much the same way that representational realism is a framework. It provides a warrant for a number of approaches that are considered constructivist in nature. Situated cognition and Communities of Practice can be seen as warranted by this framework. Enaction is remarkable in that it is the first framework to use a metaphor of mind that is backed by biological rather than technological evidence. The framework is valuable because it provides a measure for determining the internal consistency of practice that is called "constructivist." It also provides guidance for design, and guidance for the creation of research agendas, something that is often considered a weakness of the constructivist project. Enaction is sometimes referred to as a post-constructivist position.

Evolutionary Consciousness—Banathy contends that because human culture has evolved into self-reflective consciouness, we have the ability to engage in self- guided cultural evolution.

Situated Cognition—Clancey claims that situated cognition is comprised of three aspects: the social function which regulates behavior; behavioral content which relates cognition to spatial temporal settings; and the structural mechanism which coordinates perception, conception, and action. What cognition is situated in is human experience (which includes time, place, and other aspects of a dynamically changing environment as well as dynamically changing internal mechanisms). From this perspective much of the literature on situated cognition is incomplete in that the internal dynamic is often missing. Further, situatedness is often confused with environmental context. On the other hand this literature base does make the social-centeredness of learning visible.

Systems Design—Banathy defines this as a future-creating human activity where members of a system engage in creating and implementing their vision of what their system should be or in consciously redesigning it to meet changes within the community and/or its environment.

FURTHER READING

Banathy, B. H. (1996). *Designing Social Systems in a Changing World*. New York: Plenum.

Clancey, W. (1997). *Situated Cognition*. Cambridge: Cambridge University Press.

Lave, J. and Wenger, E. (1991). *Situated Learning: Legitimate Peripheral Participation*. New York: Cambridge University Press.

Reigeluth, C., Jenlink, P., Carr, A., and Nelson, L. (1998). Guidelines for Facilitating Systemic Change in School District. *Systems Research and Behavioral Science*, 15(3), 217–234.

Wenger, E. (1998). *Communities of Practice: Learning, Meaning, and Identity*. New York: Cambridge University Press.

CHAPTER 86

Teacher Thinking for Democratic Learning

BRENDA CHEREDNICHENKO

Schooling is compulsory for all young people, yet not all young people have the same experience of school nor do they achieve the same outcomes. Teese and Polesel (2003) have found that dramatic differences in schooling outcomes support social and educational inequality across the society. This chapter discusses some research in Australia which looked at the way teachers think about their students, their students' families, and communities and the curriculum. It revealed the different approaches teachers take to making curriculum decisions and uncovered some of the reasons why not all children have the same opportunities at school and as a result of their years at school. It showed that it is critical for teachers to be aware of the understanding they have about their students, the assumptions they make about what students are capable of and what things they need to learn in order to be successful in school and in the community.

In teaching, what occurs in the classroom between the teacher and the student is informed by teachers' cognitive processes: their knowledge, intentions and their understanding of students, curriculum, school organisation and the development of their professional knowledge. It is important to understand not only the social context of teaching but also the psychological context as well. Understanding how teaching and teacher thinking about learners affects learning, requires rich description and understanding of the behaviors, relationships, and the engagement in the classroom. This inquiry into the cognitive processes of and influences on teachers is needed if we are to unlock the "insider" view of teacher decision making.

The real value of learning is indicated by the way in which learners apply their knowledge. How well schools do their job can be judged by the way in which students use their knowledge and skills when they have opportunities (Eisner, 2001). Similarly teachers will make choices about what are the appropriate knowledge and skills to be taught and about the best strategies for building relationships for learning. This chapter describes the influences on teachers' thinking and decision making for curriculum. It explains the factors which help shape these choices and shows that teachers in different communities are influenced by their communities as well as their own educational background and experience. These social and psychological factors help shape the learning activities that students have in their classrooms. Research which examined teacher thinking and understanding about their students, the school curriculum, and the application of thinking skills programs in a broad sociocultural sampling of primary schools in Victoria,

Australia, is discussed here (Cherednichenko, 2000). The explicit teaching of thinking skills programs, for example, based on the work of de Bono, Bloom, or Gardner was not widespread at that time in the state of Victoria, although in 2004 there is now a very strong inclusion of these strategies in classrooms. In 1990s there seemed to be a small but growing number of schools which included a specific emphasis on thinking skills in their curriculum. There was also a clear tendency for this high demand to be in wealthier schools, which already offered a wide range of curriculum programs.

It is important for field of educational psychology to explore and understand why teachers in different communities think and behave differently toward students and curriculum and to discover whether this is based on educational knowledge or other factors. Teachers were asked to reflect on their schools and their classroom practice and to identify programs which they specifically included for teaching student thinking. Interestingly, most private schools and many public schools in well-to-do communities felt it was important to attend to the development of thinking skills explicitly in the curriculum. Very few teachers in schools in working class communities thought that their students needed or could manage thinking skills programs. Teachers in different social contexts had very different understanding of the intellectual needs and capacity of students and this seemed to very closely linked to issues of social class. A link was identified between these educational psychology issues of intelligence and learning styles and teacher thinking, knowledge, and actions and consequently to broader social outcomes of schooling.

Teachers were asked why they had "added" thinking skills programs to their class curriculum. The research also inquired about teachers' understanding of their schools, children, and families and gathered information about teacher attitudes and expectations as well as descriptions of their practices. One hundred and twenty teachers teaching in schools in a range of sociocultural communities participated in the research. The research found that a wide range of factors were considered when teachers made decisions about curriculum, including the decision to focus explicitly on teaching thinking skills or not. The findings of the research enabled some connections to be uncovered between teacher thinking about education, about their own learning experiences, the intentions of teachers as well as the sociocultural environment in which the school and its families were located.

THINKING ABOUT TEACHING AND THE SCHOOL ENVIRONMENT

Most teachers argue that any curriculum decision is guided by an essential commitment to change for improvement. There is a shared belief that all teaching can be improved, students can learn better and that this is the main job of the teacher. The potential for teachers to think deeply and critically about their teaching and then to make the changes necessary for improved educational and social outcomes is strong and has been long supported by the work of Schon (1983) and others. It is important therefore to know about the way in which teachers think about and act toward their students and communities and the factors that influence this teacher cognition and so the potential for change.

The deeply personal nature of teaching ensures that action and response are highly individualised. When the culture of the school supports conservative and traditional practices, there is a reduced ability of teachers to redirect their efforts to change outcomes. Yet in supportive and collaborative environments, school change is more readily achieved as this culture provides a basis for exploring new curriculum and an ability to implement change so that learning can improve. Teachers in similar environments do share strong cultural, social, and educational values and therefore often have close agreement about what is needed or appropriate for their students. When these cultural connections and similarities are acknowledged and explicit, schools are more readily able to provide an enriching curriculum for students, specifically for those who demonstrate precociousness. This cultural relationship or affinity strongly influences the way in which teachers understand their students and their needs and so establish learning opportunities as their own knowledge and values, the aspirations of parents and the needs and abilities of students mediate their decision making, as do differing resource and policy structures. This results in a form of curriculum selection, which commences in the early years of schooling building to reinforce a differentiated curriculum and learning outcomes for students of different sociocultural backgrounds as they progress through school.

The cultural affinity between the teachers, their students, and communities in the schools in this study was found to be a significant influence on their decisions about curriculum, more so than many other factors such as for example, quality of resources for teaching. Most teachers share a strong cultural affinity with middle-class students and less so with students of poorer communities. This translates to teacher behavior and decision making, which results in students in some communities, notably the middle-class schools, being offered a more complex, challenging, and intellectual curriculum.

Frequently it is assumed that working-class families are unable to engage fully in academic and intellectual pursuits. Families and students from working-class communities are disadvantaged as they try to access the high culture pursuits of tertiary education and the arts for example. Even when families are able to interact with prestigious cultural activities, increased social mobility is impeded unless the tools for access are developed. Equal numbers of teachers in working class and middle-class schools participated in this study, and revealed their reasons for including thinking skills as very different from each other, notably related to sociocultural issues.

Two trends were uncovered. In both the public and private schools in wealthier communities, teachers felt pressured to extend and add value to the curriculum in order to preserve the image and role of the school as catering to the intellectual needs of students and to support their academic success. Teachers understood their students well because they lived in these communities and often sent their children to the same or similar schools. A close alignment of cultural values and standards was found between parents and teachers. This meant that the teachers' actions, often unconsciously, were supporting the existing enriched curriculum. Teachers and parents held similar aspirations to students and the curriculum decisions endorsed these.

However, in poorer communities, teachers who implemented thinking skills programs did so at some risk. While most schools worked with parents to change the curriculum, in some cases there was concern about making these programs explicitly known to parents as anything which was perceived as moving away from core skill development might be unsupported. Teachers and parents' expectations and knowledge about what was good teaching and curriculum were not aligned and the teachers felt parents would not approve of some innovative practices such as thinking skills programs. Most teachers in these communities argued that these differences made change and innovation more difficult. While realising that the teaching of core skills was essential, they also wanted to instil in their students an ability to inquire, think, challenge, and solve problems so that they might engage in the world more fully, more democratically, and more powerfully. These teachers were acting against what was expected by their communities, taking conscious decisions to change what they were doing for improved learning.

The study of the teachers' reasons for introducing certain curriculum, such as thinking skills programs highlights the critical role of teacher cognition, beliefs, values, and attitudes and the external factors which influence teacher actions in shaping the curriculum. Much has been written about the role of society, schools, and teachers as powerful social structures and agents in construction of an unjust social and educational experience for young people. As they respond to government pressure and their own experience, teachers often *unconsciously* support the continuation of the unequal class system many times because they feel they do not really have the power to change or because this would mean extensive negotiation with the parents and communities about innovative curriculum. These social and cultural factors that influence teacher cognition are characterised as follows:

School Influences

Within the school environment the direct fields of influence are:

* *Educational Delivery: Teaching and Learning.* The educational program for which the school is responsible includes curriculum provision and the range of curriculum offerings which are implemented, the policies that shape the practice of curriculum, the priorities the school sets for development, the personal relationships which exist and are fostered between teachers, parents and students, and the resources which are available and the way in which they are distributed to support programs.
* *Institutional Profile: Corporate Identity of the Institution.* The school's identity and profile is developed through the School Charter and the embedded practices and policies, which define the school, such as school uniform, the interpretation of its corporate values and traditions, the location and status of the school within the market, the profile of the staff and the strategic development and visioning drives school decision making.

Community Influences

Within the community context the direct fields of influence are:

* *Community Context: Social Identity of Students.* Within the context of the school's community the identity of students is shaped by the socioeconomic conditions of the local community, which in turn are influenced by the wider context; the cultural mix and diversity of the community; the level and distribution of community services and resources; and the location of the school, in urban, industrial or rural settings.
* *Global Perspective: Government, System and Policy Macro-economic Conditions.* The overarching policies and structures of government and education systems with regard to education, economic management, and industrial relations are highly influential in the way in which schools evolve and construct their curriculum.

THINKING CONSCIOUSLY, TEACHING DIFFERENTLY

The practice described by most teachers in working class schools of this study was a shared commitment to change learning opportunities and the social and educational outcomes for students, despite a chronic lack of cultural, educational, and physical resources. Michael Fullan (1991) discusses the things that stimulate us to behave differently and explains changes in teachers' practices as being stimulated by a range of contradictions between the values of the families and the values, attitudes, and knowledge of the teachers. Because teachers take a strong interest in the educational outcomes for their students they are constantly reassessing what is needed and how what they know can be used to change the curriculum and so the outcomes.

As a consequence, teachers who are consciously able to understand the pressures that educational experiences contribute to unequal social and educational opportunities for young people, are better prepared to act and to change their own preconceptions and expectations and so, through conscious and purposeful innovation, they are able to educate for improved outcomes. In so doing they serve to diminish the relative differences in schooling and so enable more equitable social and educational outcomes for students than would otherwise be achieved. This creates a strong argument for the development of teachers who are able to understand the practices of schools and as a result make conscious decisions to move beyond a functionalist social theory of social reproduction and to consider themselves as active decision makers, along with students in the learning process.

In some settings, teachers demonstrate a metacognitive awareness of their own teaching and respond to reject the hegemonic curriculum and to initiate and implement curriculum that is outside not only the government determined curriculum, but often also the expectations of parents and community for the possibility of improved social and academic achievement of their students. Such actions require conscious decision making and civic courage on the part of teachers as they develop and implement changed programs, aiming to reach beyond the basic demands of the society for technical competence in literacy and numeracy or for welfare, as adequate focus for the educational energy in working class schools. These teachers demonstrate an ability to act in ways which reflect a *"critical constructivism"* of teaching as they seek new approaches and build new curricula.

It is argued therefore that the perceptions of teachers and their understandings of their students, their students' abilities, and their learning environments are interrelated, indeed inseparable. This has a critical impact for the work of education psychology; thinking, and action are not context-free and understanding behavior is clearly demands consideration of sociological and psychological factors, that is the sociocultural context as an integral part of teacher thinking, behavior, attitudes and actions. This research highlights the need for the construction of a new knowledge base for researching teaching, learning, and thinking. This new knowledge must be eclectic, connect the disciplines of educational psychology and sociology to understand teaching as a result of the ways in which teachers know and interpret sociocultural factors. It must be an essential component of preservice and inservice teacher education and underpin decisions about practice.

Educational psychology has a significant role to play if the school is to take a significant role in deconstructing barriers to social mobility and supporting access, rather than creating barriers and enabling exclusion. Understanding teacher cognition (as well as student learning behavior), its impact on building social and intellectual capacity is critical at both the institutional and personal level. As teachers engage in teaching practice, learning will be delivered at the point of intersection of the sociological influences outlined above and the psychological influences of teacher's thinking. Any deliberate changes in teacher practices are responses to the interpretation of family needs and wants, as well as to teacher's education knowledge and experience, and set within the framework of policy and practice at both the global and local levels of management of education. Individual action is therefore always within the context of a wide range of structures and institutional forces, so highlighting the importance of understanding the ways in which teachers think about their students and students' families and backgrounds as well as their personal goals and practices. The model for the relationship outlined in Figure 86.1 illustrates how teaching cognition (the psychology of education) filters and interprets school and community influences (the sociology of education) in deciding curriculum, teaching, and learning.

Effective change is driven by the power to make decisions and to access the appropriate resources to work against the prevailing culture to act critically to construct positive experience and outcomes. Working against the prevailing culture is difficult, but can be sustained when the innovative change is connected to cultural change and supported by systems and government policy. The perceived influences of parents and community are as powerful as the explicit impact of system and policy in supporting and inhibiting change and innovation. Without systemic and policy support for practical reform, some teachers will continue to struggle to address issues of equity and learning improvement in environments which very often serve to reduce the impact of their efforts and abilities.

Such change begins with educational psychology leading the way in supporting teachers to develop a critical understanding of personal knowledge and practice. Making this knowledge

Figure 86.1
Interpretative framework for curriculum decision making: The psychological and social context of education

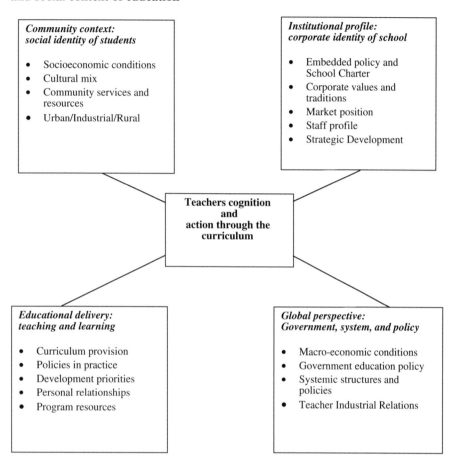

explicit and understanding the social factors that inform teacher cognition provides the capacity to make different decisions, which support better student learning and social outcomes. It is not sufficient to encourage students to be risk-takers, innovative, and change agents; the responsibility lies initially with teachers in schools and universities to be change agents in their own work.

A starting point for this inquiry with and about teacher cognition draws on a third related discipline in the form of philosophical or critical inquiry. This deep reflective inquiry has the capacity to enable individual teachers and groups of professional to challenge their accepted beliefs, values, and practices as well as strengthen commitments. There are several layers of this development, which are critical for students and teachers alike as we grow to make sense of and improve our world. They include the establishment of personal goals for learning and the way we relate to others and the world; professional inquiry, research and reflection on practice to ensure teacher knowledge is current and relevant; nurturing values of social democracy and understanding of social contexts both local and global; and participation in shared professional discourse of teaching and learning. By engaging with others in the development and critique of ideas and practices, a more humanist and holistic approach to teaching and learning can be developed, which is cognizant of and responsive to a range of social and cultural influences

Figure 86.2
Teacher thinking for democratic learning, school reform and social justice

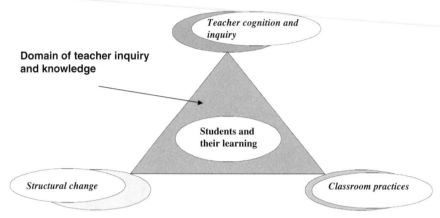

on learning. This engagement enables teachers to explicitly identify individual differences and respond appropriately to these. As well, a professional discourse of change for improvement is generated, based on professional inquiry, reflection and research.

In a climate of globalization and uncertain futures collaborative inquiry fosters civic courage and increased possibility for action and social change. The relationship between psychological influences of teacher cognition and social outcomes of schooling, as illustrated in Figure 86.2 suggests a demand for educational psychology to support teachers to learn about themselves as the basis for improving student learning:

- Personal understanding and knowledge which underpins personal practice and leads to the development of
- Professional knowledge which informs teaching practice which enables
- Student inquiry and thinking development for improved student learning outcomes which in turn support the achievement of
- Democratic and socially just schools and enhanced equity of educational opportunity.

TEACHER SELF-STUDY: ENHANCING TEACHER AGENCY

Educational psychology has both an opportunity and responsibility to support the development of more explicit teaching cognition and decision making, so that the social context of learners is a critical consideration in setting curriculum. This will result in the development of a conscious reflexivity, or awareness of thought and action. For teachers, the potential for innovation and improved learning outcomes is derived from the professional need to discover better ways to foster student learning. Teachers' deep concern for student well-being and development is evident, but the system often acts to thwart any sustained attempt at change for improvement.

Encouraging all teachers to engage in professional development is difficult and again issues of social justice and equity colour the delivery of excellent practice in every school. It is often argued that there are impediments within Australian culture to success and innovation: the tall poppy syndrome, government bureaucracy, utilitarian politics, and cultural cringe. The delivery of inequity is bound, at least in part, to the funding from the government failing to meet the needs of educating every child, and it being based on the assumption that all students come to school with the similar experience. These institutional inequities serve to diminish teachers' capacity to innovate and reform schools. Consequently, a recognition of the diverse backgrounds and experience must be attached to real resources for teachers and students.

The critical link between teaching and learning is defined as personal agency, shaped by a range of structures—curriculum, resources, and policy. Understanding the relationship between structures and agency, Giddens (2000) explains, is the basis for informed and democratic decision making. Exploration of these links must be lead through the field of psychology in teacher education so that teachers can study their own motives and thinking and consciously engage in the development of democratic practices for the direct improvement of curriculum provision. In such environments, decision making will serve the interests of students, teachers (and communities) and lead to improved learning outcomes for students. As a consequence, the social and cultural impact of improved working, teaching, and learning conditions leads to the development of shared leadership, stronger relationships, and changed practices.

Similarly, the ability to act is also shaped by knowledge and experience: knowledge of self, others, and the contextual influences. Teachers as agents of change make choices. They will act to change and disturb the curriculum, or to reinforce the existing curriculum. It is the way in which this agency is exercised, that determines the curriculum which is delivered and the impact it will have on student learning outcomes. Through teachers' study of their behavior and cognition, they will be better informed and prepared to respond to the prevailing social pressures so that professional and personal reflection leads to significant and meaningful change for students. This new direction for educational psychology, that of teacher self-study, connects teacher cognition to social improvement, strengthens reflective inquiry, and opens the way for a better teaching and learning practice.

FURTHER READING

Cherednichenko, B. F. (2000). *A Social Analysis of the Teaching of Thinking Skills in Victorian Primary Schools*. PhD thesis, University of Melbourne.

Eisner, E. (2001). What Does It Mean to Say a School Is Doing Well? *Phi Delta Kappan* 82(5), 367–372.

Fullan, M. (1991). *The New Meaning of Educational Change*. London: Cassell Educational.

Giddens, A. (2000). *Beyond Left and Right: The Future of Radical Politics*. Cambridge: Polity Press.

Schon, D. (1983). The Reflective Practitioner. New York: Basic Books.

Teese, R. and Polesel, J. (2003). *Undemocratic Schooling*. Camberwell, Victoria: ACER.

CHAPTER 87

Recognizing Students among Educational Authorities

ALISON COOK-SATHER

It is a striking phenomenon that rarely, since the advent of formal education in the United States, have students been consulted about whether or how schools are serving them. With few exceptions, adults have controlled the design, implementation, and reform of K–12 education. This practice has its roots in deeply problematic assumptions about young people's capacities and about relationships between young people and adults. These assumptions issue, in part, from the frameworks provided by educational psychology. As part of the larger project of this encyclopedia to redefine traditional notions within educational psychology, I present in this chapter an argument for recognizing students' capacities as critics and creators not just consumers of education and a parallel argument for rethinking who should learn from whom in relationships between young people and adults.

Traditional educational psychology has viewed students as disempowered participants in the educational process who must be well monitored and restricted to specific roles. According to this view, students are passive recipients and consumers of knowledge or depersonalized objects whose learning can be manipulated without their active participation in the planning and implementation of that learning. Using the concepts of recognition, authority, perspective, and listening, I argue for a reconceptualized role for students that sharply contrasts the restrictive roles promoted by traditional educational psychology.

What does it mean to use the concepts of recognition, authority, perspective, and listening to reconceptualize student role such that we recognize students among educational authorities? It means that instead of continuing to impose on students a traditional, adult-generated, agrarian- and subsequently industry-based model of education, we acknowledge the world in which today's youth live—one saturated in information technology, youth cultural media, and political currents set in motion by globalization. It means that instead of excluding students from important policy- and practice-shaping conversations, we create legitimate and valued spaces within which students can speak and to re-tune our ears so that we can hear what they say. It means that instead of assuming we know what and how students need to learn, we acknowledge their knowledge, interests, and goals and invite students to assume active roles in critiquing and reforming education. In short, it means changing the structures in our minds that have rendered us disinclined and unable to elicit and respond to students' perspectives and changing the structures in educational relationships and institutions that have supported and been maintained by this disinclination and inability.

Judging from the little but important work that has been done in this area, profound changes in role and relationship as well as in learning can result when adults listen to students. When adults listen to students, they can begin to see the world from those students' perspectives, make what they teach more accessible to students, conceptualize teaching, learning, and the ways we study them as more collaborative processes, even change what they teach and who they are. When students are taken seriously and listened to as knowledgeable participants in important conversations about schooling, they feel motivated to participate constructively in their education. Because they experience daily the effects of existing educational practices, students have unique and valuable views on education that, when elicited and shared, have the potential to transform schools into institutions responsive to rather than disconnected from the modern world.

Over the last decade some educators and educational researchers have attempted to create new roles for students and to challenge traditional notions of who has relevant knowledge about education. These long overdue efforts are important both for the essential ways in which they attend to student perspectives as well as for the ways they throw into relief the work that remains to be done. In the following discussion I evoke the historical images of students that have contributed to their exclusion from conversations about educational policy, practice, and reform. I then outline a variety of attempts to attend to student perspectives on educational practice undertaken over the last decade. I conclude with a detailed discussion of how attitudes and institutional structures need to change if we are to more consistently and fully recognize students among those with authority on educational practice.

HISTORICAL IMAGES OF STUDENTS

Although it is rarely articulated as such, the most basic premise upon which different approaches to educational policy and practice rest is trust—whether adults trust young people to be good (or not), to have and use relevant knowledge (or not), and to be responsible (or not). The educational institutions and practices that have prevailed in the United States both historically and currently reflect a basic lack of trust in young people and have evolved to keep students under control and in their place as the largely passive recipients of what adults decide should constitute an education.

Keeping the young under control and in their place took the form it has to this day after the industrial revolution in the nineteenth century. The national obsession with efficient production in all realms plugged learners into bolted-down desks and lock-step curricula through which they were guided by the teacher-as-skilled-engineer. More progressive, humanistic conceptualizations of learners based on trust in their capacities and inclinations have always run parallel to the impulse to contain and control young bodies and minds, but they have remained alternative, not the norm. Arguments that students should be nurtured and allowed to learn in their own ways at their own pace, child-centered notions of education, and alternative models, such as those in Waldorf and Montessori schools, run counter to but do not displace the dominant view of students and approaches to their education. Even these more progressive approaches do not cede students' authority comparable to adults' in imagining and designing educational opportunities.

A COLLECTION OF EFFORTS TO RECOGNIZE AND RESPOND TO YOUNG PEOPLE'S PERSPECTIVES

Calls to listen and respond to what students have to say about school have sounded intermittently since the early 1990s. Since then, a variety of efforts have been made to attend more carefully and to respond to student perspectives. In the following section I will briefly outline these efforts. While all of them represent important steps toward recognizing students as authorities, the majority of them unfold within adults' interpretive frames and thus leave ultimate authority on education in the hands of adults. Only a few strive to shift that locus of authority, include students' voices and perspectives in larger conversations about policy and practice, and also have students help define the terms of those discussions.

Constructivist Perspectives

A wide variety of pedagogical practices aggregate under the term "constructivism." I do not detail this variety here but focus rather on what all constructivist approaches have in common: the belief that students actively construct their own understandings. In contrast to the traditional transmission model of education, constructivists carefully observe their students and develop learning opportunities that allow students to explore their ideas and make their own meanings. Many constructivists also argue that teachers can improve their practice by listening closely to what students have to say about their educational processes. Basically, constructivists argue that students need to be authors of their own understanding and assessors of their own learning. Embracing this belief, many constructivists attend to student learning processes and feedback on their learning experiences with the goal of changing pedagogical practice so that it better facilitates that learning. In short, constructivists recognize students as authorities by making space for those students to be agents in their own learning.

Critical Perspectives

Critical pedagogies not only position students as active in their own knowledge construction, they also foreground the political nature of education. Critical pedagogy focuses on critiques of social injustices and inequities and calls for the empowerment of students to develop knowledge that will help them extend their understanding of themselves, of the world, and of the possibilities for changing both. Approaches to teaching and learning based on critical pedagogy are built around adult-generated topics or around themes that are relevant to and which emerge from students' own lives. They often embody multicultural and anti-racist educational theories and practices that have evolved to counter discriminatory and exclusionary tendencies in education. All approaches within critical pedagogy embrace a commitment to redistributing power not only within the classroom, between teacher and students, but in society at large. Thus, critical pedagogies recognize students as authorities by inviting them to see and change societal inequities.

Social critics access student perspectives from a different angle but with a similar goal: their aim is to critique dominant educational policies and practices, but they write as those neither in the classroom nor in the formal role of educator or educational researcher. Writing from the perspective of critic positioned outside the classroom but dedicated to illuminating the experiences of those within classrooms, social critics produce texts that appeal to a wide readership and thus help to inform the general public about students' experiences in school. And because these authors are not perceived by the public as educators—as those with a particular bias—they can present a critical angle on the classroom that could not be offered by educators, and they can be heard by the public in a way that educators cannot be. Thus, social critics call attention to the authority of students' experiences as legitimate grounds for changing educational policies and practices.

Although they share with critical pedagogues and social critics a commitment to challenging and changing current power relations in education, some postmodern feminists nevertheless caution against uncritically or unreflectively privileging student perspectives. Some feminist theorists argue that calls for listening to student voice as a central component of student empowerment actually perpetuates imbalanced power relations because they do take into sufficient consideration the complex ways that power works within pedagogical relationships. These theorists remind us that for every voice that speaks another is silent, and that we cannot simply assume or act as though our classrooms are safe and inviting spaces. There is empirical research on classrooms in which teachers have attempted to create empowering learning conditions that shows how complex and fraught such efforts are. The cautions articulated by feminist scholars who have analyzed efforts at student empowerment challenge us to examine our assumptions and motives when striving to question or change power dynamics and the structures that support them. Thus, feminist theorists challenge us to carefully consider what recognizing students as authorities really means.

Ethnographic Perspectives

Although there is certainly a significant diversity of perspectives and practices within each of the realms of constructivism, critical pedagogy, and postmodern feminist theory and pedagogy, each group has, respectively, a shared commitment that underlies its members' approaches to attending to student voices. A wide range of ethnographic researchers, those who embrace constructivist, critical, and/or feminist theories and those who do not, strive to access student perspectives from another angle. Positioned primarily outside the classroom but interested in the pedagogical interactions within classrooms, ethnographers of education take a range of approaches to integrating student voices into their own critiques of school and presenting the perspectives voiced as a legitimate impetus for change.

Using their own frames of reference, these researchers seek student perspectives to fill in those frames. They discuss the change in perspective among participants in school communities' reform efforts; they invite students who have been silenced to address issues of identity, difference, and racism; they endeavor to access students' perspectives on what significantly affects their school experiences; they explore what it means to listen to student voices and how to do so. Such work foregrounds the challenges and complexities, as well as the urgency, of efforts to recognize student perspectives. And perhaps most importantly, this work recognizes student perspectives as authoritative by including them in the larger policy- and practice-shaping conversations from which students are generally excluded but which determine their lives in school.

Students' Perspectives

All the efforts to attend to student perspectives that I have mentioned thus far unfold within adults' interpretive frames and thus leave ultimate authority on education in the hands of adults. Another group of educators and educational researchers strives to shift that locus of authority and attend to young people's own interpretive frames of analysis both within classrooms and in conversations about policy and practice. Unlike the other efforts discussed thus far, these educators and researchers employ students' voices and perspectives not only in support of their own agendas as educators and as evidence that change is needed but also as the terms according to which practice and plans for reform should be shaped.

Most striking about these efforts is that those eliciting student perspectives do not have any fixed idea about what they are going to find. Furthermore, the goal of many of these studies and revisions of practice is to inspire students to feel like and be co-researchers. Thus students speak for themselves as well as about themselves.

LOOKING TO ANOTHER PROFESSION: RECOGNIZING CLIENTS' PERSPECTIVES IN MEDICINE

Each of the outlined examples of efforts to challenge the traditional ways in which students have been positioned in relation to their education offers an important dimension to a necessarily multidimensional revision of who should be recognized as an authority on educational theory and practice. These examples offer particularly useful partial answers to questions about the purpose of education, who has the perspective and the power to decide, and how to begin to change assumptions about both. To situate these efforts in relation to other reform efforts, I want to mention briefly recent trends in the field of medicine. The ways in which some medical practitioners have reconceptualized their patients' roles offer us inspiring models in education.

Clients in the medical realm are very much like students in education: they are those whom the profession is intended to serve, but they are often those with the least agency in the service process. For a long time professionals in the medical field assumed, like educators, that they knew best how to conceptualize and deliver service. Over the last twenty years, however, the provider/client relationship and client satisfaction with service delivered have become foci for research and practice. Many doctors now argue that understanding patients' concerns, expectations, and requests is essential for health care practitioners, policymakers, and researchers. Recent research indicates that an increasing number of doctors elicit patients' perspectives both while care is being given and subsequent to delivery. There are even some nascent movements toward including patients' assessments of care in the training of medical practitioners. Because research finds that positive patient/provider relationships and patient satisfaction are positively associated with quality care, many medical researchers advocate not only attending to what their patients want but also promoting patient autonomy built on kindness and respect for the patient as a person. There is, in fact, an international movement toward what has been called "patient-centered" medicine, and research indicates that when patients perceive their care to be patient-centered, the health care provided is more efficient (i.e., there are fewer diagnostic tests and fewer referrals necessary).

These recent changes in the medical field offer evidence that it is possible to change attitudes and practices—even in a profession that has traditionally considered the adult professional to be the only one with legitimate knowledge and perspective.

A CASE STUDY OF RECOGNIZING STUDENT PERSPECTIVES

As someone who has maintained a project for the last ten years that aims to recognize students as authorities on educational practice, I can speak from inside the experience of striving to elicit students' perspectives and of learning to listen to and act on them. The project I have maintained in collaboration with high-school-based educators is called Teaching and Learning Together. Part of an undergraduate teacher preparation course, the project invites both the spoken and the written perspectives of young people into conversations about teaching and learning within the following forums: a weekly exchange of letters between preservice teachers enrolled in the course and selected students who attend a local public high school; weekly conversations among the preservice teachers in the college classroom; and weekly conversations between the high school students and a school-based educator at the high school. Through these forums this project positions high school students as authorities among other authorities, including teachers, teacher educators, and published researchers. My goal is to challenge the preservice teachers to develop beliefs and practices that are guided by what high school students, not only adult authorities on educational policy and practice, identify as critical issues in teaching and learning.

When one tries to alter established educational structures and power dynamics, one necessarily faces a variety of difficulties, which are also opportunities. This has certainly been my experience. There are the logistical challenges of connecting educational contexts (school and college) and of collaboration with school-based educators and high school students who have demanding schedules and numerous commitments. There are the psychological challenges of convincing young adults on the brink of their first careers that they have something to learn from the people they are planning to teach. There are the intellectual challenges of fostering communication between groups of students who have different ways of thinking and talking and who move in different educational cultures. And there are the personal challenges attendant upon any such deep questioning of established beliefs and practices. Before, during, and after each iteration of Teaching and Learning Together, one of my roles is to work through the disruptions such an approach prompts in a way that inspires all participants to keep learning.

These challenges spring from the fact that authority has always been assumed to belong to educational researchers and theorists. It is difficult even for preservice teachers within a project that frames high school students as authorities to learn to listen to those students. As one preservice teacher who had participated in Teaching and Learning Together put it, "being in the [college] environment for four years, I just did not think that I could learn anything from [my high school partner] . . . at the beginning I came in to the . . . project with the idea that she could probably learn something from me."

The challenge to listen at all is equaled by the challenge to learn to listen differently once one decides to listen. One preservice teacher who had participated in Teaching and Learning Together was deeply frustrated with her dialogue partner until, as she explains, "I realized that I was expecting [my partner] to speak in my language. Amid our discussions of student voice and its value, I had neglected to realize that his learning, his method of articulation, was through experience and concrete examples. I had sought to give him voice while failing to hear the sound of his individual words." It takes time and continued effort to change what are deeply inscribed ways of thinking about who has authority on education.

Experiences of and responses to published efforts to foreground student perspectives present similar challenges. Most power relationships have no place for listening and actively do not tolerate it because it is very inconvenient: to really listen means to have to respond. Listening does not always mean doing exactly what we are told, but it does mean being open to the possibility of revision, both of thought and action. At a minimum, it means being willing to negotiate. Old assumptions and patterns of interaction are so well established that even those trying to break out of them must continue to struggle. And understanding that is part of what it means to listen.

TOWARD MORE FULLY RECOGNIZING STUDENT PERSPECTIVES

Although each of the efforts I have reviewed this far has an essential element to contribute toward the goal of recognizing students among the authorities on educational practice; we must go beyond what has already been accomplished. Decades of calls for educational reform have not succeeded in making schools places where all young people want to and are able to learn. It is time to change profoundly our notions of students' capacities and who learns from whom in relationships between adults and young people.

Step One: Learning to Listen

A first step toward recognizing students as authorities on educational practice is learning to listen to those who experience schooling every day. Although students are rarely asked for their perspectives, when they are asked, they offer insights not only for teachers but also for themselves.

High school students who participated in Teaching and Learning Together as part of their teacher preparation commented on how their participation illuminated and sometimes changed their sense of themselves and their experiences in school. One student explained that "[participating in this project] made me step back as a student and just look at how everything was going on in the classroom. It made me look at how I was being taught and how teachers worked." When students better understand how teachers work—the complement to teachers' better understanding how students work—they can participate more constructively in the educational process. Reflecting on her participation in Teaching and Learning Together, another high school student described how her sense of responsibility had changed: "It made me think about how to be a better student cause it makes you think that a teacher is up there and they worked hard to come up with this lesson plan and if you're not going to put in a hundred percent then you're letting them down in a way."

When students have the opportunity to articulate their perspectives on school, they not only offer insights into that schooling that are valuable for educators. They also have an opportunity to hone their own thinking—to think metacognitively and critically about their educational experiences. And as a result of this newly gained perspective and investment, students not only feel more engaged but are also more inclined to take responsibility for their education because it is no longer something being done to them but rather something they do.

Of course students, like adults, do not always have helpful things to say. Sometimes they have nothing to say, sometimes they say things they have not thought through, and they always speak from complex positions. It is a challenge both to the students themselves and to those committed to listening to them to learn both to speak and to listen.

Step Two: Taking Action with Students

If we bring together the various commitments that characterize existing efforts to recognize students among educational authorities, we can formulate a place for taking action with students. From century-old constructivist approaches to education we can retain the notion that students need to be authors of their own understanding and assessors of their own learning. With critical pedagogy we can share a commitment to redistributing power not only within the classroom, between teacher and students, but in society at large. Like critics positioned outside the classroom, we can find ways of illuminating what is happening and what could be happening within classrooms that the wider public can hear and take seriously. Keeping in mind postmodern feminist critiques of the workings and reworkings of power, we can take small steps toward changing oppressive practices, but we can also continually question our motives and approaches in taking these steps. Like the few educational researchers who have included student voices in arguments for how to reform education, we can include student perspectives in larger conversations about educational policy and practice. And finally, we can include students', as well as adults', frames of reference in conversations about educational policy and practice; we can take seriously their frames of reference and the assertions made within them among other impetuses toward change.

With these commitments, precedents, and nascent efforts as a foundation, we can begin to think about next steps. One possibility is using existing forums. As some of the efforts outlined above illustrate, established forums and publications can expand to include students. When educators and educators-to-be learn to listen to students, they can lead the way for others to change. After carrying on an extensive epistolary exchange with a high school student focused on respect, one preservice teacher who participated in Teaching and Learning Together wrote about how her high school student partner taught her that she has "a *responsibility* to include multiculturalism and diversity in the curriculum." This future physics teacher reflected that "by keeping silent on this issue, I am teaching that only white students can become scientists." Another preservice teacher gained an equally invaluable insight after reflecting on his exchange with a high school student. This student's eloquence and metacognitive awareness had caused the preservice teacher "to underestimate my role in helping him to further explain his ideas"; but, after realizing his misreading of the student, this preservice teacher took into his career as a social studies teacher a new awareness of his responsibility, which can only be truly fulfilled by listening to students. Likewise, two years after participating in Teaching and Learning Together, teaching in a middle school, one graduate explained, "I don't think it always occurs to teachers to ask students about their opinions. But I do it as a matter of course in my classroom."

The changes in attitude and in practice these preservice and practicing teachers model are inspiring calls to more fully recognize and respond to student perspectives. And yet it is important to acknowledge that such accomplishments are not and cannot be the end of the story. We cannot ever learn, once and for all, to listen. We must continually relearn to listen—in every context, with each group of students, and with each individual student. The understanding that each time we will need to learn to listen anew should be as inspiring as it is daunting. It is our opportunity as educators to meet the very challenge we pose to our students: to learn.

Striving to change national contexts for conversation and engage in just this kind of learning, researchers can include students in more presentations at academic conferences and in more publications. The mere presence of those who are generally only talked about changes those conversations. When we as educational researchers and teachers hear directly from students about their experiences of school, we cannot as easily discuss problems in education and potential solutions in abstract or ideal terms, nor can we as easily dismiss the critical perspectives and the suggestions that students offer. Yet both conference forums and publication processes present challenges. The inclusion of students at conferences presents logistical challenges—securing permission to escort minors and addressing questions about who pays for the students' travel and accommodations, just to name a few. Publication poses other challenges, such as tackling issues concerned with who is in charge of the composing and editing processes in student-generated texts. It is not easy to adjust to the changes required. The greatest challenge, then, is how to change the terms of the conversations and practices. Unless students' voices matter and are essential to the actions we take, we run the risk of reinscribing old patterns of power distribution and approaches to change.

A step beyond including students in existing forums is the creation of new forums within which all stakeholders can come together and talk amongst themselves, each bringing a perspective that is valued and respected by all the others. Like the classroom-based projects, conferences, and publications that foreground student perspectives and invite students to define the terms of discussion, suggest directions, and propose alternatives to the status quo in teaching and learning, more forums need to be created within which students' critiques of current practices and visions for other possibilities are put first.

Thus among the most basic implications of this call to recognize students' perspectives is that there need to be sustained contexts and on-going dialogue about the meaning and nature of education. At the classroom level, at the administrative level, at the school and community levels, and at local and national policy levels, every participant in formal education needs to ask him- or herself where the opportunities for this kind of dialogue exist or could exist within his or her context. Where in the classroom? Where in the school day? Where in the administrative structure? Where at school board meetings? Where in district, state, and national forums? Specific questions educators can ask under the umbrella of this overarching question include the following:

- With whom do I speak about how education is working and how it might need to change?
- Where does the impetus for changing a curriculum or a form of interaction in school come from, and how can students be more central to that process?

- What are some important barriers to pursuing this change in attitude and practice and how can we address them?
- How might our school's or system's review and reward structures be revised so that student perspectives are not only an integral part of the feedback elicited but also a legitimate source upon which to draw in conceptualizing revisions of policy and practice?

Underlying the answers to these questions, which would necessarily vary by context, is the obvious need to rethink the logistical challenges posed by already overly constricting schedules within which all members of the school community labor. Some answers might be relatively easy, such as including a question on a standard teaching or administrative evaluation form that asks: Did the instructor make changes during the class that were responsive to learning needs expressed by students? If addressing this question, and providing evidence of change based on its answers, were not only legitimate but also required for review and promotion, the structures that currently support the exclusion of student perspectives from conversations about educational policy and practice would be changed. This move in education would be in keeping with the recognition among medical professionals that they have failed to attend sufficiently to the experiences and perspectives of those they aim to serve and the revision of their professional practices to include clients' perspectives to rectify this failure.

Cognizant of many critiques of power dynamics, I do not believe that power can or should be eliminated from any interaction. What can be changed, however, is who is invested with power and how participants in a class, an institution, or a national debate about education are supported and rewarded for participation. If, as in some of the approaches discussed here, attention to students is not only a mandatory but also a genuine response or follow-through on what is heard, then we begin to see changes in both conceptual and institutional structures.

Challenges will remain that we will not quickly overcome in including students in forums for conversation about education. Almost all the challenges reflect what may be a basic human tendency: to fall back consciously or unconsciously on long-standing assumptions and practices, what is familiar and comfortable—or even familiar and uncomfortable. The tendency to evoke or simply rely on the assumed in classrooms characterizes many researchers' and policymakers' impulse to evoke traditional, and therefore generally conservative, categories of analysis. These evocations are often made with the conscious or unconscious goal of disabling efforts to think and act in new ways in the context of educational practice and reform.

Even as we strive to change the current structures and power distribution in education, we must keep in mind that individual students move on. Just as we cannot once and for all learn to listen, we cannot once and for all consult students. This must be an ongoing process. No particular group of students can or should be invested with the responsibility for shaping educational practice and reform. However, all students should be consulted and their words and perspectives included in deliberations about schooling and school change. It is the collective student voice, constituted by the many situated, partial, individual voices, which we are missing.

CONCLUSION

The recognition of and response to student perspectives for which I am arguing here is not simply about including students as a gesture. It is about including students to change the terms and the outcomes of conversations about educational policy and practice. Such a reform cannot take place within the dominant and persistent ways of thinking or the old structures for participation. The terms of the conversations, who participates in them and how, and the ways we act on what comes of the conversations must be reconstituted. As I have argued elsewhere, to make education a viable and revitalizing process, we must reconceptualize the roles participants play and be willing not only to change the ways we think but also constitute a new language and a new culture for reforming education.

Like those in charge of the health care system, educators think that we know what education is and should be. It is in part our roles as adults, and thus those responsible in many ways for the younger generation, that condition us to think that way. However, given the unpredictable and unprecedented ways in which the world is changing, we do not know more than students living at the dawn of the twenty-first century about what it means to be a student in the modern world and what it might mean to be an adult in the future. To learn those things, we need to embrace more fully the work of recognizing students' perspectives in conversations about schooling and reform. Education has traditionally been about changing students to make them fit. Perhaps education now needs to be about changing adults to fit students and the future.

TERMS FOR READERS

Authority—An authority is one with rightful power. One who has authority has power and esteem born of others' recognition, one has competency. An authority is one who is appealed to as a legitimate source of knowledge and understanding. An authority, like an author, can create something, can participate in important decision-making processes, can make change.

Listening—To listen is to give close attention to with the purpose of hearing; to yield to advice or admonition. Thus listening is paying attention with the intention of responding, of acting in response. Listening to those who have previously been unrecognized or who have had perspectives and roles without a voice means retuning ears to hear, then being ready to act on what we hear, and then listening again and anew.

Perspective—Perspective means two seemingly different things: on the one hand, a narrow, limited, albeit valid angle or standpoint from which one looks; on the other, a wide and encompassing view. It means both the single angle and the interrelation of multiple aspects of a subject; thus it implies both looking and understanding, individual and collective.

Recognize—To know again, to admit the truth or validity of, to acknowledge. To recognize is to see and acknowledge something one has been ignoring or was not aware of—to see it and acknowledge it either for the first time or again and anew. It carries with it the implication of thinking again, of rethinking, as well as seeing, re-seeing, and seeing anew.

Role—A role is a part, a function, a prescribed piece in a performance, or the expected behavior or participation in a social interaction. A role is constituted by a collection of expectations that others have for a person occupying a particular position. It implies as well a set of rights and responsibilities as defined and approved by the system in which the person acts. In addition, role implies the existence of other roles that have bearing on one another. People occupying different roles are ascribed different degrees and kinds of power. These power dynamics affect interactions and people's sense of themselves, which are closely intertwined. They influence people's thinking about what they are responsible for, what is possible for them, and what is not. Essential here is the notion that roles are not fixed identities but rather socially constructed phenomena that can be revised.

FURTHER READING

This chapter is based on an article I published in *Educational Researcher* called Authorizing Students' Perspectives: Toward Trust, Dialogue, and Change in Education (Vol. 31(4), May 2002, 3–14). This article—which can also be found at http://www.aera.net/pubs/er/toc/er3104.htm—offers extensive research support for the claims I make in this chapter. I include below a short list of the texts that have been most influential on my work:

Dewey, J. (1964). My Pedagogic Creed. In R. D. Archambault (Ed.), *Dewey on Education*, pp. 427–439. Chicago: The University of Chicago Press.

Duckworth, E. (1987). The Virtues of Not Knowing. In *The Having of Wonderful Ideas and Other Essays on Teaching and Learning*, pp. 64–79. New York: Teachers College Press.

Freire, P. (1998). *Pedagogy of Freedom*. Lanham, MD: Rowman & Littlefield Publishers, Inc.

Luke, C and Gore, J. (Eds.). (1992). *Feminisms and Critical Pedagogy*. New York: Routledge.

Weis, L., and Fine, M. (Eds.). (1993). *Beyond Silenced Voices: Class, Race, and Gender in United States Schools*. Albany, NY: State University of New York Press.

Welch, S. (1990). *A Feminist Ethic of Risk*. Minneapolis, MN: Fortress Press.

CHAPTER 88

Critical Consciousness and Pedagogy: Reconceptualizing Student-Centered Dialogue as Educational Practice

CATHY B. GLENN

Dialogue, particularly when it is student-centered, is commonly understood by critical peda-gogues as the principal communicative means for engaging students and developing in them critical consciousness. This approach to educational practice directly challenges mainstream ed-ucational psychology models of education that privilege monologic approaches to pedagogy. As such, a critical approach often assumes that student-centered dialogue—in contrast to monologic lecturing that assumes knowledge can (and ought to) be transmitted to students—is tantamount to critical education. However, dialogue's privileged status in critical approaches to education has been critiqued as not only being difficult to facilitate in some institutional settings, but also as being uncritically appropriated without consideration of its limitations. In this chapter, those limitations are addressed and the possibilities of an alternative critical orientation and practice are explored via an ethnographically oriented case study. Using Raymie McKerrow's theory of critical rhetoric as an approach to teaching that nurtures critical consciousness without privi-leging student-centered dialogue, I analyze the strategies of one critical educator in a complex institutional setting: a classroom of over 100 students. Expressly, the focus in this chapter is an exploration of a critical communicative orientation that resists mainstream educational psychol-ogy models without uncritically jettisoning a lecture format that a critical educator may be called upon to employ in a classroom with a large student population. Ultimately, what is demonstrated in this case study, in contrast to the vast majority of critical pedagogy literature, is that critical education that resists mainstream educational psychology need not privilege student-centered dialogue in order to develop students' critical consciousness.

Mainstream educational psychology embraces a Piagetian formalism, which tends to privilege cognitive assimilation by emphasizing, in teaching practices, students' ability to understand phenomena by fitting it into their existing cognitive structures. Monologic teaching practices, which tend to privilege lecture formats, support assimilationist objectives by situating the teacher as the expert whose task is to deposit knowledge into passive and stable student-receptacles. In this model, when students are confronted with phenomena or ideas that disrupt their constructed reality, a mainstream educator will focus on helping students assimilate the new information into existing frameworks in order to resolve the tension that is created by contradictory information. It is an approach that presupposes the stability and discreteness of existing structures and, thus, tends to reify and reproduce them while eliding their interconnected constitutiveness. More than this, formalism is an objectivist educational psychology that demands students disconnect their processes of valuing, knowing, and being from each other and abstract or decontextualize those experiential processes from constitutive sociocultural constructs. Put simply, formalist educational psychology reproduces students and educators who have difficulty understanding their roles in maintaining existing constructs and the possibility of their transforming existing conditions.

Critical educators, on the other hand, recognize and embrace a postformal, accomodationist educational psychology. Accommodation, in Piagetian terms, is the move to adjust one's cognitive structures to account for novel phenomena or ideas. Rather than fit disruptive information to existing cognitive structures, a critical teacher helps students develop a critical consciousness—that is, critical educators nurture students' abilities to critically and self-reflexively reconceive their cognitive frameworks in the face of dissonant phenomena or ideas in order to make room for novelty and the possibility of change. Critical accommodation is a subversive practice that takes seriously the constitutiveness of subjectival meaning-making processes: it is a hermeneutic approach that embraces emotion and intuition in relation with intellect and reason; situates students and teachers in sociocultural contexts that are always already historical; is explicitly political in its recognition of interconnected relations and patterns among discourse, power, and identity; and, is future oriented in its anticipatory, yet open-ended and contingent orientation. From this perspective, students and teachers, together, can explore difference in classroom settings as moments of opportunity for radical change. Dialogic teaching practices are often the privileged communicative mode in which critical educators resist mainstream educational psychology's objectivist and abstractive tendencies. Instead, dialogic means are seen as essential in helping students recognize their roles in reconceiving cognitive constructs and creating the possibility of transforming sociocultural conditions.

What is at stake in the debates between mainstream and critical educators is the very psychological health and well-being of students and educators, as well as the possibility for resisting oppressive and inhumane constructs and, in the process, constructing just sociocultural conditions. These stakes are far too high to simply privilege dialogue as the only means to develop critical consciousness, especially when institutional settings may preclude student-centered dialogue. Instead, what is needed are communicative strategies that critical teachers can employ, even in the most difficult institutional settings. To that end, this chapter explores one critical educator's rhetorical strategy to engage, in a lecture format, a large number of students without abandoning her critical approach. First, in the section that follows, is an overview of critical pedagogy as it relates to student-centered dialogue and development of critical consciousness. The second section addresses limitations of student-centered dialogue, troubling the facile dialogue-monologue dichotomy, and clears room for alternatives. McKerrow's praxis-oriented aspects of critical rhetoric, as an alternative to privileging student-centered dialogue, are outlined in the third section. In the fourth section, the case study, the various teaching strategies employed are analyzed via McKerrow's concepts. In the last section, I suggest possible implications for theorizing critical pedagogy when student-centered dialogue is not a viable option. The case study analysis suggests, ultimately, that student-centered dialogue is not the only—nor is it an essential—means for helping students develop critical consciousness.

CRITICAL PEDAGOGY, CRITICAL CONSCIOUSNESS, AND STUDENT-CENTERED DIALOGUE

In general, a principle aim of *critical pedagogy* is the creation of educational conditions—by educators and students in concert—within which students are able to develop their *critical consciousness*. The pedagogical process of developing critical consciousness involves working with students to recognize, evaluate, and negotiate structures of power and knowledge. The objective of this pedagogical focus on developing critical consciousness is that students will come to understand themselves as active agents, within and as a part of those structures of power-knowledge, facilitating identification and creation of conditions for the possibility of humane change in oppressive sociocultural constructs. As part of this critical pedagogical approach, *student-centered dialogue* is viewed as essential in facilitating the development of critical consciousness. Critical pedagogy, then, is an educational orientation that directly challenges transmission models of learning, which are models that assume and privilege the possibility that knowledge can (and ought to) be transmitted unproblematically (that is, without power considerations) from educators to students. This assumption is confronted, from a critical perspective, by recognizing that knowledge and identity construction is a fluid, negotiated practice that is informed by sociocultural and economic contexts within which that negotiation takes place. A critical approach to educational practices assumes that without acknowledgement of those contexts and the power that constitutes them, their conditions cannot be addressed and their detrimental oppressive influence is reproduced, via transmission model educational practices.

At least three concepts are important to define at the outset: "critical" as it relates to pedagogy, "critical consciousness," and "student-centered dialogue." First, "critical" is an adjective that informs those words described by it with a set of assumptions embedded in critical social theory. Those assumptions include, but are not necessarily limited to, the following: (1) language mediates knowledge and constitutes subjectivity; (2) discourse is always already constituted within relations of power, which are historically and culturally conditioned; (3) "factual" knowledge is always already value-infused; (4) subject-object-concept relationships are fluid and influenced by sociocultural and economic constructs; (5) subordination of some in society is reproduced when the subordinated accept their status as natural and/or inevitable; (6) oppression, to be most fully addressed, must be recognized as occurring at multiple intersections (e.g., race, class, sexual orientation, etc.); and (7) traditional or mainstream models of research, teaching, and thought tend toward reproduction of those oppressions. Thus, "critical pedagogy" can be understood as an approach to pedagogical theory and classroom practice that includes sociocultural contextual considerations with respect to both educators' and students' positionalities in processes of knowing and knowledge construction. A critical approach to pedagogy, with an aim toward social change through educational practices, emphasizes student potentiality in contributing to transformation of oppressive sociocultural constructs and, thus, moves toward realizing human emancipation. There are various other names for this approach pedagogical theory and practice (e.g., "post-formal," "liberatory," "anti-racist," "emancipatory," "radical," "progressive," "democratic," etc.), all of which directly challenge mainstream transmission and cognitive models of educational theory and practice.

The second term, "critical consciousness" (what Paulo Freire coined as *conscientization*), is conceived as an ongoing process whereby learners (both educators and students) work together to move toward awareness (and awareness of their awareness) of oppressive sociocultural conditions. Critical consciousness enables recognition, on the part of students and educators, of their roles as active agents in maintaining oppression. At the same time, critical consciousness enables understanding of the possibility of students' and educators' roles in humanly reconstituting those oppressive conditions and realizing social justice. Because the approach challenges transmission models of learning and knowledge construction, critical consciousness differs from the idea of consciousness-raising. The latter assumes that educators can (and ought to) transmit preselected knowledge to students, "depositing" it into passive student-receptacles, thus raising students' consciousness. Consciousness-raising is understood as a top-down process, from active educator to passive student. In contrast, critical consciousness development is conceived as an active process negotiated between students and educators; it is an equalizing educational practice that understands students as active agents rather than passive objects. As part of the development of critical consciousness, students and educators work together to challenge, disturb, interrupt, and rupture prevailing power and knowledge narratives in order to develop critical capacities to recognize oppression and understand their own roles in both maintaining and reconceiving those narratives. Theoretically, the pedagogical aim of developing critical consciousness, then, is to facilitate recognition on the part of students of their being active subjects rather than passive objects. By extension, the practical objective is to create a classroom environment wherein students' own experience and lifeworlds (rather than preselected curriculum) become central, and wherein students and educators can, together, challenge the seeming "natural-ness" and inevitability of oppressed subjectivities and oppressive circumstances. The process of critical consciousness development is at the heart of current critical educational approaches, and the move toward development of critical consciousness assumes that student-centered dialogue is essential in facilitating that development.

The third concept, "student-centered dialogue," is understood as the intrinsic communicative modality of employing productive critical pedagogical practices. Dialogue amongst learners is most commonly understood, from this perspective, as an alternative to monological or lecture approaches. Ideally conceived, productive dialogical practices are employed as a direct challenge to transmission (or monologic) models of educational practices and are viewed as opening up critical communicative opportunities to students. Thus, dialogical communication practice from this perspective assumes that: (1) all learners (students and educators) are invited as potential communicative participants; (2) interaction among participants can be productively confrontational and/or cooperative in moving toward intersubjective understanding; (3) knowledge is constituted in interaction (rather than discovered) and existing power-knowledge constructs can be critically interrogated; (4) constituting more humane power-knowledge constructs facilitates embodiment of critical citizenship on the part of learners; and (5) critical, student-centered dialogue productively facilitates processes of critical consciousness development. That the dialogue is student-centered, again, challenges transmission models by drawing subject matter from students' own lives, language, and cultures, rather than from pre-existing curricula. It is a bottom-up approach that focuses on students' experiences, identities, and lifeworlds in an attempt to move away from top-down, educator- and text-centered curricula. Student-centered dialogue, then, affords the possibility that learners can constitute critical readings of dominant sociocultural constructs by situating educational practices within their own experiences. Moreover, it provides the opportunity to situate learning in historically informed sociocultural contexts from which learners can envision and enact social change.

LIMITATIONS OF STUDENT-CENTERED DIALOGUE: CONSIDERING ALTERNATIVES

Although the specific means engaged to facilitate student-centered dialogue vary among critical pedagogues who adopt this approach, affording a privileged status to student-centered dialogue currently is understood as synonymous with critical pedagogy and development of critical consciousness. The practical advantages of student-centered dialogue in the classroom have been a focal point in recent educational research and a large body of current scholarship explicates the transformative potential viewed as inherent in this critical approach to pedagogy. Scholars have addressed how dialogue can offer students an opportunity to rehearse social criticism, how sociocultural and identity issues can be addressed during dialogic processes, and how issues related to race, class, gender, ethnicity, and sexual orientation can be critically engaged when dialogue is student-centered. Scholars also point to the constitutive aspects of dialogue with respect to identity formation and this constitutive communication function is viewed as the primary means for helping students develop an awareness of their agency in affecting change in oppressive circumstances. Moreover, performing as critically thinking and speaking subjects in the classroom provides, for students, the basis for their performing as citizen-critics outside it, as well.

While acknowledging the value of a student-centered approach to critical, dialogic pedagogy, an equal acknowledgement of the possibly problematic nature of taken-for-granted assumptions of such an approach is also important. Critiques of dialogic assumptions include concerns that not all learners may be comfortable accepting an invitation to dialogue when the "rules for engagement" include a confrontational style of discourse or when cooperative or therapeutic objectives require more consensus than students are willing to support or more self-closure than they are willing to offer. Thus, some students may not view dialogue as a benign invitation; rather, they may perceive that the compulsory student-centered dialogic environment acts as a coercive force in demanding their participation in a particular style of educational practice. Without acknowledging the possibility of this reading by students, dialogue may simply reproduce the very normalizing and oppressive tendencies it seeks to challenge. Moreover, the possibility of oppressive power-knowledge constructs developing in student-centered dialogue has been critically addressed by some scholars. Critical approaches to pedagogy are understood as being explicitly political, but the politics embedded in current mainstream critical approaches are viewed as an inherent aspect of approaches that privilege student-centered dialogue. Given the political assumptions of mainstream critical approaches outlined in the previous section and the extension of those assumptions into pedagogical practices by mainstream critical educators, the possibility exists that different ideological versions of "critical" may be marginalized, overlooked, or excluded. Thus, some students (and some educators) may be forced to define their position as "critical" in a manner that situates them outside mainstream critical ideologies and this may reproduce, in dialogue, the very sociocultural and political marginalization and oppression that dialogue seeks to address.

In addition to these sociocultural and ideological concerns, some scholars have questioned whether students are as passive and whether lecturing is as monologic as is commonly assumed by mainstream critical pedagogy theorists and practitioners. Dichotomous understandings of passive-active in relation to monologic-dialogic ignore the complexity of a range of different enactments on both "sides" of those contrasts. As is suggested above, some dialogic styles may be far from egalitarian and may serve to prompt students to withdraw into passivity rather than emerge as active participations, thus, inhibiting development of critical consciousness. At the same time, different styles of lecturing may afford students the opportunity for critically active engagement rather than passive acceptance of knowledge and, thus, nurture development of critical consciousness. A risk of theoretically assuming fixed dichotomies—active vs. passive and dialogue vs. monologue—is that the variety of educational practice options that span a range of both dialogic and monologic styles may be overlooked or ignored. That risk is particularly salient for critical educators who view student-centered dialogue as an essential aspect of their pedagogical practice, but who face considerable practical limitations employing it.

One of the practical limitations of employing student-centered dialogue is class size, an aspect of critical classroom organization that is rarely, if ever, a part of scholarly discussions of student-centered dialogic pedagogy. It should go without saying that each classroom context is unique and each possesses its own promise and potential; on the other hand, each also presents distinctive contextual challenges. This recognition of contextual contingency—specifically as it relates to the number of students in a particular class—is virtually nonexistent in scholarship advocating a critical approach to teaching that uses learner-centered dialogue as the means to develop critical consciousness. Facilitating critical dialogue is not an easy task, even with a relatively small number of students; it is a complicated process that requires constant communicative (re)negotiation. For those critical pedagogues who find themselves in the context of a large classroom, that communication process becomes nearly untenable. It is crucial for those educators, then, to develop specific, situated, and localized strategies in order to retain the critical character of their teaching approach while adjusting their teaching strategies to accommodate a large number of students. One such strategy is suggested by Raymie McKerrow's theory of critical rhetoric. In the following section, an outline of the praxis-oriented assumptions of critical rhetoric is offered as it relates to the rhetorical role critical educators can play in helping students develop their critical consciousness, particularly when a large class size prohibits student-centered dialogue.

EDUCATOR AS CRITICAL RHETOR: AN ALTERNATIVE TO STUDENT-CENTERED DIALOGUE

Raymie McKerrow's critical rhetoric, as a communicative mode of resistance, subverts main-stream educational psychology assumptions. McKerrow describes critical rhetoric as a theoretical and practical enterprise encompassing divergent critical projects in its overarching critical spirit. Critical rhetoric serves to demystify and connect, through an engaged and subjective critique, seemingly unrelated societal forces of knowledge/power in order to recognize how they can create conditions of oppression and marginalization. In addition, employing critical rhetoric is a normative practice, rendering options for social action and allowing practical judgments about how to take such action. Critique, in this sense, is explicitly political, and the critical rhetor takes an advocacy stance in offering analyses. In particular, a critical rhetoric is concerned with how systems of power and domination are discursively constructed and maintained in order to construct counter-discourses that might interrupt and, potentially, transform oppressive constructs.

It is important to note that critical rhetoric does not point, at the outset, in the direction of a prescribed utopian *telos*. Rather, the critical rhetorician employs this method in an effort to sustain sociocultural critique—it is a practice that recognizes the value of critique and the open-ended nature of the possibilities of its normative outcomes. Thus, because of its nonprivileging nature with respect to outcomes, sociocultural critique employed by critical rhetoricians need not prescribe particular judgments and action. Rather, political judgment and action are contingently related to the process of critical rhetoric.

Criticism, from this perspective, is also a performance and, as such, goes beyond traditional argumentation's focus on critique as an instrument of rationality. The critic, through a critique of collected cultural fragments, performs interpretations of social conditions and, in doing so, argues for interpretations of those fragments. Critical rhetoric is also *performative* in the sense that it is part of instantiating—through repetitive iterative processes on the part of rhetors—a sense of sociocultural consciousness with an audience, thereby creating the conditions for envisioning alternatives to the status quo. Ultimately, this performance of critical subjectivity on the part of a critical rhetor demonstrates, for an audience, a process of identifying and/or creating the conditions for the possibility of humane social change.

As it relates to a critical approach to teaching, particularly with a large number of students, critical rhetoric can be conceived of as a way to foster the development of critical consciousness when student-centered dialogue is not a practical option. In a large classroom setting where a lecture-type format is most suitable, an educator who practices critical rhetoric is able to offer to students' readings of sociocultural circumstances through her/his performance of critical discourse. An educator who lectures utilizing critical rhetoric can embody and invite aspects of dialogue by critically framing sociocultural concerns and positing critical questions that encourage active engagement and multiple interpretations from diverse student populations. Critical rhetors, thus, nurture students' potential to reflect on this critique and help develop their abilities for envisioning alternatives to oppressive status quo constructs. This pedagogical function of critical rhetoric acts as a "model" of critical consciousness for students and creates the conditions for students' own critical engagement without having to prioritize student-centered dialogue in the process.

Also, when situated in a critical pedagogical approach, the open-ended, contingent nature of normative possibilities in critical rhetoric can be particularly effective in engaging students in the cognitive and affective processes necessary for critical classroom engagement. The nonprivileging normative approach, with respect to the choices created in the critical process, leaves room for students' own sociocultural and historically located analyses and applications. In other words, critical rhetoric employed by an educator *need not prescribe* what students should believe or do. Instead, employing critical rhetoric challenges students to examine the taken-for-granted assumptions that may preclude their own critical reflection on and evaluation of those beliefs or (in)action. It is the process—*the critical rhythm of sustained criticism*—not necessarily the content of the critique that students can begin to approximate when an educator employs critical rhetoric.

The following case study demonstrates, through a specific embodied example of pedagogy, how critical rhetoric performed by a particular pedagogue can foster critical consciousness on the part of a large number of students when student-centered dialogue is an impractical option.

A CASE STUDY

Dr. Michelle Wolf is twenty-year faculty member in the Department of Broadcast and Electronic Communication Arts (BECA) at San Francisco State University (SFSU). She completed her M.A. in Communication Studies at the University of Massachusetts and her PhD in Communication Theory—with a Mass Communications and Educational Psychology emphasis—at the University of Texas at Austin before relocating to California and accepting the position at SFSU. Wolf has been teaching for twenty-five years. Whether teaching thirty students or 150, her provocative style and inherently critical mode of teaching means that theoretical material introduced in class is interspersed with frequently affective, sometimes graphic, and always controversial media, and these cultural fragments are offered with a healthy measure of Wolf's own sociocultural critique. Her obvious enthusiasm for, commitment to, and engagement with students creates a welcoming classroom environment and, although also quite challenging, the environment invites critical exploration of the course material in connection with students' life experiences.

Overview of Method and Classroom Particulars

My observations of Dr. Wolf's teaching strategies, in BECA 422: "Social Aspects of Electronic Media," took place during the fall 1999 semester and consisted of approximately fifteen total hours of logged, in-class observations. The original study from which this chapter emerged employed an ethnographically oriented methodology. Specifically, along with the in-class observations, the students were offered the opportunity to contribute their thoughts and feelings about Wolf's approach and their own engagement with it by responding to a survey utilizing open-ended questions. The original project also included an oral history conducted with Wolf and a parallel autoethnographic account. The analysis section that follows, then, is based in all four methodological sources: in-class observations, students' survey responses, Wolf's oral history account, and autoethnographic material.

The population of students in this study—over 100—reflects the diversity commonly found at SFSU. The ages of students ranged from eighteen to thirty-nine; the class standings ranged from first-year students to seniors; 46 percent of students claimed Caucasian ethnicity, while 54 percent claimed diverse ethnicities; and, the gender breakdown was 52 percent female, 48 percent male.

The size of the class population in 422 significantly limited the possibility for employing student-centered dialogue. Moreover, the setting—a large auditorium-like classroom with fixed, theatre seating—contributed to the difficulties because students were focused on the front of the room and the physical environment was less than conducive to discussion and more so to a lecture or performance approach. Although some limited discussion was accomplished, Wolf primarily focused on employing other strategies to critically engage her students.

The observations focused on how it was possible that, without the benefit of student-centered critical dialogue, the students in Wolf's class were able to critically engage with the material addressed in lectures and how that engagement facilitated development of critical consciousness. In general, I observed that the level of critical engagement that would usually be reserved for smaller, more dialogically centered classes was nurtured in this large student population. Those means—as illustrated by the categories in the following section—offered the students in 422 an opportunity to critically and actively consider the material without having to frequently vocalize their thoughts in class.

Analysis

This section illustrates three conceptual categories of teaching strategies employed by Dr. Wolf: explicit cultural critique, personal self-disclosure, and spontaneous, provocative participation assignments. I offer an exemplar in each of the three categories and analyze them utilizing praxis principles of critical rhetoric in order to demonstrate its resistance to mainstream educational psychology's assimilationist tendencies in favor of a critical accomodationist approach.

Sociocultural Critique

Today's class is the second part in a unit on censorship. In addition to a lively lecture about censorship precedents and implications, we watch part of a cable program featuring a woman applying lotion to her enormous (silicone) breasts, a graphic and emotional clip from a 1970's Vietnam documentary, and a short videotaped modern primitive performance in which a man recites poetry while impaling his scrotum with needles and filling it with saline. In the last few minutes of class, we watch as a man performs oral sex on his well-endowed male partner while masturbating himself. For a class of approximately hundred students, the room seems unusually silent during the last clip. At the end of the class period, the students begin leaving the room; some are very quiet, others giggle as they make their way to the door, while still others are talking to friends in hushed, somewhat frenetic tones. It's just another day in BECA 422.

Wolf's use of controversial and dissonant media, in combination with the lectures she performs afterward, act as a model or demonstration of sociocultural critique for her students. As a critical rhetor, Wolf unapologetically advocates for and against important sociopolitical issues (censorship, on this day), and her provocative media choices and analyses of them help constitute that advocacy via her sociocultural criticism. The critical rhetorical performances stimulate students' critical engagement and reflection processes and help facilitate development of their sense of critical consciousness. In particular, Wolf's media choices spark students' critical thinking processes by immediately engaging them on an affective level, establishing a sense of investment and commitment to the topic. This direct engagement enables Wolf to prompt her students to think more deeply and critically about those topics and facilitates an opportunity for them to make connections between seemingly unrelated media images and messages and, thus, the power/knowledge constructs embedded in them.

When choosing fragments of media to combine for presentation, Wolf assumes an active rather than passive role on the part of students as audience. As such, her juxtapositions of diverse mediated fragments encourage students to engage critically and be aware of connections between them, particularly as they relate to students' lived experiences. It becomes crucial that students begin to read beyond the surface meanings of individual fragments (e.g., nude bodies, sexual acts, war footage, etc.) and try to envisage how those fragments might be related in and to broader sociocultural contexts. Wolf's choices embody critical rhetoric by recognizing that media fragments may be interpreted as polysemic (containing many meanings), instead of simply representing the one obvious meaning that requires interpretation. Students are given the opportunity—in engagement with Wolf's choices and her own critical readings—to offer readings of their own, which may challenge dominant sociocultural meanings by subverting the surface meaning-making processes.

From the perspective of a critical rhetor, description is always already evaluative and processes of understanding and knowing cannot be separated from processes of evaluation. Educators (as critical rhetors or not) choose what they will focus on, what aspects are emphasized, and those choices are always already influenced by what an educator brings to teaching. In Wolf's case, her critical perspective is always already a part of her media choices, and that perspective explicitly frames the analyses she models for her students. Unlike educators who ostensibly teach from an "objective" point of view, then, critical rhetors explicitly offer their situated points of view and invite diverse interpretations of those perspectives. Moreover, the controversial media choices, by prompting diverse readings on her part and from her students' perspectives, demonstrate the constitutiveness of meaning making through discursive processes.

Wolf's political orientation is a starting point for many students' own opinion-formation processes and critical development. For instance, her explicit capitalist critiques, her anti-censorship stance, and her feminist analyses of mediated body images trigger in her students responses that begin (or continue) the processes of critical consciousness development. Rather than imposing her perspectives on students, Wolf's analyses often spark critique of them (generally in the form of written feedback). Her students catch her critical rhythm, so to speak, and undertake the act of criticism themselves. More than this, when asked to consider options for changing what can be viewed as damaging or oppressive mediated messages, Wolf's students offer creatively fashioned alternatives, the conception of which may have been less creative if not for the critical forum in which they are allowed to develop. The criticism rendered from Wolf's open-ended orientation is, thus, not prescriptive; rather, it is a discursive process that opens space for students' own decisions about what counts when making critical judgments. Contingently oriented criticism like Wolf's, rather than fixing a set of interpretations from which to choose seeks, instead, to increase the possibilities for students' creative interpretations. For the students in Wolf's class, generation of interpretive options to status quo constructs becomes a creative process of critical invention.

In sum, these aspects of critical rhetoric, performed by Wolf, seem to confirm the notion that the performance of critical readings can act as a way to establish a critical rhythm and create opportunities for students to envision humane transformation of social structures. Wolf's explication and critique of the controversial mediated messages and images open up previously unexamined areas of analysis for students and foster the kind of critical thinking and reflection necessary for developing critical consciousness. Wolf's strategies offer a way to engage with students at this critical level without making student-centered dialogue the central aspect of her pedagogy.

Personal Experience and Self-Disclosure

Today's lecture begins a unit on body image and media representations and Dr. Wolf takes some time to relate her own experiences with body image development. She shares an abbreviated, but emotional narrative of several early life experiences; the first involved an incident of her own painful experience with facial disfigurement as the result of being hit in the face with a baseball bat. The story includes aspects of both her physical and psychological devastation and the sometimes-cruel reactions of her grade-school peers. She goes on to talk about her battles with an eating disorder and the negative self-perception of her own body image as it relates to media representations of the "model" body type and her childhood experiences. The students seem mesmerized; there is not a single student in the room who does not seem completely engaged with Dr. Wolf as she tells these stories.

Critical rhetoric is decidedly, yet self-reflexively, subjective; critique takes a stand either for or against something, often in the context of the critic's lived experiences. In the case of Wolf's self-disclosure with respect to body image and media representation, the performance of critiquing the overwhelming, and sometimes devastating, impacts of represented (and ignored) body types in media serves to model cultural critique as a deeply personal and powerfully political process. Notably, in this context, the level of Wolf's self-disclosure acts as a way to bridge the affective gap between Wolf and the large number of students in this classroom. A sense of intimacy is created when Wolf relates a personal narrative with which nearly all students can relate: feelings of insecurity, marginalization, negative self-concept, and personal pain. They can see reflected parts of themselves in her portrayal of her personal experiences and development. The level of connection this creates with her students enables Wolf to maintain an environment that nurtures a feeling of safety in which her students are free to critically explore various aspects of the concepts presented in BECA 422.

A key aspect of this critique, for Wolf, includes an explicit confirmation that feelings (in contrast to informal logic or reasoning) are a natural and necessary part of the critical process. This aspect of critical rhetoric reflects a move away from the strictly rational and traditional epistemic function of rhetoric based in general, abstract principles. Rather, critical rhetoric includes a *doxastic* sense that expands those standards to include analyses grounded in personal experiences, feelings, and beliefs. The expansion allows for a relationship between knowing and being and, in so doing, provides students with a way to explore how beliefs, knowledge, and truth are constituted. Put differently, the focus shifts away from knowledge and knowing based on abstract foundations independent of subjectivity and toward recognition of the concrete contingency of both knowledge and its constitution by individuals in relation with one another.

Wolf's critical rhetoric, by explicitly demonstrating the power of mediated symbolic representations of body images in her lived experiences, also underscores how those signs come to possess that power. With a personal connection, Wolf's critique connects mediated images with material effects in her lived experiences and, by extension, her students' lifeworlds. In this way, students begin to understand more than what a sign *is*; they come to understand what signs *do* in sociocultural contexts and how they become powerful. The shift in focus helps students connect to the topics addressed in ways that are personally significant and, in the process, prompts a level of commitment to those topics.

In sum, Wolf's use of personal narratives reflects critical rhetoric's acknowledgment that experience, feelings, and beliefs are an important part of the critical process. Her critical analyses of mediated body images also engage students in a way that includes them in the construction of transformative possibilities. By connecting with Wolf's personal experiences as they relate to the subject matter, students are invited to question how that same subject matter affects their lives, as well. This critical engagement lends a sense of immediacy to Wolf's lecture and helps facilitate critical consciousness development for students without dialogue being the central focus.

Participation Assignments

In a unit on news coverage, Dr. Wolf begins the class session with a participation assignment, a current events survey. She asks: How do people in Iraq label their ethnic group? What is the capital city of Iraq? What is the name of one other city in Iraq besides the capital? What does the terrain/land look like in Iraq? What is the weather like in Iraq? Can you name a body of water in this country? What form of government will you find there? Is there a Head of State in Iraq and what is his/her title? What percentage of the population of the Iraqi people lives in the cities? During the process of asking the questions, Dr. Wolf takes on a demanding, almost aggressive tone. It feels as if she expects that her students should know the answers to these questions and that they should have no problem responding to questions about countries that have generated such intense media attention.

After the students finish and pass their survey responses forward, she tells them the answers to the questions. In general, the students appear to be surprised, even stunned, by how little they know about such heavily covered, politically significant countries. After disabusing the students of numerous stereotypes and misconceptions about Middle-Eastern peoples, their cultures, and the countries in which they live, she spends some time explicitly critiquing what seems to be an apparent lack of engagement with and attention to the news media by those who have chosen to devote their academic time to media studies. I look around the room and it seems that every student is listening intently to the not-so-subtle critique of her/himself.

Participation assignments generally consist of either written surveys administered in class and turned in immediately before a lecture, or take-home exercises that ask students to individually connect with and/or engage in a critique of some form of media. An example of a participation survey is related here; outside participation assignments also included visiting activist websites and responding to the content, critiquing new television programming, and writing a viewer/listener response letter to a media source offering a critique about what they viewed/heard. The sometimes spontaneous—and, almost always provocative—participation assignments in this class serve at least two purposes: first, they compel students to focus attention on a subject that they, previously, may not have thought about in much depth. Second, in conjunction with Wolf's critical analyses, they move students from vague feelings about an issue or concept to working through those feelings toward more precise, critically informed thinking and reflection.

In general, Wolf's constant probing for students' thoughts, feelings, and opinions, via the participation assignments, set a critical tone in class that activated an inclination toward students' critical thinking processes. The students, through the written participation assignments, presented the products of those critical thinking processes; they understood this as their opportunity to critically respond to Wolf without extended in-class dialogue. The effect, immediately, was to engage students in the subject matter at hand and, as significantly, enable them to connect their own experiences and knowledge about the concepts and issues to a critical evaluation of the theoretical constructs discussed in the lecture.

For example, the participation survey recounted above allowed an opportunity for Wolf to critique the process of nominalization that occurs in mediated representations of diverse cultures. As part of this participation assignment, she demonstrated for students a way to critique mediated discourses that tend to obscure or neglect aspects of Iraqi culture and that, in the process, locate Iraqis as "deviant" from US-American sociocultural standards. This demonstration, in conjunction with students' participation in the survey, served to highlight how particular mediated representations become embedded in the knowledge constructs most viewers take for granted. The students' inability to name important aspects of Iraqi culture reflects the process of the knowledge construction of US-American media and their own lack of critical engagement with that construction and the assumptions therein. Wolf's lecture session afterward challenges students to re-examine those assumptions that underlie the processes of how they come to understand mediated cultural representations.

Finally, critical rhetors also recognize that absence is as important as presence in constructing knowledge, particularly as it relates to understanding and interpreting mediated discourse. The power to discursively erase the existence, in mediated representations, of different ethnicities, genders, classes, and sexual orientations, is derived precisely from its absence in relation to what is present. Wolf's critique of mediated body images (described in the previous section) also included an account of what is left out of those images and the effects of that discursive erasure. In the context of the participation assignment in this section (along with that in the previous section), the critique served to help her students develop a more sophisticated, critical level of awareness—critical consciousness—when viewing mediated images of cultures constructed as deviant from US-American norms. At the same time, Wolf's performance of that critique allowed for the development of critical consciousness without the benefit of student-centered dialogue.

SOME IMPLICATIONS AND DIRECTIONS

In this study, several aspects of negotiating critical engagement with a large number of students without prioritizing student-centered dialogue were explored. This exploration suggests several strategies that can help facilitate critical consciousness development on the part of a large number of students (and, perhaps, smaller student populations, as well). Wolf's intentional and risky stimulation of her students through explicit cultural critiques and controversial media choices, open and honest self-disclosure, and spontaneous, provocative participation assignments all promoted critical engagement in diverse and particularized ways in her classroom. Likewise, students' understanding of, and responses to, her intentions and approach indicates that the performance of critical rhetoric, on the part of educators, offers an alternative to privileging student dialogue while maintaining the ability to nurture students' critical consciousness development. Moreover, this case study demonstrates that a critical approach to pedagogy can resist mainstream educational psychology's assumptions without privileging one model of critical pedagogy. Rather, critical approaches to pedagogical theory and practice are diverse. Thus, critical educational practices, variously interpreted, can take the form of a range of schools of thought: post-formal, democratic, Socratic, feminist, hermeneutical, Marxist, neoliberal, and/or post-structuralist. Critical pedagogical theory and practice understood from this perspective, then, is far from a homogenous approach. This case study, in the context of a classroom of over 100 students, provides some promising results in support of this view.

First, the size of this student population uniquely contributed to communicative dynamics in some surprisingly effective ways. The distinctive setting with its fixed seating and large number of students—a setting traditionally considered problematic in terms of critically engaging students—seemed to actually promote the possibility that Wolf's risky, dissonant, sometimes confrontation style would be critically effective. With respect to cultural critique and controversial media, the large room and number of students may have helped to dissipate uncomfortable feelings that, in a smaller classroom, would be more problematic. The forceful approach may be more effective when the environment is not so intimate and the students are allowed to silently explore their thoughts and feelings around the concepts and issues without being compelled to share, publicly, those thoughts and feelings.

Second, with respect to self-disclosure, the personal nature of Wolf's narratives takes on a public performance character that helps alleviate the potential that students will feel personally confronted. In this setting, students were able to disassociate themselves from the personal implications of self-disclosure for Wolf while, at the same time, witnessing a personal narrative in which they felt safe to engage, evaluate, and on which they could privately reflect. In a smaller classroom, the personal-academic boundary may be too blurred for comfort if the students feel too personally confronted by an educator's personal disclosures. In this context, however, that boundary remained in place while still offering an affective bridge to critical reflection.

Finally, with respect to participation assignments, when the survey questions were consistently intended to point out a particular lack of awareness or information on the part of students and that insisted student reconceive their own cognitive frameworks, the larger classroom provided a sense of anonymity thereby fostering a sense of safety within an otherwise provoking environment. In a smaller classroom, this forceful a tactic could prompt students to feel they have an individual responsibility to come up with the "right" answer/opinion/feeling or face public exposure and embarrassment if they offer what might perceived as the "wrong" answer. In this context, however, students could recognize and respond to the challenge without being put publicly on the spot to respond to it.

The analysis offered in this chapter begins construction of only a first layer of understanding of one unique and powerful educator's rhetorical strategies for critically engaging a large number of students without the benefit of student-centered dialogue. And, without question, Dr. Wolf's pedagogical strategies are risky and the approach she takes may not be suitable for some educators. Diverse student populations, various classroom limitations, and institutional constraints are but a few of the contingencies with which individual educators must contend when choosing pedagogical strategies, risky or not. Moreover, utilizing intentionally provocative media, personal self-disclosure, and seemingly confrontational participation assignments requires sober consideration of possible student responses to such stimulation. Certainly, Wolf's twenty-five years of experience with this approach assists her in facilitating critical engagement with her students and, by her own account, having "lots of confidence" and "knowing what you're doing" are crucial in fostering the kinds of positive experiences she experiences with students. Clearly, the possibility that students may initially respond negatively can be uncomfortable for others with less experience or, perhaps, less of a tolerance for risk, vulnerability, and uncertainty. However, every teacher takes risks when critically engaging students and, explicit or not, those risks make each one of us vulnerable and render the "outcome" of our pedagogical strategies uncertain. It is within the fertile liminal spaces of that uncertainty that those teachers and students who are willing to risk can create the lush conditions for the possibility of transformation.

Comparison studies are needed, of course, in other settings and with other educators and students. Gradually, the findings could be pulled together and further conceptions and strategies could be added to the tentative categories discussed in this study. Moreover, for educators who approach pedagogy critically, this study offers a starting place for theorizing how it is possible to resist mainstream educational psychology's objectivist and abstractive tendencies and retain critical aspects of their teaching, even in the most challenging institutional settings. The theory of critical rhetoric suggests a framework from which to begin that theorizing work in order to more fully understand how to practically develop students' critical consciousness in diverse classroom contexts that seemingly preclude critical approaches to teaching.

FURTHER READING

Burbules, N. C. (2000). The Limits of Dialogue as a Critical Pedagogy. In P. Trifonas, (Ed.), *Revolutionary Pedagogies*. New York: Routledge.

Kincheloe, J. L. (1999). The Post-Formal Critique of Educational Psychology. In J. L. Kincheloe, S. R. Steinberg, and P. Hinchey (Eds.). *The Post-Formal Reader: Cognition and Education*. New York: Garland Press.

McKerrow, R. E. (1989). Critical Rhetoric: Theory and Praxis. *Communication Monographs*, 56, 91–111.

CHAPTER 89

Homeschooling: Challenging Traditional Views of Public Education

NICOLE GREEN

A FAMILY PORTRAIT: PAUL AND HELEN

I was welcomed enthusiastically as I entered the home of Paul, Junior High student, and Helen, Paul's mother. As I took off my coat and shoes, Paul expressed excitement about the fact that I was interested in his homeschooling experience and, along with his mother Helen, we immediately ventured upstairs to his schoolwork area. Paul invited me to sit next to him at his desk, which comfortably fits a computer and allows enough space for Paul to read and write. Helen showed Paul's timetable and organized subject folders while he began to confidently navigate the school's website.

Paul, Helen, and her husband have been involved in the homeschooling Virtual program for less than one year, following eight years in the public school system. Being enrolled in the Virtual program means that Alberta resources are used and assessment involves regular contact with the teachers and the completion of assignments, unit tests, and projects. Paul has a different teacher for each subject and a support teacher visits twice per year. Helen chose the Virtual program, in which the course delivery is the responsibility of the teacher, because

I can help him out but I can't be his teacher . . . I mean I guess to a certain extent I am his teacher because I am the one who sets out what he does during the day and if he does have any problems he asks. So yeah I guess I am [his teacher] but I try not to look at it like that. Like I said, I am his Mum and that's where as I just as soon stay but I am willing to make the effort and to make the difference . . .

Helen describes her relationship with the homeschooling program positively, stating that the school atmosphere is welcoming and the teachers are very approachable. Helen appreciates the educational support from the school, as well as the opportunity Paul has to enrol in Tae Kwon Do. Helen explains that Tae Kwon Do has provided him with a different side of discipline and respect and interaction with peers. The family also enjoys skating and creek walks as part of the Physical Education program.

As well as experiencing a delightful morning of conversation with Paul, I observed this intelligent young man completing his Mathematics, Language Arts, and Computer lessons his mother had outlined for him to do. On one occasion he called his mother to the room for assistance, after trying to work out the problem independently by looking in other text resources. By half past eleven, promising that he would read his Science text that evening when his parents were out, Paul's schoolwork was done. When Paul completes his school work, usually by one o'clock, he then has the afternoon to enjoy his favourite TV shows, reading his favourite books about Science, World War II, and the Harry Potter series, and building with his unimaginable amount of LEGO construction pieces. Paul spoke of the desire to become an architect, a goal reflected in his elaborate and detailed LEGO structures he has planned and built over a period of time. Paul also shared his satisfaction with homeschooling throughout the day during our conversations, "the teachers are very nice and helpful. The main expectation is for students to do the best they can . . ."

INTRODUCING THE INQUIRY

With my interest in examining the narratives of families and children in an effort to understand their experience of distance education in Queensland, Australia, I chose to conduct an inquiry into homeschooling in Alberta, Canada. The purpose of the research was to inquire into three families' experiences of homeschooling and explore issues of teaching and learning by analysing and interpreting their experiences.

The inquiry was carried out in collaboration with three families enrolled in a well-established homeschooling program. Observations and interviews were conducted in the families' homes. I believe it is necessary to highlight that I am consciously taking responsibility for the analysis and interpretation I present. You have already been introduced to Paul and Helen. Throughout the chapter, Christopher, Samuel, Luke and Lynn, and Nadine, Brett and Sarah will also be introduced through a family portrait. There could be multiple perspectives of homeschooling experiences in Edmonton, Alberta, and I am openly mindful about only offering several perspectives on the following pages, remembering that these families' lives did not begin the day I arrived nor did their lives end as I left. This chapter will share some of the themes and patterns which emerged, demonstrating how the families' homeschooling experiences suggest that educational practices in public schools can marginalize students who do not understand behavioral codes, who do not have possession of dominant cultural knowledges, or who fail to reflect the widely accepted norms of learning and development outlined by mainstream educational developmental psychology. Thus, with my interest in issues of teaching and learning, educational psychology themes emerged as important and relevant in the inquiry with families who homeschool, especially in relation to the families' experience with public education prior to their decision to teach and learn with their children at home. The families' public school experience did not adequately address the diverse needs of the students when they used a curriculum and worked within school cultures that represented a modernist perspective of promoting sameness and overcoming difference. From the families' narratives, it appears that curriculum and teaching practices in their public schools reflected an educational psychology focus in which working collaboratively and in context to pedagogically respond to the students' affective and interpersonal lives was not attempted.

THE PRESENCE OF DEVELOPMENTAL EDUCATIONAL PSYCHOLOGY IN ALBERTA

The early twentieth century marked the introduction of the discourse of educational development psychology and continues to greatly influence educational practice today. My observations in Alberta have led me to see that there is an educational movement going "back-to-basics," resulting in a conservative curriculum. Knowledge is viewed as a commodity where students develop a base of knowledge. This core knowledge predetermines student learning, with the content "stated" as outcomes that are measurable and identify what students are expected to know and do. Concepts develop linearly, from the simple to the complex, and suggest developmental appropriateness based on white, middle-class assumptions. I have heard numerous stories from teachers faced with high stakes standardized testing, which evaluates and ranks students and, eventually, schools and teachers. While the standardized tests assess and interpret student progress, it is important to highlight that they do not measure diverse student characteristics, only mathematical and language and literacy academic performance in grade three and mathematical, language and literacy, science and social studies in grades six and nine. The autonomy of many teachers is greatly lessened as they feel it necessary to adequately prepare students by "teaching to the test" and the outcomes based curriculum, which assumes behaviorist and cognitivist perspectives from educational psychology traditions.

EXPERIENCING EDUCATIONAL DEVELOPMENTAL PSYCHOLOGY

From educational psychology's perspective, the students in each family in my inquiry did not meet the predetermined ages and stages of human behavior and development defined by the school curriculum and culture of the school and classroom when they were enrolled in public school. It appears that the students challenged the educators' beliefs and knowledge about dominant modernist views of children and learning. Often this knowledge is engrained as "truth" by educators' own schooling and socialization experiences.

Paul, Christopher, Samuel, Luke, Nadine, and Brett demonstrated alternative models of cognitive, social, emotional, and physical development, which was not accepted or catered for during their public school experience. In various ways, Helen, Lynn, and Sarah described their children's abilities as invalidated by the educators in their public schools. The families' experiences in public school caused them to feel different, defected, or not belonging because the students manifested learning and behavior contrary to the "truth" determined by educational psychology research present in the school curriculum and operating as school culture.

The families' experiences point to the need to rethink the Western view of intelligence, and physical, social, and emotional behavior, which focuses educators' attention on the fixed and innate descriptions of what students *should* be doing and how students *should* be behaving in age-defined classrooms.

This chapter will show how the students' experiences in public school shaped their relationships and capacity to succeed in schooling due to the educators' uninformed understanding of human diversity. Different aspects of the families' homeschooling experiences will be discussed, highlighting how they are able to educate within an understanding of human possibility that ventures outside the limitations explained by educational psychology and outlined in school curricular documents. The chapter concludes with suggestions of the ways we can seek alternative possibilities in public schooling where caregivers, teachers, children—school communities—learn to respect, hear, and appreciate each others' knowings, unknowings, unique abilities, and ways of being in the world.

THE LINGUISTIC DISCOURSE OF ABILITY

During the short time I spent with each family, Paul, Christopher, Samuel, Luke and Christopher, Nadine and Brett demonstrated their individuality, unique personality, personal histories, and hopes. What was interesting from the interviews with the students' parent (in all cases, this was "Mom") was the way in which they talked about their children. The parents spoke from multiple perspectives, of their children's personal and academic abilities, challenges, interests, and desires. Helen spoke for approximately ten minutes to answer my question, "tell me about your child."

Paul is a challenge everyday. He is a very intelligent young man. He absorbs everything that he reads or sees on television that is educational. He loves to learn. My son is also ADHD and that has been a difficult challenge in regards to any type of schoolwork . . .

While the parents' words spoke of a "rich" child, their descriptions of their children's learning disabilities and physical impairments could also highlight a "poor" child. However, they described these needs in terms of their formal education prior to homeschooling. The parents appeared to use language of the dominant discourse to talk about their children as equal but different. By talking about their child/ren in this way, the parents were demonstrating their discomfort with the categories used in school that reflect the modernist view of the child. According to the parents, their children were judged in the school system by measuring them against standardized categories. In contrast, the parents' descriptions were not presented negatively or the children were not described as "needy" —

Of course, Paul is classed as a learning disability but I've never let my son feel that at all. I will not have my son labelled because there is nothing wrong with him. He just has, every so often, short circuits, which can totally make a total different child at one point or the other . . . the Principal at (the) Junior High School is where I first actually got any kind of comment from a teacher in regards to homeschooling. They were the ones that mentioned, well they said maybe you should home school Paul because he doesn't seem to be fitting in.

From the conversation with Paul's mother, it seems that the educators at Paul's school associated his behavior with a lack of compliance and competence, demonstrating a constructed view of human capacity aligned with educational psychology's descriptions of human beings and who they are and should be through different stages of development.

Paul's experience shows how a classification reduces a student's vast capabilities into one label or several words. The coding which occurred in order to label Paul as "ADHD" became the means of removing him from his classroom, peers, and community school—"he doesn't seem to be fitting in." The question needs to be asked, is it the child who should "fit" the school or should the school accommodate each child within a community of learners?

UNDERSTANDING SCHOOLING

Helen, Lynn and Sarah reported that they were the last person they would have thought would homeschool their child/ren. Each parent highlighted the time when they problematized the educational processes their child/ren were a part of. The decision to educate their children at home was not precipitated by a specific incident; rather, the decision took months, and sometimes years. It is important to note that the participants do not object to public schooling as a whole but rather to specific parts of the education system. Typically, the process began with a general dissatisfaction with some element of the public school, which led to an investigation of alternatives. Helen shares her thoughts,

I just seemed to really pay attention more and more of how things worked in the public school. Now I realize that there are a lot of kids and it's hard to cope with. Okay, so I understand the other side too but what about the kids? What happened to the concept of kids? I really became aware of this in the last three years of my child's stay at public school and I just didn't like it anymore. I thought, no, this is not what I what I want to teach my son...I wanted him to have the opportunity to learn exactly the way he learns best...

The parents tried very hard to work with the staff at their children's school, however, in the end, the parents decided that the only way to preserve their children's self-concept and confidence was through homeschooling. Lynn speaks of her experience,

I was reading a book by Dobson, James Dobson, called bringing up boys, and in there he doesn't necessarily advocate homeschooling but he does say in a round about way that, if you are having some trouble, it might be something you might consider. I had never, never, never! considered homeschooling. I was the last person that probably would have ever home schooled but, based on how Christopher was doing and, also after reading the book, I thought well maybe it is something we should consider.

The parents claimed that they have a right and responsibility to protect their child/ren from harmful influences, viewing learning as a journey and only partially related to schools. The decision to homeschool was not easy for any of the parents I conversed with. Sarah explains,

All I have to do is look at the families that are considering it and I see the conflict in their brain, and the way they are talking and the emotion in their voice and how difficult a decision it is. I remember that, it is tough.

Advocacy was a discussion topic in all the interviews with the homeschooling families. The parents spoke of the need to advocate for their child/ren's emotional well-being, and to advocate that homeschooling is not "damaging" their child/ren's opportunities for successful lives and social well-being.

UNDERSTANDING THE INDIVIDUAL

Helen, Lynn, and Sarah spoke first of academic reasons for choosing homeschooling, in different ways, however, by the end of my visit, it became clear that their decisions were based on their children's experiences of negative socialization. The school program and environment were described in terms of the interactions and relationships between children and children, and children and staff, which, in turn, affected the students' emotional well-being and identity, and the parents' relationship with the institution.

If the child and childhood are only knowable in relation to the persons and environment in which they are situated, than the children of the families in my inquiry did not benefit from inclusion in school. One child was isolated and alone in his peer group due to a lack of support in addressing difference; another child's self-confidence was affected due to experiencing a lack of success in school and always failing to fit in. Another child became introverted and shy once she began school; she always thought she was "stupid" in school. The students' experiences highlight that the children were divided among their peers as well as within themselves as they participated in learning environments that failed to recognize them first and foremost as complex and interdependent human beings.

An understanding of identity, both across groups and within individuals, as understood as complex and multiple, fragmented and ambiguous, contradictory and contextualized, reflect the narratives told to me. However, the legacy of the Piagetian tradition remains to delineate that the students' academic performance and behaviors can only be explained by their own individual ability. Rather than using a language of relationship, connectedness, and community, traditional educational developmental psychology distances itself by focusing on learning and development

as an individualistic phenomenon. As the families' experiences demonstrate, the students func-
tioned in their public school classroom environments within communities, in connection with the
social environment and within interrelationships, not merely as isolated entities. According to the
families' account of their reasoning for choosing homeschooling, the public school educators'
understanding and evaluation of the students could be seen as a disconnection with the students'
complex interactions of everyday life in varying contexts. While individual students bring a
unique disposition to the class, Vygotsky and neo-Vygotskian research, for example, has shown
the importance of learning places and the social engagements, which occur in those places to
provide the context for learning to happen. Lynn shares her experience,

*When Christopher would come home from school, he would just unleash fury. We couldn't control him. He
would run over anyone and everything in his path. From 4 o'clock to bedtime was absolute chaos in our
house. But after he got home schooling and he realized that it wasn't as fast paced, it was just him and me.
There weren't distractions; it wasn't like you've got to get this done today, he calmed down a lot ... We were
able to take the time, longer time ... If they can't do it in a year, then they don't do it in a year, they take a
little longer.*

When Paul, Christopher, Samuel, Luke, Brett and Nadine began their schooling at home, it appears that dramatic changes occurred in their learning capabilities. Perhaps a better interpretation,
outside of educational psychology's perceptions, would be that the students' learning capabilities
were hindered by, or fostered through, the dynamics of the interactions in the educational process.

A FAMILY PORTRAIT: CHRISTOPHER, SAMUEL, LUKE, AND LYNN

*Christopher, Samuel, and Luke welcomed me with conversation and gifts as I entered their
home. They had many stories to share and toys to show me. Especially proud was Christopher, who
enjoys creating different objects from Kinex construction. He enthusiastically showed me his photo
album, a record of digital photos taken of his creations. A School Project Fair was approaching
and the boys excitedly shared this upcoming experience during different conversations throughout
the day, as well as their involvement in swimming and other family experiences.*

*The boys' school day began when Lynn, their mother, invited us to the kitchen table just after
9:00 am. Each day, the boys start with a music and handwriting program the school is trialling.
The structured program has been successful with the three boys as the music encourages a flow
in their handwriting and an external motivator to practice the letter formations. The remainder
of the day continued with a very strong sense of routine for Christopher and Samuel, both
in Elementary, and Luke, in Kindergarten. I had the pleasure of observing and participating
in religious studies, spelling, phonics, story writing, report writing, mathematics, science, and
social studies. The boys are also learning to play the piano as part of their music program. The
day's schoolwork was divided between two recess periods and lunch. Once Luke had completed
his one hour of structured writing and math work in the morning, he entertained himself with
reading, drawing, and playing with his toys while his older siblings continued with their formal
learning. Christopher and Samuel usually complete their schoolwork by lunchtime and all three
boys then enjoy outdoor play for a large part of the afternoon with their next-door neighbour.*

*The family have been involved in the homeschooling program for eighteen months and Lynn
describes her experience metaphorically,*

For me, as a Mum, I'm thinking it's like jumping off a wall, landing in frozen water, hoping you can swim
and then realizing that you can swim, and making it to shore and realizing it really wasn't that bad after
all. ... It's like, oh! I made it, it's not so bad, I can swim back now!

Lynn has chosen to enrol Samuel in the basic program as he is working independently most of the time and is moving ahead at his own pace. By selecting a basic program for Samuel, Lynn assumes 100 percent of the instruction, delivery, evaluation, and responsibility for the program of studies. Samuel's program is supervised by a teacher who facilitates this program through discussion with Lynn and Samuel, visits twice a year and offers resource assistance. Christopher is in the blended program to access extra guidance from a teacher in the homeschooling program. Lynn appreciates the need to be responsible to a teacher and having the extra support while she continues to address the different ways her son's learning preferences and abilities are catered for.

PEDAGOGY OF HOMESCHOOLING

As highlighted, Helen, Lynn, and Sarah pedagogically decided to improve their child/ren's academic and social environment. The ways in which they developed their homeschooling program can be viewed in terms of their own individual constructions of the child and childhood, learning, and education based on their past experiences.

Helen, Lynn, and Sarah placed a very high value on education and alluded to the notion that it was preparation for life and work, reflecting a modernist view of education. For example, Helen spoke often of the importance of achieving success and that success is measured by the need to learn certain knowledge and skills. Helen's narrative speaks of long-term objectives, that the focus they have taken for Paul now will have a long-term pay-off, that is, success later in life,

I think my biggest thing is to be able to know that I accomplished something that makes a big difference in my son's life. That's where I see where my experience is going. And I hope I can do that for him and me, you know, do it in the best way I can so that he succeeds. As long as he does, I know that I have. That's what a parent's supposed to do so I think it's going to be a very big thing when he finishes grade twelve and he graduates . . .

While the parents' energies focused on pedagogy, which improved their child/ren's academic and social environment, their narratives also highlighted that their child/ren are potential contributors of society. However, the parents were not willing to sacrifice their children's present to reach the goal of a successful future. If the future were more important than the present, they would probably have kept their children at school where the "expert" teachers would have given them the "knowledge" they needed to be successful. Sarah shares her experience,

I know that what they learn is from discussion and there is a lot going on in the world now. A LOT going on in the world now and in discussing it and stuff like that and finding out about it, it's how do you make learning interesting? How do you make them want to learn? That's more our responsibility than what they actually learn. It's giving them that desire to learn. . . . And HOW to go about getting your information and stuff like that. If they know that, they're going to learn for the rest of their life and they're going to enjoy it. A lot of kids go through school and they hated learning since they failed one test in grade one, you know.

PEDAGOGICAL KNOWLEDGE

Educational developmental psychology has traditionally focused on transmission from teachers to students. The transmission of facts, societal values, specific skills and attitudes, rather than recognizing topics such as classroom pedagogy, teachers and learners, thinking and learning as interrelational and relevant to psychosocial and cultural processes.

It was interesting that the parents in the inquiry spoke predominantly of learning from their child/ren. From my short time with the families, and what each parent expressed to me in the interview, it appears that understanding and learning from their child/ren meant predominantly understanding their temperament styles, learning preferences, work habits, and personal time rhythms. Helen advises,

I think the biggest thing is it all depends on how your child learns. So, you know, you deal with it that way, look at it that way. Well, how is it that my son, or my daughter, can learn better. Well, I know which way he can so let's see if we can, you know, get it to work out so he's still learning what he needs to learn but his way, or her way, which, for kids, I think makes the most biggest, fun thing of it all is they're doing it their way, nobody's telling them they can't do it that way.

While routine was important for both Helen and Lynn, the routine was based on their child/ren's personal rhythms as they had learned the importance of this aspect of their children's learning style and preference. Time and routine in the families' days allowed for time not to hurry through the curriculum and their child/ren were not expected to continue learning at the one pace.

SEEKING ALTERNATIVE POSSIBILITIES IN PUBLIC SCHOOLS

This section of the chapter suggests that the insights gained from three families' experience of homeschooling may prompt educators in rethinking their pedagogical decision-making, practices, and relationships in students' and families' educational lives.

An Educator's Responsibility

How educators provide learning opportunities and the ways in which they respond to learners is reflective of their beliefs about knowledge, human behavior, and ways of learning. Educators are continually making moral choices, making difficult decisions, however, quite often these are based on observations filtered through a lens of educational psychology they bring with them as a result of their own educational experiences as a learner in public schools and university settings. I believe an educator's growth will be in his or her own personal responsibility first. Educators must reflect on who they are, their assumptions and biases about race, class, gender, and ability, in order to allow their students to be who they really are. In community, this involves educators reflecting on who they are in relation to others. Following this process, educators can begin to destabilize dominant discourses and critique material and challenge teaching/research practices in a more informed context.

Communities of Reconceptualization

I believe seeking alternative possibilities for education in public schools involves communities of pedagogues who have concerns or issues, and who are willing to attempt the development of new ways of thinking and teaching that prepares parents, school educators, and students with the complexities of classroom life. Such issues and concerns may include the ones raised in this chapter by Paul, Helen, Christopher, Samuel, Luke, Lynn, Sarah, Nadine and Brett.

When Paul, Brett and Christopher, specifically, failed to meet the linear expectations described by developmentalism, they were evaluated as students in need of remediation or adjustment. Their public school experience resulted in their social exclusion because their behavioral, intellectual, physical, and emotional selves did not mirror what educational psychology, school curricular, and school culture had deemed as appropriate. The families' narratives spoke of many children and many childhoods and all three parents pointed to the tension between the concept of development as a universal phenomenon (the dominant view), a predetermined linear sequence that all must follow to achieve full human potential, and the recognition of their child/ren's diversity, competence, and complex and interrelated personalities. The success of the students' homeschooling education indicates that the educators in the public school setting supported a narrow and limiting perspective, while the parents could see alternate ways of viewing their children and thinking about the educational experience.

Stating that Paul does not seem to fit, speaks to me of the educators at Paul's school possibly not being able to rely on the authority and certainty of developmental psychology they had in the past relied on. The alternative could have been to use this knowledge of Paul as a beginning to further understanding of the realities of his familial and educational life, and to collaborate in providing ways his classroom and school can be more inclusive of *all* students. In all the families' experiences, the students demonstrated that they had capabilities the educators would not have thought possible. If all the students in this inquiry could have also been involved in democratic dialogue and decision-making when issues and concerns arose at their community school, perhaps their experience of public school would have been different.

Discussing the importance of individualizing learning, or planning for each child's preferred learning styles and routines, or the importance of children developing a love of learning, speaks to me of the parents and public school educators willingness to work with and accept, without questioning, a school curriculum and school culture, based on educational psychology, which states the "best" schooling processes and outlines what is developmentally appropriate. The alternative could have been to use the families' experiences as a beginning to constantly and persistently look into how "truths" are produced, to open up new possibilities, to ask new questions, and to challenge old beliefs. Rather than focusing on individuals, one possibility could have been for the parents and educators to uncover any shared common commitments and discuss ways the school curriculum and school culture can contextualize learning for children and the expectations we have of them.

The conversation with the three parents uncovered that they do not reject modern knowledge as a whole; for example, they are continuing to use Alberta curriculum resources, and they are focused on their children's future contributions to society. However, the parents did construct and deepen their understanding about how things really were in school for their child/ren rather than conforming to a standard of acceptance. Thus, the inquiry has drawn attention to the insights and knowledge parents have and the ways in which these insights and knowledge are valued in leading to a deeper understanding of children. In homeschooling programs and public school communities, it is of importance to explore parent's image of the child/childhood more directly as a way of constructing and deepening their understanding of their own pedagogical work. Furthermore, the inquiry has caused me to realize the necessity to include youth in inquiries of reconceptualizing alternatives to education in public schools. As one of the students reminded me so articulately during the observational visit, "*if you interview my Mum, you have to interview me. You can't know everything about homeschooling if you don't talk to the kids.*" The parents' also spoke of the many ways they learned from their children, highlighting that community conversations would not be a complete conversation without youth's participation, visibility, and inclusion.

A FAMILY PORTRAIT: NADINE, BRETT, AND SARAH

I arrived early and had the pleasure of joining Nadine, an elementary student, Brett, a high school student and Sarah, their mother, for breakfast. The 'school day' began at around 9.30 am when Brett's hired support and family friend Julie arrived. The two disappeared downstairs to work on Brett's high school social essay, while Nadine stayed at the kitchen table and began working on phonics, followed by mathematics. Nadine worked through her elementary textbooks as Sarah and I talked about some of the experiences they have had with homeschooling. Sarah has been homeschooling her children for eight years and explains that the virtual program meets her needs,

very well . . . things I want my kids to know, I teach them. And they give me a lot of flexibility in the virtual program too, which is good. And another thing which makes it so neat is that it takes all the discipline out of the teacher's job description, they don't have to do any of that stuff so then you have this really cool relationship with these kids where the teacher is assisting in the learning and that's it . . . I like having them come out, they seem like really neat people.

I also had the opportunity to observe Brett and Julie before lunch and left with a sense that these two make a great team. As they discussed, edited changes, listed choices, made decisions and searched for definitions, they continued open and friendly conversations. Julie supports Brett three days a week for four hours per day. As well, Brett drives into town to be tutored in Mathematics two days per week and spends an afternoon with a mentor. Brett is a mature young man who has faced many physical challenges in his life. He enjoys weekends with friends playing computer games and is involved in work experience at his Church, providing the PowerPoint presentations to accompany the service. I was also fortunate enough to view his incredible artistic work designed with computer technology. Brett has two dreams for his future, working with computers and becoming a pastor. Nadine loves to sing and dance and I felt welcomed by her smiling nature throughout the day. She attends drama and choir and will begin swimming in the spring. Nadine enjoys her afternoons and is able to keep herself busy reading and working on the computer with the mathematics, phonics, and musical programs. At present, she is following her interest in George Washington and American history and shared with me a book she is reading on the topic.

On the day I was visiting with the family, they were excited about two concerts being held, one that evening and one the following, in which both Nadine and the family's eldest daughter (who is attending college), would be involved. Sarah's husband took the afternoon off work for the occasion of the concerts and we enjoyed lunch together—and my first taste of homemade rhubarb and strawberry pie!

Places and Spaces for Seeking Alternative Possibilities in Public Schools

The families' experience in the inquiry has emphasised how important it is for educators to continually question the existence of constructions so greatly influenced by educational psychology, and to be increasingly attentive to our own wisdom and intelligence which results from experiences of being in relation with learners, families, colleagues, and community members. I believe problematizing developmental educational psychology knowledge and the processes in our educational system, which are quick to recognize the "poor" or deficient child, is a long process of reflection, making connections and considering possible alternative ways of viewing education, learning, and development. It involves risk-taking and an engagement with the body of knowledge informed by educational developmental psychology in relation to school communities' lives.

In Italy, the municipality of Reggio Emilia makes possible forums, which bring children and all pedagogues (parents, teachers, and other community members) together for understanding and planning for the experience of education. We cannot begin to replicate a practice which exists in a cultural and political setting on the other side of the world. However, the inquiry has suggested that we, too, can be continually asking, in a discourse of meaning making, what do we want for our children here and now and in the future without relying on the language of progress which was born during the Enlightenment period?

From my teaching experience, parents want to be involved in the formal education of their child/ren, as do the families I spent time with. In my own experiences of talking with people from my different work and social communities, I have had conversations with individuals expressing concerns that supporting homeschooling means de-legitimizing public school teachers' knowledge and professional skills. If home educators are viewed more effective than public school educators, then public education will be further compromised. This was not the sense I received from the homeschooling program the families were enrolled in. From our conversations it seemed that Helen, Lynn, and Sarah believed that both they and the staff desired each other's involvement in the homeschooling experience. All three parents valued an open relationship with the staff working at the homeschool program and appreciated the support which was provided. There appeared to be no one privileged voice of authority, in fact, the parents highlighted their own learning from their child/ren, learning from the staff of the homeschooling program, learning from the curriculum, and continual lifelong learning. The parents began on a steep learning curve; however, with experience and the support of the staff in the homeschooling program, they shared a strong pedagogical relationship and appeared to value coming together, with the child, in learning.

Helen, Lynn, and Sarah did struggle with the image of themselves as teacher and themselves as parent and the difference between the two. Perhaps this struggle comes from the language we use in education to describe the relationship between children, parents, teachers, and the classroom learning, in particular, the language that distinguishes the role of teacher and the role of parent. Language such as "parents as partners," "parents as first teachers," "the school and community in partnership," and "parent helpers" was used throughout the interviews to describe different roles and relationships, and also the same roles and relationships.

Helen, Lynn, and Sarah spoke of themselves as parents knowing their children best; that they are a big part of their child's education whether in public or homeschooling, provoking thought about the extent to which staff in schools accept and act upon the possibility that many parents/caregivers have close knowledge of their children's educational lives, despite the fact that they have no formal teacher training. Furthermore, does this language affect a parent's involvement in their children's educational lives in formal schooling? How is this view formed? What role do parents see themselves as having in school communities? Why do we separate the role of teacher and parent? Are we not all pedagogues? How could children benefit from the educational insights of both professional educators and parents on school landscapes?

CONCLUSION: THE CONTINUAL NEED FOR RECONCEPTUALIZATION

The three families in the inquiry provided the opportunity to have another view, a different perspective, of curriculum and teaching practices in public schools through the sharing of their experience of homeschooling. When school practices focused on typically developing students, the public school educators of the students in the inquiry could be described as failing to see, or choosing to ignore, that intellectual, physical, emotional, and social ability takes many forms and involves many different aspects. In critique of educational developmental psychology, this chapter has argued that educators need to seek a more informed understanding of students' abilities and educational and familial lives so that learning and development, in all its complexity, can be better facilitated.

Past history and experience has shown that many pedagogues prescribe to a long and linear list of principles of child development and learning. In attending to the inquiry's findings, I believe it is so important for school educators to seek an alternative, in which dialogue is open and ongoing with families and youth. Rather than accepting many children fail to succeed in education without inquiring into individual and cultural differences in students' learning and development, pedagogues can come together in communities of reconceptualization using a language that encourages continual dialogue and critical inquiry in an attempt to undermine the assumptions, biases, and preconceived abilities of students outlined by educational psychology.

TERMS FOR READERS

Homeschooling—There were approximately 60,000 to 95,000 elementary and secondary home-schooling students in Canada during 2000–2001. In the homeschooling program in Edmonton, parents choose this form of schooling over other schooling options for a variety of reasons. Within Alberta, there are three organizations offering different support and services to homeschooling families: Alberta Home Education Association, Alberta Distance Learning Centre, and the School of Hope.

Considerable research on homeschooling in the United States has clarified the historical development of home education, parents' reasons for choosing a form of education other than traditional schooling, comparisons of home education to public or private education, and home education demographics, yet there has been very little inquiry into learning at home in Canadian contexts.

Modernist Education—This education system is shaped and influenced by industrial production and economic market processes. Education is viewed as providing training in certain forms of skills, sensibilities, values, and knowledge, in the process of preparing individuals in their role as contributors to society. Thus, it is believed that the more educated the society, the more rational individuals within society are, the more progress that is possible.

Neo-Vygotskian Research—Research focusing on an attempt to understand the cognitive processes of the individual within an environmental context. Rather than focusing on outcomes, sociocultural accounts of learning and development attempt to understand the processes that occur in specific learning contexts.

Pedagogue—Someone who educates. Dahlberg, Moss, and Pence (1999) propose the notion of pedagogues and children as citizens and co-constructors of knowledge, identities, and values. This is contrasted with the idea of educators as technicians, cultural transmitters, and facilitators in age-appropriate activities. Pedagogues are informed by, but not determined by scientific knowledge and technical processes.

FURTHER READING

Arai, A. B. (2000). Reasons for Homeschooling in Canada. *Canadian Journal of Education*, 25(3), 204–217.

Cannella, G. S. (1997). *Deconstructing Early Childhood Education: Social Justice and Revolution*. New York: Peter Lang Publishing, Inc.

Dahlberg, G., Moss, P. and Pence, A. (1999). (Eds.). *Beyond Quality in Early Childhood Education and Care: Postmodern Perspectives*. London: Falmer Press.

Kincheloe, J. L. (2004). Into the Great Wide Open: Introducing Critical Thinking. In J. L. Kincheloe and D. Weil (Eds.), *Critical Thinking and Learning: An Encyclopedia for Parents and Teachers* pp. 1–52. New York: Greenwood.

Kincheloe, J. L., Steinberg, S. R. and Villaverde, L. E. (1999). (Eds.). *Rethinking Intelligence: Confronting Psychological Assumptions about Teaching and Learning*. London: Routledge.

Mayberry, M., Knowles, G. J., Ray, B. and Marlow, S. (1995). *Homeschooling*. California: Corwin Press, Inc.

CHAPTER 90

Activity Theory as a Framework for Designing Educational Systems

PATRICK M. JENLINK

INTRODUCTION

The field of educational psychology has made significant progress in the study of individuals' learning; much has been learned about basic structures and processes of individual cognition (O'Donnel and Levin, 2001). However, paradigmatic arguments concerning cognition challenge existing assumptions that promote considering the individual learner in isolation. Relatedly, cultural-historical activity theory (CHAT) has been moved to the forefront as a theory of learning, which elevates the focus from learner in isolation to learner at the level of collective activity. The purpose of this chapter is to examine cultural-historical activity theory in relation to systems design of learning environments. The concern of design, as Brown (1992) notes in her discussion of "design experiments," is a multilevel and multifocus activity in which psychological, curricular, instructional, interpersonal, activity, organizational, and often also physical aspects are jointly considered with the purpose of constructing viable learning environments. Salomon (1996) in arguing for a reconfiguration of the field of educational psychology's main mission, explicates in particular that the mission should be to "explain, guide, but particularly *design*." It is this focus presented by Brown and Salomon on "design" that instructs, in part, the purpose of this chapter.

Cultural-historical activity theory will be introduced as a framework for analyzing and designing educational systems—analyzing human activities that take place in cultural contexts, meditated by language and other symbol systems and designing educational systems as goal-directed systems in which cognition, behavior, and motivation are integrated and organized by goals and the mechanisms of self-regulation. The approach used in this chapter will distinguish between short-lived goal-directed actions and durable, object-oriented activity systems; explicate the function of consciousness and its relation to related cognitive activity (noting the unity of consciousness and behavior in terms of inner mental concepts and dynamics), and elaborate a framework informed by cultural-historical activity theory that can illuminate our understanding of the nature of learning as well as animate the design of educational systems toward that understanding and the transformation of educational processes and activities.

SYSTEMS DESIGN AND ACTIVITY THEORY: A CULTURAL-HISTORICAL SYSTEMS PERSPECTIVE

Systems design is largely communicative in nature, depends on discourse as a semiotic tool for mediation within the cognitive, cultural, and creative activities essential to overcoming deep sociohistorical patterns of learning that are woven into the fabric of human activity and educational systems. The use of cultural-historical activity theory (CHAT) as a framework for designing educational systems, learning systems in particular, represents a sociocultural and inquiry-oriented perspective that illuminates the relationship between design as a human activity system and the sociocultural context in which the design activity unfolds. The design activity, as described in Banathy's concept of systems design (1996), is mediated by conversation and language forms of semiotic mediation. Mediation of design, through the use of cultural artifacts like discourse and language, represent actions within the human activity system of design. The mediational role of conversation and use of other symbol-based systems in systems design is supported by cultural-historical activity theory, which presents a systemic view of design activity (Engeström, Miettinen, and Punamäki, 1999). The semiotic nature of discourse and language within communities of design practice, as well as learning communities, enables participants to transcend formal cognitive and cultural patterns that often marginalize and disadvantage voices of difference. Essential to the design of complex activity systems for learning is the ability of participants to acknowledge the dialectical contradictions that have emerged in their past or present activity system(s), while also acknowledging the importance of creating dialogical relationships toward the goal of designing new systems.

Discourse and language systems—semiotic tools of mediation— underlie the process of both learning and systems design. The framework of cultural-historical activity theory suggests that mediational artifacts such as language and discourse do not exist inside or outside of individual consciousness; rather they reside on the borderline between oneself as designer and the others who are also designers and users. Learning, as is the case with designing learning activities, is "a process of social negotiation or collaborative sense making, mentoring, and joint knowledge construction" (Zhu, 1998).

CULTURAL-HISTORICAL ACTIVITY THEORY AND HUMAN ACTIVITY SYSTEMS

In society, the nature of, and capacity for, human activity is endlessly multifaceted, mobile, and rich in variations of purpose, context, content, process, and form (Engeström and Miettinen, 1999). The social structure of society is not characterizable as something standing alone, apart from the activity and people that created it. Rather, "society forms the individuals who create society; society, that is, produces people, who produce society, in a continuous dialectic" (Bhaskar, 1989). Human activity forms systems that, with their particular social languages and other cultural artifacts such as discourse and physical tools, do not operate independently one from another. They interact dynamically, forming systems of interrelated and interdependent activity, with particular goals and purposes. The meaning of activity as related to social systems design and activity theory will be examined, using the idea of educational systems design as a context and referent. Human activity systems related to educational systems design will be explicitly referenced to further contextualize the meaning of activity.

Human Activity Systems

Checkland (1981) suggests that human activity systems may best be understood as structured sets of activities that are notional, expressing some purposeful human activity that could be found within the real world. Banathy (1996), elaborating on Checkland's perspective of human activity system, posits the example of idealized system design as a type of human activity system that is purposeful in nature and which can be used to create a new system that could exist in the real world. Relatedly, Checkland and Scholes state that

The emergent property of a defined human activity system is the ability, in principle, to pursue the purpose of the whole... within it activities and structure concerned with communication and control so that the [human activity system] could in principle (were it to exist) adapt and survive in a changing environment. (Checkland and Scholes, 1990).

Individuals are active participants in multiple activity systems, often in complex arrays of roles and responsibilities. The idea of multiple roles in various activity systems is made more problematic by the fact that activity systems constantly interact with other activity systems in a complex dialectic of boundary work. The complex dialectic of the boundary work found in human activity systems pervades conscious human activity, often giving rise to tensions that drive changes in an activity system and its participants, individually and collectively. Because activity systems constantly interact with other activity systems, and because as noted, "participants themselves have many affiliations (identities, subject positions) with many other activity systems, ongoing social practices constantly change as tools-in-use are appropriated across boundaries and eventually are operationalized... to transform activity systems" (Russell, 1997). The notion of transforming activity systems gives support to Banathy's (1996) ideal of social systems design as contributing to the transformation of society through transcending old systems. Activity may also be understood from the viewpoint of activity theory (Engeström, Miettinen, and Punamäki, 1999).

Cultural-Historical Activity Theory

Cultural-historical activity theory (CHAT), with its philosophical and historical roots in the classical German philosophy (from Kant to Hegel), in the writings of Karl Marx, and in the theorizing emerging from the cultural-historical school of Russian psychology most often associated with the research of L. S. Vygotsky, A. N. Leont'ev, and A.R. Luria, presents a framework of understanding activity in human systems. Recent work with activity theory in the fields of human cognition, cultural psychology, and communication through the research of Michael Cole, Yrjö Engeström, and Ritva Engeström draws attention to the similarities in social systems and educational systems design and the sociohistorical and sociocultural foundations of activity theory.

Through the framework of CHAT, in the context of educational systems design, participants in a human activity system are guided by object or motive-based expectations of creating an ideal educational system. The creative activity is mediated by use of cultural artifacts that might be any combination of rule-based, role-based, symbol-based, cognition-based, discourse-based, process-based, and technology-based tools. A primary example is the use of ideal systems design technology, systems language, and design conversation in the design of an ideal educational system. Also critical to the framework, which guides the systemic change process, are sociocultural rules that are aligned with the object or motive based expectations. Essential in this framework is membership in a community of stakeholders seeking to design a new ideal for the educational system—a design community. Membership in the community by the facilitator and stakeholders is balanced through a division of labor that seeks to authentically engage all participants in the systemic change process. Serving, as center for this framework, is a set of beliefs adopted by the participants that serves to provide social coherence for the design community.

Figure 90.1
Cultural-historical Activity Theory as a Framework for Design

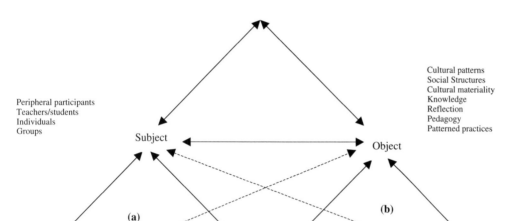

Discourse
Critical reflection
Inquiry activity
Knowledge - cultural, formal, etc.
Technical tools – computer, software
Symbol-based tools - Language
Process-based tools
Diversity-based – multicultural

Mediating
Artifacts and Tools

Cultural patterns
Social Structures
Cultural materiality
Knowledge
Reflection
Pedagogy
Patterned practices

Peripheral participants
Teachers/students
Individuals
Groups

Subject

Object

(a)

(b)

Socio-cultural
Rules

Diversity-rich
Community

Differentiation of
Labor

Traditional academic rules
Pedagogical rules
Language rules
Mediated agency rules
Diversity-based rules
Knowledge rules
Cultural capital rules
Discourse rules

Cultural-historical contexts
School
Classroom
Social groups of participants
   - teachers
   - students
Social languages
Mediated agency
Legitimate peripheral membership

Collective activity
Cultural activity
Cross-cultural activity
Individual work
      vs.
Distributed work
Roles/status
Power issues

   Cultural-historical activity theory, as a framework for understanding the meaning of human activity systems, is based on a relational dynamic between the subject, object, mediational artifacts (or tools), sociocultural rules, division of labor, and community structure of a human activity system (see Figure 90.1 for an elaboration). Community refers to those who share the same general object; rules refer to explicit norms and conventions that constrain actions within the activity systems; and division of labor refers to the division of labor of object-oriented actions among members of the community.

   As a sociocultural theory of human activity and learning, activity theory focuses on interaction among and between people as a primary source of communicative action resulting in objectivation of human subjectivity through social action. Activity systems are complex interrelated sets of actions and activities or practices, situated within sociohistorical and sociocultural contexts.

The top triangle in Figure 90.1 represents an element of the activity system that defines the subject, object, and mediating artifact(s) relationship. The subject(s) of any activity is the person(s) for whom the activity is created. The object is the motive or intentioned outcome implicit and explicit in the activity. The mediating artifacts or tools are cultural in origin and serve to mediate the subject's actions and activities as the object is transformed through objectivation, and human subjectivity (social languages, forms of economic and political organization, cultural and ethical norms, ideals for social systems) is embodied in the intentioned outcome or product. The second triangle in the lower left of Figure 90.1 represents an interrelated element of the activity system. This element depicts the relationships between the subject(s), the sociocultural rules of the community (related to the object, goal, outcome—see (a) in Figure 90.1), and the designated community made apparent. The third triangle in the lower right of Figure 90.1, represents the relationship between the object(s) or intentioned outcome(s), the community in which the subject is a member, and the division of labor respective to the particular activity. The division of labor might be thought of as role differentiation by subject(s) within the community (see (b) in Figure 90.1). The community's culture produces, uses and transforms artifacts as individuals and the collective engage in activities. Connected, the three triangles form a framework for analyzing and designing human activity systems such as educational systems. In this framework, activity theory is elaborated as a complex set of interrelated and situated relationships that enable participants to accomplish a goal.

Cultural-historical activity theory explains an activity, (such as those related to educational systems design, design of learning environments and experiences, and cognition and learning), as a unit that is instructed by a socially defined goal and animated by the execution of some specific actions that have evolved or have been created to attain that goal (Cole and Engeström, 1993; Leont'ev, 1978; Russell, 1997). As such, activity involves patterns of communication with others related to the setting and the goal, and thus, mastery of a set of symbolic tools (such as systems language), discourse tools (such as communicative action and design conversation), or perhaps process tools (such as educational systems design). In an activity, each of these elements influences the individual's and the collective's actions, practices, and understandings. It is important to reiterate that the various components of the activity system do not exist in isolation from each other. Rather, "they are constantly being constructed, renewed, and transformed as outcome and cause of human life" (Cole, 1995).

Through the integrated lens of activity theory and human activity systems, society may be seen to exist only in virtue of human activity, activity that is conscious. Consciousness gained and expressed through activity brings about change, though social changes need not be consciously intended. Importantly, Bhaskar notes that "society, then, is an articulated ensemble of tendencies and powers which ... exist only as long as they (or at least some of them) are being exercised ... via the intentional activity of human beings" (1989, p. 79). People, in their conscious participation in activities and social practices, "for the most part unconsciously reproduce (or occasionally, transform) the structures that govern their substantive activities" (Bhaskar, 1989, p. 80). Production and transformation are related to the externalization and internalization of activity in society.

Externalization and Internalization

Integral to understanding the importance of cultural-historical activity theory and the design of educational systems are two basic processes of externalization and internalization, explained as operating continuously at every level of human activity. Internalization and externalization focus on the production and transformation of culture and society. Engeström and Miettinen explain that "Internalization is related to reproduction of culture; externalization as creation of new artifacts makes possible its transformation. These two processes are inseparably intertwined" (Engeström and Miettinen, 1999). Relatedly, the principle of internalization/externalization suggests that the shaping of external activities results in shaping internal ones. The importance of these two concepts and their inseparability is further explained by Bhaskar as he examines society as already being in existence, and thus "any concrete human praxis, if you like, act of objectivation, can only modify it; and the totality of such acts sustain or change it. It is not the product of their activity (any more than their actions are completely determined by it)" (1989, p. xx). When considering the design of an educational system —that is, learning environments and the learning experiences therein—within society, it is important to see society as already existing, and that an educational system already exists. But society or an educational system as a social system within society exists only by virtue of human activity. Therefore, "people do not create society, for it always preexists them. Rather it is an ensemble of structures, practices and conventions that individuals reproduce or transform. But which would not exist unless they did so. Society does not exist independently of conscious human activity" (Bhaskar, 1989, p. xx). Relatedly, designing learning environments, and more specifically the learning experiences that animate the cognitive development of students, requires an understanding that internalization/externalization processes regulate human actions/interactions within cultural activities. The use of semiotic tools (language, discourse) and other intellectual or psychological tools to mediate design serves to instruct the design imperatives for creating alternative levels of consciousness in the learner, facilitate higher levels of mental activity, and transform existing systems.

Importantly, if we apply this understanding of conscious human activity to the design of learning systems, we become aware of the critical role that designing activity systems of learning play in transforming existing learning experiences, rather than reproducing them. As Bhaskar explains, social structures are products of social activity, they may be viewed as objects of transformation through conscious human activity. "And because social activities are interdependent, social structures may be only relatively autonomous. Society may thus be conceived as an articulated ensemble of such relatively independent and enduring structures; that is, a complex totality subject to change" (Bhaskar, 1989, p. 78).

DESIGNING EDUCATIONAL SYSTEMS—LEARNING ENVIRONMENTS/EXPERIENCES

Designing educational systems, for purposes of this discussion, focuses on the design of complex learning systems or learning environments, and the various learning activities that enable individuals to learn. Returning to Brown (1992) briefly, design in relation to cognition is concerned with multilevel and multifocus activity, and the creation of alternative learning experiences that consider the whole learning environment and the social interaction of individuals within the environment as well as through the interconnected activities that situate learning experiences. In this sense, design, as a form of social systems design, is a communicative process among individuals that enables collective action(s) of learning, creating, constructing knowledge, mediating meaning and understanding, etc. These actions lead to the creation of change in and/or of the social system; the transfer of the conception of a new or alternative system into action. Banathy further elaborates that the designer's main tool is subjectivity, which includes social practice, community, interest and commitment, ideas and ideals, the ethics of the system and the moral idea, affectivity, faith, and self-reflection" (Banathy, 1996, p. 164).

As identified in the examination of cultural-historical activity theory (CHAT), the embodiment of participant's subjectivity is a critical element of the social change or transformation process. Subjectivity as a design element enables the object of design to be realized, particularly when the object is to create a complex social system for learning.

A defining characteristic of systems design is that the design process is inquiry oriented and is a form of discourse, practical in nature and based on social language or symbol systems. This discourse is communicative in action, seeking to bring participants into inquiry-based activity that is focused on creating an alternative or new system. Banathy defines systems design, in the context of human activity systems, as "a future-creating disciplined inquiry," an inquiry that "people engage in design in order to devise and implement a new system" (1996, p. 42). Again, returning to Brown (1992) briefly, the idea of creating an alternative, viable learning system, that is multilevel and multifocus is concerned with a disciplined approach to inquiry in the experimenting of design and cognition.

Educational systems design is based on an ideal systems design approach. Incorporating Banathy's notion of the "ideal" as a focal point, the new educational system is created by "those who serve the system, those who are served by it, others who have a vested interest in it, and all those who are affected by it" (1996, p. 195). The characteristic of users creating or designing the ideal system—user-designers—is a critical component of designing learning systems. From this perspective of systems design, the subjects, that is, the learners, of the design activity (see Figure 90.1) are the same individuals who are the vested owners/users of the system. Therefore, systems design reflects an authentic participation of learners/users in "the design because they genuinely and deeply care about the future state of their system" (Banathy, 1996).

An examination of ideal systems design as delineated by Banathy suggests five interrelated and interdependent design spaces that are critical to designing a new system. Each space represents a design space in which participant inquiry and design conversation are situated, and includes the following: exploration and image creation space, design information and knowledge space, design solution space, evaluation and experimentation space, and modeling space. Jenlink (Jenlink, 1995; 1999, June) provides a contrasting yet complementary view of systems design in suggesting that the process includes: contextualization of the system, design of new system and system implementation processes, implementation of system, and critical inquiry and system learning. Together, these form a multidimensional design space in which design activity unfolds. Also critical in this view of systems design is self-renewal and evolution of consciousness as critical processes implicit and explicit in the design; contributing to the participant's ability to transform social structures and transcend existing systems as the ideal is created and realized through the actions of participants. During the design process, consciousness moves through, or perhaps more accurately along, a developmental and evolutionary path reflecting different types of consciousness in social action including: perspectival, interpretative, critical, ethical and moral, self-reflective, integrative, creative, collective, self-renewing, and evolutionary (Jenlink, 1999, June). Each type of consciousness relates to different design activities, with particular focus on forms of conversation, objects of the design process (see Figure 90.1), design maturity of stakeholders, particular social language, and sociocultural rules that govern or influence the social action of participants engaged in design activities.

Systems design of a whole, complex learning system, such as a classroom, requires a focus on the ideal learning experience for each student, inclusive of the cultural-historical, epistemological, pedagogical, ethical and moral considerations for all learner(s) (this can be compared to sociocultural rules in Figure 90.1). Issues of equity, social justice, and caring provide a constant tension in the design process to create the ideal educational system. The dialectic boundaries set by interacting activity systems, the concern for continued reproduction versus transformation of social structures, and the need to address issues of moral, intellectual, and social responsibility in an increasingly problematic society affirm the importance of using an ideal systems design approach to creating new educational systems. The importance of conversation and language as semiotic tools in the processes of designing complex learning systems, requires designers to see learning/design of learning through multiple perspectives of cognition, as well as understand the nature of existing societal structures, the dialectic boundaries of activity systems, the cultural and cognitive patterns of the participants and their communities, and the sociohistorical and cultural artifacts implicit/explicit therein, while simultaneously contextualizing the design of the learning system and/or interrelated sets of activities and experiences.

SEMIOTIC MEDIATION: CONVERSATION IN/AS DESIGN

In the design of learning systems, mediation is the instrument of cognitive change. This mediation can take the form of the textbook, visual material, classroom discourse patterns, opportunities for second language interaction, types of direct instruction, or various kinds of teacher assistance. Regardless of form, mediation is embedded in some context that makes it inherently sociocultural processes (Engström, 1991; Tharp and Gallimore, 1988). Semiotic mediation, as Mahn (1999) explains, is the "mediating function of language and other symbolic systems." Designing learning systems and activities in which learning experiences are shared by students, requires mediation through the use of discourse as medium of design and the use of language as a semiotic tool necessary to mediating cultural-historical activities and the design of new activities. Semiotic Mediation is integral to designing learning systems; it situates itself in both the design of the system as an integral design feature of the system. In this sense, the use of semiotic mediation enables designers to examine the ways that individuals appropriate social symbol systems and to reveal that internalization was transformative rather than transmissive. The semiotic mechanisms (including psychological tools) mediate social and individual functioning and connect the external and internal, the social and the individual (Vygotsky, 1981; Wertsch and Stone, 1985).

In this sense, conversation as semiotic mediation is different from other forms of tool-mediated action in number of ways. First, while conversation (i.e., dialogue, discussion, etc.) require utterances and use symbol systems (i.e., language), the action that is performed is one of "meaning," making or exchange. Second, it is not the coparticipants who are the object of the "speaker's utterance act," except in the sense that what is spoken is directed toward other participants. Third, conversation that is significant to the design of learning systems is a constructive process that results in a socially constructed design experiment for learning, which must be implemented to determine its viability.

Through semiotic mediation, the dynamic development of learning systems/experiences and the recognition of learners' immediate development needs are clarified through the concept of zone of proximal development. This concept highlights a central tenet in sociocultural theory— the interdependence of individual and social processes in the coconstruction of knowledge (John-Steiner and Mahn, 1996).

Semiotics and the Zone of Proximal Development

The goal of design, instructed by cultural-historical activity theory, is for learners to experience learning through activity-based experiences concerned with growth and development of cognitive capabilities, and transformation consciousness. Designing learning systems, and therein learning experiences that support learners' development of capabilities so that they can learn to do without assistance things that they could initially do only with assistance, requires, as a design consideration, an understanding of the Vygotsky's (1978) notion of the zone of proximal development. Formally, this approach comprises designing learning experiences within the learners' zone(s) of proximal development (ZPD).

Zone of proximal development (ZPD) refers to the "distance between the actual developmental level as determined by independent problem solving and the level of potential development as determined through problem solving under adult guidance or in collaboration with more capable peers" (Vygotsky, 1978). Within the zone of proximal development, learning is focused not on the transfer of skills to the learner but on collaboration between an expert person and the learner that enables the learner to participate in sociocultural practices (Lave and Wenger, 1991). From this perspective, "the development of cognitive structure happens when the individual internalizes a complexity that was formerly distributed over the system that she/he operates within." (Hansen, Direkinck-Holmfeld, Lewis, and Rugelj, 1999).

Design is a formal learning activity, requiring semiotic mediation, much that same as the mediation required learners in the zone of proximal development. Just as peer interaction is crucial to learning because it set up circumstances in which learners perceive an internal need to reconcile different perspectives to resolve conflicts of interpretations, peer or coparticipant interaction in designing learning systems shares an internal need to reconcile different perspectives of cognition and learning, As designers of learning systems, there is a need to design learning experiences that meld the cognitive and social aspects of learning without subordinating either to the other (Rogoff, Radziszewska, and Masiello, 1995).

Conversation and Design Semiotics

Conversation as semiotic mediation in design, draws from the work of Banathy (1996), Jenlink (1995; 1999, June), Jenlink and Carr (1996) and Horn (1999). Conversation, in the context of designing learning systems, is viewed largely as a communicative action, providing a medium through which participants in the design process may engage in a multidimensional inquiry leading to the creation of a new system of learning activities. Design, and therein conversation, acknowledges multiple forms of social discourse. As such, design conversation is viewed, in of itself, as a dynamic system comprised of different forms of discourse, each with a particular purpose and mediational importance as semiotic tool in the system design activity.

Design conversations occur as socially constructed processes of communicative action, situated within multiple interrelated design activities. Bringing this social action into being requires something more to be exchanged within the discourse than just those intersubjective understandings (or misunderstandings) that belong to the flow of the discourse. "That 'more' consists of what is being talked about, the referential and semantic contents of communication."(Engström, 1995). In the design of a learning system, the social languages and coconstructed meanings as well as the ideals generated serve as the referential and semantic contents of communication.

When examined through the lens of activity theory (see Figure 90.1), the communicative action, practical discourse, and inquiry-based orientation of design conversation reveals a deeply complex array of rule-based social actions. These actions are mediated and governed by discourse and social language that is politically and cultural charged in the contexts of its origins. Returning to Brown (1992), design, as a series of communicative and social actions, occurs within the larger dynamic of the design activity system, and is concerned with the whole of the learning environment. Design, in of itself, is an activity system with the purpose of designing learning environments and activity-based learning experiences. It is comprised of interrelated and interdependent events, activities, actions, and processes. Each event and activity of the system seeks to transform a particular object into an intentioned outcome—creating the ideal educational system. This transformation or objectivation, using stakeholder subjectivity as a tool, draws into play issues of social justice, equity, difference, voice, consciousness, and ethical and moral responsibility.

The semiotic mediation of design through conversation or discourse requires an understanding of different forms of discourse as mediational tools. The "meta" nature of design conversation reflects a dialogic "betweeness" that connects various disciplinary perspectives as well as the recognition of differences that populate social systems. Critically evaluating the complex nature of systems design, and examining the sociohistorical and sociocultural context in which the design process is situated problematizes systems design. Given the socially charged nature of discourse and language that influences the activity systems of schools, the forms of conversation, communication, and language systems needed for designing learning environments/experiences must be aligned with the needs of the learners. This becomes even more apparent when considering the need to overcome or transcend the patterns of cultural reproduction that seek to maintain social structures that reify educational systems. To accomplish the design of learning systems, four forms of discourse are examined in relationship to design conversation as a meta-conversation.

Discussion. Perhaps the more common discourse found in social activity, discussion is often more pragmatic, giving way to patterns of advocacy, political posturing, and a fragmentary boundary (Jenlink and Carr, 1996). Discussion discourse is more subjectively influenced by opinion and supposition, and often characterized by patterns of rigidity and being closed to sharing personal or professional viewpoints for scrutiny by others. Discussions are often rule revealing, positing nonnegotiable viewpoints in adversarial and debate like interactions. Through this relation, social rules are surfaced by the participants as each attempts to win the other over this her/his point of view. Sociocultural rules that often come into play include competition, move-oppose, conversation as battle or aggressive confrontation, non-listening, non-suspension of assumptions, and active judgement. As Isaacs notes, "the challenge of this space is to change the meaning of the trauma that arises, both individually and collectively." (Isaacs, 1999). Patterns of conversation often reflect boundary setting, political posturing, defensive routines, and heated exchanges. The language of discussion is often positional, politically charged with advocacy for personal positions, unilateral control, and aligned with social structures that are familiar and provide safe ground from which to argue a particular position. The consciousness that seems to dominate this type of discourse is positional, fragmentary, and advocacy in nature.

Discussion discourse provides a transitional discourse between monologue and the more dialogic types of discourse. The importance of discussion, as a rule revealing discourse, is that participants, individually and collectively, are brought to a level of conscious awareness of the unique perspectives that each person has. This perspectival consciousness is important to the evolution of the design conversation, particularly as the importance of difference is brought into play in the designing of the ideal educational system. The danger with discussion is that if participants remain in the discussion cycle too long, fragmentation and loss of collectivity is often experienced as rigid boundaries set in motion dialectical opposition to sharing and honoring differences.

Dialogue. Dialogue, as a form of discourse, is critical to the systems design process. Whereas discussion is perhaps the more pervasive form of discourse found in social activity and educational settings, dialogue is crucial to bringing the participants to a level collective and transformational consciousness in the systems design process. Dialogue is differentiated into two types by Isaacs (Isaacs, 1999) who sees reflective dialogue as rule reflecting, and generative dialogue as rule generating. Banathy's (1996) identification of strategic and generative dialogue as foundational to design conversation builds on the notion of generative dialogue as rule generative, noting that generative dialogue "is applied to generate a common frame of thinking, shared meaning, and a collective worldview in a group" (p. 215). In contrast, Banathy states that strategic dialogue "implies communication among designers that focuses on specific tasks of seeking solutions." (1996, p. 215).

Each type of dialogic discourse encourages and sustains relational patterns in the larger conversation, patterns essential to creating an integrative and collective consciousness in the participants and across the social activities of systems design. In dialogue, the social language reflects respect, diminishing of dialectical and positional boundaries, sharing meaning and knowledge construction, collective identify and acceptance of personal worldviews. Patterns of conversation move to openness toward others, listening deeply, suspension of judgment, disclosure of personal beliefs and assumptions, caring, concern for equity and justice, and a focus on community. Sociocultural rules are cultural-historically bound systems, that is, they are situated in and bound by cultural and ideological systems of belief that have a temporality, a historicity. As such, in consideration of designing complex learning environments, and relatedly the learning experiences that animate the system, rules must be examined with respect to the origin and/or ideological or theoretical boundedness of their origin. Relatedly, in designing new or alternative systems for learning, rules are coconstructed and collectively respected as communicative and social action that inform the design activity as well as become imprinted in the learning activities that form the educational system. Dialogue as form of discourse, in each of its types, is a critically important social discourse that enables the design conversation to serve as the creative and generative medium through which the user-designers create the ideals. As Isaacs further explains, the generative dialogue, while the rarest of dialogic discourse, "is the one where people cross over into the an awareness of the primacy of the whole . . . this is the space where people generate new rules for interaction, where they are personally included" (Isaacs, 1999). Dialogue serves as a critical nexus in the forming of systems design as meta-conversation.

Ethical. Ethical discourse is a governed by social rules of right and wrong. As Banathy states, ethical discourse is focused on "values, morals, and ethics . . . among the stakeholders" (1996, p. 181 and 215). Stakeholders, as user-designers, must focus not only creating the ideal educational system, they must engage in explicit discussion, aimed at finding common ground and developing consensus. Ethical discourse replaces the aggressive and often conflicting discussion discourse with an "informed and value-based exchange of ideas and perspectives."(1996, p. 181 and 215). Ethical discourse sets boundaries by mutual agreement as to what the ideal system should or should not embody. The social language of this discourse is characterized by personal and collective codes of right and wrong, equity, social justice, and consideration for difference. The conversation patterns of ethical discourse are reflected in Banathy's statement that "we each bring with us to the ethical discourse a wide variety of values and moral attitudes. Although this creates a more complex discourse, it also empowers the conversation with the capacity to deal with increased complexity" (1996, p. 181 and 215). Ethical discourse in design creates reflects a social awareness of variant cultural-historical conditions that shape individual and collective identities of students, and which define equity in learning. Sociocultural rules, in ethical discourse, set boundaries of what is right or wrong (socially and culturally as well as epistemologically and pedagogically), and reflect concern for such issues as related to social justice, equity, and related issues of diversity. Semiotic mediation of design, using CHAT as a framework, would reflect a concern for the learner and her/his needs in relation to the objective of the activity being designed.

Postformal. Postformal discourse "includes an expansion of the awareness of self in relation to others, and a critical awareness of the communication process in relation to how it emancipates or constrains our relations with others" (Horn, 1999, p. 364). Grounded in the postformalism of Kincheloe and Steinberg (1999), postformal discourse is a dialogue about power, " a dynamic investigation of our selves, our relations with others, and the political implications of the type of conversation in which we are engaged" (Horn, 1999, p. 364). This form of discourse shares a similarity with dialectical discourse in that it is grounded in a critical perspective of responsibility for social and cognitive activity, guided by inquiry into social structures of culture based on a critical hermeneutic of power relations. Postformal discourse surfaces a critical consciousness on the individual and collective level of design activity. This critical consciousness is concerned with issues of social justice, equity, diversity, etc., similarly to ethical discourse, however it draws to the foreground of design activity the cultural-historical origins of cognition and learning, focusing on the processes, contexts, and etymological origins of knowledge.

Postformal discourse is guided by the four elements of a postformal structure including patterns, process, etymology, and contextualization. Conversational patterns in postformal discourse include facilitative, constructive, collective, critical voice, and a focus on sociohistorical and sociocultural relationships that exist between knowledge, knowledge construction, and user-designers. In postformal discourse, the elements of dialectical and discussive discourse surface as participants engage in examining personal perspectives and individual worldviews. This serves the meta-conversation of design by creating an awareness of perspectives, thus leading to a per-spectival consciousness essential to generating a quality and energy essential to ensuring that voices of difference are included in the design of an ideal system.

Semiotics and Responsive Design

As a tool for semiotic mediation, design conversation is a complex discursive activity that embodies multiple forms of discourse, and which must be culturally responsive to the needs of the audience for whom the design is targeted. As a culturally responsive practice, design requires a focus on both the design of learning environments, broadly speaking, as well as learning experiences situated within, to support learning. As such, design conversation necessarily focuses on the cultural-historical contexts in which learning is situated. Culture is central to design, as is language, in that contemporary perspectives view learning as changes in the quality of participation in cultural practices (Cole, 1996; Rogoff, 1990; Wenger, 1998). These practices are historically inherited, and are also socially mediated and negotiated through interpersonal relationships among individuals in pairs and in groups (Lave and Wenger, 1991; Rogoff, 1994). Semiotic mediation of design must consider the language systems and other cultural-historical artifacts of the learner, as information in design of the learning experiences. As designers, a primary challenge is to learn and understand the cultural contexts of origin, the cultural worlds of students (Lee, 2003).

DESIGNING LEARNING ENVIRONMENTS/EXPERIENCES:
ACTIONS AND ACTIVITY

The design of a learning environment or learning experience, in relation to creating a human activity system, defined, is defined in part by the nature of actions that are illustrated in the design. In cultural-historical activity theory, the distinction between short-lived goal-directed actions, that is, the actions that animate or otherwise give life to an activity, and the more durable, object-oriented activity is of central importance. Design, mediated by conversation as a semiotic tool, is focused on the independent actions as well as the activity system. To further explicate, an activity is comprised of sets of actions that the participant (designer or learner) engages in to accomplish each activity, often simultaneously with other actions and activities. An action is a set of interrelated processes that enable the participant to mediate their work in systemic change while creating the ideal system. A process may be understood, then, as a set of procedures and principles that a participant uses as part of each process, again, often times simultaneously with other procedures, principles, processes, actions, and activities. Finally, a procedure may be understood as steps that the participant take toward completion of a procedure, and principles may be understood as causal relationships that help one to understand phenomena and make decisions necessary to perform processes well. Activities, from a cultural-historical perspective,

A historically evolving collective activity system, such as denoted by a learning environment, seen in its network relations to other activity systems, is complex. Goal-directed actions, within an activity, are relatively independent but subordinate to the activity, and eventually only when interpreted against the background of entire activity systems. Activity systems realize and re-produce themselves by generating actions and operations, as part of a culturally bound system (Engeström, 2000).

REFLECTIONS ON CHAT AND DESIGN

The design of complex whole learning systems, such as a classroom, as well as the learning experiences within that system, requires a concern for the learner as s/he is situated within the cultural-historical nature of the "whole" system. Cultural-historical activity theory offers a framework for understanding the complexity of design in relation to cognitive development and the design of learning experiences that provide the learner, within her/his zone(s) of proximal development, with the psychological as well as cultural tools necessary to mediating learning.

Designers of learning environments and learning experiences may guide the design processes by drawing on cultural-historical activity theory as a framework for responsive design As semiotic mediational tool, design discourse is socially and culturally charged with the rules and social languages of the respective contexts of origin. Stakeholder subjectivity is recognized as a primary tool in the generative process of creating an idea system. The critical and developmental role that discourse takes in mediating the creative process is made apparent as human subjectivity challenges the existing beliefs and social structures that represent the old system. Mediating tensions as well as overcoming dialectical boundaries set by interacting activity systems further informs the importance of design conversation in educational systems design. Taking on the responsibility of the main mission of educational psychology, that of *design* as Salomon (1996) argues, brings to the foreground the importance of adopting new perspectives of cognition, such as cultural-historical activity theory, and engaging in new as *design experiments* for learning.

FURTHER READING

Banathy, B. H. (1996). *Designing Social Systems in a Changing World: A Journey Toward a Creating Society*. New York: Plenum Press.

Bhaskar, R. (1989). *Reclaiming Reality: A Critical Introduction to Contemporary Philosophy*. London: Verso.

Brown, A. L. (1992). Design experiments: Theoretical and Methodological Challenges in Creating Complex Interventions in Classroom Settings. *Journal of Learning Science*, 2, 141–178.

Checkland, P. (1981). *Systems Thinking, Systems Practice*. New York: John Wiley & Sons.

Checkland, P., and Scholes, J. (1990). *Soft Systems Methodology in Action*. New York: John Wiley & Sons.

Cole, M. (1995). The Supra-Individual Envelope of Development: Activity and Practice, Situation and Context. *New Directions for Child Development*, no. 67, 105–118.

Cole, M. (1996). *Cultural Psychology: A Once and Future Discipline*. Cambridge, MA: Harvard University Press.

Cole, M., and Engeström, Y. (1993). A Cultural-Historical Approach to Distributed Cognition. In G. Salomon (Ed.), *Distributed Cognition: Psychological and Educational Considerations*, pp. 1–46. Cambridge, UK: Cambridge University Press.

Engström, R. (1995). Voice As Communicative Action. *Mind, Culture, and Activity*, 2(3), 192–215.

Engström, Y. (1991). Non Scolae Sed Vitae Discimus: Toward Overcoming the Encapsulation of School Learning. *Learning and Instruction*, 1(3), 243–259.

Engström, Y. (2000). Activity Theory As a Framework for Analyzing and Redesigning Work. *Egronomics*, 43(7), 960–974.

Engström, Y., and Miettinen, R., (1999). Introduction. In Y. Engström, R. Miettinen, and R. Punamäki (Eds.), *Perspectives on Activity Theory*, pp. 1–16. New York: Cambridge University Press.

Engström, Y., Miettinen, R., and Punamäki, R. (1999). *Perspectives on Activity Theory*. New York: Cambridge University Press.

Hansen, T., Direkinck-Holmfeld, T., Lewis, R., and Rugelj, J. (1999). Using Telematics for Collaborative Knowledge Construction. In P. Dillenbourg (Ed.), *Collaborative Learning: Cognitive and Computational Approaches*, pp. 169–196. Amsterdam, The Netherlands: Pergamon.

Horn, R. A (1999). The Dissociative Nature of Educational Change. In J. L. Kincheloe, S. R. Steinberg, and P. H. Hinchey (Eds.), *The Post-formal Reader: Cognition and Education*, pp. 351–377. New York: Falmer Press.

Isaacs. W. (1999). *Dialogue: The Art of Thinking Together*. New York: Currency.

Jenlink, P.M. (1995). Educational Change Systems: A Systems Design Process for Systemic Change. In P. M. Jenlink (Ed.), *Systemic Change: Touchstones for the Future School*, pp. 41–67. Palatine, IL: IRI/Skylight Training and Publishing, Inc.

Jenlink, P. M. (1999, June). *Crossing Boundaries, Changing Consciousness, Creating Learning Communities: Systems Design as Scholarly Practice in Educational Change*. Paper presented at the ISSS Conference, Asilomar, California.

Jenlink, P. M., and Carr, A. A. (1996). Conversation As a Medium for Change in Education. *Educational Technology*, 36(1), 31–38.

John-Steiner, V., and Mahn, H. (1996). Sociocultural Approaches to Learning and Development: A Vygotskian Framework. *Educational Psychologist*, 31(3/4), 191–206.

Kincheloe, J. L., and Steinberg, S. R. (1999).A Tentative Description of Post-formal Thinking: The Critical Confrontation with Cognitive Theory. In J. L. Kincheloe, S. R. Steinberg, and P. H. Hinchey (Eds.), *The Post-formal Reader: Cognition and Education*, pp. 55–90. New York: Falmer Press.

Lave, J., and Wenger, E. (1991). *Situated Learning: Legitimate Peripheral Participation*. Cambridge, MA: Cambridge University Press.

Lee, C. D. (2003). Toward a Framework for Cultural Responsive Design in Multimedia Computer Environments: Cultural Modeling as a Case. *Mind, Cultures, and Activity*, 10(1), 42–61.

Leont'ev, A. N. (1978). *Activity, Consciousness, and Personality*. Englewood Cliffs, NJ: Prentice-Hall.

Mahn, H. (1999). Vygotsky's Methodological Contribution to Sociocultural Theory. *Remedial and Special Education*, 20(6), 341–350.

O'Donnell, A. M., and Levin, J. R. (2001). Educational Psychology's Healthy Growing Pains. *Educational Psychologist*, 36(2), 73–82.

Rogoff, B. (1990). *Apprenticeship in Thinking: Cognitive Development in Social Context*. New York: Oxford University Press.

Rogoff, B. (1994). Developing Understanding in the Idea of Communities of Learners. *Mind, Culture, and Activity*, 1, 209–229.

Rogoff, B., Radziszewska, B., and Masiello, T. (1995). Analysis of Developmental Processes in Sociocultural Activity. In L. M. W. Martin, K. Nelson, and E. Tobach (Eds.), *Sociocultural Psychology: Theory and Practice of Doing and knowing*, pp. 125–149. New York, NY: Cambridge University Press.

Russell, D. (1997). Rethinking Genre in School and Society: An Activity Theory Analysis. *Written Communication*, 14(4), 504–554.

Salomon, G. (1996). Unorthodox Thoughts on the Nature and Mission of Contemporary Educational Psychology. *Educational Psychology Review*, 8(4), 397–417.

Tharp, R. G., and Gallimore, R. (1988). *Rousing Minds to Life: Teaching, Learning, and Schooling in Social Context*. New York: Cambridge University Press.

Vygotsky, L. S. (1978). *Mind in Society: The Development of Higher Psychological Processes*. Cambridge, MA: Harvard University Press.

Vygotsky, L. S. (1981). The Instrumental Method in Psychology. In J. V. Wertsch (Ed.), *The Concept of Activity in Soviet Psychology*, pp. 124–144. Armonk, NY: Sharpe.

Wenger, E. (1998). *Communities of Practice: Learning, Meaning, and Identity*. Cambridge, MA: Cambridge University Press.

Wertsch, J. V., and Stone, C. A. (1985). The Concept of Internalization in Vygotsky's Account of the Genesis of Higher Mental Functions. In J. V. Wertsch (Ed.), *Culture, Communication, and Cognition: Vygotskian Perspectives*, pp. 162–179. New York: Cambridge Press.

Zhu, E. (1998). Learning and Mentoring: Electronic Discussion in a Distance-Learning Course. In C. J. Bonk and K. S. King (Eds.), *Electronic Collaborators: Learner-Centered Technologies for Literacy, Apprenticeship, and Discourse*, pp. 233–259. Mahwah, NJ: Erlbaum.

CHAPTER 91

Reconnecting the Disconnect in Teacher–Student Communication in Education

B. LARA LEE

> Thinking beings have an urge to speak, speaking beings have an urge to think.
> —Hannah Arendt

INTRODUCTION

Most educators enter the classroom environment trained to teach within their designated disciplines. Unfortunately, far too many are unprepared to engage their students in authentic dialogue grounded in equity, justice, and respect for differences. What makes such a condition most grievous is that educators are first and foremost interpersonal communication practitioners in the classroom serving as social agents within a moral domain. In other words teachers are expected by "society" to teach "right from wrong." Meaningful communication is often absent from the classroom environment denying students opportunities to critically dialogue about vital social issues that impact their lives, or to explore and develop a healthy sense of Self, build experienced social interaction with others, as well as question and discover the world that they must live and successfully navigate in. The consequence is a disconnection in teacher-student communication.

This chapter emphasizes the implementation of a more expansive interdisciplinary approach toward the field of educational psychology and specifically preservice training for educators that joins together curriculums and curricula that integrate psychological, educational, and multicultural approaches. Such means allow for the investigation of existing assumptions that have been traditionally understood and explored within the field of educational psychology, but that now require a significant shift to respond to more contemporary rapidly changing social climates and diverse student populations.

In this chapter, I demonstrate how human alienation is attributed to a communication disconnection within the teacher-student dynamic in education. My purpose is to address the current communication disconnect, discuss the pivotal role of communication in education as well as convey two progressive, democratic teaching approaches grounded in dialogue and critical inquiry or dialectic engagement for reconnection within the teaching and learning process and teacher-student relationships. Altogether, a teaching grounded in transformative communication is examined and advocated. This approach encourages positive self-fulfilling prophecies for student success; educator vitality while discovering common-bond experiences tied to authentic human dialogue, ways of knowing and being to transform existing standardized mechanisms based on institutional academic talk and scripted teaching and learning processes that oppress both teacher and student.

In sum, I argue for radical change within existing preservice teaching and learning, educational theory, and classroom practice that denies the pivotal role of communication and dialogue in teaching and learning. Transformative communication and teaching can revive the human spirit and necessitate dead teaching, lifeless teacher-student communication, and unmindful learning. The sacredness of teaching must be recovered.

DISCONNECTION

Missing Communication Preparedness

All educators, no matter the pedagogy or praxis must negotiate and traverse various borders, barriers, and intersections of communication and human interaction while attempting to create a learning environment conducive to individually unique students with their own particular lived experiences, frames of reference and human expression. Both teachers and students must confront their fear of self-disclosure and verbal intimacy to engage in more meaningful communication in education.

Many educators learn either explicitly or implicitly to maintain a safe emotional distance regarding the lived experiences of their students as well as critical social issues that may become too personal, emotional, or controversial. Students quickly understand and see the wall that is built between themselves and their teachers. What occurs, then, is a *communication disconnect*, or gap, within the teaching/learning process and relationship. The disconnect causes a stifling or suppression of human emotions, memories of lived experience, and voice for all concerned. Communication training is at the epicenter, at the very core of the radical shift needed to prepare educators.

Here is the challenge, within this collaborative environment—hard-hitting, tough issues, questions, and conversations must be tackled to strengthen critical thought processes, cognitive development, and engaged learning by allowing teachers and students to get involved in real dialogue about social norms, beliefs, rituals, and customs that dictate what can or cannot be said and done in everyday life. Meaningful teaching and learning cannot happen, if students are not encouraged or allowed to communicate their genuine thoughts, feelings, and experiences, or teachers are silenced by administrative policy.

Communication, dialogue, and critical inquiry encourages educators to become transformative intellectuals that make teaching and learning come alive through mutual participation, collaboration, and discovery—rather than be dulled and limited by educational systems that practice rote teaching and learning that silences student voices and expression of individual lived experiences. Part of the dulling that occurs in educational preservice training and practice is attributed to the exhaustive rules, regulations, and punishments that are routine in schools, and all of which, silence dialogue and critical inquiry.

The classroom should be a wide space for a community of learners to practice peaceful social relations and democracy by embracing diversity in education and society in such a way that individuals have the freedom to be fully human, to speak their lives, and to live with greater dignity as unique human beings. Teachers and students need the freedom to make errors and corrections throughout the learning experience. Education must feed the soul, or rather the mind, body, and spirit—the entire person. If not, learning becomes prepackaged, lifeless, and begins to numb thinking, feeling, being, and without doubt, harms collaborative teacher-learner relationships. Any hope for meaningfully successful student outcomes within and outside of the classroom are greatly reduced or lost, altogether.

Teacher–Student Dissatisfaction with Education

Too often the teaching–learning dynamic is one suspended on alienation, mistrust, false competition, and disrespect while cresting on the diminishment of the Self. I have taught students of Business, Communication, Education, Gender and Women's Studies; and within single-sex and coeducational environments. Amazingly, students share similar feelings about their right to speak and be heard in the classroom. Surveying students over the years, the response is frightfully consistent in conveying that teachers are authority-centered, egotistical, and have no care or regard for student thoughts, views, or counterpoints on any given topic.

My experience has been that students fear not being heard, listened to, or stated differently, they fear social and intellectual rejection by other students, and importantly, by their teachers. Another area of enormous complaint by students is that they claim existing educational requirements and course content have little bearing on their real lives, experiences, and aspirations. They see no connection between what is being taught and what is being lived.

Consequently, learning must be relevant to the popular culture, race, class, and gender issues as well as familial, friendship, and relationships that so dramatically influence student's lives. Otherwise, they will tune out and turn off. We make a grave error in education, if we deny the compelling, external, larger world influences that have the power to preoccupy the minds, attentions, and interests of our students. Education must represent the lived world and be dedicated to promoting social and academic competence and in developing sociocultural understanding, if the field of educational psychology is to successfully meet the rapid changes in society, and student lives.

Simultaneously, teachers feel unheard, undervalued by administrators and unappreciated by students and their families or caregivers. They claim that their students range from listless unresponsiveness to aggressive hostility, with only the occasional interested and prepared student. Still further, educators are enslaved by mechanized educational systems that forbid creative, groundbreaking, or pioneering dynamic teaching. Subsequently, educators become disillusioned with the profession and, with their ability to affect meaningful learning and teaching for positive social change. The consequence then becomes that a high number of potentially qualified, dedicated teachers leave the field for more lucrative and lesser stressed-filled careers to be replaced by oftentimes inadequately trained teachers, or by those entering the field laterally from other vocations without the necessary educational grounding.

In sum, tensions arise in the classroom when teacher aspirations collide with student expectations—making the need to talk openly—profoundly imperative. We must discontinue teaching methods and approaches that are practiced in isolation and without understanding of the impact of every day lived experiences and realities. If not, we close off important possibilities for wider social awareness, recognition of common-bond experiences, and social-human development for students. Inadequate guidance and socialization frequently prevails in teaching through communication barriers.

Politics, Power, and Hierarchy of Language

In this section, I provide only a few, yet dramatic examples of the power of language and social interaction. Language is rooted in politics and social hierarchy wherein hegemony or dominant viewpoints, and beliefs are publicly broadcasted, taught, and adopted as if these biased assumptions were completely normal, appropriate, and relevant to everyone's lived experiences. Such power in language demonstrates how systematically and administratively, diverse perspectives in lived experiences or cultural expression can be made invisible or altogether erased. The field of Education is not exempt from such a condition of power imbalances. As teachers, we should not accept a dominant discourse that refuses to recognize or denies the social and political elements taught in education and within the larger society.

Educators must be aware, and teach their students that a politics of language controls people and their roles in a given society. Most often politics are based upon a social framework grounded in capitalism that divides individuals according to financial and material wealth, education, race, sex, and class privilege. Similar politics of power resides in the classroom. Human beings consciously or subconsciously carry around the fear of rejection or loss of face in social interaction.

Since the educator's primary role is that of communication practitioner, I draw from the work of Brown and Levinson wherein they demonstrate that politeness in communication is used when there is the perception or belief that unequal positions of power and authority are present in social relationships. The teacher-student dynamic is such an example. Traditionally, power is marked in education by teachers speaking, and acting with authority contrasted by students listening, inactive and passive participants. Such politics serve to maintain unequal positions of power in education and perpetuate conflicts.

Language is so powerful that it can maintain grievous social inequities, racism, sexism, homophobia, and hatred for difference regarding any kind of cultural identity and experience. The politics and power of language dictates that who is given authority to speak and be heard while others remain muted or silenced. Public discourse conveys who holds a privileged status and power within institutions and society.

For example, feminist theory reminds that women have long had to negotiate and resist silence imposed upon them by the dominant class. Significantly, women's ways of learning, living, and being reflect their own unique speaking style and patterns that have been historically defined and stereotyped as being weak, and less authoritative and credible than the male standard used to measure or analyze effective communication.

Another example is that people of differing cultural and ethnic diversity suffer at the hand of dominant expectations in communicative practice. Students who do not demonstrate skill in the English language are labeled as ESL or students whose second language is English. They often experience discriminations or missed opportunities due to biased evaluations of their intellectual and academic ability. Such prejudiced evaluations undermine the self-worth and human potential of many students.

The politics and power of language is maintained through social hierarchy. Customarily those holding power and status are viewed as possessing superior abilities and importance than those occupying positions lower down on the social hierarchy. Such events can even occur in education, if we fail to practice democracy of dialogue in teaching and learning.

Rejection Anxiety: Race, Class, Gender, and Sexuality

The existing fragmented approach toward race and ethnicity within mainstream education must be carefully examined to reveal the levels of often male, (but also female) Eurocentric and heterosexual class privilege that ignores the presence and value of diversity and multicultural experiences. This effort to reproduce a singular view of cultural and ethnic identity must be addressed and corrected through education. As the United States rapidly expands its landscape of culturally diverse citizens, no educator should be ill-informed or unprepared to address issues concerning the politics of race, identity, and culture. Nor should they be ill-equipped to communicate and socially interact with a wide range of student lives and experiences.

Eurocentric or predominately white privilege continues to dominate the vastly diverse student terrain. Educators and students don't enter the classroom environment free of preexisting frames of reference, biases, and prejudices. In actuality, each person contributes to the learning environment either negatively or positively based upon individually adopted ideologies that regulate thinking, communication, social interaction, and behavior that tend to follow along the lines of some embedded or adopted belief system. Significantly language and communicative styles reflect those interior or personal values and assumptions learned during early childhood development and are engrained over the years unless otherwise challenged by social consciousness or educational awareness.

Consequently, the classroom dynamic becomes filled with a diversity of Selves, thoughts, words, modes of being, and lived experiences. Such a potentially volatile climate requires that educators have interpersonal communication competency to negotiate through a wide range of issues; and possess the capacity to respond to classroom interactions and student interactions with an emotional intelligence and maturity involving the human spirit of compassion, care, and tolerance for difference.

As educators, we cannot simply declare an awareness of diversity among our students, without applying communicative action supportive of such a claim. A reform of thinking and practice must occur, beginning with how educators are trained, how they project their identities; and how they allow a diverse population of students to project their identities.

The Hidden Curriculum in Education and Society

Supporting the existence of the politics, power, and hierarchy of language within education is what is often referred to as the hidden curriculum in education. This undercurrent of dominant power and ideologies is found, if not in all, at least most, educational institutions wherein the beliefs and values of a dominant group are broadcasted or transmitted to students through specific administrative missions and regulations, mandated curriculums and approved curricula.

This is the case, whether the classroom is single-sex or coeducational, the hidden curriculum is grounded in cultural hegemony. Cultural hegemony impacts and shapes beliefs that influences our identity, sense of self, and place within the social hierarchy. Educators must be trained to be aware and understand its power to construct a particular and intended worldview that may advantage some students, while disadvantaging others. What makes cultural hegemony so potent in its influence is that over time, the messages broadcasted eventually are perceived as natural and normal—worthy of our teaching and support.

Awareness of the hidden curriculum should serve to remind us that education cannot be imposed upon students through mechanized, rote processes without their active participation and voice. The hidden curriculum in education suppresses the questioning of the role of education as a moral agent dictating beliefs, values, and ideologies as well as constructing social identifies. Still further, intelligence is ruled, controlled, and constructed according to manufactured IQ tests and scoring that reduce student ability to a number, while labeling them as being intellectually superior or deficient without giving consideration to the potentially many intelligences that students possess that cannot be empirically measured.

Finally, as educators we must become skilled in recognizing how we have been shaped and influenced by a hidden curriculum in education and society that is grounded in social class, patriarchal or male-privileged hierarchy rooted in cultural hegemony. Even our ways of knowing, believing, learning and living are replete with the residue of the hidden curriculum in education. Considerable attention and effort is given through education in maintaining the status quo that may mask oppressive power and inequality. Healthy and competent communication begins to repair the breech of disconnection addressed throughout this chapter.

COMMUNICATION

What Is Communication?

Communication is not an innate or rather automatic quality. We are not born with the ability to communicate verbally and particularly, to communicate with effectiveness and competence, but rather it is a learned process that continues throughout our lives. There is a never-ending human drive to speak and be heard. Communication is how we as individuals attempt and struggle to make sense and meaning in our lives. As translated from the Greek, communication literally means to share, have fellowship, and communion with others to form community. Significantly, to form communion requires that the act of mindfully, present, listening be part of the communicative interaction. This crucial detail is often ignored or overlooked within communication practices and relationships.

At its basic, original starting point, communication affirms the humanity of others and ourselves; as well as impacts the quality of our lives, daily. Communication is not simply a process of sending and receiving messages, but rather, it is continuous transactional human engagement that involves the entire person—mind, body, and spirit and significantly, personality and emotions.

Underpinning our need to communicate and experience human verbal contact and intimacy is the want to belong, be loved, and to love others. We must tell our lived stories to discover, build identity, and claim selfhood. Through the projection of our voices, we claim empowerment that our thoughts, experiences, and lives do matter and have meaning in the larger social community. Significantly, communication and social interaction are tied to the hierarchy of human needs that range from simple to complex. To be alive, is to hear our words and voices resonate within our physical beings, thoughts, and actions; and to gain feedback and reaction to those sensations and experiences from others. Communication signals our presence in the world.

COMMUNICATIVE SOCIAL INTERACTION

We create and maintain social identities, images, and Selves through an exchange of words or interpersonal communication. We have often heard that each of us wears a mask that covers the real Self to protect egos from harm. Such devices are used because we clearly understand that all citizens must abide by civil, legal, and social rules that dictate our movement in society. From a sociological perspective, daily living is bound up in rituals that regulate our individual and collective behavior. Over time and with experience, these rituals and moral rules begin to mold our human identity.

Social interaction oftentimes reflects the politics of language and hierarchy of power in society. Interestingly, much of the role playing and maintenance that we engage in daily, is wrapped up in a social construction of reality that is often imposed upon us by dominant social powers. In other words, oftentimes, we tend to abide by, and obey rules, regulations, and dictates of personal interaction that have been socially constructed, or manufactured; and we internalize these constructions as they were absolute, unquestionable truth.

Functional Conflict

A profoundly important element of communication and social interaction that is often under-addressed, ignored, or misunderstood is the role of conflict in the course of human social interaction. Conflict does indeed have a constructive place within our communication lives. However, to remain in a state of conflict is destructive. Let me explain. Communicative conflict can raise important issues and actually connect diverse people moving them on the path to achieving harmony and community. It can help to bring issues and problems out in the open for deeper discussion that could lead to resolution or reconciliation.

For example, educators have aspirations for their teaching and students have expectations about their learning such mixed goals can create a site for potential conflict. Communication drives social interaction and too often, the paths of intent for teachers and students run parallel without actually meeting and connecting because neither truly knows and understands how to genuinely talk and listen to the other, but only to argue their viewpoint. We must next examine how communication and social interaction impacts individual lives or Selves.

UNDERSTANDING THE SELVES

Considerable research bears out that we are not comprised of one Self, but of many Selves making us highly complex beings that at times defy definition. Every person has undergone environmental and relational experiences that involved elements such as styles of attachment with significant caregivers ranging from positive, healthy, constructive familial relationships to negative, destructive, and unhealthy caregiving. From a psychological and sociological perspective, through these relationships we learn and adopt social roles, receive and adopt social labels, and come to understand our sexual biological anatomies and gender-role expectations. We then see ourselves in relationship and context with others.

Each of these stages of development and experience is accompanied by our communication practices and those received by others in our lives that range occur within various communication climates that range in a continuum from highly constructive or highly destructive influences on the development of the Selves. Through early, mid, and late adolescent experiences and relationships we should have learned how to express emotions, develop kinship, build healthy identities and experience affection and love. But as we know, childhood experiences can be fraught with dysfunctionalism, varied hardships as well as toxic communication climates.

All of these factors directly impact how we elect to engage in self-disclosure and relational intimacy, which can be highly open or purposefully hidden to others. Our approach clearly depends on our ability to give and build trust with others. Based upon those unique variables within the human condition, each of us perceives, interprets, and evaluates messages sent and received, otherwise known as communication. Grounding each of these human elements is the various methods of communicating, that each of us adopts to frame and project our sense of Selfhood, identity, and persona that we want others to see and accept.

FEAR OF SELF-DISCLOSURE AND VERBAL INTIMACY

Most members of a given society fear rejection. So as stated earlier, they tend to engage in acts of communication politeness to avoid having their face or Selves attacked, embarrassed, and reduced in any way, socially. Altogether, individuals generally try to function in public with minimal face loss, when communicatively interacting. For this reason, we construct and maintain communication boundaries to help us regulate the impact of incoming and outgoing communicative messages. Importantly, boundaries may appear to be invisible, but when they are crossed or violated—misunderstanding and conflict can erupt.

Our levels of communication intimacy and disclosure are grounded in early childhood experiences; as well as our ongoing need to protect our identities. Most individuals become skilled at maintaining social distance or developing masks that protect them from psychological, social, emotional, and even physical harm. The existing educational system and teaching methods frequently invade the protective mechanism that both teachers and students adopt for emotional safety. Yet, self-disclosure is absolutely necessary toward building a community of engaged learners, a space where progressive teachers and students teach and learn through a discussion of sharing lived experiences.

Two fears generally emerge in the classroom. First, most educators do not want to be placed in a position wherein they appear to be less than academically prepared and knowledgeable. They already work within a vocation that provides precious little respect, without engaging in self-sabotage by inviting students to further demean them. Therefore, many teachers will guard their Selves and their space to ensure that their intentionally projected identities and images are out of harms way. Such a need for safety and protection adds to the alienation and disconnection that customarily comprises the teacher-student relationship. Teachers elect to lecture from scripted, well-planned. and rehearsed material to avoid challenge and potential discredit. Granted, there are indeed exceptions, but I am speaking of the rule.

Second, students are in an environment that is constantly testing, evaluating, and measuring if they have intellectual acuity thereby inciting hostile competition for the right to be affirmed by the teacher and deemed to be a good student. Oftentimes, students opt not to participate rather than be made to feel "dumb" and incapable by other students and specifically, their teachers. Learning is a process of trial and error, yet too often there is a pretense of a false perfection that stops teachers and students from being themselves for fear of embarrassment or humiliation if they may behave in human ways and make mistakes. Unfortunately, conventional, nonprogressive education is not an arena conducive to self-disclosure and verbal intimacy.

RECONNECTION

Bridging the disconnection gap within the teacher–student dynamic requires three transformative elements: communicative practices grounded in democracy of voice and human agency, democratic/progressive and anti-oppressive/liberatory teaching methods, and approaches known as critical pedagogies that use dialectic discussion. I have demonstrated the importance of genuine, meaningful communication and dialogue. Now let us examine two transformative models of education that promote reconnection among teachers and students.

Progressive Democratic Education

John Dewey grounded his progressive model of education in the conviction that individuals should have the right and opportunity to participate within the social consciousness of society. All should practice and participate in democracy. A progressive teacher attempts to meet students where they are in their learning and lived social experiences, and seeks to transcend socially imposed distinctions of classism, race, and gender. Dewey believed that the greatest freedom one could posses was freedom of the mind and the right to obtain and experience freedom of intelligence, choice, and action. Ultimately, he held the commitment that education must reflect the lived experiences of the outside world connecting psychological and sociological processes, of which, both held equal importance.

Liberatory Anti-Oppressive Pedagogy

Dewey's fundamental model has been enlarged and expanded through the work of Paulo Freire, which also advocated democracy and freedom in education and society. He was opposed to the banking method of education, which he found to be an oppressive pedagogy or approach toward teaching. This is a method of teaching that reduces students to depositories or receptacles of information lectured or banked into the minds. Such a model discourages critical inquiry and human agency. Students are reduced to objects of teaching rather subjects in command of their learning.

Many oppressions exist within society, however, anti-oppressive education deals with those explicit and implicit lessons found in a hidden curriculum that perpetuates intolerance, hatred, and teaching that contradicts democracy and freedom in learning and impedes social justice. By contrast the progressive model of education proposed is one grounded in dialogic encounter and dialectic engagement. These models of education function to promote human dignity and social justice. To implement the two models of education proposed above, I recommend the following.

DIALOGIC ENCOUNTER

Learning is enhanced through active student participation. This communicative practice promotes co-agency in building community, collaboration, and understanding of cultural difference and experience. Yet, much of teaching today silences student voices. As conveyed earlier, the primary role of an educator, in my view, is that of communication practitioner facilitating a dialogue rooted in dialectic interaction or critical inquiry to engage in self-reflection in order to reach higher levels of understanding and seek personal truth, on a given issue. Together teachers and students learn through a dialogue that assists them in naming and understanding the larger world with all of its diversity and complexities.

Dialogic encounter moves beyond just dialogue and gives us an opportunity to address the interior memories of our lived stories; and provides us opportunities to reflect upon the exterior social influences that impact our individual lives. Such an element of dialogue functions to convey a more complete text of lives. This form of dialogue best occurs when a community of learners attempts to build an environment of trust. The progressive educator earnestly attempts to bridge the gap that separates individuals from genuine connection and understanding.

DIALECTIC ENGAGEMENT

The dialectic encourages the classroom to be a location of democratic practice and freedom of expression in interrogating critical social issues that impact daily living, opportunities, justice, and so forth. Dialectic engagement supports transformative teaching and learning through serious intellectual thought and discussion. This approach allows us to question if teaching and learning is coerced, enforced, and objectively positioned, or if it is fully participatory and highly proactive in questioning prescribed, systematic, and authorized knowledge.

Dialectic engagement or critical inquiry helps students name and question their world and life; while verifying and determining the correctness, validness, and credibility of eternal, authoritative, knowledge that students are expected to adopt and internalize. The outgrowth of such efforts is enhanced participation, humanity, and dignity. Such a partnership increases student efficacy of voice and action while reducing uncertainties that evoke predatory competition, distrust, and alienation. Significantly, dialogic encounter and dialectic engagement counteract the forces of the hidden curriculum, political power, social hierarchy, dominant ideologies and hegemony that are implemented to maintain the dominant status-quo and culture that suppress and silence views of difference and dissent.

CONCLUSION

In this chapter I have earnestly tried to demonstrate the communication disconnect that exists among teachers and students in education wherein communication can either cause disconnection or reconnection. I provided concrete examples of the sources, reasons, and practices that cause disconnection and dividedness. These examples were followed by conveying fundamental elements of human communication, social interaction, development of the Selves and the human fear of rejection. Two key models of education grounded in democratic/progressive and anti-oppressive/liberatory education were proposed that poignantly address as well as be pragmatically implemented through in preservice training that is grounded in communication, revised educational theory and classroom practice that implement dialogue and critical inquiry wherein both teacher and students are active participants in the educational process, while remaining communicatively connected.

My hope is to convey and demonstrate that such an education can encourage teachers and students to compose lives of meaning, connection, and truth. Preservice and established educators, I encourage you to consider the following possibilities so that you and your students can stave off the disconnection that can so easily disrupt harmonious teacher-student relationships. First, investigate and promote preservice training courses and labs in Interpersonal Communication and Conflict Resolution. Second, require service learning in areas of educational emancipation, social justice, and civil equity. Third, commit to ongoing professional development in emotional and spiritual intelligence involving an ethic of compassion, care, and tolerance.

TERMS FOR READERS

Anti-oppressive Education—Educational pedagogy and praxis that specifically deals with those explicit/implicit lessons found in a hidden curriculum that perpetuates intolerance, hatred; and teaching, contradicts democracy and freedom in learning, and impedes social justice.

Dialectic Engagement—Critical inquiry that interrogates or examines social issues, dominant ideologies, and hidden lessons in education and society.

Dialogic Encounter—An environment and approach that promotes community and collaboration in teaching and learning to discover differences and common-bond experiences in everyday lived experiences

Emotional Intelligence—An appropriate level of emotional (and communicative) response to a given issue that arises in communication that does not violate, harm, or destroy the Self of another.

Hegemony—Dominant social norms, frames of reference, ideologies, and mandates imposed on the less powerful that are eventually internalized and adopted as natural.

Hidden Curriculum—The implicit/explicit social norms, values, beliefs, and regulations that are transmitted to students through education.

Multiple Intelligences—A vast number of human capacities that cannot be accounted for through standardized measurement and assessment.

Progressive Education—Educational ideology and practice founded in dialectic engagement and dialogic encounter in the promotion of social justice and equity.

Spiritual Intelligence—Ability to practice compassion, care, and tolerance for differences in human uniqueness and experience.

Styles of Attachment—Relationships practiced and adopted in adolescence ranging from highly positive to highly negative communication and social interaction.

FURTHER READING

Anderson, M., and Collins, P. (2004). *Race, Class and Gender*, (5th ed.). Belmont, CA: Thomson-Wadsworth.

Dewey, J. (1916). *Democracy and Education*. NY: MacMillan

Freire, P. (2001). *Pedagogy of the Oppressed*. NY: The Continuum International Publishing Group, Inc.

Giroux, H. (1988). *Teachers As Intellectuals*. Westport, CT: Begin & Garvey.

Goffman, I. (1967). *Interaction Ritual*. NY: Pantheon Books.

Goody, E. (Ed.). (1978). *Questions and Politeness*. NY: Cambridge University Press.

Greene, M. (1998). *The Dialectic of Freedom*. NY: Teachers College, Columbia University.

Noddings, N. (1992). *The Challenge to Care in Schools: An Alternative Approach to Education*. NY: Teachers College Press

Palmer, P. (1998). *The Courage to Teach*. NY: Jossey-Bass.

Wood, J. (2003). *Interpersonal Communication and Everyday Encounters*. (3rd ed.). Belmont, CA: Wadsworth Publishing Company.

CHAPTER 92

The Rise of Scientific Literacy Testing: Implications for Citizenship and Critical Literacy Skills

MARY FRANCES AGNELLO

INTRODUCTION

Given the movement of standardized testing and more frequent testing of students during grades K–12, it can be taken for granted that testing and literacy testing in particular are normal, to be expected, and should be part of the educational and social routine of students in the United States. Higher stakes and expectations of educators and students have exerted demands on the curriculum and the work day of teachers and students that might be expected if we assumed that the testing of reading and writing and other academic skills is and should be taken for granted. This article sets forth four movements that have contributed to the rise of scientific testing in general and scientifically based reading instruction and research. These four movements include (1) the movement of psychology toward a verifiable human science, (2) the development of intelligence quotient and other forms of testing and measurement, as well as the study of reading and reading instruction within the field of psychology, (3) the exertion of power over teachers as technocrats within bureaucratic schools, and (4) the political demands for teacher and student accountability.

Much has been said about the inequities of testing, the racial bias of testing, and the irrelevance of testing to life and even many aspects of schooling. However, what is *not being said* may be as important as that which is. Or perhaps, there is dissent about testing practices that is not being acknowledged by policy makers and lawmakers. The manner in which little or no attention is being paid to the important "other discourse" about the expense of testing, the reduction of education to test preparation, the irrelevance of one exam to life problems, and the loss of excitement about learning and education helps to ensure that compliance with the social practices of testing contributes to the stability of economic and political structures formed by and for special interests. Michel Foucault advocated the discovery of how such practices came to be taken for granted through a normalization process that occurs across social structures, throughout organizations, and in the discourses that emanate from these various institutions. So, how did we come to these places in our history and society where testing is taken for granted and learning to read and write across the curriculum is geared toward the tests that show success or failure of teachers and students engaged in the work of teaching and learning? I propose that we can better understand the rise of scientific literacy testing by understanding the development of science, the history of psychology that led to scientific legitimacy of measuring human capacities, the bureaucratization of schools and control of teacher work, and finally the manner in which testing satisfies through scientific verification the accountability of educational services rendered and received.

The following discussion will address these four areas of social and educational progress as grounded in European scholarship and the six values (progress, Republican virtue, nationalism, faith in reason, natural law, and freedom) held dear by the founding fathers who put governance and social structures into place in the late eighteenth century. The framers of the Constitution had knowledge of the writings of John Locke, whose influences are present in letters of Thomas Jefferson and John Adams. Newtonian physics and other scholarship by George Berkeley, James Mill, and other philosophers' writings contributed to both philosophy and psychology as we know them today. Writings by Aristotle, Rene Descartes, Wilhelm Wundt, Francis Galton, Ivan Pavlov, John B. Watson, Alfred Binet, and Charles Darwin cannot be underestimated in their influences on the study of the connection of the mind and body, experimentation, mechanistic views of human functions, the intelligence movement, and evolution of man as an organism. The following sections will synthesize the contributions by some of these and other scholars whose works, synchronized with the power and influence of policy makers, have led to our present-day practices of scientific literacy testing.

THE MOVEMENT TOWARD PSYCHOLOGY AS A VERIFIABLE HUMAN SCIENCE

Philosophers whose studies spanned the gamut from spiritual topics to natural sciences to governmental theories were curious about human reflexes and the senses. Aristotle wrote about the objects that were perceptible by each sense in the *Five Senses* (384–322 BC). As opposed to Plato, who believed that truth could be found in the mind rather than in the world of matter, Aristotle found truth and matter to concretely exist in the real world. He could separate himself from that which he was attempting to understand. For him the world could be studied through the sensory perceptions that man could formulate about the reality around him. Modern-day assessments of Aristotle's contribution to psychological process point to his explanation of the powers of the rational soul to understand, constituting the highest level of existence. Aristotle is credited with an all-inclusive view of man's existence including physical, psychological, and moral as a unitary system, unrivaled until the seventeenth century. His view of studying reality constituted the foundations for psychological study until the use of empirical science emerged during the Renaissance.

During the Renaissance, as the authority of the Church was being challenged, scientific discovery unraveled the truths of the deistic-centered universe. Copernicus studied planetary motion to arrive at his heliocentric theory, later verified through empirical observations by Kepler, Galileo, and Newton. As the de-centering of humanity and the earth in relation to the rest of the universe and to God along with Charles Darwin's theory of evolution removed mankind from the center of earthly existence, scientists attempted to understand the species of man as one of many found in the natural order. This order could best be explained through scientific observation.

The reliance on reason as a source of knowledge found efficacious scientific practices involving observation. Such observation became the basis of empiricism. Francis Bacon's work was seminal in organizing the approach to scientific study, involving careful and controlled observation. Isaac Newton's method relied on observations to explain causal events. Psychologists emulated Newton's views of the orderly universe, transferring the thought that mental activities must be ordered by the same system of laws. Rene Descartes taught that the study of bodily processes was the province of physiology and the study of the mind belonged to psychology, thus first defining psychology's subject matter as the mind. This concept is also important when we discuss the view of learning and learning literacy specifically as a mental activity divorced from the external world in which we learn or become literate. A whole body of scientific study grew up around the psychological processes of reading, later to be confronted by Deweyian and Freirean scholars, as well as sociolinguists and anthropologists who viewed reading and writing as socially grounded. Among other thinkers who concerned themselves with sensory specification were Isaac Newton, John Locke, Charles Bell, Ernst Weber, Hermann Ludwig Ferdinand von Helmholtz, and Edward Titchener

In addition to being credited or blamed with carrying forward the dualism of Aristotelian separateness of the mind and body, Descartes studied visual perception, the interaction of the mind and brain, and mechanism in human action. James Mill, also interested in the concept of mental mechanics, wrote an essay of that title in 1829. John Stuart Mill wrote an essay called "Mental Chemistry" in 1843. These philosophical and psychological players were concerned with the brain—its thinking, responding, and control or connection to human activity. The view that the mind worked mechanistically helped to establish the view of the human body as a machine, "an automaton" that could be stimulated and controlled, and eventually its component parts were studied in controlled experiments legitimized by their scientific rigor.

Scientific rigor, as it interfaced with the tenets of classical liberalism, established a formidable basis for the power and knowledge relations that have come to dominate American/Western thinking. A brief overview of the six tenets of classical liberalism puts into perspective the views of nature and man's *progress* toward perfectibility. An understanding of these six tenets is helpful for understanding the ease with which science would come to dominate in social theories and practices informing education, democratic government, and economy. The view of natural law to explain the order of the universe and the world, and particularly as *natural law* was informed by reason and later science, as well. Natural law was adapted by the early American philosophers to describe the relationships of human beings as not subjugated one to another. It was natural to those seeking the bourgeois revolution to break from the politics of the monarchy in the quest for human *freedom*. Such freedom was embraced by the American Revolutionists to question the place of the individual in the new political system. As the freedom of the individual from the whimsical policies of the King became the priority of the founding framers of the new Constitution and Bill of Rights, natural law was invoked as based in *reason*. Later science would replace reason as the legitimate framework within which social theory would operate. The confidence that the founding fathers had in their *Republican virtue* as their moral guide gave them the impetus with which to strive for a good life and a good society, invoking the powers of the Protestant godhead to found its identity within the international community. *Nationalism*, or love and dedication to country, became a more widespread phenomenon in the contexts of the nation state. The rise of science inspired by Enlightenment thought gave leaders with goals of social control, capitalistic gain, and development of the frontier a fertile laboratory in which to conduct the governmental experiment in republican democracy within the new nation state. Although the political ties of the United States and England were redefined, the intellectual thought of the English philosophers remained an American mainstay. Similarly, English thought would lead to the rise of psychology and the furtherance of psychology as a science.

THE RISE OF PSYCHOLOGICAL SCIENCE AND DEVELOPMENT OF INTELLIGENCE QUOTIENT TESTING

The mental mechanism model of the brain and nervous system in writings by George Berkeley, David Hume, David Hartley, James Mill, and others led to "psychophysics" and "new psychology." These schools of thought believed in careful measurement of human responses to various stimuli. Eventually, a split between those psychologists who would or would not discuss "consciousness" (in some ways similar to the same split between advocates of whole language and phonics reading philosophies) contributed to become the mainstay of psychological debate. Yet, work by Charles Darwin, William James, and Sigmund Freud muddied the scientific waters of the field. Darwin's work had far-reaching effects in all areas of study; James's work as religious, spiritual, and related to consciousness was difficult to categorize; and, of course, Freud's work, subjected to scientific scrutiny, withstands as well as falters in some areas. However, scholarship leading to "Gestaltpsychologie" and the advent of behaviorism brought psychology, particularly from the perspective of John B. Watson, into experimentation based on learned and unlearned responses. Although B.F. Skinner's work was often more philosophical and utopian than psychological, he is also credited with the stimulus/response explanation of human behavior.

As the desire to sort human beings and the view of the "survival of the fittest" promoted capitalism and its practices, including the establishment of a meritocracy and a ruling class, Darwin's theory of evolution was embraced. Such synchronicity occurred because American ideology ascribed to the self as creator of success and the need for the individual to take care of oneself and one's business. An extension of this perspective to human productivity and potential for perfectability became normalized as psychological testing became a predictor of student success at school. Student learning was invoked as a way to measure human achievement and success. Later, *assessment*, often associated with property value, was applied to student achievement. Student accomplishments were reified as the "worth" of students was indicated by their test scores: the nineteenth-century work by Galton, and several who worked on test development— James McKeen Cattell on Mental Tests, 1890; Hermann Ebbinghaus on the Completion Test, 1897; Stella Emily Sharp on a Test of Mental Testing, 1899; Charles Edward Spearman on General Intelligence, 1904; William Stern on the Mental Quotient, 1912; and Binet on testing of students in Paris to determine the probability of their school success and studies of memory, 1894.

The layering of the concept of the evolution of the species, as well as the possibility of better understanding intelligence by its measurement put into place, essay by essay, the building blocks of the foundations of broad-based social applications of testing that would be done in the Army through the use of the Alpha Beta test in 1904. Much of the development of the tests was done by Arthur S. Otis, whose work was published by the World Book Company in 1921.

Harcourt, another big name in test publishing, was founded by Aflred Harcourt and Donald Brace, who were friends at Columbia in New York. The duo emerged as publishers of world-renowned writers, as well as a leading textbook publisher. Focused on publishing high school textbooks, the company merged with World Book, whose expertise was in the elementary school market. What became Harcourt Brace Jovanovich acquired The Psychological Corporation in 1960 through the World Book Company, and became one of the foremost producers of testing materials. In late 2003, the company changed its name to Harcourt Assessment Inc., uniting its two divisions into one operating company. The name PsychCorp will remain the brand imprint for certain testing products. The growth of this company, as well as other publishers and their connections to the power of large corporations, helps to steadfastly solidify the commercial power of testing. The union of the power of psychology as science to create, to innovate, and to legitimate in psychological testing with the commercial success and stability of the publishing business is a large component of the rise of scientific literacy testing.

Also important to the understanding of the rise of scientific literacy testing is a comprehension of the development of the study of reading within the field of psychology. The area of scientific reading research has been said to have originated with Javal's work in 1879. He was actually interested in eye movement during reading and contributed a body of work to what is essentially at least a part of the physiology of reading. Later Frank Smith said if the light would go off, the stuff of reading would still remain in the mind, insinuating that the eye is not the key to understanding reading. Of course, there is reading for the blind and disabled through the Braille system, among many other areas of studies of unusual and/or problematic reading issues.

As we know, sociologists and anthropologists also have contributed significantly to expanding the meaning of literacy as well as to the notion of literacy as sociocultural phenomena that can be determined and nurtured in one's social environment according to one's needs. Others, like Paulo Freire and the second-generation criticalists, approach literacy as politically grounded, determined, and mandated. I will withhold the sociocultural and political discussions of literacy for another occasion and attempt to focus on what appears to have been important landmarks and names in the development of the *science* of reading, especially in the field of psychology, in what will not begin to do justice to the field of study. The remainder of this part of the discussion will attempt to touch on what are deemed important strides in the study of reading from a psychological perspective.

In a centennial dedication to the scientific study of reading, Harry Singer (1985) described four areas of groundbreaking study in the field of reading as perception, cognition, components of reading, and patterns of ability. Javal's studies found that the high school student's eye is in motion only 6 percent of the reading time, while the remainder of the time is spent on fixation pauses. His view was that the more quickly and efficiently that the reader could process what the eye had perceived into long-term memory, necessarily involving interaction between the reader's knowledge and text data, the better reading would be achieved. Cattell (1886) postulated that a component in the speed of reading is the size of the unit of perception. Work in cognition done by Huey (1908) demonstrated that as readers mature, they perceive verbal relationships across sentences, referred to as "chunking." Important in these findings is that verbal relationships across sentences remain in long-term memory, determining the meaning a reader makes of text. Thus, while analysis of syntactic structures is important, it is not as consequential as the reader's comprehension of text. The study of the components of reading later focused on comprehension and speed of reading. In 1921, Gates published a study that found these two components to be related yet separate functions. His studies led to later theorizing that processing print at a rate where words are identified automatically enables better comprehension because more time can be spent on understanding than doing what has recently been called *decoding*.

As more studies and theories were formulated, patterns of ability came to be an important area of inquiry. Findings were mixed and evolved a view that readers vary their speed and style of reading based on the kind and difficulty of the material being read, as well as on the purposes for the reading. Further investigation led Gates (1927) to diagnostic tests that subsequently gave way to a view of the importance of different types and processes of reading and a multiplicity of factors studied by Monroe (1932). Holmes was the first to test this hypothesis statistically; his finding was that two students could be equally successful in reading by using different combinations of abilities. Later the view that reading was developmental from the primary through the high school grades led to graduated difficulty of reading instruction throughout the schooling years.

In the 1960s and 1970s, learning theory and reading theories and research intersected to concentrate on comprehension and instructional strategies. The SQ3R strategy included Survey, Question, Read, Recite, and Review as a way to tackle text. Other strategies promoted included advance organizers, hierarchical organization, directed reading activity, questioning strategies, mathemagenic behavior (a term coined by Rothkopf meaning learning processes), summarization of text, and teacher attitudes. As many students of teacher education advance through their course work, they learn these and other strategies for reading instruction.

Other knowledge areas affected the way that scholars implemented the study of reading and reading instruction. Contributions from several academic areas include input from psycholinguistics, sociolinguistics, and linguistics. *Phonics*, or the relationship between letters and sounds, cannot be underestimated in its effects on reading instruction. Susan Glazer (1998) describes "political undertones" three decades ago to do phonics instruction. Because she understood the political importance placed on phonics, she said she knew she had "better" teach phonics although she had some misgivings about such an all-inclusive view of how reading instruction should occur. The same phonics movement has resurfaced as part of scientifically based reading instruction in the early twenty-first century. In the era of No Child Left Behind, teachers presently are under the same pressure. They know they must teach letter-and-sound correspondences and sounding out of words or they will incur the wrath of school officials. The disciplining of the hierarchy of educators occurs from mandates for educational excellence articulated by President George W. Bush extending down from the education bureaucrats who decide which school districts will receive No Child Left Behind reading grants to the State to the Regional Educational Centers to the Independent School District Administration to the local campus administrator to the reading department to the reading teacher.

With the history of educational research and instructional strategies developed from the tip-of-the-iceberg-of-psychological studies mentioned here over the last century through the present, there has indeed been a normalization process of educational testing for normal, abnormal, and special students across the United States. The practice of testing is not only definitive in its determination of those who have succeeded in learning what they need to know, but also in diagnosing the placement of students who have been deemed abnormal, and even gifted or supranormal. Testing is a logical outcome of reliance on science, industry, and progress in the United States. Testing within states, across states, within nations, and across nations helps to fuel the fires of international competition, in many ways more important than the Olympics have been historically to gain glory for the state or nation.

TEACHERS AS TECHNOCRATS

To be able to discuss the relationship of teachers and bureaucratic educational practices often associated with the rise of industrialism, centralization, and hierarchization of the disciplines associated with the educational profession, it is important to understand the rise of modernity. With the increased legitimacy extended to science, scientific principles, and psychology as the science that would help lead an evolving population toward desired goals of progress, and Taylorism (scientific principles of management), teachers found themselves on the bottom rung of the ladder of expertise to make decisions regarding the implementation of educational policy. As workers on the assembly line of education, they were expected to pour knowledge into the empty heads or vessels of their clients. In the modern industrial world, where output, production, and profits are the priority, education's workers in the trenches, the teachers, were to be held accountable for their work. "Good" management and goal-oriented materials that would be tested helped to assure that the prescribed curricula would be taught.

In the Freirean view (1970), teachers were expected to do banking education entailing the deposit of knowledge into students' accounts. When the test or the audit for accounts showed a balance or near balance between what the teacher had deposited and that which the student could verify existed in the student account, successful learning had occurred. If such a balance did not appear, the teacher had not done the work. Most recently teachers' jobs are on the line if their students do not perform at least satisfactorily on the grade exit exams in Texas. So, in essence, the teachers' accounts must now also measure up to the deposits made by higher echelon educational officials' mandates for curriculum focus. With a centralized exam and curriculum that ensures success on that exam, teacher and student work could be efficaciously controlled.

The early movement toward centralization of public state-controlled education was implemented by the efforts of Horace Mann, who argued that women, because of their nurturing roles as mothers and caregivers, would be the best school teachers. It was no accident that the economic plan he proposed would pay these female teachers salaries equivalent to one third of what their male counterparts would earn. The concern in Mann's early to mid–nineteenth-century centralization project also aligns along industrial progress at about that time.

Big business and corporations developed similar kinds of urban landscapes that Thomas Jefferson had found so abhorrent in the late eighteenth-century Europe and England. For Jefferson, the yeoman farmer would have been the economic backbone and a stabilizing force in the political culture of the United States. Fifty years later, the notions of social progress fueled by capitalism and special-interest politics found the United States in similar situations with urbanized areas, with a revolutionized economy built on the factory system. As the goals of profit making drove the industrial world, business owners looked for more and better ways of managing workers and their production for maximum earnings. Frederick Winslow Taylor, champion of scientific management principles, stated his views for removing the expertise from the workers' domain, thereby simplifying the necessary work to produce the desired results. He stated his aims as removing all decision making from "the shop" and determining from above in the work hierarchy what should be done and how long it should take to achieve it.

Similar business management principles guided the thinking of school policy makers. During the centralization of the nineteenth and early to mid–twentieth centuries, small one-room and autonomous schools consolidated, and management of teachers, students, and knowledge that was to be taught was overseen by the administration. The history of teacher education encompasses the rise of the science and business management principles. Formerly an entity unto itself occurring within the normal school of Horace Mann's age, teacher education found itself part of the teachers' college and later the university, usually in lower-status position to educational psychology and administration.

Despite the formation of teachers unions and the rhetoric calling for professionalization of education and the good work that many teachers do, teachers are still managed, reformed, and essentially have little decision-making power about school administration or the curriculum. The mandates of No Child Left Behind, 2001, and other formal and informal policies put the exam into place to ensure "failsafe" success of teachers. If basal readers, packaged education programs, practice tests, the test, and a curriculum overrun with testing strategies and preparations can determine student success, teacher intelligence and professionalism do not matter. The teacher is merely an instrument for passing the knowledge along to its recipients. This view of education has been shown time after time to be efficient for test score achievement but not necessarily for teaching and learning that might be considered most important in a caring, empathetic, democratic, and egalitarian society. Postmodern criticalists, descended from feminist and critical scholars, promote a kind of literacy advocated by Freire called critical literacy. Such literacy would engage students and citizens in political discussion and decision making that could help to transform the lives of those least educated, usually the impoverished in a society.

THE ACCOUNTABILITY MOVEMENT

Historians of education often point to the Russians' launching of Sputnik (1957) as a turning point in American education. Because the Russians had superceded Americans in their space exploration, U.S. education policy makers changed the focus of education to math and science, with little attention given to the liberal arts. Within a utilitarian framework that informs mainstream educational policy, education is associated with worker preparation and national security. Advocates of utilitarian education (and liberals would argue the conservatives who wish to dismantle public education) find testing to be the manner in which student, teacher, administrator, school, district, city, and regional success at teaching and learning can be measured accurately. As technology moves to the forefront of human, business, and international communication and production, discourses promoting technological education predominate in discussions of educational attainment. Essential elements of teaching and learning prescribe teacher lesson plans. Practice tests, test preparation, and curriculum that prepare students for testing success have become the emphasis in educational attainment of late. Critical thinking exercises with multiple-choice answers respond to the need for critical thinkers in our work society. Little, if any effort, is put on citizenship development, as discourses to achieve on tests and obtain high credentials for entrance into the best schools and universities drive education machinery.

Such a delimitation of educational discourse narrows the scope and discussion, "Of what purpose is education?" The delimitation of literacy as related to the discourse of scientific reading further reduces the scope of education. The manner in which such limits on the discussion of education is further amplified becomes clear when we consider how scientifically based reading research was a requirement in the application for federal reading grant monies by low-achieving schools. In the No Child Left Behind grant application, the verbiage for teaching reading to youngsters was required to reflect phonics, phonemic awareness, and scientifically verifiable methods of manifesting that student success had been achieved in reading. The power and knowledge arrangements described by Foucault to determine certain knowledge as truth and to favor certain discourses is a helpful analogy to invoke here. Power and knowledge arrangements of corporate power and money, the politicians who are vested in the webs of the publishing business, and the discourses that prescribe to the public what kinds of literacy, reading and writing, and education, in general, are to be implemented, remind us that testing is an ubiquitous obstacle to education for purposes other than testing. The importance of literacy to Jefferson was directly connected to citizenship. In the present day, literacy is taught in the academic area of language arts; it is not taught in the social studies, where government and citizenship are purportedly taught. Literacy as the exercise of and articulation of personal and communitarian desire for social justice, inclusion, and access is lost as literacy becomes the ticket to test success.

The rise of scientific testing of literacy has been a gradual development. It begins with the following and is implemented at all levels of teaching and learning: the rise of science, the rise of psychology as science and the study of reading as a psychological endeavor, the regard for reading as a psychologically testable skill, the de-professionalization of teachers, and the rise of high-stakes testing as the determining measure of educational success. Accountability tests are staged at every step to ensure that proper teaching and learning occur. We indeed are being disciplined by the test, by science, by reading instruction, and by scientific reading instruction. Educators and concerned citizens feel the need to ask how we got this way and what can be done about it. I have attempted to explain how we got this way; now we as a collective must decide what we will do about it.

TERMS FOR READERS

Critical literacy—literacy that is focused on community and political involvement, the exercise of political power, the use of reading and writing to contribute to one's social community and/or to transform one's world.

Literacy—Reading and writing in general. The focus here, however, is on reading specifically.

Scientific testing—Of or related to standardized testing with a history grounded in psychological study, development, and implementation in educational institutions.

FURTHER READING

Cattell, J.M. (January 1886). The time it takes to see and name objects. *Mind, 11*, 63–65.

Freire, P. (1970). Pedagogy of the oppressed. New York: Seabury Press.

Gates, A. I. (September 1921). An experimental and statistical study of reading tests. *Journal of Educational Psychology, 12*, 303–314.

Huey, E.B. (1908). *The psychology and pedagogy of reading.* New York: Macmillan.

Monroe, M. (1932). *Children who cannot read.* Chicago: University of Chicago Press.

Singer, H. & Ruddell, R.B. (Eds.). (1985.) (3rd edition). *Theoretical models and processes of reading.* Newark, DE: International Reading Association.

What Are We Measuring?
A Reexamination of Psychometric Practice and the Problem of Assessment in Education

MARK J. GARRISON

Whether one is in college to obtain a bachelor of science degree in psychology, a superintendent preparing a report to a school board, or a university admissions officer, data collected from educational and psychological tests are typically emphasized. The results of IQ tests are said to measure student intelligence, achievement tests are presented as measurements of subject mastery, and entrance exams are given as measurements of ability to succeed in college, to take only three common examples. The words *measure*, *measures*, or *measurement* appear, by my count, at least 135 times throughout the federal *No Child Left Behind Act*, the provisions of which rely more than in any other time on the results of standardized tests. It is widely believed that this law represents a fundamental change in the structure and function of education in the United States, with test scores constituting a key mechanism to bring about and justify this change.

But what if educational and psychological tests and the data they yield are not measurements at all? This essay explores this possibility and the profound implications it has for debates surrounding the validity of educational and psychological tests and the problem of assessment more generally.

THE NEED FOR AN ALTERNATIVE PERSPECTIVE

As the role and significance of standardized testing increases, especially in education, debates about the validity of this technology are once again highlighted in both academic and lay circles. Yet, an assumption typical of both critics and supporters of standardized testing is that such tests *measure something*. This belief is evidenced by the frequently heard question, what is being *measured* by an IQ or a standardized achievement test? And while some object that scores on standardized academic tests are proxies for knowledge and acceptance of the dominant Western middle-class outlook, others advocate that educational tests measure social and emotional domains critical for success in life, in addition to more traditional measurements of academic prowess. In both cases, again, the assumption is that something (culture, ability, personality) is being, or should be, measured.

The assumption that psychological and educational tests measure *something* is as old as the tests themselves, and it is an assumption that is rarely if ever challenged, although it is noteworthy that Alfred Binet, the inventor of what is known as the IQ test, acknowledged that his test was not in fact a *measurement*. Yet, he nonetheless continued to speak about and present his instrument as just that: a scale for the measurement of intelligence. Foreshadowing arguments of future psychometricians, he justified this inconsistency by claiming—without explanation—that it was of practical necessity.

That an entire field (what is referred to here as psychometry) could be handed over so much authority and financial support, in part at least, on the basis of measurement with evident uncertainty of what is being measured is in fact baffling, and perversely irrational in my view. How is it that so many of us have taken for granted that measurement is taking place when there is so much disagreement over what is being measured? It may in fact be the case that this assumption of measurement has enabled psychometric practice to withstand periodic, intense, and what now appears to be mounting criticism. Constructing alternatives to psychometric practice may, in turn, depend on efforts to reexamine the significance and legitimacy of psychometry's claims to measurement and the nature of assessment more generally.

Popularized critiques of testing are typically predicated on the assumption that a key problem lies with the *misuse* of educational and psychological tests and specious interpretations of the *meaning* of test scores. For example, so-called hereditarians use the same standard—the IQ test—as so-called environmentalists do; the rub is in the *use* and *interpretation* of *scores*. One group posits the primacy of genes in differential academic performance between so-called races; the other retorts that such group differences in test scores prove the negative impacts of poverty and discrimination on intellectual development. Psychometric practice has actually flourished in this context, eagerly developing concepts and methods—such as construct validation—for determining the proper use and meaning of test scores, a project that garners further institutional and fiscal backing. Psychometry's response to these challenges over the past four decades has also served as a basis upon which to maintain its legitimacy as a science and thus its instructional power.

In this essay, I suggest a different direction. I argue that psychometry fails to meet its claim of *measurement* and that its object is not the measurement of nonphysical human attributes, but the marking of some human beings as having more worth or value than other human beings, an act central to and part and parcel of the legitimacy of a particular kind of hierarchical social system known as meritocracy. Psychometry's claim to measurement serves to veil and justify the fundamentally political act of marking social value, and the role this practice plays in legitimating vast social inequalities.

DEFINITIONS OF PSYCHOMETRY

According to the *Oxford English Dictionary* (*OED*), psychometry literally means measuring the soul, or "mind measuring" ("psycho" refers to mind while "metric" refers to measurement). The first reported use of the word, the *OED* continues, appeared in 1854, where psychometry was defined as the "faculty of divining, from physical contact or proximity only, the qualities or properties of an object, or of persons or things that have been in contact with it." The *OED* gives sense 2 as follows: "The measurement of the duration and intensity of mental states or processes" with the following quote from Francis Galton, an early eugenicist and proponent of differential psychology: "Psychometry . . . means the art of imposing measurement and number upon operations of the mind, as in the practice of determining the reaction-time of different persons." (Galton's choice of the word *imposing* should not go unnoticed.) And finally, the *OED* offers this definition of psychometrics, a definition with more contemporary flare: "The science of measuring mental capacities and processes; the application of methods of measurement to the various branches of psychology."

The literal, etymological meaning of psychometry is a useful place to begin. What would it mean to *measure mind* (let alone soul)? Is mind (or soul for that matter) the kind of thing one has more or less of? Or, to start with the more contemporary definition, are all mental capacities such that they exist in gradation, such that they come in different amounts? For example, is it correct to say that one is thinking or not thinking, or are there different degrees of thinking? Is a theory of mind needed in order to determine if mind can be measured and, if so, how metrication—the basis upon which numbers are assigned to phenomena—can take place? The issues raised here are fundamental from the point of view of both the theory and practice of measurement, and addressing them serves as a useful starting point for deliberating on the nature of measurement and the status of psychometry as a science.

Possibly one reason for the absence of a broad discussion among academics and the public concerning measurement of nonphysical entities is that the limited amount of material available on this question is highly technical. Fundamental problems in the philosophy of science such as the nature of knowledge and scientific objectivity are at issue; ability to contend with complex mathematics is also typically required. Yet it is, I think, possible to develop a broad and accessible discussion of measurement. It is also the case that psychometricians generally avoid the problems posed by measurement of nonphysical entities in the name of being practical. But we must ask what practical problem rendering psychological and educational tests as measurements solves? In this regard, it is absolutely necessary to go into the nature of measurement if so much of educational reform is contingent upon the results of what are given as measurements. A final difficulty with this topic is the language itself, where the word *measure* has numerous meanings and uses in the English language; *measure*, for example, can refer to the results of a measurement, or simply any standard, whether used in measurement, assessment, or comparison.

THE NATURE OF MEASUREMENT

Measurement deals with the dialectical relationship between quantity and quality. The central theoretical concept of measurement is *magnitude*, defined as the property of relative size or extent. Simply stated, measurement deals with the question of *how much*.

The common expression "how much" suggests the dialectical unity of quantity and quality in measurement. A magnitude (which is represented by a standard) is a known quality that is also known to exist in degrees. Measurement is integral to determining points at which quantitative changes lead to changes in quality, for example, the point at which an increase in heat transforms water into steam. Psychometric efforts to determine at what point scores on a particular test make a person qualified represent this *logic*, even if the reality is that what are known as cut scores are in fact arbitrarily determined.

A standard is a tool used in assessment, comparison, and measurement. Common, everyday standards of length and weight represent known magnitudes. Yet, a standard (say the meter) must be theoretically and technically fit for the measure of objectively existing properties of a thing or phenomenon. Once accomplished, this allows for *different* objects, processes, or phenomena to be compared in relation to the same magnitude, such as weight, length, heat, et cetera. It is also the standard that allows for equivalence, or calibration.

It is important to emphasize that while a standard is necessary for measurement, at least initial theoretical work is presupposed for it to be able to accurately represent magnitudes. For example, there needed to be a conception of the qualitative aspect of heat before its measurement could take place. Once such theoretical knowledge is at least initially established, measurement becomes possible.

Contrary to what seems to be conventional wisdom, the key issue here is not that of precision. The claim to measurement is the claim that laws governing quantitative and qualitative change can be accurately represented mathematically. This is the criterion of being *isomorphic*. For a measurement system to be valid there must be a correspondence between elements, relations, and operations of the mathematical and substantive system in question. This correspondence is exemplified with the additive principle "One can take 10 feet and add it to 10 feet and obtain 20 feet." Notice that individual test items cannot be shown to be equivalent in this manner. While there are exceptions to and debates about the universality of the additive principle for measurement (e.g., with heat phenomena) the example stands for my purposes here.

Psychometry, in contradiction to this definition, renders measurement as the mere application of number systems to objects, processes, or phenomena, a process that has no necessary reference to the empirical world. This is the notion of measurement as social convention. Many critics have thus designated psychometry as "measurement by fiat." Without too much difficulty, one can find psychometricians admitting that the ability of test scores to truthfully reflect quantities of a characteristic of interest is suspect.

If this definition is accepted as the basis for practice, any rule-based assignment of numbers to phenomena could claim measurement. Common practice in the social sciences has it that a questionnaire, for example, in which the respondent expresses his or her attitude with the aid of numbers, is as an instance of *measurement* of preferences.

In addition to the idealist assumptions underpinning pscyhometry's definition of measurement is the field's tendency to imbue data with properties of the testing procedure. One cannot assume a scale to be a property of that which is measured if that scale is a necessary consequence of the method of analysis. The relevance here to educational and psychological testing is striking. It is not permissible to argue that intelligence (or any purported characteristic of individuals) is normally distributed in a population on the basis of the normal distribution of scores, for such a distribution is demanded by the statistical methods most commonly used in test construction and analysis.

Most important for our purposes here, theoretical work determines if the property or quality under investigation *can* be measured. The development of measurement has generally progressed from classification based on quality, to topology or the comparison of qualitative aspects of phenomena, to metrication and thus measurement. Classification concepts such as "cold" become topological when comparisons are used, such as "colder *than*. . . ." Such concepts not only establish sameness (or difference), but also make it possible to compare at least two objects that possess a given property; this in turn makes it possible to arrange such objects into a sequence. Given the difficulties associated with their methodology, questionnaires—to continue with the above example—are at best topological in nature.

While topological concepts provide a transition from classification to measurement, it is important to note that classification (or differentiation) itself is not measurement. This is contrary to what is commonly asserted in contemporary textbooks on psychological and educational testing. The ability to differentiate and rank on the basis of common properties does not in itself allow one to claim that the extent of that property can be determined. In this way, the common presentation in social science texts of levels of measurement—nominal, ordinal, and so on—makes the fundamental error of presuming mere classification to be a form of measurement.

Thus a key problem, one pointed to above with the definition of psychometry as *mind measurement*, is the assumption that the mind or a purported faculty or function of mind is a property capable of gradation. There are, however, many properties that do not permit gradation (i.e., they are *not* magnitudes) such as *Pilsner, feline, wooden,* and *human*. In other words, the psychometric dictum of E.L. Thorndike (the famous early twentieth-century psychometrician) that if something exists it must exist in some amount is patently false.

Yet, Thorndike's premise may have great social and political significance. We know that human history is riddled with cases of some humans beings designated as less human, or not human at all; *humanness* has been given as something individual persons and groups have *more or less of*—a key presupposition of the eugenicist's project of a "master race." The U.S. Constitution made this presumption when it rendered African slaves and Native peoples as only holding a fraction of the value of white Europeans. Such designations are based on the claim that some human beings have less intelligence, ability, or otherwise valued attribute, than other human beings, and, on that basis, they have been rendered less human, of less value, and in some cases, a threat to civilization itself. Such designations are to serve as justifications for the inequalities and crimes bound up with slavery, colonialism, and capitalism more generally.

Most readers will accept at some level, however, that education is something that can be graded. Clearly some students learn more of a particular subject matter than others, and clearly people obtain, both officially and in practice, different levels of education or expertise in different fields, and so on. In this way, measuring educational achievement seems less problematic than measuring mind or intelligence. Defining content areas such as math and delineating levels of mathematical knowledge seem relatively simple by comparison.

The project of measuring academic knowledge in practice, however, appears particularly fixated on ranking *human beings* and less on determining degrees of knowledge *per se*. For example, norm-referenced achievement tests offer results in terms of percentile ranks, not delineations of what a student does or does not know about a given field of study, let alone diagnoses of the cause of any difficulty. Put another way, scoring in the 70th percentile only indicates how well one did relative to the norm; it does not indicate 70 percent of required material was mastered. Thus the test remains at the *topological level*, where percentile results indicate only that, for example, Sue performed *better than* Joe; the preceding semantics suggest that the object is in fact the ranking the worth or value of persons, and not what they know or can do as such. It is not uncommon to hear educators move seamlessly from reporting student grades to designations of students as "good" and "bad" suggesting that differential academic performance reflects some moral order. Using the above example, when one says *colder than*, the comparison is in terms of *temperature*; to say *better than* suggests comparison is in terms of *worth*, where grades and tests scores are the currency by which such value is negotiated and ultimately exchanged.

The same problem exists with so-called measurements of ability. By virtue of being norm-referenced, such tests only provide rank-order information on the basis of students' ability to furnish what are considered correct responses to test prompts. This ranking does not in any way permit the claim that "cognitive ability" is therefore being measured because ranking is itself not measurement. In this way, present-day achievement and ability tests cannot measure any property of individuals or groups: their object is to rank-order the value of individuals and groups.

A further difficulty lies in the fact that there is no evidence that the numbers produced (test scores) correspond to (are isomorphic with) what we understand to be laws governing mental processes and functions, or the dialectical relationship between qualitative and quantitative aspects of these processes or functions. It appears to me that the level of theoretical knowledge we do have is both at odds with psychometric assumptions—ones derived from the discredited notion of *faculty*—and insufficient to permit measurement, should that indeed even be necessary for advances in educational psychology.

STANDARDIZED TESTS: TOOLS FOR MARKING SOCIAL VALUE

The above analysis suggests that standardized tests are not tools in measurement. Here I advocate that they be explored as standards for assessing or marking social value. But before the notion and significance of social value is explored relative to assessment, it will be important to explore the significance of the distinction between measurement and assessment, especially as the latter has developed in education.

Assessment and Measurement

While it is common to suggest that measurement is simply a more precise form of assessment, not to mention that the words *measure* and *assess* are given as synonyms in many thesauruses, the latter is in my view a distinct although certainly related undertaking. According to the *OED*, the words *assess* and *assessment* have been, for almost the duration of their 600 years in use, bound up with notions of taxation, tributes, and fines. It is not until the nineteenth century that assessment is used in the general sense as a synonym for estimation or evaluation. And it is only as a manifestation of the fields of education and psychology in the twentieth century that the now common meaning of assessment is derived. Thus the *OED* gives the fifth sense of the word as, "The process or means of evaluating academic work; an examination or test." Interestingly, the word assessment is presented as almost synonymous with the word examination or test. And the increasingly practical role psychology played in contemporary institutions gave rise to notions of assessment as this one: "To evaluate (a person or thing); to estimate (the quality, value, or extent of), to gauge or judge." Examining the development of the use of the word we find this quoted from the Office of Strategic Services' 1948 publication, *Assessment of Men*: "A number of psychologists and psychiatrists attempted to assess the merits of men and women recruited for the Office of Strategic Services." In this way, assessment has historically related to judgments of *value* (originally in the form of taxation) with the more recent developments specific to judging the value or deservedness of human beings. Furthermore, assessment seems focused on determining quality (as in designations of good, authentic, etc.) not *how much* quality. Even the notion of *good enough* appears as qualitative in nature, and is recognized as an assessment, not a measurement.

Further examination of the word suggests that not only is it bound up with judging human value in particular, but that it also explicitly recognizes social hierarchy as a variable. *Assess* is a form of the Latin verb meaning to "sit with." In an educational assessment, the assessor *sits with* the learner and *assigns value*. In this way, assessment is predicated on human relationships in a way that measurement is not. The word's alternative meaning clearly suggests the importance of social position when it states that this person who "sits beside" (as in an assistant-judge) is one who "shares another's rank or dignity" and who is "skilled to advise on technical points." It is also then important to point out that assessments are now bound up with what is called professional judgment.

Standards

Standards are the foundation of both assessment and measurement. In measurement, the object of the standard is magnitude, the abstract expression of the extent of qualities of things or phenomena. The object of the standard in assessment is value; the *relation* here is between subject and object. With measurement, the magnitude makes possible the grasping of the *relation* between quality and quantity. Standards in assessment make possible the judgment of value by stipulating boundary points as indicators of quality (merit, worth, goodness, authenticity). In fact, official educational assessment operates on the basis of establishing desired qualities and their vertical classification, or placement in vertically structured category systems with the assistance of numbers. This is what is being delineated when it is said that the task of validity is to determine the meaning (value) of test scores. The validity discourse about test score meaning relative to testing purpose is based on value not residing in things or phenomenon themselves, *but in their relation to subjects*. Length, however, is a property of an object. It might be useful to delineate standards in measurement as *absolute*, while standards in assessment are *relative*.

The confusion between measurement and assessment is not insignificant, having both scientific and ideological importance. Scientifically, the confusion over what is measurement is bound up with confusing properties of objects with properties of numbers (a good example being the normal curve) and social relations and the properties of those objects or phenomena in the relation (a good example confusing individual ability with competitive standing). These mistakes are functional for masking the workings of the values system in official testing practices and the power involved in designating some human beings as more valuable than others.

THE ASSESSMENT OF SOCIAL VALUE

This notion of social value, derived from one of the founders of sociology, Emile Durkheim, signifies how value is socially attached to groups as well as to structural positions via status duality (good or bad) and spatial duality (high or low). This duality of the *good* and the *bad*, the *high* and the *low*, constitutes the two levels of value duality within a system of vertical classification or ranked categories. Within such a system all individuals and groups are then placed in either the *sacred* or the *profane* position; theoretically, they are mutually exclusive categories.

It seems to me that marking virtue (good or bad) and talent (high or low) constitute the object of standardized test–based assessment within a hierarchically structured social system premised on the idea of merit—that one's position in the hierarchy is earned or deserved. With this understanding, educational testing appears as an elegant example of vertical classification. Because students do not typically come to school with official labels, in part as a presupposition of public education for all, academic achievement and ability are constantly assessed, assuming great social significance. Herein lies one reason for the ubiquity of testing and the basis for it being equated with opportunity.

Ranking human worth on the basis of how well one competes in academic contests, with the effect that high ranks are associated with privilege, status, and power, suggests that psychometry is premised not on knowledge of intellectual or emotional development but on Anglo-American political ideals of rule by *the best* (most virtuous) and *the brightest* (most talented), a *meritocracy*. Marking virtue gives rise to status duality, marking talent gives rise to spatial duality; the linkage to social structure is the argument of social value. Western political thought since the eighteenth century postulates talent as concomitant to virtue, and thus its signifier. As just one example, Southern Europeans were once barred from immigrating to the United States, in part on the basis of their low IQs; the argument of the psychologists was that those who lack intellectual capacity inevitably gravitate towards immoral and criminal behavior. A high score on an IQ test, however, suggests a student is worthy of being trained to play social roles with high status and power—the high score suggests the high status, worth, or virtue.

It appears that assessment—the use of standards in the judgment of value—is a feature of the earliest forms of stratified human society. Sociologists point out that there have always been arrangements for formally recognizing the capacity to perform important social roles and to exercise their associated social status and power. Notice that there are in fact two capacities at issue here. The first is the capacity to perform the role itself (functional competency), and the second capacity is to exercise the role's *associated social status and power* (what might be called social competency). It is this second ability, which may be the ultimate object of assessment via standardized tests in education, a conjecture that is supported by the relatively strong correlation of test scores with socioeconomic status (note the uncritical replication of social value in the notion socioeconomic status) compared to the relatively week correlation of ability and achievement tests with performance outside academe.

Precision as Value

In addition, economic historians have shown that the precision of a standard signifies the degree to which a thing or phenomenon is valued. For example, in societies where land was relatively abundant, the system of area measures tended to be poorly developed. The same tendency is observed with measures of weight. Thus the more valuable the object, the finer the standard employed; as the value of the object increases for a culture, the finer its standard.

This general proposition can be seen at work with social value if we take the example of driving a truck versus becoming a physician. Driving a truck can be said, on this basis, not to be of great social value, for the standard to obtain such a license is not very fine, or precise, even though the safety of millions of travelers and billions of dollars worth of products are at stake. One either passes or fails the relevant tests; unlike with the SAT and ACT no elaborate hierarchy exists. Academic achievement and ability, the standards for entering medical school, are thus highly valued, reflected in the fineness of their measure. The great effort towards precision is not aimed at measurement, but instead constitutes a means by which to identify and produce value; for example the value of a credential can be inflated simply by making it more difficult to obtain. That there is a great deal of fineness in the standard of the second and not in the first suggests which is held in more esteem by the dominant culture. We might expect this situation to change radically if truck drivers somehow got themselves involved in making transportation policy. That is, those who are deemed to occupy sacred positions (good character, high ability) are fit to make decisions, to decide on the all important questions of who, what, where, and when.

Thus notions of ability, of capacity, are bound up with social positions, for ability must have a place for it to be manifest. This *quality or state of being able* manifests itself in the "physical, mental, or legal power to perform," according to *Webster's*. Note that ability can signify both a power inhering in persons (functional competency) as well as legal power, or being formally allowed to do something (social competency). It is in the context of the present society that mental power stands as one justification for legal power. It is significant that the etymology of *ability* is from the Middle English *suitability*. In this regard, standardized test–based assessment can thus be thought of as the judgment of individual worth relative to a structural slot or social position—what is deemed of value and who is deemed of value—the meeting place of which is variously achievement or ability. That is, achievement and ability signify both places and persons, as in someone (an individual) who becomes rich (a social position). Note as well that suitability can take individuals or positions as its object—is the individual suitable to the position, is the position suitable for the individual.

The emphasis on abstruse academic exercises, I think, are aimed at judging the ability to exercise a role's attending social status and power—for example, is the person capable of "good judgment"—and not so much the functional capacities demanded by the role. Employers often prefer a college to a high school graduate for jobs requiring minimal formal education on the assumption that a college degree signifies the virtues of perseverance, honesty, and so on. That is, official educational assessments seem overly concerned with the second capacity identified above. Because the role of truck driver currently has little associated status or power, licensure procedures need only focus on the functional ability itself.

Exercising status and power demands a particular set of aims and values, or else the stability of that status and power is threatened (it is this stability of the status quo that seems to be the referent of "good judgment"). Abstruse academic exercises constitute values that reflect a definite world outlook. For example, within Euro-American thought, written competitive exams reveal a person's ability to delay gratification. Proponents of written competitive exams often put considerable stress on the moral argument at both the individual and the national level. Examinations are a test of common sense and of character as well as of basic academic knowledge and skill. It was assumed that success on such exams demanded perseverance and good character, all of which would in turn bring legitimacy to institutions that employed such exams. In fact, much of this discourse is found in the infamous 1983 U.S. Department of Education report, "*A Nation at Risk*," with its talk of "excellence" and "commitment to a set of values" as the basis of "the learning community."

SUMMARY AND IMPLICATIONS

The long-standing debate as to whether standardized tests accurately measure *merit* (worth) is simultaneously a frank admission that standardized tests aim to assign value to human beings—to determine who is worthy of what type of education—and a block to grasping fully the significance and implications of such a project. Standardized tests are not designed to accurately and fairly select, certify, and monitor via measurement of specific competencies or abilities, but rather to legitimate the hierarchy and inequality that results from such acts via the *assessment of social value*. Thus it may be more useful in analyzing psychometry to view it as political theory, as a formal justification for a system where, in the words of the famous psychometrician E.L. Thorndike, "the argument for democracy is not that it gives power to men without distinction, but that it gives greater freedom for ability and character to attain power."

Possibly the first implication of this understanding is to reject any form of assessment that functions to differentially value *human persons* or *groups*. Let me be clear: the issue is not in recognizing that humans differ in their abilities, interests and so on (although such difference are not, in my view, the problem they can be made out to be). The problem emerges when such differentiation is systematically linked to a hierarchical social structure and the reproduction of that structure. In this way, it is racist practice to rank the value and worth of *human beings*.

Thus there is a need for assessment in education to establish a new starting point, one predicated on the equal worth, dignity, and rights of all human beings and human cultures. Those working to develop assessments in the service of education must vociferously reject the linking of academic prowess with notions of bad or good, fit and unfit to govern. A student's worth as a human being does not turn on whether or not they can perform this or that academic task. In this way, the link between assessment and social value must be broken. The institutional arrangements standing behind talk of *good students* must be replaced with arrangements where the *work* of teachers, students, and the community as a whole is judged by teachers, students, and the community as a whole on the basis of whether or not this work is serving to prepare youth to solve the problems they and their society face, to contribute to society. Ranking some human beings as being smarter and better than other human beings contribute nothing to education or society; it merely serves to justify and exacerbate the various forms of inequality that are now intensifying. Thus, the slogan here might be evaluate *work*, not *people*; people have inherent dignity and rights irrespective of their ability to carry out this or that type of work. Because work is ultimately social, it is work undertaken together that should be evaluated both by those who engaged in and are affected by such work.

This is in my view some of what the above analysis suggests about the basis upon which assessments should take place. In fact these starting points may be evident in recent efforts towards alternative or authentic assessment, in particular those inspired by the notion of multiple intelligences which recognizes and values a broad range of human abilities and achievements in nonhierarchical terms. Possibly this is the reason that the powers that be have so consistently thwarted such efforts.

The analysis presented here also has profound implications for the present standards and accountability movement, especially as embodied in the *No Child Left Behind Act 2001* (NCLB). It suggests to me that strategies opposing *NCLB* on the basis that it does not provide enough funds to meet legal requirements misses the fact that *NCLB*, and in particular its testing mandates, are in themselves attacks on public education and those who attend and work in public schools. By marking so many of the nation's schools as failures, the law is functioning to devalue public education. This discrediting is necessary if new arrangements are to be put into place, such as charter schools and voucher schemes. Efforts to alter the sense of the value of public education might function to assimilate Americans to a lower standard of education, not to a higher one. For if the society does not organize for universal public education—publicly financed and publicly controlled—the overall level of education will decline. In this way, standards in educational assessment not only are bound up with attempts to differentially value human beings and thereby justify inequalities, but are presently serving to devalue the notion of public education itself by marking the institution as a failure.

SUGGESTED READING

Berka, K. (1983). *Measurement: Its Concepts, Theories, and Problems* (A. Riska, Trans.). Boston: Kluwer.

Nash, R. (1990). *Intelligence and Realism: A Materialist Critique of IQ*. New York: St. Martin's.

Ward, A. W., Stoker, H. W., and Murray-Ward, M. (Eds.). (1996). *Educational Measurement: Origins, Theories and Explication* (vol. 1). Lanham, MD: University Press of America.

CHAPTER 94

Curriculum, Instruction, and Assessment in a Reconceptualized Educational Environment

RAYMOND A. HORN JR.

INTRODUCTION

How are curriculum, instruction, and assessment different in a reconceptualized educational environment? The best way to answer this question is to first provide a brief summary of how these three aspects of teaching and learning are done in traditional classrooms. This summary will be followed by a discussion of how these three aspects of pedagogy are manifested in a reconceptualized environment, and then the chapter will conclude with an example of a lesson or student activity that reflects reconceptualized educational theory and practice. This discussion will focus on curriculum, instruction, and assessment; however, to better understand how these aspects of teaching and learning are manifested in different educational environments, the roles of those involved in the teaching and learning process also will be examined.

CURRICULUM, INSTRUCTION, AND ASSESSMENT IN A NON-RECONCEPTUALIZED EDUCATIONAL ENVIRONMENT

Before the No Child Left Behind Act (NCLB), an analysis of curriculum, instruction, and assessment would find significant variation in how these three were done from school to school. However, the federal mandate has had a normalizing and standardizing effect on pedagogy. The most significant normalizing agent is the mandate for the use of standardized tests to measure student achievement. Even though there is not a national curriculum assessed by one national testing system, to meet NCLB requirements so that they can keep receiving federal educational funds, the states have had to develop statewide curriculum in certain disciplines. Student achievement of this curriculum or disciplinary standards is measured by standardized tests that have met federal guidelines. The result has been the implementation of statewide standardized curriculum and assessment, and in a less formal way, a move toward the development and assessment of a national curriculum that has resulted in a technical rational definition of curriculum. In addition, the federal government has required states to develop specific accountability structures for student achievement. Most significant are the highly qualified teacher and average yearly progress requirements. Accompanying these accountability requirements is the imposition of stringent penalties for noncompliance. Another significant federal requirement is the promotion of quantitative research–based practice as the basis for decisions about teaching and learning.

In a standards and accountability environment as fostered by NCLB, the ultimate accountability mechanism is the standardized test score. Student scores are used to determine the effectiveness of students, teachers, and schools in meeting the state mandated levels of test scores. Essentially, the test scores are to tell the whole story of pedagogical effectiveness. Class rank, grade-point average, portfolios, or any other assessment tools are subordinate to the determination of educational effectiveness by a standardized test. Failure to perform at the predetermined federal and state levels can result in students' not being allowed to graduate, teachers being dismissed, administrators fired, and the control of schools taken from local school boards. Performance failure has resulted in schools being closed, privatized, and placed under state-appointed officials.

In the NCLB environment, disciplinary experts develop the state-mandated curriculum. To various degrees, this curriculum development process can be exclusively controlled by outside experts (i.e., university-level professionals, think tanks, and disciplinary professional organizations), or a similar process that allows a degree of input from practicing teachers in the various disciplines. However, seldom are teachers allowed a significant role, and generally student and parent participation is minimal at best. Once in place, the mandated curriculum is enshrined as the canon, and deviation from the curriculum can be justified only after the mandated curriculum has been successfully taught. Documented outcomes of the imposition of mandated curriculum include curricular fragmentation, curriculum displacement, curriculum reductionism, and a rigid adherence to curriculum alignment.

Curricular fragmentation occurs when curriculum is reduced to a series of disconnected facts. Because of the focus on the correct answering of specific and unconnected factual information on the standardized tests, curriculum is no longer viewed as interconnected and holistic. As a response to this testing focus, the pragmatic and expedient pedagogical strategy is to develop a factoid focus, or concentration on the teaching and learning of curriculum as discrete and unconnected factual information.

Curriculum displacement occurs when the tested school curriculum takes precedence over nontested curriculum. In this case, certain disciplinary areas become expendable in light of the amount of time that is available to guarantee appropriate student achievement levels on the tested curriculum. Often, the fine arts, physical education, social studies, and other programs that meet the functional purposes of education, such as driver education, vocational education, and family and consumer science, are displaced from the curriculum because of the need to use their time for test preparation. For example, as testing time approaches, some schools require teachers in these areas to devote class time to remediation activities related to the tested curriculum and the development of test-taking strategies.

Curriculum reductionism takes place within the tested disciplines. Disciplinary curriculum that will be tested is stressed at the expense of other information within the discipline that will not be tested. In fact, tested content is often divided into categories of essential knowledge and nonessential knowledge, with an instructional emphasis focused on the essential knowledge. Of course, essential knowledge is defined as the discipline's knowledge that has the highest probability of being on the test.

Somewhat related is curriculum alignment. This refers to the practice of making sure that the written curriculum is what is taught and tested. The purpose of curriculum alignment is to streamline the pedagogical process by making sure that extraneous information (i.e., information that is not part of the written curriculum) does not compete with the time that is used to teach and test the mandated written curriculum. A rigid application of curriculum alignment finds no place for impromptu or creative infusions of curriculum in either the written, taught, or tested phase of the teaching and learning process by either the teachers or students. This pedagogical restriction works against the enhancement of curricular authenticity and relevance that may occur when the curriculum, instruction, and assessment is situationally changed by teachers or students to enhance instructional relevance.

The focus of instruction is constantly negotiated between student-centered, teacher-centered, and test-centered techniques. In a standards and accountability environment as defined by NCLB, the most efficient pedagogical strategies are teacher-centered and test-centered. The use of student-centered instruction infers that student differences and needs will inform and mediate the nature of curriculum, instruction, and assessment. Since in a standardized test environment the test content is predetermined, it is more efficient for the teacher to transmit knowledge or be directive in focusing student learning on what is most important—learning what will be on the test. Student differences that involve learning styles, cognitive styles, cultural differences, command of the English language, disabilities, or other special needs are irrelevant because none of these differences are factored into the testing process. Because of this disregard for student difference (mainly because all students regardless of these differences must take the test), students are decontextualized and objectified. Just as all of the tests are standardized, students are stripped of their individuality and viewed as an essentialized and homogenized group in that only their individual test scores define them as individuals.

In order to achieve instructional efficiency, instruction tends to emphasize the use of direct instruction models. Memorization, rote learning, test taking skills, and repetitious instructional activities tend to be the norm; simply, because they offer a greater potential for test achievement. Lower-level thinking skills are also emphasized, and higher-order thinking, cooperative learning, and student creativity are closely monitored to ensure time on task, content coverage, and determination of the correct answer. Constructivist techniques and strategies may be used but are also closely monitored, because in the end, there is a correct answer that may not coincide with the students' construction of meaning.

In general, efficiency models of education are more focused on control. The organizational hierarchy is well defined, with sharp boundaries between administrators, teachers, and students. To enhance the efficient delivery of mandated curriculum within the time available to prepare for the test, many schools attempt to control instruction through the use of prescriptive commercially prepared instructional products that are characterized by scripted lesson plans, lesson plan banks, programmed instruction materials, and other teacher-proof materials and lessons. In addition, student motivation is an object of control. Many schools rely on extrinsic motivational strategies to foster appropriate student attitudes toward test preparation and performance. In a return to the scientific management of schools, school time is also highly controlled. Besides curriculum displacement, time is rescheduled for remediation purposes. Students whose progress lags behind, as determined by diagnostic tests, have their school time restructured to accommodate remediation activities. These repetitious drill activities may occur throughout the school day by displacing other curriculum, or be structured activities after the regular school hours, on Saturdays, and during the summer break.

Another aspect of NCLB is the growing requirement for schools to base their instruction on only quantitative research-based strategies. NCLB defines research-based strategies as those supported by randomized longitudinal quantitative studies. Not included in this definition are qualitative research studies, action research by educators, and descriptive statistical quantitative studies of short duration and small samples that cannot be generalized to the larger student population. Building on the research mandate of NCLB, the federal government has restructured its professional research organizations to accommodate and promote this restrictive definition.

In the NCLB environment, the assessment of curriculum is a simple issue because of the total focus on state standardized tests. Teacher-made assessments, authentic assessment, and the use of multiple assessments are all subordinated to the standardized tests. Student performance on these standardized tests is not only evaluated by whether students answer the questions correctly, but their overall performance rating is determined by arbitrary cutscores or passing scores (i.e., a number on a score scale that determines whether a test has been passed). Because of this arbitrary process of setting the passing scores, some states periodically change their tests when scores tend to be high. Many have criticized the use of cutscores because government officials can change the cutscores at any time for any reason. Also, these arbitrary performance levels can have a great impact on students and schools. For instance if a cutscore is set at 80, some testing experts have argued that there may be no significant difference in a child's learning from a 77 to a score of 80. Because the purpose of these tests is to compare all students in a state, the tests must be able to reliably account for student differences involving variables such as place (i.e., rural, urban, suburban, underfunded schools, well-funded schools), individual difference (i.e., intelligence, disability, culture, language, socioeconomic status), and local instructional differences. This need to generalize test results is problematized by the fact that some tests have yet to be proven statistically reliable and valid in their assessment of students.

In an attempt to accommodate these reliability and validity issues, test content is manipulated to enhance the score spread. Score spread allows students to be statistically ranked and sorted. The more spread out the scores, the easier it is to sort the students. One technique in establishing score spread is to eliminate questions that were to frequently answered correctly. In this case, schools and students are punished for their ability to effectively teach to the test. Other problems with the validity of these tests include test pollution and teaching/testing mismatches. In test pollution, the validity of the test results is adversely affected by the teaching of test-taking skills, the use of practice tests, and the use of other test preparation strategies that are designed to enhance student achievement through the question-answering process rather than through the correct understanding of the tested information. The issue of teaching/testing mismatches involves the difference between what information is on the test and the information that is taught in schools. If students are not taught what is on the test, then they do poorly, not because of their own effort but because of this mismatch. The solution to this problem is twofold. First, teachers can anticipate the test content and teach to the test. Second, test preparation materials can be purchased or developed that closely aligns with test content. In any case, either practice once again has significant consequences for curriculum and instruction, and more important the students and schools.

Finally, the impact of this type of educational system on the roles of the educators and students is significant in our comparison to a reconceptualized environment. In this technical rational system, administrators function solely as managers whose primary responsibility is to ensure appropriate student test scores. The administrator's role as instructional leader is sharply defined by the standardized test requirement. The role of teachers in the teaching and learning process is greatly affected by the standards and accountability environment. One requirement of NCLB is that all teachers must be highly qualified. This noble and commonsense requirement is subverted by the federal requirement that the definition of highly qualified teachers is solely determined by their performance on standardized tests. Most of these tests are related solely to disciplinary content knowledge. Other indicators of teacher expertise such as administrative evaluations geared to the local context, teacher experience, and student and parent feedback are subordinated to the test performance requirement. Many alternative teacher certification programs designed to fill teacher shortages are solely focused on content tests with a minimal emphasis on pedagogical knowledge. In this type of environment, teachers function as deskilled technicians whose sole responsibility is to make sure that the appropriate content is taught in the required amount of time. Teachers are considered deskilled when they must operate within a narrow range of specialized knowledge and skills. In this situation, teachers become content specialists rather than content generalists who can make interdisciplinary connections. Generally, the power of teachers is limited to decisions about how best to carry out the curricular and assessment mandates of the states.

In rigid technical rational standards and accountability systems, students are viewed as the receptors of knowledge that can be transmitted to them through direct instruction or constructivist activities that are contrived so that students will arrive at the correct answer. Generally, students are limited in how much they can participate in the decision-making process concerning teaching and learning. Their role is akin to the role played by workers in the traditional factory system in that they do what they are told to do by the manager/expert/administrator/teacher. This lack of ownership and empowerment within the teaching and learning process has well-documented negative effects such as high dropout rates and high levels of student anxiety. In addition, some students, due to a narrow instructional focus on tested content and repetitious remediation, experience a reduced engagement with curriculum and critical thinking skills.

THE RECONCEPTUALIZED EDUCATIONAL EXPERIENCE

In a discussion of a reconceptualized educational experience because of the significant foundational differences between this view of education and a technical rational view, it quickly becomes apparent that curriculum, instruction, and assessment cannot be viewed as separate components of teaching and learning. Unlike the reductionist alignment process in which curriculum, instruction, and assessment are viewed as separate and discrete aspects of the educational process that need to be aligned in order to enhance the efficiency of the educational process, a reconceptual view sees these three components as inherently and ubiquitously integrated. Therefore, other concepts will be used to organize an explanation of the reconceptualized educational experience. These organizing concepts include a focus on critical thinking, attention to context and social constructivism, an interdisciplinary and holistic orientation, authentic assessment, and teachers and students as scholar-practitioners.

Before discussing the characteristics of reconceptualized education, it is important to clearly establish the fundamental purpose of a reconceptualized education. Of course, as is the idealistic purpose of all education, the purpose of reconceptualized education is to prepare individuals to have full, rich, and productive lives. More fully defining this purpose requires a look at the nature of society in which the individuals will exist, and the knowledge, skills, and dispositions that they will need to acquire in order to fulfill this purpose. Writing in the context of preparing students to function effectively in the economy of the digital age, one scholar proposes the needs that must be fulfilled by education. Students need to acquire a digital-age literacy in science, mathematics, technology, and visual information and culture. In addition, in order to manage complexity, they need to be inventive, curious, creative, and risk-taking. They need to acquire skill in higher-order thinking, teamwork, leadership, and problem solving—all within an ethical sense of personal and social responsibility (Thornburg, 2002, p. 59).

To say the least, this is certainly a significant challenge for any educational system. Most individuals would agree that any student who acquires this skill and knowledge certainly would be well prepared to effectively engage the complexity of the future. Furthermore, let us add to this wish list an overriding concern for social justice, an ethic of care, and the promotion of participatory democracy. From a pragmatic viewpoint, any educational system will have difficulty achieving such a lofty purpose if faced with inequitable educational funding, systemic poverty, racism, and a myriad of other conditions that complicate and confound the education process. However, these conditions are precisely why all of this knowledge, skill, and critical awareness need to be the central focus and purpose of public education.

Proponents of reconceptualized education will argue that their educational perspective offers the greatest potential to maximize the achievement of this purpose. They attempt to realize their purpose through pedagogies that empower and emancipate; standards that require the engagement of complexity; accountability systems that are equitable, just, and caring; and educational systems that are attentive to individual needs and local and global contexts. The characteristics of such an educational system are as follows.

A Focus on Critical Thinking

The term *critical thinking* has quite different definitions depending upon the purpose of education. If the purpose of education is to control the educational process in order to promote a specific viewpoint or reproduce a specific arrangement of power, then critical thinking may be defined as the higher-order thinking skills of analysis, synthesis, and evaluation that are to be learned and used within narrow contexts with the sole purpose of finding correct answers and validating the predetermined conclusions of experts. If on the other hand the purpose of education is to empower and emancipate, then students are encouraged to use these processes to expand contextual awareness through problem posing and problem solving through research, challenge simplistic solutions, and uncover injustice, a lack of care, and undemocratic policy and practice.

In this reconceptual definition, critical thinking is inherently critical in its concern for social justice, an ethic of care, and democratic participation. It is also technical in relation to the development of higher-order thinking skills within this critical context. It is also contextually holistic in the understanding that the primary function of these skills is to increase the complexity of the situation in which they are employed. In addition, a reconceptualized view of critical thinking requires an awareness and critique of the values that are imbued within all human activity. One consequence of the inclusion of values is the concomitant inclusion of emotion. Unlike the positivist separation of reason and emotion, reconceptualized critical thinking understands that reason and emotion are interrelated and interconnected, and therefore, analysis, synthesis, and evaluation must engage a situation or problem as having both a logical and an affective dimension.

Critical thinking is not used as a normalizing agent so that students will fit into the preconceptions of the dominant group, but instead is a best practice that facilitates the development of critical and creative thinkers who can think out of the box. Through the use of divergent and lateral thinking as well as convergent and linear thinking, students make connections that allow them to see the deep and hidden patterns in which all human activity is nested. To achieve this potential, students learn how to think not what to think. An integral part of problem posing, pattern detection, and making connections is the ability to engage in continuous critical reflection. Critically reflecting upon process, conclusions, actions, and consequences is an integral part of reconceptualized critical thinking. In a reconceptualized context, critical thinking is posed as using analysis, synthesis, and evaluation in the critical reflection process that is a fundamental aspect of the praxis process of action–critical reflection–action.

In reconceptualized curriculum, critical reflection as the recurring theme in all critical thinking activities is inherently metacognitive in nature. Metacognition is the awareness of one's thinking processes—how one constructs questions, solves problems, makes decisions, organizes daily activity, and all of the other cognitive activities that mediate our desires and actions. A deep, broad, and critical understanding of the consequences of our actions is not possible without this metacognitive reflection.

In conclusion, reconceptualized curriculum requires a constant use of critical thinking in relation to the developmental level of the students. The acquisition of facts, data, and information is always in the context of critical thinking. Instead of collecting and learning facts as an isolated activity followed by critical thinking, the collection of information occurs within the critical thinking framework. In their lessons, teachers pose problems or situations that require students to form questions, gather information, employ higher-order thinking in the analysis of the information, pose and test solutions, and throughout this whole research-based process engage in critical reflection. Or, in a less linear sequence, teachers ask students to gather information, formulate questions, detect problems, analyze, reflect, synthesize, and evaluate—all done continuously and dynamically as deemed relevant by the teacher and student.

Attention to Context and Social Constructivism

A reconceptualized view of education is attentive to context—the context of the individual student, the context of place, and the act of learning in context. This view is fundamentally a social constructivist view. In this context, student thinking and learning (i.e., their construction of meaning) is unique to each student and to the specific circumstances of the context of the situation in which the learning takes place.

First, a reconceptual view is sensitive to student diversity and difference that manifests itself in forms involving gender, race, ethnicity, social class, lifestyle preference, sexual preference, language, special abilities, and disabilities. In addition, all of these forms are mediated by the political, social, cultural, economic, and spiritual contexts in which the students live. Adding even more complexity to the teaching and learning process is the increasingly pluralistic nature of society, which problematizes monocultural educational practice. To educationally accommodate these differences, reconceptual education employs instructional diversity through an attention to other individual differences that may manifest themselves as multiple intelligences, cognitive styles, learning styles, and emotional responses within and to the learning process. Because each student is viewed as unique, the resultant pedagogical strategies must be student-focused, humanistic, and personalized.

A second consideration involves the place in which the learning occurs and the student exists. Reconceptualists are aware that the concept of place mediates and informs all teaching and learning, and that there are many places that affect the educational process. Place can include the culture of the individual classroom, the school, the family, the neighborhood, the city, the region, and the world. The characteristics of place enter the classroom with students, teachers, mass media, business activity within the school context (e.g., business-supported educational programs, marketing aimed at students as consumers) and governmental regulations. A reconceptual view recognizes that teaching and learning cannot be isolated from these characteristics and, in fact, they overtly and covertly influence all aspects of the educational process. Often referred to as hidden curriculum, these characteristics and influences offer the potential for authentic and relevant education to occur.

Reconceptual teachers situate information within the conditions or places in which students find themselves, thus fostering authentic educational activity. Reconceptual teachers understand that by situating learning within the places that influence their students, their students experience learning that is mediated by change. Situated learning is important because, when learning is situated within real-world contexts, knowledge, inquiry, and learning processes are not static and controlled entities but change as the learning context changes. This engagement with change requires the learner to engage change, the dynamic nature of the construction of knowledge and use of skills, and the complexity that is created by change. In this way, learning becomes less an artificial exercise conducted within the minds of students and more an authentic learning exercise within the world in which the students live. This is truly authentic education because there is no separation of knowledge or learning contexts from the social, political, economic, cultural, and historical forces that mediate real-life situations.

Besides the motivational value of engaging curriculum within the authentic context of their local place, students gain more complex understandings about their home, neighborhood, and city. Utilizing their critical thinking skills and critical dispositions, students can take the opportunity to develop the capacity to democratically participate within their local context. Within this authentic learning context, disciplinary knowledge as well as abstract concepts such as social justice, caring, and democratic participation take on a concrete and visceral meaning. Understandings gained within the authentic context can lead to learning activities involving praxis, in which students formulate action plans, critically reflect, take action, and engage in further critical reflection. Active learning in context positions knowledge, skills, attitudes, and values within an authentic context rather than in the artificially decontextualized context of formal learning. In this social constructivist context, teachers creatively and situationally develop instructional strategies and course content that requires students to individually and cooperatively engage the knowledge that they already have with the knowledge that they are expected to learn.

Based on the social constructivism of Vygotskian theory, the social context of learning is an essential element in reconceptualized education. This social context recognizes both teacher-and-student and student-and-student interactions as the fundamental social contexts of teaching and learning. The importance of this understanding is seen in the continuous use of observational learning, situated learning, cooperative inquiry and problem-based learning, cognitive apprentice-ships, and dialogic and generative conversation. Reconceptual education promotes cooperative group work as a fundamental organizing structure for teaching and learning. Within the group context, students learn to work collegially with others; critically critique their own and their colleague's ideas, values, and assumptions; and recognize their fundamental interconnection and interrelationship with others in all human activity. Another important conversation goal of reconceptual education is to foster an awareness of the different types of conversation and their consequences. Different types of conversation are essentially different types of text that mediate our understanding of human activity and the consequences of our subsequent actions that are based upon our interpretation of these texts.

An Interdisciplinary and Holistic Orientation

In keeping with its critical pragmatic and postformal orientation, reconceptualized education views all aspects of teaching, learning, and knowledge as holistic in nature. This orientation not only views curriculum, instruction, and assessment as integrated components of the educational process, but also views the curriculum as interdisciplinary rather than as separate disciplinary fields. Obviously, science, math, social studies, etc. are discrete and separate fields, but in the context of teaching and learning, a reconceptual view finds it necessary and more effective to construct learning activities that require the learner to engage these separate disciplines in a holistic context. In this reconceptual view, disciplines are integrated and synthesized, thus eliminating any hierarchical arrangement of disciplines in which some are privileged over others. This positions the student for more authentic engagements with disciplinary knowledge, and creates the potential for the occurrence of more complex student understandings. Through interdisciplinary study, students have the potential to make more complex epistemological connections, and detect more complex patterns of human activity.

The promotion of interdisciplinary learning requires interdisciplinary teaching. In reconceptual education, teachers learn, plan, and teach in interdisciplinary teams. In order for students to make holistic connections, teachers must also make these connections. While individual teachers may be disciplinary specialists, they reconceptualize their disciplinary understanding to be part of an interdisciplinary understanding that engages human activity in more complex ways. Another benefit of interdisciplinary teaming involves pedagogical diversity and complexity. In the interdisciplinary teaching context, each individual teacher brings pedagogical techniques specific to their discipline, and collectively these teachers construct a reconceptualized pedagogy that is synergetically powerful in its ability to foster a holistic student understanding of content, critical thinking and metacognition, authentic situated learning, and a postformal engagement with the phenomenon under study.

Reconceptualized education also defines *interdisciplinary* to refer to the integration of theory and practice within a critical context. Besides integrating the content of different disciplinary areas, teaching and learning within and between disciplines is reconceptualized to bring together theory and practice within authentic learning contexts. As students engage learning in authentic real-world situations, they use disciplinary theory in an interdisciplinary context to inform and mediate the experiences of their practice. Conversely, the experiences that they encounter within their practice are used in a critical critique of the theory. As students engage theory and practice as dynamically interrelated forms of understanding, they do so within a critical and pragmatic context. In a sense, they simultaneously engage in two levels of thinking: one that requires critical reflection on content and process and another that requires an assessment of the critical consequences of the theory and practice in relation to issues of social justice, caring, and democratic participation.

Authentic Assessment

In order to assess the reconceptual goal of holistic understanding of human activity and natural phenomena, assessment must be authentic and multiple. Authentic assessment requires a formative and summative evaluation of student learning within the context of real-life problems and situations. The goal of authenticity in the assessment of learning is to determine how well students have applied content, skills, and attitudes in these real-life contexts. The idea of authentic assessment is in contrast to the formal idea that students can apply the learning that they experience in the decontextualized and artificial environment of the classroom to the real-life situations that they will encounter at a later time. A reconceptual view questions the effectiveness of formal assessment because of this disconnect between learning and the authentic application of the learning. Situated interdisciplinary learning directly connects the acquisition and understanding of content, skills, and attitudes to real-life situations. Therefore, only assessment that occurs naturally with instruction and is directly related to the situated/real-life context can provide a valid and reliable assessment of student achievement.

To capture the complexity of the learning process over time, which includes student engagement with all of the interdisciplinary content, skills, and attitudes within the real-life context, multiple assessments are required. Being student-centered, reconceptual education is interested in student achievement over time. Student growth in learning is a better indicator of teaching and learning effectiveness than a once-a-year decontextualized assessment such as a standardized test. In order to assess the holistic nature of student learning over time (i.e., a semester, a year, the length of a program), many and diverse assessment strategies are necessary. These can include traditional forms of assessment such as report cards, standardized tests, and teacher-constructed tests. Also included can be portfolios, scoring rubrics, peer and self-assessments, journals, and parent conferences. The use of multiple forms of assessment provides a fuller picture of not only student acquisition of content, but also of student cognition, affect, and ability. No one method of assessment can provide a valid and reliable assessment of such complex concepts such as teacher effectiveness, school effectiveness, and student progress.

An often-cited goal of education is to develop life-long learners. A reconceptual view of this goal recognizes that an integral part of the learning process is the ability of an individual to assess her or his own learning by herself or himself. If students do not learn appropriate assessment strategies in school, how can they accurately assess their learning when they are not part of a formal learning environment? From a pragmatic viewpoint, while in school, students must learn how to assess themselves through the use of multiple and authentic assessment strategies. These strategies need to be multiple because in real-life contexts, assessment at various times needs to be immediate and long-term, both of which require different assessment techniques.

Also, to function independently individuals need to be able to self-assess rather than rely on external assessments by other individuals. Authentic assessment strategies need to be acquired because when the assessment need arises, it will be in a real-life context, not in a decontextualized classroom context. How then are these requirements of multiple and authentic assessment in later real-life situations best met? The answer is found in how professionals engage in assessment. They use journals, rubrics, portfolios, and peer and self-assessments.

Teachers and Students as Scholar-Practitioners

Reconceptualized education requires teachers and students to perform roles that are quite different from their roles in a technical rational system. One term that can be used to capture this very different role is scholar-practitioner. Scholar-practitioners are individuals who have the attitude and ability to utilize scholarly and experiential knowledge and skills, viewed by them as dynamically interrelated entities, in their understanding of phenomena and in their solution of problems. Teachers as scholar-practitioners are not the deskilled technicians of technical rational systems, but individuals who as scholars can use scholarly knowledge and skills to better understand and shape their practice. They are practitioners who can use their practical knowledge to critique the formal theory and the theory that emerges from their practice. Above all, scholar-practitioners are critical in that the theory that they engage and the practice in which they are involved is critically interrogated with a fundamental concern for the promotion of social justice, an ethic of caring, and democratic participation. Through their scholarship and practice, they are not micro-managed individuals but self-empowered professionals who engage in a critical praxis in their classrooms, schools, and communities.

Teachers such as this are skeptics and critics who, through their critical interrogation of social phenomena, strive to facilitate the construction of egalitarian, caring, and democratic communities. In the context of educational communities such as the classroom, the school, and the larger community in which the school is nested, they use their interdisciplinary orientation, critical thinking, and postformal perspective to construct effective and egalitarian pedagogical environments. As researchers, they are bricoleurs who utilize a wide range of inquiry methods and knowledge bases to build egalitarian communities through the use of a critical pedagogy. They understand the situatedness of their own teaching and learning, and critically reflect upon their understandings as they are socially constructed in relation to the changing context of their place and their social interactions with others. They are critically pragmatic in that they are consequence focused, and critically interrogate their actions and the consequences of their actions. They value self-assessment and engage in continuous authentic and multiple assessment of themselves and their activity.

Likewise, students in a reconceptualized educational environment are scholar-practitioners in training. Unlike technical rational systems, students are empowered and active constructors of knowledge within authentic contexts. As student researchers, they are personally empowered through a critical pedagogy that requires them to experiment, discover, create, problem-solve, think, and act. By developing cooperative skills and dispositions, they learn the value of fostering community and the necessity of critically focused participation within a community. Through authentic assessment, they experience the validation and empowerment that is the result of personal growth. And in the end, they are transformed into life-long learners.

FURTHER READING

Thornburg, D. (2002). *The New Basics: Education and the Future of Work in the Telematic Age*. Alexandria, VA: Association for Supervision and Curriculum Development.

PART IV

New Visions—Postformalism:
Education and Psychology

CHAPTER 95

Race in America: An Analysis of Postformal Curriculum Design

JOELLE TUTELA

What happens when students and teachers become empowered? When teachers become more actively involved in curriculum design and integrate their interests and knowledge into their subject matter, their classes are more likely to engage student participation. As a teacher of social studies, I wanted to demonstrate that history can be interesting, even exciting, and—most important—relevant, when historical events and persons are viewed through multiple lenses. I wanted history to "come alive" for my students, but found that they were not interested in its study because, in their experience, it had been taught as disjointed facts that generally dealt with dead white men. As such, they found it hard to relate to the subject. The memorization of facts requires low levels of thinking; certainly, it does not elicit creativity. By departing from a one-dimensional approach to the past and engaging students, challenging them to use higher levels of thinking and draw from their cultural awareness, the reshaped curriculum could empower students to view themselves as active participants. An interdisciplinary approach that engages multiple points of view is more likely to initiate and sustain engagement, so that a multidimensional picture becomes possible. Imaginative approaches to studying the past excite student curiosity and invite a genuine investment in learning.

Postformalism can break the chains of a sterile, one-dimensional approach to the study of history. Postformalism is rooted in democratic post-Cartesian ways of observation and evaluation and seeks to expand human rationality and knowledge (Kincheloe, 2001, p. 341). By deconstructing the typical pedagogical approach to history, teachers can invigorate students, encourage them to participate in the learning and stimulate new insights about the past as it relates to both the present and the future.

My approach to surmounting the constraints of the Cartesian method was to integrate the study of history with the fine arts. As an educator, and an artist, I know that works of art not only are aesthetic entities but also are purveyors of knowledge about our economic, political, and cultural circumstances. Using art as a springboard to the examination of history enlivens the subject matter. Art humanizes. Art adds emotional challenges, thereby attracting and holding student interest. I determined that the best way to integrate fine art into the history curriculum was to transform my classroom into an artist's studio, filled with the tools for the creation of "masterpieces." My students became my apprentices. In concert, we would create art. In concert, all of us would be enriched.

Just as a master seeks to improve her craft, I decided to engage members of the community to collaborate in the construction of my studio/classroom. I collaborated with the Director of Education at the Montclair Art Museum to create "Crit and Create: Race in America." As an apprentice learns from the master, students taking Crit and Create: Race in America learned to (a) analyze art and primary sources, (b) examine several perspectives, (c) become familiar with the techniques artists use to create their art, and (d) utilize their new knowledge and skills to create their own monument to race in America. There are several stages in the design and implementation of Crit and Create: Race in America. Each will be described and related to postformal thought.

STAGE I: PREPARING THE CANVAS

The first stage in Crit and Create was the creation of a calendar of the events in concert with the school calendar and the museum calendar. This proved to be more problematic than originally anticipated because I wanted to cover so much. An examination of the school calendar brought home how little time there is in one marking period! I met with the Director of Education from the Montclair Art Museum to devise a schedule that would honor both of our commitments while serving to achieve our teaching objectives. Gary Schneider and I wanted our program to

- validate alternative teaching and assessment methods to stimulate higher thinking;
- demonstrate that making the community an extension of the classroom improves student involvement;
- illustrate that studying art improves visual literacy and problem-solving skills;
- show that studying art and its relation to the humanities spurs student reflection on their values and heightens their social consciousness; and
- create an environment in which those with a minimal understanding of art become both comfortable with, and enthusiastic about, art.

To accomplish these objectives, we scheduled three in-school and out-of-school events for students and the museum staff. The culmination would be an evening opening, at the museum. By considering the museum as "our backyard" and a major educational resource, students began to understand that "emotionally derived knowledge" is as important as "rationally derived knowledge." This partnership with the museum staff encouraged students to develop satisfying and meaningful connections with the larger society and to forge bonds between the two worlds.

Using the community as a direct extension of the classroom provides a strong foundation for intellectual and emotional development and reflects postformal thinking; it improves both the student's life and the life of the community (Kincheloe 2001, p. 343). Through community involvement, students enhanced critical thinking as they reflected on classroom activities and developed commitment to social issues. Students witnessed first-hand that what they learned in the classroom really does relate to real life. Crit and Create expected students to immerse themselves in both the artistic and the societal environment. It also provided positive role models and experiences that required them to practice and hone their communications skills.

After my conversations with the Director of Education of Montclair Art Museum, I met with the principal, Elaine Davis, to inform her of the new partnership and the new approach to teaching history through an investigation of the arts. She was pleased at the prospect of expanding the classroom into the immediate community, of students working in cooperation with museum personnel, and of students becoming "masters" in more than one discipline.

To fund Crit and Create, I wrote a grant proposal to the Montclair Fund for Educational Excellence, which is committed to funding educational program that incorporate creative initiatives. Montclair Fund for Educational Excellence typically supports programs that enhance student learning by the application of nontraditional approaches. Fortunately, the grant proposal was accepted, perhaps because Crit and Create mirrored the foundation's educational mission. The *interconnectedness* of student learning—in addition to learning from the teacher and classroom activities, learning from one another and from members of the community at large—is a major component of postformal thinking.

After the logistics had been finalized came the artistic challenges. I would equip my fledgling artists with a "palette" so they could begin to create their "masterpieces." This comprised two phases. *One*: the students learned "primary colors": studying the history and vocabulary of racism in America. *Two*: the students learned "complementary colors": studying the language and techniques of artists and as well as an overview of art history.

During the first two weeks of the marking period, students studied "primary colors." To ensure that they had a clear understanding of race in America, I developed lesson plans that integrated materials and activities to promote cognitive development and comprehension of a spectrum of historical events, described from a variety of perspectives.

Students in *Crit and Create* began their studies by examining group interaction and the dynamics of oppression. Each student was asked to determine his/her "social identity" and "membership" and compare these to those listed in the chart below (Adams 1997, p. 70).

Social Identity	Membership	Status: Agent	Status: Target
Race	Black, White, Latino, Asian, Native American, Biracial	White	All Others
Gender	Female, Male, Transgender	Male	All Others
Economic Class	Poor, Working Class, Middle Class, Upper Middle Class, Owner Class	Upper Middle Class, Owner Class	All Others
Age	Young, Young Adults, Middle-Aged Adults, Elderly	Young Adults, Middle-Aged Adults	All Others
Sexual Orientation	Heterosexual, Homosexual, Bisexual	Heterosexual	All Others
Religion	Christian, Jew, Muslim, Hindu, Buddhist	Christian	All Others
Physical Ability/ Disability	Nondisabled, Disabled	Nondisabled	All Others

This activity required students to examine their backgrounds with regard to race, gender, economic class, age, sexual orientation, religion, and their physical condition and to view themselves as members of several groups. They also confronted the concepts of "agents" and "targets," in order to better understand the dynamics of power in America. In discussing these issues, students recognized the complexity of relationships within our power structure. This activity provided students with the opportunity to overcome the limitations of monological formalism and afford them with new ways of thinking about themselves and others.

Building on acquired knowledge and working in small groups, students developed working definitions of: *discrimination*, *prejudice*, *race*, *ethnicity*, *racism*, *individual racism*, *active racism*, *passive racism*, *target*, *agent*, and *ally*. Regular group interactions provided opportunities for developing a clearer understanding of these terms and how they are applied to individuals, groups, and society as a whole. These interactions also enabled students to take ownership of their learning and provided opportunities for them to express their point of view—two key aspects of postformal thinking.

To develop a critical lens for students to grasp the complexities of the relationships between individual consciousness and culture, students examined a timeline of key events (1819 to 1990) in the struggle for racial equality in the United States (Adams, 1997, pp. 105–107). The timeline helped students gain an overview of the racial categories that had been constructed and legislated by North Americans of European descent to justify privilege and colonialism, even theft and murder. In asking students to examine the history of racial segregation in the United States, it became apparent that they also needed to understand the importance of the individual responsibility and to reflect on the more sinister aspects of American history.

As a corollary of this examination, students were encouraged to reflect on, and talk about, strategies that might be effective in preventing the abuse of power. In addition, students were encouraged to reevaluate simplistic responses to complex questions. The focus, at this juncture, was an analysis of the role of race, gender, religion, and class in the greater context of historical events. To heighten student awareness of historical events from numerous vantage points—race, gender, religion, and economic class—students gave presentations about the inequities they had found in their lives. This exercise underscored the importance of bringing one's own cultural and ethnic awareness to the study of history.

To initiate a dialogue of racial issues in contemporary America, students viewed and then analyzed the film *Do the Right Thing*, written and directed by Spike Lee. Although the scenario is fictitious, the film alludes to racism and bigotry in contemporary America and their tragic, often-violent, consequences. Students leveraged what they had learned from the film to articulate their understanding of the complexities of contemporary urban life, especially for people of color. One of their assignments was to write a movie review. To prepare for this assignment, students were asked to evaluate previously held opinions in light of new-found information and to investigate the duality and ambivalence inherent in the film's characters and in their actions. In many cases, students who had thought they possessed clear-cut solutions to the conundrum of racism discovered their own turmoil and prejudices. This consciousness of their ambivalence.

To enhance understanding of various perspectives of race, gender, and class, and to create an environment in which my students *wanted* to do their homework, I compiled a reader that included African-American voices from the eighteenth century through the present. I included articles that would appeal to my students, so that they were motivated to do their homework and pleased to discuss what they had learned. I also gave my students choices in their additional readings; the only requirement was that they select three relevant articles each week, read them thoughtfully, and write a response. Providing choice empowered my students, giving them opportunities for independent investigation of areas of interest, and encouraging them to reconsider their perspectives and prejudices. These readings engendered awareness of the power of the word, especially when it emanates from subjugated voices, to paint accurate—if somewhat darker— pictures of one aspect of America's past.

Students now were somewhat prepared to understand America's complicated racial history. Now it was time to add the "complementary colors." Most students taking *Crit and Create* had had no formal artistic training. With this in mind, I started with the basics. Students were asked to look at selected works of art and answer straightforward questions: *What do you see? Do you like what you see? If you like it, why? If you do not like it, why not?* Through simulation, students were introduced to the seven key categories that guide most art critics when they review a piece of art: *Physical Presence, Personality, Historical Circumstances, Tradition, Language, Viewpoint, and Conclusions.*

To introduce the specialized argot that comes into play when describing and analyzing artwork, students were asked to describe a painting as if they were reporting a car accident. This aided them in achieving objectivity. I converted my classroom into a gallery, *Faux 215*. On the walls, I hung replicas of: mosaics, frescoes by Giotto and Fra Angelico, and paintings by Van Gogh, Duchamp, Monet, Picasso, Magritte, and Pollack. As they examined these pieces, I provided an overview of the principles governing realism and abstraction. Before entering the new gallery, students crowded in the hall in front of the gallery to review museum directives designed to guide their behavior. In *Faux 215*, students had fun applying their new vocabulary and their newly acquired insights as they attempted to review a painting in the manner of an art critic from *The New York Times*. Students were required to review two paintings, applying the seven key categories of art criticism, and to present their reviews to the class. The simulation required students to consider how we arrive at opinions, and it made them active, often enthusiastic, participants in a new arena—guided analysis to reach an informed evaluation. Further, students were obliged to leave the comfort zone of a more traditional social studies class and to envision themselves in a new role, that of art critic.

Gradually, the students began to feel comfortable with their new "palette." The next investigation was an examination of the monuments that have helped shape the United States landscape. Students read and analyzed the article, "Lies We Tell Ourselves," by James Loewen. Among other things, Loewen describes how historical markers "distort our understanding of the past and warp our view of the world. . . [because] Americans like to remember only the positive things, and [because] communities like to publicize the great things that happened in them" (Loewen 2000, p. 20). By asking students to think about an essential controversy—"Who gets memorialized and who gets ignored?" (Loewen 2000, p. 20)—I was, in effect, asking them to become aware of a pervasive mode of thought—the Eurocentric, patriarchal, and elitist viewpoint—and to consider what might be done to empower and give voice to another perspective, that of the non-Eurocentric, non-patriarchal, non-elitist—in other words—the subjugated and the disaffected. Joe Kincheloe maintains in his introduction to this encyclopedia, that students with their new lens would be able to remove their ideological blinders and demand multiple perspectives in their studies.

Students then were asked to consider the function of selected monuments by asking themselves the following questions:

• What is the difference between a monument and a memorial?
• Why do we build monuments? What are the motivating factors?
• Why do we create monuments that commemorate tragic or horrific events?
• What function(s) does (do) such monuments serve for survivors? For the fallen?
• For society as a whole? For posterity?
• Why do we build monuments to commemorate heroes or heroic events?
• Who should have say in the design and building of monuments?
• Who and what are memorialized by a specific community. Who and what are ignored? Who decides these important questions?
• How do monuments simplify the past? How do they "sanitize" the past?
• What important messages do monuments convey about the society that created them?

This critical examination enabled students to uncover the human motivations for building monuments and the ability of monuments to communicate not only to the societies that created them but also to future generations. These individual examinations, and the ensuing group discussions, helped students ponder the complexities of the modern world and the uses and abuses of power. In the course of this unit, students viewed slides of monuments found throughout the United States. The Statue of Liberty, Washington Monument, The Minute Man, Thomas Jefferson Monument, The Lincoln Memorial, The Korean Memorial, The Vietnam Veterans Memorial, and The Civil Rights Memorial were examined and discussed in order to better understand the role each plays in shaping our landscape and our attitudes. Students commented on each monument and recorded the salient points of their discussions.

These slides helped the students think more critically about the meanings and the influences of our national monuments, broadened their knowledge of this genre, and increased student appreciation of their importance—both as aesthetic entities and as expressions of national consciousness. The discussions also helped students understand that artists—through their works—represent the attitudes of the time and place in which they live. To stimulate greater involvement, students designed a book cover that represented a person and/or an event they wished to commemorate. This created the opportunity to consider what was important to them and, in their presentations, to attempt to convince others of the logic of their choice and the importance of the person/event being remembered. Students took a walking tour of our school, Montclair High School and its grounds to examine its monuments. This heightened their awareness of the local landscape. After reviewing their findings, students realized that much of the school's landscape had been totally foreign to them, since they neither recognized the persons commemorated by the bas-reliefs sculptures nor the connection of these figures with of Montclair High School. For the most part, all that they had seen were figures of white men and a few white women. Students then were asked what monuments *they* would create to add to the school's landscape. This exercise enabled them to voice their concerns, to "lobby for their cause." In keeping with the tenets of postformalism, students reflected on the fact that these particular monuments commemorated only one dimension of the community at large. This was problematic for most students of color. They wondered why the school's landscape was not populated with figures of: Martin Luther King Jr., Mahatma Gandhi, Maya Angelou, W.E.B. Dubois, Frederick Douglas, Ida B. Wells, Harriet Tubman, Jacob Lawrence, and Langston Hughes, to name a few.

As apprentices hone their skills by learning from the master, it was important that my apprentices learn to research all of the skills and history of art from the perspective of an artist. To initiate this unit, students viewed a PowerPoint presentation that provided an overview of the traditional canon of Western European art, beginning with cave paintings and ending with contemporary conceptual art. The presentation gave the students an inkling of how Western art and its functions have changed over the past seven centuries. They also gained an appreciation of the fact that artworks tell a visual story of culture—that they reflect the major beliefs and pervasive behaviors of a specific society at a specific period. I was mindful that the artists represented were white males; nevertheless, the intent was to introduce the traditional canon and then bridge to a more pluralistic, inclusive approach. For many of my students, this was the first time they had been introduced to art history, the first time they had viewed these works of art. This activity provided a grounding—however basic—of the subject, and was undertaken so that my students could understand the continuum that has led from primitive expression to contemporary expression Further, the overview emphasized the usefulness of an interdisciplinary approach to the subject.

The overview began with color slides of the Lascaux cave paintings (France) and of the Great Pyramids (Egypt) to underscore the story-telling functions of art. Students then viewed the works of Giotto, Da Vinci, and Michelangelo whose paintings—commissioned by the Roman Catholic Church—served a didactic function: to educate an illiterate populace by conveying religious and ethical messages of the Old and New Testaments. Portraits of the nobility of Spain, immortalized by Velázquez and Goya, brought home that, at one time, only the personal histories of the wealthy and politically powerful could live on by virtue of magnificent paintings that had been commissioned by these noble families. By the nineteenth century, most artists no longer were the protégés of their wealthy patrons, the Church and the aristocracy. With their obligation to their powerful patrons annulled, many were drawn to depicting a more "democratic" middle-class milieu. Works by Ingres and Manet were shown to illustrate this movement. With the invention of the camera, numerous artists began to move away from realistic depictions of their subject matter and looked inward for new inspiration. Artists became interested in iconoclastic interpretations. With this in mind, students viewed the art of Picasso and Duchamp. By the middle of the twentieth century, increasing numbers of artists had rejected the constraints of representational art and were deconstructing their art into the basic elements of paint, canvas, and gesture. Students were exposed to the works of Pollock, deKooning, and Rothko, leading exponents of the startling new ethos, and then to those of American artists, Rauschenberg, Johns, and Warhol, who focused on portraying the more mundane aspects of contemporary life in radically new ways. Moving closer to the present, "ideation" took on new importance. That pure idea, not expressed in tangible form, can be art found its expression in works by artists like Kosuth and Baldessari.

Learning about this evolution in art helped students comprehend that art literacy should not be one-dimensional, and that a multidimensional approach can improve critical consciousness. Students also came to understand that one purpose of art and the humanities is "to open our minds to more alternatives and to ambiguities in the way we see the world" (Feinberg 2000, p. 13). Just as philosophers seek to understand and express human existence through words, artists make sense of their world through pictures.

STAGE II: CREATING THE WORK OF ART

With some understanding of art history, my students were better prepared to study additional examples of contemporary art. For our first in-school event, the Director of Education from the Montclair Art Museum, visited our class to discuss selected works of several minority artists whose subject matter is race. This expansion of the artist's cultural base was an "eye-opener" that helped students understand "the insight to be gained from the recognition that divergent cultures use art to highlight both our social constructs as individuals and the limitations of monocultural ways of making meaning" (Rose and Kincheloe 2004, p. 97). To help students grasp these multidimensional implications of art and the complexity of human existence, students viewed a PowerPoint presentation of the work of the contemporary artists: Whitefield Lovell, Willie Cole, Shirin Neshat, Kara Walker, Tseng Kwong Chi, and Jimmy Durham. Students were able to identify the symbols used by these artists and to articulate the intellectual and emotional impact of their symbolism. These artworks, by subjugated voices, once again inspired students to confront the multiple perspectives of the American experience. Willie Cole uses discarded objects—for example, irons and ironing boards—to comment on his personal history and that of his culture. His sculptures, reminiscent of the slave trade, convey a strong African-American message of his heritage. The works of Shirin Neshat depict the lives of Muslim women in the Middle East. Binary opposites positions invite questions about the viability of her country's mores and cultural institutions. Tseng Kwong's self-portraits provide trenchant commentary on Western ignorance about Asians; in his black and white photographs, Kwong, in a gray Mao suit, wearing sun-glasses and sporting an ID badge stands in front of trite tourist attractions such as the Statue of Liberty, Niagara Falls, and The Hollywood Sign. His work compels the viewer ponder the dangers of stereotypical thinking as it relates to East-West relationships, both personal and global. Many of these artists, in confronting the complex and inflammatory issues of race and gender, want their art to open minds. They want their audiences to consider alternative ways of viewing the world and how they relate to that world. (Feinberg 2000, p. 13).

This discussion following the presentation focused on the fact that artists incorporate their perspectives on race and gender in their art to coerce the viewer to come to terms with these issues. According to art historian, Jonathan Feinberg: "using works of art as illustrations of cultural constructs and sociopolitical forces. Critical theory derives from philosophy and theoretical orients sociology. Cultural studies resembles traditional history with an emphasis on broad social forces, such as race and gender, and with an infusion of language from critical theory" (2000, p. 18). The presentation, and ensuing discussion, led students to the realization that they wanted to create a monument—to be exhibited at the Montclair Art Museum. They already knew their subject matter: Race in America.

Students now were fairly familiar with some of the techniques contemporary artists use to communicate personal, cultural, and political messages. They were ready to transfer this under-standing to the selection of their materials. They considered the use of the ordinary artifacts of daily life. They now understood that such objects could be manipulated in order to shed new light on familiar situations, to question what had been taken for granted, to open the minds of *their* audience. Students were better able to observe their surroundings and their attitudes and behaviors from multiple perspectives. Given this broader understanding of their world, it was time to "roll up their sleeves" and create! Students participated in an artist-in-residence program, in which a local architect, Barry Yanku visited our class to show the students how to transform an abstraction—their concept—into a concrete entity—their monument. Based on the readings and discussions in class, the students had chosen an event—the death of Emmett Till in 1955—that they wished to commemorate. Their choice had been guided by their conviction that this tragic event had sparked the civil rights movement. The architect helped the students construct a model, using Federal Express boxes. The students wanted to understand how architectural space can be used convey the emotional impact of a brutal act. After thoughtful discussion, they decided to juxtapose a square with a circle to express oppression (despair) and freedom (hope). The square represented the oppressiveness of racism that confronted Emmett when he visited his relatives in Mississippi. The circle represented the ideals of freedom as embodied by the courageous civil rights workers in the Deep South. Half of the circle had a window that let in light (hope). In contrast, half of the square was windowless and dark (despair). The completed monument, which stood three stories in height and 30 feet in width, was positioned at the main entrance in front of Montclair High School. An entrance permitted students, faculty, and other members of the community to enter this architectural space. Having integrated artistic expression (the arts) with social consciousness (the humanities), the students had deepened and expanded their ability to think critically. They also had harnessed their creative energies tell an important story—one they felt had been overlooked.

Now it was time for the apprentices to take a two-hour guided tour of the Montclair Art Museum in order to apply their knowledge of art history and art criticism to the world at large. Their new lens was a greater appreciation of art. They were able to ask insightful questions, and to understand the answers to their questions. They were able to interact in a meaningful way with their tour guide. As they toured the permanent collection, they were comfortable discussing some of the works and their responses to these works. This was a successful culmination to all that had preceded it; the museum was the logical setting in which students could relate what they had learned in class to the world outside the classroom.

STAGE III: DISPLAYING THE WORK OF ART

Now it was time for apprentices to become masters. They needed to transition from learning about art to creating a work of art, from learning about monuments to building one. Students brainstormed about people and events worthy of commemoration and to the reasons for their choices. Students had to consider the intended function(s) of the monument, the message or messages they wished to convey, the nature of their audience, and the most effective way to communicate their message(s) to that audience. In addition, students had to write a statement that propounded their rationale for the creation of the monument and to describe the artists and artistic movements that had influenced their thinking.

I met with each student individually to discuss how to best display their monument. This one-on-one interaction encouraged each student to further investigate prevailing attitudes towards race and to develop his/her own voice. The assignment served to promote constructive effort to improve race relations. The students had learned to cultivate multiple ways of seeing. They had considered American monuments from the perspectives of race, gender, and class. The subjects of their projects included, to name just a few: a) whether Nat Turner was villain or hero; b) whether the lynching of a white middle-class male can be justified; c) what exactly does it mean to be Puerto Rican; d) what is our society's ideal image of female beauty; and e) recognition of the significance of the actions of several African-American competitors during the 1968 Olympics. It was opening night. Everyone was dressed in his/her Sunday best. Instead of taking an ultimately meaningless multiple-choice test, the students were presenting their findings regarding *Race in America in the Twentieth Century* to more than 150 people. Instead of being confined to assigned seats, students were interacting, in animated fashion, with interested adults, fielding questions, excitedly describing their projects I had metamorphized. No longer teacher, I was, for now, their mentor and coach, and I looked to them to learn what *they* had learned about *Race in America in the Twentieth Century*. As they took an active role in this museum event, my students had moved beyond the linear Cartesian approach to observation and evaluation. They had learned immeasurably from their own lives, from the multiple perspectives of history and of art, and from the community. They had gained an understanding of the interrelationship of human consciousness and culture. And, most important, they had become, at least for this evening, proactive citizens. This is what can happen when both students and teachers are empowered.

CONCLUSION

Crit and Create: *Race in America* examined the use of an interdisciplinary approach to teaching and assessment, as well as guided student interaction with the greater community, to determine whether this method could empower students to achieve a higher order of thinking. A hermeneutic approach to curriculum design made it possible for students to become active participants in the learning process. Students were asked to examine aspects of racism in twentieth century, to study this cultural phenomenon through the eyes of an artist, and create an artwork (in this case, a monument) in response to what they had learned.

The interactions between students, art, history, and the greater community created an enriched learning environment. It provided numerous occasions for students to gain a deeper, broader understanding of the multidimensional world in which we live. It helped them gain a deeper, broader understanding of history and art and how both affect, directly and indirectly, their lives. Students were profoundly enriched by participatory democracy, contributing to the curriculum, applying their newly acquired knowledge and skills to artistic creation, developing their voices and using these voices to communicate with the community.

In response to the age-old question, what is the purpose of education, I would answer thus: a) encourage students to increase their social and cultural awareness; b) require them to apply multiple perspectives to learning; c) design and implement activities that encourage them to think critically; and d) create a nurturing environment that elicits critical questioning and inspires the hunger to always learn more. We must listen closely to our students. We must be genuinely interested in each of them. Their likes and dislikes. Their fears and aspirations. We must learn what interests them and transform their interests into bridges that lead to further investigation and discussion. If we gather beautiful "patches" from each one of our students, we can create a beautiful "quilt" –one that warms all of them, leaving no one out in the cold!

FURTHER READING

Adams, Maurianne Bell, Anne Lee and Griffin, Pat. (Ed). (1997). *Teaching for Diversity and Social Justice*. New York: Routledge.

Berger, John (1977). *Ways of Seeing*. New York: Penguin.

Feinberg, Jonathan (2000). *Art Since 1940 Strategies of Being*. New Jersey: Prentice Hall.

Greene, Maxine (1995). *Releasing the Imagination*. San Francisco: Jossey-Bass Publishers.

Kincheloe, Joe (2001). *Getting Beyond the Facts. Teaching Social Studies/Social Sciences in the Twenty-first Century*. New York: Peter Lang.

Loewen, James (2000). Lies We Tell Ourselves. *World* (Magazine of the Unitarian Universalist Association).

Rose, Karel and Kincheloe, Joe. (2004). *Art, Culture and Education*. New York: Peter Lang.

CHAPTER 96

Upside Down and Backwards: The State of the Soul in Educational Psychology

LEE GABAY

> You need chaos in your soul to give birth to a dancing star.
> —Nietzsche

While we all seem to have an idea about what "soul" is, there are many ways of conceiving of and describing it. As Madison suggests in *The Hermeneutics of Postmodernity*, knowledge is not a passive copying of reality but rather an active construction or constitution of it: each individual creatively interprets reality but there is no absolute truth or reality. Aristotle defined the soul as the active intellect or core essence of a being that was indeed part and not separate from the body. Similar to Aristotle, Buddhism teaches that all things are impermanent and constantly in a state of flux, and thus people are changing entities. Philosopher Anthony Quinton explores the ontological (being in the world) question of who or what a person is by conceiving of the soul as a series of mental states connected by continuity of character and memory that embody the essential constituent of personality. St. Augustine explored an introspective method where perception is intelligence combining with the soul. Alluding to this he wrote, "Noli foras ire, in te redi, in interiore homine habitat veritas" (Deep within man there dwells the truth).

Soul, which is the etymological basis of the word *psychology* (psyche, "soul" or "mind," *ology*, "study of"), and by extension also of educational psychology, appears to be sadly missing from the rigorous domain of study that is its namesake. Psychology asks questions about the life of the mind and its unique perception of the world. As a discipline, educational psychology explores the mind's cognitive processes with the aim of developing an individual's capacities and potential to be successful in a specific society or culture. With its given theoretical positions and important influences on learning and instruction, educational psychology is serving a primary pedagogical function affecting both mental and external behaviors. However, to get a genuine understanding of the functions of teaching and learning that take place within formal school environments, soul is a necessary ingredient, providing a space for intellectual knowledge, reflection, imagination, memory, creation, and mystery. These are the qualities that characterize soul and are completely disregarded by the mechanistic tradition in educational psychology. This essay is a treatise on the importance of reincorporating soul into how we approach education.

Schools are gradually developing clear and rigorous academic standards for what every child should know and be able to do. In an increasingly competitive and industrialized global economy there is a legitimate need for a comprehensive effort in making sure students are given the opportunities to achieve locally, nationally, and worldwide. In developing both reliable and valuable assessments of individual growth, educational psychology needs to encompass and include a soulful critical epistemology that thoughtfully embraces issues of race, class, and gender. It is not an easy task to critique the paradigm of knowledge production within this culture while maintaining legitimacy and allow opportunities for many conceptual frameworks and relevance in curriculum. Educational psychology often defaults into unreflective crass positivism with its theoretical and epistemological assumptions that disregard specific lived experiences with significant cultural pluralism and empirical justice needed to build a world community. Unfortunately, there are central social questions that educational psychology entirely ignores. Do we want our students to be leaders or to be led? Are we building a nation of audience members or are we enculturating actors and activists? It is important as teachers, researchers, and educational psychologists to delve more thoroughly into critiquing our social and political circumstances. The role of educators is to look critically into forms of subjugation and oppression and include an ideological framework that is both multilogical and rigorous to see how these approaches are manifested in the classroom.

In examining educational psychology's curriculum programs and teaching metholodogies, I am reminded of Hegel and his ideas against absolutes and his notions that the self is constructed through the interaction with others. As Hegel asserts, given the ever-changing nature of knowledge, it cannot be reproduced. By looking at cultural histories, practices, and meanings, poststructuralist critiques of epistemology focus on the characteristics and understanding the essence of knowledge. A positivistic epistemological stance is deeply connected to simplistic notions of totality with its concept of "universal truth" and assumption that there are fundamental characteristics and values which all humans and societies share. The positivistic approach to knowledge is the story of forms of domination, fear tactics, intellectual limitation, and Western patriarchy. Western society and educational psychology are based around the precepts of rationalism, reliability, and familiarity—all apparently crucial to notions of totality. Lost are the intrinsic elements of motivation, cultural difference, and individualism.

The yearning for concrete, verifiable knowledge in traditional epistemology, at the expense of that which is more instinctive or free flowing, seems an all too common pitfall. What is possible is narrowly defined and what is impossible is broadly stated. As a result, development of the creative spirit and innovative ideas, which should be the lifeblood of educational psychology, is eliminated. The quest for soul is blocked as a result. These beliefs speak volumes about our culture and the limited values we hold. It is indeed a tall order to work against the tendencies of this country. Epistemology seems to intimidate because it disrupts reality and a comfortable sense of the truth. To advance from our current narrow worldview we need to go to places of discomfort. Educational psychology in particular and its entrapped soulful essence cries to take advantage of new mediums, open up older ones, and continually dismantle realities. As teachers and students, we must all be rebels—indeed there is nothing conformist about the journey to know the soul and the self. Unfortunately, many teachers feel helpless, powerless, and are often complicit with directives spawned by traditional mechanist educational psychology because the problems are so great.

Jimi Hendrix is widely considered to be the most important and influential electric guitarist in the history of popular music. Jimi Hendrix played the guitar backwards and upside down. As a self-taught lefty he held the instrument that would soon redefine for a generation what guitar playing could be. In stark contrast to what can be a traditional positivistic approach to how to play the guitar when one is left-handed, his style emerged from his having improvised a manner of playing that best fit his physical needs and musical intuition. His ambition to nurture his gift, free from constraints of the imposed dominant society, enabled a musical revolution. If Hendrix were a current music student, I doubt the cognitive perspectives that characterize educational psychology that ignore the numerous ways students spontaneously think, feel, act, and learn would enable him get away with literally turning the genre around. His unique way of expressing his genius would somehow been trampled with the needs of standards-driven testing procedures and strict methodology that would have prevented him from expressing his soul.

With Hendrix in mind, and the implications for pedagogy, educational psychology needs a healthy session of self-reflection. It seems frightening that so many of us need to relinquish our cultural and ethnic identities to gain success in academic endeavors. There are more victims than beneficiaries when linear forms of carefully tailored, unthreatening knowledge that fails to approach issues from many angles is provided. Educational psychology has developed a "formula" for learning, and the more this formula is used as the only "valid" means of teaching and learning, the more it becomes a form of intellectual redundancy. Schools, curricula, and pedagogical practices have to encourage the inclusion of new languages by welcoming different grammars and creating new music (so to speak) for souls forgotten or silenced by educational discipline and potentially by society at large. Does this mean that educators should encourage children to turn their musical instruments upside-down? Not necessarily. But should it exclude the possibility that a beautiful sound could emerge from an instrument held in an uncommon position? Absolutely not. Educational psychology appears to have misplaced a diverse and nuanced generation in a complex and often confusing society. There are egregious blind spots in our curricula. To begin to remedy the intellectual redundancy (the "anti-Hendrixness") of our current educational system, we must rebel: Our goal should be to create imaginative alternative strategies that allow us as teachers and students to embark on the journey to uncover and come to know our soul.

In *Pedagogy and the Politics*, Henry Giroux asserts that we must question the kind of society in which we want to live and what kind of teachers and pedagogy can be informed and legitimated by a view of authority that takes democracy and citizenship seriously. In reframing these questions, we should search ourselves to discover what we want and how we want to get it. Giroux refers to teachers as "transformative intellectuals" and schools as "development spheres." Thus, thinking, doing, producing, and implementing gives teaching the dialectical meaning that such a vision requires, or in the Jimi Hendrix sense, turning the educational psychology genre upside-down and backwards. To become a transformative intellectual, a phenomenological hermeneutic universal of soul is required. Soul seems to resonate, weaving itself through postformal educational psychological questions suggested by Kincheloe in *The Post-Formal Reader* of how we should deal with the meaninglessness and sociopsychological pathology that affects all of us individually and institutionally with the intention of developing a more holistic psyche expression and production or transmission of knowledge.

Soul is part spirit, desires, and self-esteem. Soul has rage, passion, grace, elegance, sensuality, sexuality, anger, longing, loneliness, confusion, transcendence, and spirituality. G.B. Madison elegantly broaches this subject in *The Hermeneutics of Postmodernity* by stating that there does indeed exist a "soul" and a "body," but the body is a human body only by being the very foundation of the soul, the visible expression of a "spiritual" life.

Soul allows us to approach problems in a new way by adding an element of creativity. Creativity is transformative knowledge through its quality of seeing things in a new way, or updating an older concept, and perceiving connections between the unconnected. Its vision could be dynamic, stimulating, chaotic, or even wrong, but at least it brings new life energy and takes risks by expanding individuals' and communities' worldviews. A unique aspect of creativity is that it is an all-inclusive domain—rich or poor, healthy or sick, creativity is an infinite commodity where all can take as much as one wants to ultimately produce or enact new epistemological paradigms. It is not enough, however, to create a culture that encourages creative thinking. Educational psychology also must develop mechanisms that channel creative energy and give our students a sense that their ideas are being listened to by both encouraging and rewarding this type of thinking. Pedagogy needs to put in place a system that can evaluate, act on, build upon if necessary, challenge, and handle even the wildest creative ideas.

A natural by-product of spiritually and soul is celebration. Most religious denominations include music and dance and celebration in their own dogmas. They take the mysteries of life and celebrate the journey with much fanfare. Likewise, transformative knowledge is a celebration: it has the potential to create universes through its joyous reconnection to the soul and spirit by facilitating the restoration of unity and an element of respect.

The restoration of soul to pedagogy will require more than just a change in the outlook toward creativity and celebration. Irrelevant curricula make good teachers bad; for teacher as well as student, agency is essential. Both need to engage in determining what is worth learning—not merely to survive or nurture dependence on the existing system—but to become independent of it. Offering a curriculum that is focused upon breaking the built-in structural antagonisms, thus changing the hegemonic dynamic while maintaining legitimacy, is something that Joe Kincheloe and Ladislaus Semali richly explore in *What Is Indigenous Knowledge?* The pursuit of multilogical perspectives that these authors describe is particularly useful for discovering one's soul. I have drawn upon multilogical perspectives not only to inform my own teaching and learning, but also to consider myself from the dimensions of critical complexity, agency, poststructuralism, essentialism, phenomenology, ideology, positivism, and constructivism. Ultimately, in relying upon frameworks designed to rigorously question and reexamine all of my assumptions, I have come into much closer contact with my soul.

> For what profit is it to a man if he gains the whole world, and loses his own soul? (Matthew 16:26).

Education and schooling are distinct and all too often not interchangeable. Education begins at birth and continues throughout life. Educational psychology, a subdiscipline of psychology dedicated to the positivistic study of cognitive processes and behavior, provides the foundation for the formal learning environment of schools. The primary purpose of schooling is to assist the individual to better develop his or her full potential as well as the knowledge and skills to interact with the environment in a successful manner. Teaching is not *giving* knowledge or skills to students; teaching is the process of *providing opportunities* to produce their own knowledges. Certainly schools need to discover/allow for new ways to learn. There's nothing more radical, there's nothing more revolutionary than learning what one wants to, and not what one ought to. Cognitive theories can never accurately describe how intelligence is expressed. Each situation is specific and idiosyncratic. The search for the soul has the potential of liberating teachers and students into a new paradigm to seek new literacies and personal ones at that. *In Pedagogy and the Politics of Hope*, Giroux explores the valuable link between what a student learns in the classroom and the environment in which she functions outside of school, stating that teachers need to understand how experiences produced in the various domains and layers of everyday life give rise to the different "voices" students use to give meaning to their own worlds. Whether it is hip-hop, free verse, slam, or any other yet-unlabelled form of verbal self-expression, the new poetries will continue to come and old ones will be reinvigorated. These languages must reflect the social and cultural life in the classroom. In this structure for postmodern learning, students need to be asked how they interpret the world and be encouraged to use their power in both school and society. Similar to batteries and milk, ideas get outdated; likewise, curricula need to have freshness dates inscribed or, like The Constitution, provide a built-in clause for revision or openness for interpretation. New curricula are like a mouthwash for the soul: they may provide minty freshness to the way people feel about the world.

In reconsidering the kinds of curricula we implement in our instruction, we need always to return to the question of whose interest is served, and how we can actively engage all of our students' talents, imagination, and skills into the learning process. What matters to the students should be a starting point for our discussion, and one that needs to take place with the students present. The idea of a national mandate to teach "appreciation" of specific subjugated groups (African Americans, women, Latinos, etc.) in a particular month irrespective of whatever else may be going on in the world or in the lived experience of students holds all the elements for utter lack of student interest and, worse, mockery. Positivist curricula simplify serious issues, producing chewable pills that force-feed subject matter to students. In the end, these efforts are undermined by designating which days to think about these topics. Districts have scheduled ceremonies to promote ideas that teachers and students may or may not find relevant or interesting or in any sense worthwhile. Therefore, again, the question of whose interest the curriculum serves arises. Yet if we teachers fail to teach the proscribed curricula according to mandate we are considered politically incorrect, un-American, lazy, or just plain wrong. As such, fear is what motivates so many into contrition. It is mostly "shoulds" and fright that sustain such arcane notions of pedagogy. Picture someone standing in front of a room, reading about a bunch of people whom they should know about. E.D. Hirsch and his cultural literacy crew would be the only ones applauding. In many cases history should be on walls, monuments, and in pictures, not in mandated instruction. Where is the soul in that?

Bob Dylan stated that the most powerful person in most situations is the one standing in front of an audience with nothing more than a guitar and a microphone because we necessarily get to hear the voice and the speaker. Not what they should be, but rather what they are—not playing a persona but actually living the material. A man standing behind a pulpit can start wars, bring peace, instill love, and make us think. Emotion, challenges, and thought should be welcome in student assemblies otherwise I would suggest calling Assembly Time "Group Regurgitative Teaching and Learning that Amounts to Nothing Save for Walking Book Reports."

In *Researching Lived Experience*, Van Manen acknowledges that people change and his understanding of human science rejects notions of positivism. Lived experiences connect us to the lived world. A transformative intellectual makes it real for them as hermeneutics is a dialectical and phenomenology is always autobiographical by necessity because we are socially infinite. By choosing our lenses and placing our emphasis this leads us to things that matter to us or, in other words, to the things of the soul.

Educational psychology should allow for critical faculties to divide differences into different learning categories and sort through the contradictions or our mandates. All too often I see a teacher annoyed by the distance from his students, matched only by a thirst for political instruction that allow students to see the world their way. Souls need to be emancipated, in students' work and their classes: as a teacher I need to listen to the singing of different but unified songs from my students.

The ability to liberate teachers and students into new paradigms is my working framework of the new and improved educational psychology. The unique lenses that learners bring from experience that informs their epistemology is rich and full and needs to shine in all pedagogical structures. The ability to ask questions, challenge, explore, and discuss ideas is essential to any educational pursuit. Education is not just information, it is critical thinking, and it is soul.

Soul is a person's a gift, and for numerous reasons we don't give it away too often because people might not place upon it the right value or, in many educational settings, value it at all. I know many students whose genius needs to be exposed but are reluctant to give themselves (souls) away, justifiably fearing that if they are too open there's a cost to their personal life and a cost to the class as well.

The methodology of critical complexity is crucial in the study of educational psychology. John Dewey challenged us a century ago to engage the individual in pursuing education for democracy and democracy in education. Dewey and many others who followed were more interested in the spiritual conflict that preceded them and the mental conflict that followed. Soul invites this journey into a space of fever, where knowledge is exposed and revealed. Soul furthers directions that investigate what it means to feel and move. The learning/creative process is unpredictable, and noisy and unsure of where it is going. This is revolt. A soul can change everything—socioeducationally and politically. Within each individual, you have a universe— voice and body—that yearns to demonstrate what it is capable of experiencing and accomplishing. Schools need to adopt a humble educational psychology that falls to earth a bit and restores divinity back to our students. Each classroom needs to showcase these voices whose ways of knowing don't necessarily translate into the conceptual apparatus. Amplifying them bigger than the buildings themselves, where real tears are cried, individuals' rhythm and music sing out their hearts, turning classroom into opera. If we allow this to happen, pragmatism will no longer be immune, nor could it resist new possibilities.

Pedagogy needs to embrace what is relevant. We've got to make great ideas that challenge, and thrive on the exhilaration of these challenges. As we change shape, so does the world. Once something is experienced it is difficult to return to a prior state. Thus, soul is a very strange. It can make you happy, and it can make you sad. It's a weird wave to ride. Situated in the middle of that wave, with not much light at the end of the tunnel, is frightening uncharted waters, which don't necessarily portend rough seas. What panics me is educational psychology's obsession with positivistism, with caricature—the left, the right, the progressives, the reactionary. Taking people on rumor. To further the aims and philosophy of pedagogy, the industry needs to find the light in our students, because that will help our cause of breaking down the differences between having what you want and doing what you want. As educators we need to provide the most precious thing to our students, and that is called hope.

These are complex problems and demand complex solutions. Educational psychology too often amounts to total appeasement: you can't satisfy every uncertainty, so it adds up to being steamrolled by positivism. Every problem cannot be solved at the negotiating table. At any rate I think that bringing back the emancipatory element of soul to educational psychology is an idea that is a simple situation of right or wrong

We seem to be very afraid of what we don't understand. When we can't understand something we turn to our assumptions. This is usually when we begin to reduce and simplify complex ideas, situations, and people. For instance, it is easier to say a student is "bad." It is more daunting when they are complex and individuals, not easily defined. I have a student, Kiana, who is a fourteen-year-old misanthrope. She is moody, nasty, a poor speller, and hated by the entire staff. Her mouth can be just that lethal. She is also very charming and a great dancer. Truth be told, it would be almost easier to have no hope for Kiana than to deal with her heartbreaks and infrequent successes. It takes endurance and maybe some courage to deal with her uncertainties. I can't say that I enjoy working with her nor that I really understand her, but I do know that she is more than just "bad."

There are events that have happened in this amazingly complex world that sometimes are mean and we crave reasons and answers when bad things happen to good people. If something gives us comfort, then it is good. We all deserve it. We want to believe in something that is not so bad. I certainly am not immune to the temptation of positivism. I am sure that there is an element of reductionism in my way of thinking, particularly when I think about the misfortunes that I've seen and experienced. It is clear that some things are difficult to grasp and the desire for answers is powerful. Many of us as individuals turn to religion or spirituality to find solace. However, as a culture we seem to instinctively draw on a monolithic epistemology.

Correlation is not causation; thus as a field of study educational psychology's epistemology must not be positivist in its approach as ideas cannot be reduced or decontextualized to controlled variables. The standards and testing that are common in today's educational practices wants cognitive development to run quick, cheap, and efficient, but these things have no business in my version of knowledge production, as the ramifications can be dangerous.

We must therefore embrace the whole of society. Many thinkers and writers are disavowing spiritually diverse aspects of learning. The self-justifying dogmatic epistemologies currently in use neglect the others modes of thinking and learning, and we cannot lose sight of the human factor. These positivistic powers seem to be allergic to abstraction. They want to tell instead of being shown, they want to dramatize rather than debate, and their arguments are constructed as absolutes.

Poststructuralism allows us to begin to address complex questions. Using the tools that post-structuralism provides has the potential for granting access to the soul. A poststructuralist acts to both comfort the afflicted and, more important, afflict the comfortable, thereby looking through a framework that is smart, stimulating, and fair in terms of power and justice. Kincheloe supports this assertion in *Critical Pedagogy* when he writes that poststructuralism rejects any form of universal conceptions of the world. In regard to pedagogy, this includes linguistic values and high forms of smartness. A poststructuralist's job is to bring in new tools and work to avoid bourgeois, ethnocentric, and misogynist practices.

The purpose of a poststructuralist discourse is for teachers, researchers, students, and citizens of the globe to generate discussion of critical issues that have been ignored, destroyed, or silenced. This must be done with rigorous methods and accountability and include many interpretations of what knowledge is. Looking at and trying to understand the forces that shape and often limits one's control is the very root of critical theory.

Perhaps the most useful poststructural approach is phenomenology. Phenomenologists realize that a person is always interpreting through his own personal lens. What makes phenomenology unique is that every instance has the potential to be phenomenological; it depends upon your awareness and perspective of this aspect of human lived experience. The contextual experience or "lived situated" is the quintessence of what it means to be human and to conduct research on human beings. One cannot look at phenomenology without context. It is therefore always autobiographical as well as by necessity a reflection of things. As Van Manen has stated in *Researching Lived Experience*, phenomenological research consist of reflectively bringing into nearness that which tend to be obscure, that which tend to evade the intelligibility of our natural attitude of everyday life.

The value of phenomenology lies in getting us to reflect upon our experiences in the richness of experience at the micro, meso, and macro level. Although Van Manen does ignore the issue of power in his take as there is no sociohistorical macro-analysis of forces that contribute to human suffering. The nature of true pedagogy is reflective. The use of phenomenology in pedagogy is certainly reflective in revealing our own locations in the web of reality.

The enactivist approach is also a useful tool in our search for the soul. From an enactivist standpoint, there is no way to prepare for or plan any human interaction. The moment-to-moment interpretation, in which we improvise our response to one another, offers the potential to define our own genius or limitations.

The description of the above approaches is not to suggest that these are the only approaches to reclaiming soul in our teaching, learning, and living. Alternative epistemological approaches do, however, provide a more respectful and inclusive means of thinking about the kinds of curricula we hope to teach that will help our students reengage spiritually with learning.

> The future is unwritten (The Clash).

As educators we must ask ourselves what it is that we want to be remembered for. Do we hope to just identify and articulate the problems of the world (alone, a worthy task) or will we aid in fixing them? Can we take extreme actions and drastic measures to challenge things and become emissaries of pedagogy? How far will we go? In the end, where is the soul? Where did it go? Why should we care? Should we care at all?

These are good questions. Unfortunately I don't have the answers. In *The Hermeneutics of Postmodernity*, Madison states that it is the transintentional element in a work that makes it a classic, a living classic, that is, a work which is capable of having a life of its own. Therefore the concept of imagination is a way of understanding how the world is constructed. It also holds within it a certain promise for the future. To achieve this it would help to have great hope for yourself, family, friends, and the world. Hope and creativity are the embodiment of promise. This is the ingredient for imagination. The quest for educational psychology is to awaken the spiritual in our hearts, desires, and feelings. Ideas sometimes happen by accident, but they don't survive by accident. It takes will, intent, a sense of shared purpose and a tolerance for differences and even fallibility, both others' and our own. This helps to even and perhaps beat the odds by continuing to do transcendent work and remain relevant, energetic, and powerful.

The United States is a cultural canyon of red and blue unwilling or unable to bridge the whiteness that created the divide. We have always been a nation of interdependent and interconnected social challenges. Time and space are always changing and knowledge is more than just space and time; it is boundless, endless, and infinite. People participate in creating the universe and therefore should not be told what to think.

What is true for you is not necessarily correct for me. However it is our responsibility to know ourselves, as we are each living expressions of truth. It is my hope that we are all longing for respect and hunger for beauty. It is also necessary to have the courage to get dirty and embrace this mess, as it is equally vital to live in spaces of danger and risk. Self-doubt makes us fragile and real. This discomfort can help us get where we need to go.

People are as transformative as we are mercurial. Surely there is always an element of reductionism in any research or way of thinking, so as an educator I am mindful to be humble and self-critical in relationship to both my living and working world. I must also tell myself daily that I cannot underestimate the strongest forces of the universe: the voice and soul.

FURTHER READING

Giroux, H. (1997). *Pedagogy and the Politics of Hope*. Boulder: Westview Press.

Kincheloe, J. L. (1999). *The Post-Formal Reader: Cognition and Education*, eds. S. Steinberg, J. Kincheloe, and P. Hinchey (pp. 4–54). New York: Falmer Press.

———. (2001). *Getting Beyond the Facts*. New York: Peter Lang.

———. (2004). *Critical Pedagogy Primer*. New York: Peter Lang.

———. (2005). *Critical Constructivism Primer*. New York: Peter Lang.

Madison, G. B. (1988). *The Hermeneutics of Postmodernity: Figures and Themes*. Bloomington: Indiana University Press.

Semali, L., and Kincheloe, J. (Eds.). (1999). *What Is Indigenous Knowledge?* New York: Falmer Press.

Quinton, A. "The Soul," in Personal Identity. *Journal of Philosophy*, 59 (15), 393–409.

Van Manen, M. (1990). *Researching Lived Experience*. Albany: SUNY Press.

CHAPTER 97

Critical Constructivism and Postformalism: New Ways of Thinking and Being

JOE L. KINCHELOE

For many years I have been concerned in my work with the intersection of the social and the cognitive. As I lay out in the introduction to this encyclopedia, at this intersection rests the origins of *postformalism* and a critical cognitive theory. The understanding of constructivism and critical constructivism helps us make sense of the educational/psychological world that surrounds us. In the twenty-first century the idea that teachers need to understand the complexity of the educational world is almost a radical proposition in and of itself—many educational reformers see no need for teachers to be rigorous scholars. Indeed, the No Child Left Behind reforms demand disempowered, low–cognitive-functioning teachers who do what they're told and often read predesigned scripts to their students. Ray Horn and I assert in *Educational Psychology: An Encyclopedia* that such actions are insulting to the teaching profession and are designed ultimately to destroy the concept of public education itself. The study of constructivism and critical constructivism induces us to ask important questions. What is the purpose of schools? How do we organize them for maximum learning and higher orders of cognitive activity? What is the curriculum and how do we conceptualize it? How do we understand the relationship connecting mind, school, and society?

THE IMPORTANCE OF THEORY IN CRITICAL CONSTRUCTIVISM: GROUNDING A TRANSGRESSIVE EDUCATIONAL PSYCHOLOGY

Such psychological and pedagogical questions cannot be answered thoughtfully without the help of diverse theoretical knowledges. Please note that theory is defined here not as that which indicates the proper way to teach or to learn but as a body of understandings that help us make sense of education and cognition, their social and political implications, and how we as educators fit into this complex mix. In the social theoretical domain, for example, we might ask how the existence of socioeconomic inequality along the lines of race, class, gender, sexuality, religion, and language influence our answers to these questions of educational psychology. What happens to our answers when we bring an understanding of power to our analytical table? What is the effect of social theoretical insight on the subjectivity and context dependency of knowledge production? Might, for example, the knowledge emerging here help shape the way we answer questions about the curriculum? In this context we begin to understand the forces that construct knowledge and mind. This is central to understanding constructivism and critical constructivism and their relationship to a transgressive educational psychology.

Thus, the insights of critical constructivism change the way we approach cognitive and educational activities. In transmission-based conceptions of teaching there is no reason to study the learner. Teachers in such pedagogies are given the curriculum to teach. They simply pass designated knowledge along to students and then test them to see how much of it they remember. In a critical constructivist school the identities and cognitive dimensions of students matter. Children and young people enter the schoolhouse with extant worldviews, constructed by their experiences and the social contexts in which they have lived. These perspectives actively shape school experiences, thinking, and learning. Indeed, they help shape all the interpretations students make about the world around them. If teachers are serious about teaching such students, critical constructivists contend, they must gain a sense of these prior perspectives and how they shape students' relationship to schooling.

Any learning must be integrated with these prior perspectives. It is a naïve view of knowledge and cognition that believes that transmitted knowledge deposited in the mind can be later taken out unchanged and uninterpreted. Such knowledges merge in complicated ways to shape idiosyncratic perspectives. Students, like all human beings, see the world from the perspective of previous experiences and knowledges. Critical constructivists study these knowledges, these interactions, and their effects. One of the reasons that I wrote *Teachers as Researchers: Qualitative Paths to Empowerment* was because of the need of teachers to come up with systematic ways to study and understand the construction of their students' consciousness and its effect on their life in schools. Without such knowledge, teachers can easily retreat into a transmission model of pedagogy and a filing-cabinet view of the mind.

Critical constructivists argue that traditional forms of reason and theory-as-validated-truth often contribute little to answering the most basic questions of pedagogy and cognition. How does scientific explanation help us answer the question, what is the purpose of schools? Social theory viewed in relation to pedagogical and cognitive theories in this context profoundly enhances the ability of educators to evaluate the worth of particular educational purposes, articulations of curriculum, beliefs about sophisticated thinking, and evaluation practices. These theoretical modes help teachers and students escape the well-regulated administered world that unbridled rationalism and scientism work to construct. Critical constructivists use these theoretical tools to sidestep new models of social control that put a chokehold on individual and social freedom, in the process decimating teacher professionalism. Concurrently, they use such tools to evade the stifling effects of mechanistic models of the mind.

Whether we know it or not, all of us are theorists in that we develop and hold on to particular views of how things work. Such views insidiously shape our action as lovers, parents, citizens, students, and teachers. Critical constructivists understand this reality and argue that the social, cognitive, educational theories we hold must be consciously addressed. Such conscious awareness allows us to reflect on our theories, explore their origins in our lives, change them when needed, and consider how they may have unconsciously shaped our teaching, thinking, and our actions in the world in general. Thus, we come to better understand—as great educators always should— the ways the world operates and how that operation shapes education, definitions of intelligence, educational policy, the curriculum, the lives of teachers and students, and who succeeds and who doesn't in schooling. Critical constructivists are painfully aware that many forces in the twenty-first century are at work to remove such insights from the realm of teaching. Such understandings are more important than ever in the bizarre dominant-power–driven educational cosmos of the twenty-first century.

While constructivism and critical constructivism are theories of learning, I see them as this and much more. Constructivism/critical constructivism involves theoretical work in education, epistemology, cognition, and *ontology*. In my delineation of a critical constructivist postformalism I argue for a unified theory where all of these dimensions fit together and are synergistic in their interrelationship. For example, it is hard to pursue a critical constructivist pedagogy without the grounding of critical constructivist epistemological and postformalist cognitive theories. In this unified context, critical constructivism becomes a Weltanschauung, a worldview that creates meaning on the nature of human existence. In this way critical constructivism comes to exert more influence in more domains than it has at this juncture.

CRITICAL CONSTRUCTIVISM AS EPISTEMOLOGY: PHILOSOPHICALLY GROUNDING A TRANSGRESSIVE EDUCATIONAL PSYCHOLOGY

Modernist philosophy has been trapped in an epistemology that locates truth in external reality. Thinking and cognition in this context has often become little more than an effort to accurately reflect this reality. Indeed, Cartesian–Newtonian–Baconian thought is seen as simply an inner process conducted in the minds of autonomous individuals. The thoughts, moods, and sensations of these individuals are separate from their histories and social contexts. If thinking is to be seen as a mirroring of external events, the need for a theory of critical constructivism and an understanding of the shaping of consciousness is irrelevant. In this epistemological framework the ability to conceptualize has little to do with culture, power, or discourse or the tacit understandings unconsciously shaped by them. From the Cartesian perspective, the curriculum becomes merely a body of knowledge to be transferred to the minds of students. More critical observers may contend that this is a naïve view, but the naivete is recognizable only if knowledge formation is understood as a complex and ambiguous social activity. Mind in the critical constructivist/postformalist framework is more than a repository of signifieds, a mirror of nature. A critical constructivist epistemology assumes that the mind creates rather than reflects, and the nature of this creation cannot be separated from the surrounding social world.

Knowledge emerges neither from subjects nor from objects but from a dialectical relationship between the knower (subject) and the known (object). Drawing from Piaget, this dialectical relationship is represented by the assimilation–accommodation dyad. Employing the conceptualizations, critical constructivist teachers conceive knowledge as culturally produced and recognize the need to construct their own criteria for evaluating its quality. This constructivist sense-making process is a means by which teachers can explain and introduce students to the social and physical world and help them build for themselves an epistemological infrastructure for interpreting the phenomena they confront in the world. Critical constructivists realize that because of the social construction of knowledge, their interpretations and infrastructures are a part of the cosmos but they are not in the cosmos. As a result, when the recognition of the need arises we can always modify our viewpoints.

Thus, the Cartesian–Newtonian–Baconian conception of truth and certainty is rejected by the epistemology of critical constructivism. We can never provide a final construction of the world in a true sense, apart from ourselves and our lives. As living parts of the world we are trying to figure out, and we can only approach it from the existing cognitive infrastructures that shape our consciousness. Limited in this way, we can see only what our mind allows. With this restriction we are free to construct the world any way we desire. This is not to say, however, that the outcomes of our construction will not be confused and they could even be destructive. We may, for example, adopt a worldview such as the medieval Europeans'. In this view of the world, sanitation was irrelevant and thousands of individuals died as a result of the Black Plague. Obviously, this was not an adequate construction of the nature of the world. This recognition confronts us with calls to develop a way of determining valid constructions of reality.

All that critical constructivists can do in response to such a need is to lay out some guiding principles for judging which constructions are more adequate and which less adequate. The constructions

- are consistent with a critical ethics of difference—a theoretical orientation that accounts for cultural difference, the complexity of everyday life, and the demands of a rigorous democratic education. Grounded on a detailed awareness of a bricolage of indigenous knowledges, African American epistemologies, subjugated knowledges, the moral insights of liberation theology, our critical ethics of difference seeks more complex approaches to understanding the relationship between self and world. How do students and teachers come to construct their views of reality, critical constructivists ask in this ethical context. Guided by the critical ethics of difference, educators come to understand the social construction of world and self. In this context they focus on the forces that shape individual perspectives. Why are some constructions of reality and moral action embraced and officially legitimated by the dominant culture while others are repressed? Asking such questions and aided by a rigorous understanding of knowledge production, critical educators grasp how schools often identify, sometimes unconsciously, conceptions of what it means to be educated in the terms of upper-middle-class white culture. Expressions of working-class or nonwhite culture may be viewed as uneducated and ethically inferior. Drawing upon a variety of discourses, critical constructivists separate conventionality from just, democratic, egalitarian ethical behavior.

- resonate with emancipatory goals—those who seek emancipation attempt to gain the power to control their own lives in solidarity with a justice-oriented community. Here critical constructivists attempts to expose the forces that prevent individuals and groups from shaping the decisions that crucially affect their lives. In this way greater degrees of autonomy and human agency can be achieved. In the first decade of the twenty-first century we are cautious in our use of the term *emancipation* because, as many critics have pointed out, no one is ever completely emancipated from the sociopolitical context that has produced him or her. Concurrently, many have used the term *emancipation* to signal the freedom an abstract individual gains by gaining access to Western reason—that is, becoming reasonable. The critical constructivist use of emancipation in an evolving criticality rejects any use of the term in this context. In addition, many have rightly questioned the arrogance that may accompany efforts to emancipate "others." These are important caveats and must be carefully taken into account by critical educational psychologists. Thus, as critical constructivists who search for those forces that insidiously shape who we are, we respect those who reach different conclusions in their personal journeys. Nonetheless, critical theorists consider the effort to understand dominant power and its effects on individuals to be vitally important information needed in the effort to construct a vibrant and democratic society and to reconceptualize the field of educational psychology.

- are intellectually rigorous and internally consistent—does the construction in question provide a richer insight into the phenomenon than did other constructions? Is the construction thorough in answering all the inquiries it raises about the phenomenon? Is it sensitive to the complexity in which all phenomena are embedded? Does it expand our consciousness in relation to the phenomenon? If the individual constructing a body of knowledge can answer these questions in the affirmative, she or he is on the way to a rigorous and consistent construction.

- avoid reductionism—the rationalistic and reductionistic quest for order refuses in its arrogance to listen to the cacophony of lived experience, the coexistence of diverse meanings and interpretations. The concept of understanding in the complex world viewed by critical constructivists is unpredictable. Much to the consternation of mechanistic educational psychologists there exists no final, transhistorical, nonideological meaning that psychologists strive to achieve. As such critical interpretist, postformal educational psychologists create rather than find meaning in enacted reality, they explore alternate meanings offered by others in similar circumstances. If this wasn't enough, they work to account for historical and social contingencies that always operate to undermine the universal pronouncement of the meaning of a particular phenomenon. When researchers fail to discern the unique ways that historical and social context make for special circumstances, they often provide a reductionistic form of knowledge that impoverishes our understanding of everything connected to it. The monological mechanistic quest for order is grounded on the Cartesian belief that all phenomena should be broken down into their constituent parts to facilitate inquiry. The analysis of the world in this context becomes fragmented and disconnected. Everything is studied separately for the purposes of rigor. The goal of integrating knowledges from diverse domains and understanding the interconnections shaping, for example, the biological and the cognitive is irrelevant in the paradigm of order and fragmentation. The meaning that comes from interrelationship is lost and questions concerning the purpose of research and its insight into the human condition are put aside in an orgy of correlation and triangulated description. Information is sterilized and insight into what may be worth exploring is abandoned. Ways of making use of particular knowledge are viewed as irrelevant and creative engagement with conceptual insights is characterized as frivolous. Empirical knowledge in the quest for order is an end in itself. Once it has been validated it needs no further investigation or interpretation. While empirical research is obviously necessary, its process of production constitutes only one step of a larger and more rigorous process of inquiry. Critical constructivism subverts the finality of the empirical act of knowledge production in its support of a transgressive educational psychology.

POWER SURGE: SELF, COGNITION, AND TEACHING

The Cartesian–Newtonian–Baconian view of self cannot stand up to the epistemological assault of critical constructivism and postformalism. Taking the concept of the inseparability of the knower and the known one step further, postformal educational psychology examines the socially constructed dimensions of language and discursive practices. French social theorist Michel Foucault observed that discourse referred to a body of relations and structures ground in power dynamics that covertly shape our perspectives and insidiously mold our constructions. Russian theorist Mikhail Bakhtin complemented Foucault's observations, maintaining that power functions in a way that solidifies discourses, in the process erasing the presence of unorthodox or marginal voices. After Foucault and Bakhtin the notion of the autonomous self free from the "contamination" of the social is dead; as language-using organisms we cannot escape the effect of the influence of discursive practices and the power that accompanies it.

In this context, postformalists engage in the excitement of attaining new levels of consciousness and "ways of being." In a critical constructivist context, individuals who gain such an awareness understand how and why their political opinions, religious beliefs, gender role, racial positions, or sexual orientation have been shaped by dominant perspectives. What I have called a critical ontological vision helps us in the effort to gain new understandings and insights into who we can become. Such a vision helps us move beyond our present state of being—our ontological selves—as we discern the forces that have made us that way. The line between knowledge production and being is blurred, as the epistemological and the ontological converge around questions of identity. As postformalists employ the ontological vision we ask questions about ethics, morality, politics, emotion, and gut feelings, seeking not precise steps to reshape our subjectivity but a framework of principles with which we can negotiate. Thus, we join the quest for new, expanded, more just, and interconnected ways of being human—a central feature of the quest of postformalism to become more than we presently are.

A key dimension of a critical ontology involves freeing ourselves from the machine metaphors of Cartesianism—from mechanistic psychology. Such an ontological stance recognizes the reductionism of viewing the universe as a well-oiled machine and the human mind as a computer. Such ways of being subvert an appreciation of the amazing life force that inhabits both the universe and human beings. This machine cosmology has positioned human beings as living in a dead world, a lifeless universe. Ontologically, this Cartesianism has separated individuals from their inanimate surroundings, undermining any organic interconnection of the person to the cosmos. The life-giving complexity of the inseparability of humans and the world has been lost and psychological studies of people abstracted—removed from context. Such a removal has exerted disastrous ontological effects. Human beings, in a sense, lost their belongingness to both the world and to other people around them.

Armed with such ontological understandings and grounded epistemologically on critical constructivism, postformal teachers direct student attention to the study of discursive and other power formations in the classroom. They are empowered to point out specific examples of power-shaping discursive formats and the ways that power subsequently works to shape consciousness. For example, consider a postformal history teacher who exposes students to the patriarchal construction of American history textbooks and school district curriculum guides. The teacher uncovers an approach to teaching American history that revolves around the principles of expansionism, conquest, and progress. The westward movement of America is a central organizing theme that serves to focus the gaze of the student on the "impediments to civilization," for example, Natives, "unusable" land, other nations such as Mexico and England, etc. In this context student consciousness is constructed to ignore the ethical dimensions of empire building, to identify those different from us as the "other," as inferior enemies. A nationalistic consciousness is constructed that not only exonerates the sins of the past but also tends to ignore national transgressions of the present.

Another term for the Cartesian mode of analytical reasoning is *reductionism*. This method has formed the basis for Piagetian formalism and the forms of analysis that have dominated education. Cartesian reductionism asserts that all aspects of complex phenomena can best be appreciated by reducing them to their constituent parts and then piecing these elements together according to causal laws. This reductionism coincided with Rene Descartes' separation of the mind and matter/body. Known as the Cartesian dualism, human experience was split into two different spheres: (1) the "in here"—an internal world of sensation and (2) the "out there"—an objective world composed of natural phenomena, for example, IQ. Drawing on this dualism, scientists asserted that the laws of physical and social systems could be uncovered objectively. The systems operated apart from the "in here" world of human perception, with no connection to the act of perceiving.

Forever separate, the internal world and the natural world could never be shown to be a form of one another. Critical constructivism and postformalism reject this Cartesian dualistic epistemology and posit an alternative to the Western traditions of realism and rationalism. Briefly, realism presumes a singular, stable, external reality that can be perceived by one's senses. Rationalism argues that thought is superior to sense and is most important in shaping experience. Critical constructivism contends that reality, contrary to the arguments made by proponents of realism, is not external and unchanging. What we know as reality cannot be separated to the nature of the perceiver. Change the perceiver, her background, and location in the web of reality and we get a very different picture of reality. In contrast to rationalism, critical constructivism maintains that human thought cannot be meaningfully separated from human feeling and actions. Knowledge, critical constructivists assert, is constrained by the structure and function of the mind and can thus be known only indirectly. The objectivism, the separation of the knower and the known implicit in the Cartesian tradition, denies the spatial and temporal location of the knower in the world and thus results in the estrangement of human beings from the cosmos.

Postformalists pick up on these epistemological insights, arguing that traditional social sciences promote a form of cognition suitable for an alienated age and an alienated people. The dominant expressions of the social sciences and educational psychology serve to adjust students to sociocultural alienation rather than helping them overcome it. Descartes argued that knowledge should be empirical, mathematical, and certain, and the orientation toward research that emerged worked to exploit the forces of nature in a way that destroyed the landscape of the earth. As a result of this objectivist epistemology, we now inhabit a human-made, artificial environment. Emerging from this tradition was a psychology untroubled by the manipulation of human beings and an educational system that utilized psychology to mold students in a way that would foster efficiency and economic productivity. Such goals were typically pursued at the expense of creativity, social justice, and democratic impulses.

Thinking and learning, from the perspective of the reductionists, are developed by following specific procedures, specific measurable psychological processes. The acts are operationally defined and then broken into discrete pieces—we first learn the symbols of chemistry, the place of the elements on the periodic chart, the process of balancing chemical equations, the procedure for conducting a chemical experiment. It would be disorderly and "scientifically inappropriate" to think in terms of where chemistry is used in our everyday lives before these basics were learned, the reductionists argue. Reductionists fragment data; teach to standardized tests; develop content standards; standardize the curriculum; and utilize basals, worksheets, and sequential methods. Such reductionist methods facilitate the development of materials and the training of teachers. It is far easier to write a workbook based on a fragmented form of knowledge with a list here and an objective multiple choice test there than it is to create materials that help connect individual student experience to particular forms of disciplinary and transdisciplinary knowledge. Indeed, it is far easier to train a teacher to follow specific, predefined, never-changing steps than it is to encourage a reflective stance concerning the points of interaction connecting student experience, critical concerns with justice and equality, and diverse forms of information.

Critical constructivists believe that in teaching and thinking the whole is greater than the sum of the individual parts. They reject reductionist task analysis procedures derived from scope and sequence charts. Rejecting definitions of intelligence grounded upon a quantitative measurement of how many facts and associations an individual has accumulated, critical constructivists and postformalists maintain that there are as many paths to sophisticated thinking as there are so-phisticated thinkers. The best way to achieve higher orders of cognition is to research particular students, observing the social context from which they emerge and the particular ways they under-take the search for meaning. In this process, postformal teachers set up conditions that encourage student awareness of their own self-construction, their unique skills and experiences. With such awareness students can work with diverse individuals including their teachers to facilitate their own further growth via their insight into their own prior growth.

Many reductionist teaching strategies emerge from research studies conducted in strictly con-trolled laboratory settings that have little to do with everyday classrooms and everyday learning in general. Informed by their own practical knowledge and the practical knowledge of other teachers, postformal teachers question the generalizability of laboratory research findings to the natural setting of their own classrooms. These teachers have suspected the inapplicability of such decontextualized research all along, but positivist research community was not so insightful. The mechanistic mainstream of educational psychology assumed that laboratory research findings were the source of solutions that could be applied in every classroom setting.

Mechanistic psychological researchers failed to understand that every classroom possesses a culture of its own—a culture that defines the rules of discourse in classroom situations. Thus, all classrooms are different, critical constructivists and postformalists contend, and as a result the use of standardized techniques and materials with their obsession with the parts instead of the whole is misguided. In these unique, particularistic classrooms of postformal teachers, form follows purpose as students are protected from premature instruction in precise forms. Interest and passion are cardinal virtues, as student rational development is viewed as simply one aspect of thinking. Learning and thinking problems, moreover, are not viewed simply as the products of aptitude but of complex interactions between personalities, interests, social and cultural contexts, and life experiences. Thus, in its recognition of the complexity of learners and learning situations, critical constructivism and its cognitive cousin, postformalism serve as antidotes to mechanistic reductionism.

THE INSEPARABILITY OF COGNITION AND SOCIOHISTORICAL CONTEXT

Thus, a key theme of postformalism emerges: consciousness and cognition cannot be separated from the sociohistorical context. All cognition and action take place in continuity with the forces of history. Critical constructivism understands that contextualization is inseparable from cognition and action. The role of a postformal educational psychology is to bring this recognition to the front burner of consciousness. With such awareness we begin to realize that consciousness is constructed by individual agency, individual volition and by the ideological influences of social forces—it is both structured and structuring. Psychologists from diverse traditions did not traditionally understand the ambiguity of consciousness construction and social action. They failed to discern the ways that power was inscribed in language and knowledge and the implications of this for the production of selfhood. Individuals are initiated into language communities where women and men share bodies of knowledge, epistemologies, and the cognitive styles that accompany them. Thus, the manner in which our interpretations of the world are made is inseparable from these contexts, these language communities. The sociohistorical dimension of consciousness is often manifested on the terrain of language.

Because of these linguistic and other factors hidden from our conscious understanding, individuals are often unaware of just how their consciousness is constructed. The schemas that guide a culture are rarely part of an individual's conscious mind. Usually, they are comprehended as a portion of a person's worldview that is taken for granted. It was these ideas that Italian social theorist Antonio Gramsci had in mind when he argued that philosophy should be viewed as a form of self-criticism. Gramsci asserted that the starting point for any higher understanding of self involves the consciousness of oneself as a product of sociohistorical forces. A critical philosophy, he wrote, involves the ability of its adherents to criticize the ideological frames that they use to make sense of the world. I watch my colleagues and myself struggle as postformal teachers to engage our students in Gramsci's critical philosophical task of understanding themselves in a sociohistorical context. Many of us are frustrated by our students' lack of preparation for engagement in such a rigorous introspective and theoretical task. No matter how frustrating the job may be, we have to realize how few experiences these students possess that would equip them for such a task. Indeed, life in *hyperreality* produces experiences that undermine their ability to accomplish such undertakings.

A critical constructivist epistemology and a postformal cognitive orientation are very important in the effort to engage in an ideological critique of self-production in hyperreality. Such a critique interrogates the deep structures that help shape our consciousness as well as the historical context that gave birth to the deep structures. It explores the sociohistorical and political dimensions of schooling, the kind of meanings that are constructed in classrooms, and how these meanings are translated into student consciousness. Students of cognition often speak of student and teacher empowerment as if it were a simple process that could be accomplished by a couple of creative learning activities. One thing our ideological critique of self-production tells us is that the self is a complex, ambiguous, and contradictory entity pushed and pulled by a potpourri of forces. The idea that the self can be reconstructed and empowered without historical study, linguistic analysis, and deconstruction of place is to trivialize the goals of a critical interpretivist educational psychology, it is to minimize the power of the cognitive alienation that mechanism produces, it is to ignore history.

In this sociohistorically contextualized postformal effort to uncover the sources of consciousness construction, we attempt to use such insights to change the world and promote human possibility. In the spirit of our critical ontology we work to reconstruct the self in a just, insightful, and egalitarian way. In this context postformal teachers search in as many locations as possible for alternate discourses and ways of thinking and being that expand the envelops of possibility. In order to engage in this aspect of the reconstruction of self, students and teachers must transcend the mechanist conception of the static and unified self that moves through life with the 106 IQ—it is 106 today, it was yesterday, and it will be tomorrow. While the process of disidentification is urgent, we cannot neglect the search for alternate discourses in literature, history, popular culture, the community, subjugated and indigenous knowledges, and in our imaginations. My friend Peter McLaren tells me that we need to find a diversity of possibilities of what we might become by recovering and reinterpreting what we once were. While we might use this to change our conception of reality, we must see this change of conception—this change of mind—as only the first step in a sets of actions designed to change what is referred to as reality.

TERMS FOR READERS

Hyperreality—Jean Baudrillard's concept: the contemporary cultural landscape marked by the omnipresence of electronic information. In such a landscape, individuals begin to lose touch with the traditional notions of time, community, self, and history.

Ontology—The branch of philosophy that studies the nature of being, that asks what it means to be in the world.

Postformalism—A sociocognitive theory that blurs boundaries separating cognition, culture, society, epistemology, history, psychoanalysis, philosophy, economics, and politics. Postformalism transcends much of the cognitive theory typically associated with Piagetian and many other theories of cognitive development. While more positivist and mechanistic cognitive science has associated disinterestedness, objectivity, adult cognition, and problem solving with higher-order thinking, postformalism challenges such concepts. In this context postformalism links itself to the concept of alternate rationalities. These new rationalities employ forms of analysis sensitive to signs and symbols, the power of context in relation to thinking, the role of emotion and feeling in cognitive activity, and the value of the psychoanalytical process as it taps into the recesses of (un)consciousness. In the spirit of critical theory and critical pedagogy, postformalism attempts to democratize intelligence. In this activity, postformalist study issues of purpose, meaning, and value. Do certain forms of cognition and cognitive theory undermine the quest for justice? Do certain forms of psychological research cause observers to view problematic ways of seeing as if they involved no issues of power and privilege?

CHAPTER 98

Intelligence Is Not a Thing: Characterizing the Key Features of Postformal Educational Psychology

ERIK L. MALEWSKI

To pursue postformal alternatives in educational psychology is not a wholly new venture, as it builds upon a foundation of enacting critical consciousness in pursuit of social justice: (1) the use of postmodernism to critique metanarratives, curricular understanding to advance dynamic notions of teaching and learning that take place both within and outside of formal schooling, (2) critical pedagogy to highlight the role of social institutions in shaping youth culture, (3) teacher criticality to create a context for heightened consciousness and "wide-awakeness," and (4) indigenous knowledge to critique banking models of education that forego contextual relevance in pursuit of universal truths. I agree and weave these properties into a tentative description of a postformal educational psychology that seeks to understand how intelligence functions through critical interrogation of the very tenets that anchor the field, highlighting the ambiguous, contradictory, paradoxical, and complex agendas that compose theories of cognition.

Of key importance, postformalism is deeply concerned with the ways intolerance and authoritarianism are further enabled through the Enlightenment concepts of reason and rationality, the very intellectual frameworks used to support the logic that competency based curriculums will lead to equity in public schooling, further masking the ways cognition is shaped by race, class, gender, and sexual orientation in a symbolically and materially inequitable society. Postformalism asserts that just theories of educational psychology place at their core appreciation of differences in cultural style and intellect, the ways of knowing around which meaning is made, reclaiming that significations of intellect are cultural and specific to context and identity. In addition to representation, postformal educational psychology seeks to understand the core state production of inequitable attachment of value to the ways meaning is made and through the examination of such productions seeks to redress unequal assignment in ways that maximize participatory democratic practices. In other words, postformalism seeks not only critical interrogation of formal, developmental theories but also moves to create tentative constructions of cognition that provide increased possibilities for just, sustainable, and caring cultures that forgo dominant, universal narratives and principles of operation that incite pathology, self-hatred, and other forms of sociocultural denigration among those living on the borders.

Postformal thinkers, recognizing that formalism offers a skeleton around which discursive constructions can be tentatively thread, retain the principles of participatory democracy and libratory ethics as a method of theory building that calls into question reductive mandates regarding learning assessment, forms of evaluation that squelch criticality and work to maintain conventional power relations, instead weaving around the tenets of democratic practice border knowledge emanating from the voices of the oppressed. It seeks a celebration of difference and multiplicity, leading to revolutionary realities that unite critical consciousness with liberatory teaching practices. Hybrid theories of educational psychology take from formalism and postformalism as if theoretical toolboxes and utilize each of the modalities to revolutionize how we think about human thought in education. While the description of postformalism as a disposition that values multilogicality can confuse readers searching for definitive answers and easy solutions, there remains no concise definition of postformalism; intelligence is not a thing. Instead, postformalism offers an amazing opportunity to engage in transformative theories of human aptitude as a poststructural tool that becomes emancipatory when wedded to participatory democratic paradigms capable of identifying injustice, challenging hegemonic articulations, and elevating subjugated ways of knowing.

MULTILOGICALITY AND INTELLECTUAL ENACTMENTS

As the reader might note, postformalism is itself an enacted terrain that remains alive through its fluidity and malleability. Owing to a foundation in feminism, cultural studies, poststructuralism, and queer and critical race theory, with scholars that include Hall, Derrida, Adorno, Marcuse, Foucault, Jameson, Kristeva, and Lacan, among others, a language was created that positioned cognition within economic, political, and social practices and concern over their ability to induce self-hatred, loathing, subjugation, and deprivation among those bearing selected cultural styles and manners of being. Educational psychology has been transformed through extensions of Freudian theory; historical recounts of trauma, gender, race, and social practice; threading postmodernism upon personal psychology; and Kincheloe and transcendence of developmental theories that recognize the important intersection of cognition and social group identifications in a symbolically and materially unequal world. In particular, the work of Kincheloe marked the start of a hybrid understanding of postformalism that retained a language of critique while also grafting on generative elements such as deconstruction, etymology, and problem detection that interfaced well with the need to expand critical consciousness, a shift in realties that allows teachers to promote antiracist, antisexist, anticlassist, and antihomophobic social and educational curriculum and pedagogical practices. Working from a postformal disposition, educational psychology pulls from each of these domains as if theoretical toolboxes from which various ideas can be threaded together to offer new and unforeseen descriptions of intellect proposing radically divergent ways of witnessing human reality, from art, music, and literature to applications involving the integration of science, technology, and liberation ethics. Those who embrace postformalism recognize that educational psychology, like human thought, involves imagination and play and the insight that comes from using emotion to envision cognition as contingent, idiosyncratic, exceptional, and laden with power relations.

Postformalism might best be characterized as a disposition or attitude because it is more a reaction to the near ubiquitous character of formalism and its principles and rules than itself representing any formative, authoritative body of scholarship or set of doctrines. As a result, postformalism is constituted by debate and deliberation and dominated by local narratives that often work in solidarity against hegemonic articulations while falling short as theoretical propositions that involve a quest for universal status and therefore silence the voices of the oppressed. It can be said that postformalism challenges reductive essentialism, instrumental reason, and canon building. While recognizing that presuppositions allow for hybrid theoretical forms that avoid the pitfalls of overt relativism, propositions are not beyond question but rather invite dissenting voices, exposing postformal foundations to ongoing deliberation over the assertions made in its name, questions that bring cause for humility. Clearly some could relate formal presuppositions to the beginning dialogue in Plato's *The Symposium* and postformal precepts to the interventions that occur with the entrance of Dionysius. Others find in postformalism a melding of the pre-formal with the formal to form a hybrid synthesis, possibly an emphasis on uncovering the tacit relationships and hidden assumptions that reveal larger life forces within the universe. Such universalizing discourses, as Eve Sedgewick described them in the 1990 book, *Epistemology of the Closet*, when thought of tentatively, open up the possibility for seeing relationships between ostensibly different entities as opposed to minoritizing discourses that tend to reduce narratives into their most simple parts. The emphasis of the latter on reductionism as a precursor to examination limits the opportunity to see relationships in the relentless search for establishing control and reason. As Kincheloe, Steinberg, and Hinchey explained in *The Post-Formal Reader: Cognition and Education*:

We might be better served to think of the mind not in terms of parts, but in terms of connecting patterns, the dance of interacting parts. This initial consciousness of the 'poetic' recognition of this dance involves a nonverbal mental vibration, an increased energy state. From this creative tension emerges a perception of the meaning of the metaphor and the heightened consciousness that accompanies it. Post-formal teachers can model such metaphoric perception for their students (1999, p. 69).

It is with explanation that we can find a clear relationship between the description of postformal educational psychology that Kincheloe offers and phenomenologist Alfred Schutz when he highlights a "fundamental anxiety" associated with an expressed concern that our lives might be essentially meaningless, that through our interaction on this earth we might impress so little as to leave without having mattered at all. Such anxiety does not have to lead to paralysis but can be a psychologically motivating factor, spurring ideas for projects and plans of action. Through the generative process of making such plans, arranging ahead for their enactment, and bringing them to fruition we can recognize how cognition involves the creation of identifications within particular social contexts in which our lives take place. Postformal educational psychology embraces such understanding.

While the postformal movement in educational psychology is certainly in alignment with other paradigms of thought, engaged in critique of theories of intelligence that attempt to bracket our culture, a process of neutralization that can be evidenced in the work of Jensen, Murray, and Herrnstein, it joins forces with Baudrillard and his opposition to one-dimensional depictions of reality; Dewey and his critique of positivism; and Foucault and his insistence on power as recurrent at the point of human interaction—it also seeks to move beyond these points, recouping these oppositions and extending these insights toward the generative process of tentatively describing intellectual possibilities. The work of Kincheloe, Steinberg, and Hinchey in *The Post-Formal Reader: Cognition and Education* (1999) and Eisner in *Curriculum and Cognition Reconsidered* (1994) provide valuable insight into the transformations that occur in educational psychology when postformal dispositions not only offer a language of critique but spaces of opportunity for reenvisioning cognition as a sociocultural construct and, therefore, the key to an effort to end symbolic and material inequities. In response to the success of modern, formal movements and the terror invoked through the certainties of metanarratives, we need more than "reactionary countermoves," responses based on the underlying assumptions regarding developmental psychology that fail to extend beyond the binaries established in the reasoning of the preceding position. As such, the totalizing structures stand in the way of the imagination that arises from the unrestricted play of ideas, the "wide-awake-ness" that comes from opening up opportunity, providing self-direction, and setting a person free. As Greene engages a postformal imaginary in her book, *Releasing the Imagination: Essays on Education, the Arts, and Social Change*:

We who are teachers have to strive against limits, *consciously* strive. The alternatives are not to be found in a rediscovery of untrammeled subjectivity or in acceptance of total determinism. A dialectical relation marks every human condition: it may be the relationship between the individual and the environment, self and society, or living consciousness and object-world. Each such relation presupposes a mediation and a tension between the reflective and material dimensions of lived situations. Because both dimensions are equally significant, the tension cannot be overcome by a triumph of subjectivity or objectivity: the dialectic cannot be finally resolved (1995, p. 185).

The postformal, following Greene's disposition, works toward theories of educational psychology that move youth into a symbolically and materially rich life where they actively seek self-direction and work to understand the conditions of their own existence. In the search for self-direction horizons are breeched and lived rationalities are formed, intellect is enacted and developed. In the search to understand the context where we live experiences are clarified, the social, political, and economic practices that shape subjectivities are recognized and one begins the journey toward understanding the ways their location in the web of reality shapes individual thought and the range of opportunity believed possible. Postformal education offers a critique of reductive theories of intellect that equate learning with information transmission, canon building, and establishing metanarratives, the concepts that undergird conventional cognitive theories and continue to bolster false binarisms in educational psychology, the recycling of the biology/culture debates that foreground the perpetuation of race, gender, class, and sexual orientation discrimination through neoliberal, neoconservative, and neocolonial politics, the repetitions that mark the boundaries of intelligibility around the capacities of dominate cultures. Postformal education refuses to be restricted by rules, conventions, and bifurcations that work in dialectics without synthesis, linear forms of logic that result in either/or rationalities.

A TENTATIVE DESCRIPTION OF POSTFORMAL FEATURES

The following section further delineates six key features of postformalism that are representative but by no means conclusive on the shift occurring in educational psychology:

Exploring Multilogicality

Researchers and practitioners of postformal educational psychology recognize that the highest forms of cognition involve self-examination, asking questions regarding what is known, how it was assessed, how it came to be known, and whether or not it was embraced or rejected. Postformalism shares this element of multilogicality with other cognitive theorists that emphasize multiple intelligences but adds additional dimensions to the disposition. In order to transcend formality, it becomes important to examine our own position in the web of reality through the study of our traditions, customs, and rituals and draw these particularities into relation with the historical traces of intellect and production and circulation of knowledge. Recognizing the relationship between the particularities of experience and larger social and educational practices, it is possible to become critically aware of the cultural forms embedded within each of us. Postformal thinkers who are concerned with epistemology and etymology will identify with the notion of genealogy, dimensions for examining the origins of knowledge that include the processes involved in describing the social forces that shape what constitutes knowledge as well as subjectivities and identifications.

Engaging Problem Detection

The reduction of intelligence to problem solving has long been a problem of formalism the effects of which can be evidenced in the everyday curricular practice of presenting preformed riddles with the aim of drawing closure at existing solutions. When the focus is on problem solving, students become trapped in reductive politics of instrumental rationality and cause and effect linear logic where students learn to seek out given solutions to given problems, an appeal to explicit orders of reality by curriculum developers that suggests the best solutions to social, political, and economic ills already exist. When the work of children and youth is reduced to the search for extant answers, the opportunity to engage in meaningful and potent acts of improvisation associated with creatively defining problems are thwarted. The focus on problem solving in curriculum as well as learning assessment fails to attend to the process of questioning that leads to the establishment of the problem in the first place. Postformalism embraces problem detection as a process that involves imaginatively coming to critical consciousness through determining the character of a dilemma in explorations of the relationships between ostensibly different elements, charting associations that are more holistic and capable of moving us toward symbolic and material equality.

Recognizing Implicit Orders

The idea of "looking beyond convention" helps us understand an aspect of postformalism that illuminates hidden forces and tacit assumptions with notions of explicit and implicit curriculums. Explicit or formal curricular orders involve easily recognized patterns, events that seem to occur with little variation and consistently within similar physical spaces. Through patterns that arise out of simple comparison and contrast, the explicit curricular order is often the product of the sorting and categorization function of formal cognition. Of a different order, implicit curriculums address a much deeper sense of reality. It is the tacit level of operation in which the interspaces of relationships become evident, where two ostensibly different entities are shown to be part of a larger web-like structure of reality. Recognizing the value of interspaces as worth analysis in their own right, Perrow in his 1999 book *Normal Accidents: Living with High-risk Technologies*, a study of nuclear power plant disasters, highlighted their important role in understanding tightly coupled organizations. Drawing from postformal forms of analysis, he examined the difficulty in knowing, knowledge that shifts in the interspaces between intention and reception, difficulties in intelligibility the effects of which he termed "normal accidents," and the errors that occur among discursive realities that exceed attempts at relational understanding.

Unearthing Tacit Knowledge

Postformal thinkers look beyond substantive reality to access our hidden assumptions and work to make subjugated knowledge visible. In Perrow's study of nuclear power plants mentioned above, explicit curricular orders were in place for sharing information across the organization. What Perrow found, however, were deeper implicit orders of reality that involved recognizing the significance of the interspaces between thoughts, the discursive moments where the nonrational occurs: tighter controls by leadership result in increased errors and what was believed to have been communicated effectively utilizing a formal, transmission model of reality, was caught up in implicit curricular orders, the cacophony of multiple competing, contingent realities, heard differently or simply not heard at all. Similarly, in the classroom, postformal educational psychology recognizes the importance of implicit curricular orders where tacit realities are searched out in hermeneutical pedagogies that encourage students to seek out meaning, draw relationships between ostensibly different things, and engage in problem detection that leads to composing inchoate the dynamics of a dilemma prior to the positing of its solution. Aware of the importance of poststructural analysis, teachers not only teach content but also explore the implicit orders of curriculum textbooks. For example, in a history text, a teacher might highlight the implicit dominance of white supremist capitalist patriarchical realities enfolded in the order of the information. Most often, required history textbooks further reinforce metanarratives involving the themes of exploration, conquest, and oversight. On the periphery, if addressed at all, remain secondary orders that involve historical issues such as the civil rights movement, women's issues, and the history of the labor movement. Teachers who recognize the influences postformal educational psychology has on classroom curriculum place an emphasis on uncovering implicit relationships and themes.

Releasing Imagination

The postformal abilities of the mind can often be understood through artists, artistry, and the ability to reenvision what has been erased from the social imagination. Visionary leaders recognize curriculum and instruction as the crafting of different realities and share in their creation with students. The formal curriculum becomes only one reality among many and imagination the only limit to the pursuit of the highest orders of cognition. Kincheloe, Steinberg, and Hinchey delineating the ability of postformalism to access tacit understandings assert in *The Post-Formal Reader: Cognition and Education*, "Formal thinking has not been attuned to such a reality possibly because the expansionist, conquest oriented goals of the Cartesian-Newtonian paradigm emphasized the explicit order of things" (1999, p. 68). Dominant paradigms in educational psychology in the process of attending to recognized patterns and locations have worked to subjugate alternative realities—under explicit orders politics, democratic practices, material distribution, class bias, symbolic elitism, and environmental racism, among others, when discussed are fragmented out into their simplest parts and decontextualized rather than illustrated as relational within a larger web of sociocultural practices.

Challenging Praxis

Postformalism and its counterparts in critical pedagogy have illustrated that little is as it seems when analyzed beneath its outer layer. Teachers who recognize the impact of formal curricular orders on educational realities understand that, for example, heterosexism cannot be taught solely as an issue of whether or not gay and lesbian identified people should be allowed to marry but must address the ways that heterosexuality functions as a economic, political, and social form that is enfolded in the deepest elements of our organizational lives and the realities constructed for those whose daily lives involve dismissal, neglect, and the rendering of their needs and experiences irrelevant. When postformal thought is applied to educational psychology wholly different realms of reality are made visible. Imagine postformal forms of assessment that begin with problem detection and the process of piecing together the relationships between ostensibly different social realities, learning assessments that transcend ongoing attempts to mark winners and losers whether individual students or labeling a failing school. Teachers who embrace an etymological search to understand how intelligence functions historically and in the current milieu as a social, economic, and political force set new terms for teaching and assessment that place culture and difference at the core of curriculum, understanding that cognition is not a universal category but an enacted and contingent phenomenon shaped by identity, social context, and the particularities of place.

This tentative description of postformal educational psychology transpires from a particular vantage point within educational psychology and is also shaped by the position and identifications of the author. Understanding that any description of higher order thinking does not constitute closure on the subject, this chapter acts as another guidepost on the journey toward understanding cognition as a personal-sociocultural production, a postformal attempt to draw individual ways of knowing into relationship with symbolic and material practices and the search for their equalization. If postformalism offers anything to educational psychology it is a device for peeling back the layers of reality, revealing uncommon truths and tacit assumptions and the relationships between ostensibly different realities.

TERMS FOR READERS

Critical Consciousness—The phrase refers to the ability to perceive social, economic, and political oppression and to take action against such subjugation in organizations, culture, and social consciousness. Critical consciousness involves exposing the systemic elements that lead to banking models of education where students are passive recipients of knowledge; educators enforce pedagogies involving drilling, memorizing, and repeating information; knowledge is thought of as a gift from the educated to the ignorant; teachers, administrators, and officials choose the curriculum and students adapt to it; and students are rewarded for storing information in ways that the most successful students are those who lack the heightened awareness necessary to intervene in society for the pursuit of social equality.

Intellectual Enactment—This term refers to theoretically informed actions that are guided by certain values and principles. Intellectual aims under postformalism are not simply about self-improvement or establishing a career trajectory. Instead intellectual enactment emphasizes actions guided by a moral disposition that furthers human well-being and improve the quality of life. Postformalism is not a complete denial of cognitive truth but recognition that intelligence, perception, and thought involve competing truths that most appropriately might be guided moral and ethical considerations grounded in critical notions of participatory democracy.

Liberatory Teaching Practices—This term refers to the development of critical consciousness in students and teachers through dialogic interactions that involve the reciprocal process of expressing experiences and understandings of social justice theme. From this angle, instructors often pose problems to the class that bring learners to heightened understandings of social, economic, and political issues and enfolded power relations. Liberatory teaching practices involve dialectical pedagogies that thread personal knowledge and understanding with critical perspectives and disciplinary scholarship within a search for self-direction and understanding the conditions of one's own existence.

Multilogicality—This term describes the interplay of many competing, overlapping, and incommensurable ways of knowing that illustrate the complexity of perception and analysis. Multilogicality aims for the exploration of numerous axes of reason that hold differing values in society to illustrate the myriad ways human beings reason. Through attending to more than one form of knowing, multilogicality illuminates the ways in which particular forms of reason, such as bodily and emotional intelligence, have been historically subjugated.

Postformalism—The term belies easy categorization but can be safely stated that postformalism attends to alternate ways of conceptualizing cognition and human understanding. Postformalism acts as a response to formalism's search for definitive sets of rules and principles of cognitive operation. As a reaction, postformalism unearths the idiosyncrasies and abnormalities subjugated by the domination of developmental, formalist logic.

FURTHER READING

Brookfield, S. (1995). *Becoming a Critically Reflective Teacher*. San Francisco: Jossey Bass.

Freire, P. (1972). *Pedagogy of the Oppressed*. Harmondsworth: Penguin.

Gilligan, C. (1982). *In a Different Voice: Psychological Theory and Women's Development*. Cambridge: Harvard University Press.

Greene, M. (1995). *Releasing the Imagination: Essays on Education, the Arts, and Social Change*. New York: Jossey Bass.

Sinnott, J. D.(1984). Post-Formal Reasoning: The Relativistic Stage. In M. L. Commons, F. A. Richards and C. Armon (Eds.), *Beyond Formal Operations: Late Adolescent and Adult Cognitive Development*, pp. 298–325. New York: Praeger.

CHAPTER 99

Unpackaging the Skinner Box: Revisiting B. F. Skinner through a Postformal Lens

DANA SALTER

I did not direct my life. I didn't design it. I never made decisions. Things always came up and made them for me. That's what life is.

—B. F. Skinner

While researching for this article, I was struck by the almost apologetic tone that recent biographies of Burrhus Frederic Skinner have taken. Challenging their readers to look past the two prevailing stereotyped images of the mad scientist in the white lab coat obsessively experimenting with either rats and pigeons in his "Skinner Box" or his own child in his infamous "Baby Tender," the argument is made that the true genius of Skinner can and must be observed in the questions he sought to answer through his experimentation. This is where many biographies begin a myopic tribute to Skinner's work and vision that not only decontextualizes his work in terms of its historical location and relevance, but concurrently adds to the mythology surrounding Skinner's theories of behavior. Thus, the question begs to be asked: What is it about Skinner's theories that continue to spur a rich spectrum of critique sixty years after the initial publication of his work? One thing to keep in mind while reading his work is that Skinner built upon the works of Ivan Pavlov and John B. Watson in creating his theory of operant conditioning. He directly translated his observations to the field of education and thus cemented education's love affair with uncritical, positivistic, sequential, quasi-scientific, stimulus-reward based, technologically aided instructional design. This gross over simplification of Skinner's work is not meant as a trite critique but as an entry point into a discussion of the far reaching impact of his work on education, psychology, and educational psychology specifically. The decontextulization of Skinner as a researcher has led to the biographical apologists seeking to mollify and the over zealous critics seeking to vilify Skinner's work. I'd like to begin by unpacakaging the mythology of B. F. Skinner by examining his work through various lenses that may help to contextualize his work in order to better examine its current far reaching consequences in the field of educational psychology.

UNPACKAGING THE SKINNER BOX

Any study of B. F. Skinner must note that he, himself was conflicted about his own theories. Later in his career he would question some of his early experimentations and an example of this critique can be observed through the dialogue of his characters in his book *Walden Two* (1948). However, it is this experimentation that launched the study of educational psychology as we know it today. The unpackaging of Skinner begins with placing him in a historical context. Skinner grew up on a pre-World War I and II world. Industry was king/ queen and anything that needed to be fixed, including social ills, could be broken down into pieces in order to fix the whole. Fredreick Taylor's *The Principles of Scientific Management* provided a "science" for breaking work down into parts that could be efficiently delegated and regulated. In the realm of society and education, Edward Thorndike's work in psychology and intelligence was widely regarded as a breakthrough in testing and curricular design for education. Social efficiency was the science of the day. In the world that followed the two world wars, the United States was faced with among others, two very important philosophical questions. First, how do we control the behaviors of a people so collectively damaged by the violent physical and emotional devastation of war? Second, how do we educate this postwar population for an industry that needs docile skilled workers while simultaneously educate to quell the social unrest? This was fertile ground for a way of viewing behavior in which control was not only attainable but externally modifiable. Enter B. F. Skinner. Skinner felt that because it was difficult, if not impossible to measure and control the inner thoughts that contribute to the control of behavior, focus should be placed on the more observable and thus controllable outer behaviors that can be modified with conditioning.

Without having previously studied psychology, Skinner began his career in the Department of Psychology at Harvard University. Anxious to try new ideas that focused on research that related behavior to experimental conditions, Skinner found a mentor in an equally ambitious William Cozier in the Department of Physiology at Harvard. Cozier postulated a study of animals that focused on observable, measurable behaviors and not the less measurable mental processes of the animal. Skinner was a tenacious experimenter and created many apparati in which to perform his experiments. His immensely popular "Skinner Box" was a result of this experimentation. The box was a specially devised cage for a rat that had a bar or pedal on one wall that, when pressed, caused a little mechanism to release a pellet of food into the cage. As he noted in his book *The Behavior of Organisms* (1938), this box was to represent all environments. The crucial aspect of this box was his discovery that a rat's behavior in the box seemed to be a reaction based upon the effects of the action and not on a stimulus that preceded the action, as postulated by Pavlov and Watson. This led Skinner to coin the term *operant behavior* to describe the act that is dependent on the consequence and *operant conditioning* to describe the process of organizing the reinforcement variables responsible for creating the new action or behavior. His extrapolation from these experiments informed his work in the fields of human behavior and education as outlined in his book *The Technology of Teaching* (1968). The field of programmed instruction is a direct descendent of Skinner's work.

EXAMINING THE PACKAGING FOR WHAT'S MISSING

Examining the packaging that surrounds Skinner's translation of his theory of operant conditioning into the field of education reveals what's missing and ultimately dangerous about Skinner's modernist theories. Programmed instruction has at its core the over-simplified, non-complex, reductionist mentality of operant conditioning that deliberately attempts to factor out the notion of the complexity of human thought and interactions' influence upon learning. Skinner's translation of animal behaviors observed in his "fabricated" lab environment to the classroom setting is based upon two key assumptions. These assumptions are that all behavior can be controlled and all learning can be broken down in to components that when linearly sequenced, equal learning and social sorting (related to Darwin's theory of natural selection). This formal modernistic view of learning speaks to the empirical nature of Skinner's theories.

These assumptions are the linchpin holding Skinner's theories together. Skinner referred to himself as a Baconian scientist in attitude and in his philosophy of research. This worldview is seductive for its superficially magnanimous appeal to experience as observed through the coupling of experimentation and observation. However, this appeal is uncritical in that only certain aspects of an experience are deemed "valuable" and thus "measurable" and therefore ultimately "applicable" and "translatable." As noted in the introduction to this book, the idea that consciousness could be measured was deemed to be absurd when viewed through a positivistic/mechanistic lens. Therefore, in the prevailing reductionist thought popular at the time Skinner postulated his theory, consciousness was a variable that could be discarded. Skinner's theories emphasize an exclusive cause and effect binary relationship definition for human behavioral interactions. Kincheloe argues in *The Post-Formal Reader* that this Cartesian-Newtonian worldview attempts to break consciousness, knowledge and by extension, behavior down in order to try to understand its parts. The rigidity of this reduction is what made Skinner's work so appealing to the field of education and psychology. Any outcome that didn't fit the experimental norm was discarded or viewed as abnormal. Behavior thus became predictable and modifiable. Programmed instruction allowed for the sequencing of the steps needed to complete any problem. There was no room for other ways of learning. There was no space for difference. And yet, "one size fits all" education still had problems.

Skinner's work has fed the fire of many "reforms" in education. In researching this chapter, what struck me was the lack of space in the discussion of learning for alternative views on the psychology of learning. So many movements, including the current "No Child Left Behind" movement, are built upon the foundation of operant conditioning. The rational is that there is a right behavior and a wrong behavior and through a correct sequence of standards we can condition students to get the correct answer. And if they don't . . .

POSSIBILITIES IN THE PACKAGING

The results of Skinner's theories are everywhere: from the school bell to summon children to school, the bells to signal the change in classes, stickers for attendance, candy for doing well on a test, in-prison good behavior reward incentives, Pizza Hut Bookit! reading programs, advertising gimmicks: "Buy 1, Get 1 Free!, dog training programs, and the educational standards movement are all infused with adaptations of Skinner's theories. These instances are not all bad or all good. Moving beyond a binary/dualistic language for exploring the realm of human behavior is the goal of a postformal approach to the study of behavioral psychology. A postformal approach to the psychological exploration and study of behavior rejects a hyperrational, false-objective, laboratory-equals-reality notion of behavior. As Kincheloe and Steinberg note, a postformal approach to the study of behavior and its relation to learning acknowledges past and present historical situatedness in relation to meaning and understanding—it is be elastic. This postformal approach invites, as explained by Freire, a dialogical conversation that calls into question the various assumptions under girding Skinnerian behaviorist theory. This historically situated and critical dialogical questioning of the psychology of behavior opens up the space for more possibilities for understanding human actions. Fighting reductionism a la Skinner's theory is a key component of postformalism. Looking at Skinner's theory through a postformal lens, his reductionist fortified theory of behavior cultivates a fractured, fragmented, and disconnected understanding of how and why behaviors occur, let alone responses to any other questions that arise about behavior. Thus, as Kincheloe and Berry explain in *Rigour and Complexity in Educational Research,* a rethinking of the methodologies for experimentation in the understanding of the psychology of behavior is in order. A multilogical multifaceted research agenda will combat the limitations of the monological reductionist world in which the psychology of behavior has resided. This postformal approach will transition the research surrounding the study of the psychology of behavior from a modernist Cartesian-Newtonian part-to-whole mentality to a postformal multilogical and methodological approach.

B. F. Skinner was a complex person with a complex idea: the consequences of behavior determine the probability that the behavior will occur again. This incredibly layered statement was swept up in the swell of a moment in the history of the United States where people were looking for "logical" and "rational" responses to their cracked rose-colored glasses. Conversely, psychology was seeking to be viewed as a legitimate "hard" science in a world where science equaled "objective" observable facts. Skinner's theory grew out of and was a vanguard for this view of science. His translation of his observations and theory to the field of education was based upon an assumptive and uncritical view that education in the 1950s was not succeeding because it was not stimulating, delayed the gratification for the student and it was too subjective. Opening up the dialogue for a postformal rethinking of behaviorist theory will open the space for alternative ways of understanding behavior.

No longer will it be a myopic socially efficient means to an end. It can be a springboard for other ways of thinking about how the psychology of behavior informs multiple aspects of being and how the complexity of being informs behavior. Take a moment and read Skinner's quote at the beginning of this piece. This quote is from a point later in his life and yet is rarely mentioned in association with Skinnerian theories. The inherent contradictions in this quote, when compared with his earlier works concerning behavior and consequence, are quite fascinating; and yet, without a postformal critique that champions and welcomes a fluidity and complexity in research and not only invites by required concurrent reflection, this quote would be reduced and relegated to a realm of variables inconsistent with the observable truth.

CHAPTER 100

Postformalism and Critical Multiculturalism: Educational Psychology and the Power of Multilogicality

JOE L. KINCHELOE

In 1997 in *Changing Multiculturalism* Shirley Steinberg and I offered an evolving notion of critical multiculturalism that attempted to address and avoid the problems of more mainstream articulations of multiculturalism. Drawing upon critical theory and the tradition of an evolving criticality along with a variety of scholarship from ethnic studies, cultural studies, sociology and education, critical multiculturalism is concerned with the ways that individuals are discursively, ideologically, and culturally constructed as human beings. Indeed, critical multiculturalism wants to promote an awareness of how domination takes place, how dominant cultures reproduces themselves, and power operates to shape self and knowledge. This position makes no pretense of neutrality as it openly proclaims its affiliation with efforts to produce a more just, egalitarian, and democratic world that refuses to stand for the perpetuation of human suffering.

Critical multiculturalism is uncomfortable with the name, multiculturalism, but works to redefine it in the contemporary era. Indeed, the first decade of the twenty-first century cannot be understood outside the framework of fast capitalism, transnational corporations, corporatized electronic and ideologically inscribed information, mutating and more insidious forms of racism and ethnic bias, and a renewed form of U.S. colonialism and military intervention designed to extend the political, economic, and cultural influence of the twenty-first century American Empire. It is my argument in this chapter that the postformal reconceptualization of educational psychology is well served by a familiarity with critical multiculturalism.

In particular, a critical multiculturalism is profoundly concerned with what gives rise to race, class, gender, sexual, religious, cultural, and ability-based inequalities. Critical multiculturalists focus their attention on the ways power has operated historically and contemporaneously to legitimate social categories and divisions. In this context we analyze and encourage further research on how in everyday, mundane, lived culture these dynamics of power play themselves out. It is at this ostensibly "innocent" level that the power of patriarchy, white supremacy, colonial assumptions of superiority, heterosexism, and class elitism operate. Critical multiculturalism appreciates both the hidden nature of these operations, and the fact that most of the time they go unnoticed even by those participating in them and researching them. The invisibility of this process is disconcerting, as the cryptic nature of many forms of oppression makes it difficult to convince individuals from dominant power blocs of their reality. Such subtlety is matched by cognizance of the notion that there are as many differences within groups as there are between them.

In the twenty-first century the increased influence of right-wing power blocs have elevated the need for a critical multiculturalist approach to knowledge production in various academic disciplines including, of course, educational psychology. The geopolitical and military operations to extend the American Empire have been accompanied by disturbing trends in knowledge production that hold alarming implications for the future—the future of research in particular. Critical multiculturalists are aware that such knowledge work possesses a historical archaeology in Western culture and U.S. society. David G. Smith (2003) in "On Enfraudening the Public Sphere" in *Policy Futures in Education* argues that the twenty-first-century American Empire is constructed not only around territorial and natural resource claims, but in hyperreality, epistemological claims as well. Tracing the epistemological claims of the empire, Smith studies Western knowledge from the cogito of Descartes to Adam Smith's economics of self-interest. With the merging of Descartes rationalism with Adam Smith's economics the West's pursuit of economic expansionism is justified by the concept of liberty. Educational psychology cannot ignore these dynamics in the middle of the first decade of the twenty-first century.

Postformalists who employ the bricolage described in this chapter have carefully examined this Enlightenment reason and its relation to oppression and social regulation. Proponents have maintained for centuries it is this form of reason that frees us from the chaos of ignorance and human depravity. It is this reason, they proclaimed, that separated us from the uncivilized, the inferior. Smith (2003) argues that it is this notion that supports a philosophy of human development or developmentalism used in psychology and a variety of other discourses to oppress and marginalize the cultural others who haven't employed such Western ways of thinking and being. Often in their "immaturity" these others, this rationalistic developmentalism informs us, must be disciplined even ruled in order to teach them to be rational and democratic.

This psychological developmentalist story about the contemporary world situation conveniently omits the last 500 years of European colonialism, the anticolonial movements around the world beginning in the post-World War II era and their impact on the U.S. civil rights movement, the women's movement, the antiwar movement in Vietnam, Native American liberation struggles, the gay rights movement, and other emancipatory movements which inform our critical multiculturalism and postformalism. In other work I have argued that the reaction to these anticolonial movements have set the tone and content of much of American political, social, cultural, and educational experience over the last three decades. In the middle of the first decade of the twenty-first century these forces of reaction seemed to have gained a permanent foothold in American social, political, cultural, and educational institutions.

The future of knowledge is at stake in this new cultural landscape. Few times in human history has there existed greater need for forms of knowledge work that expose the dominant ideologies and discourses that shape the information accessed by many individuals. The charge of critical multiculturalists and postformalists at this historical juncture is to develop forms of knowledge work and approaches to research that take these sobering dynamics into account. This is the idea behind my articulation of the bricolage (J. Kincheloe and K. Berry, (2004) *Rigour and Complexity in Educational Research: Conceptualizing the Bricolage*) that will be discussed later in this chapter. Attempting to make use of a variety of philosophical, methodological, cultural, political, epistemological, and psychological discourses, the bricolage can be employed by critical multiculturalists and students of educational psychology to produce compelling knowledges that seek to challenge the neocolonial representations about others at home and abroad.

CRITICAL MULTICULTURALISM IN A POSTFORMAL EDUCATIONAL PSYCHOLOGY

Critical multiculturalism is grounded on the theoretical tradition of critical theory emerging from the Frankfurt School of Social Research in Germany in the 1920s. Seeing the world from the vantage point of post-First World War Germany, with its economic depression, inflation, and unemployment, the critical theorists (Max Horkheimer, Theodor Adorno, Walter Benjamin, Leo Lowenthal, and Herbert Marcuse) focused on power and domination within an industrialized, modern age. Critical theory is especially concerned with how domination takes place, the way human relations are shaped in the workplace, the schools and everyday life. Critical theorists are valuable to the postformal reconceptualization of educational psychology as they promote an individual's consciousness of himself or herself as a social being.

Advocates of a critical multiculturalism make no pretence of neutrality. Unlike many theoretical approaches, critical multiculturalism exposes its values and openly works to achieve them. In this context an educational psychology informed by critical multiculturalism is up front about its desire to construct a psychology of justice, which promotes school practices that encourage intelligence and egalitarianism. Thus, critical multiculturalism is dedicated to the notion of equality and the elimination of human suffering. Operating on this foundation, postformalists ask what is the relationship between social inequality and the suffering that accompanies it and the learning process. The search for an answer to this question is a central concern of a postformalism informed by critical multiculturalism.

Working in tandem with subordinate and marginalized groups, postformalists attempt to expose the subtle and often tacit psychological and pedagogical assumptions that privilege the already affluent, and subvert the efforts of the poor and socially and culturally marginalized. When schooling is viewed from this perspective, the naive belief that education provides consistent socioeconomic mobility for working-class and nonwhite students disintegrates. Indeed, the mechanistic educational psychological notion education simply provides a politically neutral set of skills and an objective body of knowledge also collapses. This appreciation that both cultural pedagogy (media-generated education in an electronic society) and schooling don't operate as neutral, ideologically innocent activities is central to a postformal educational psychology grounded on a critical multiculturalism.

Connecting a postformal educational psychology to the multiple perspectives of critical multiculturalism, means moving beyond the conservative and liberal assumptions that racial, ethnic, and gender groups live in relatively equal status to one another and that the social system is open to anyone who desire and is willing to work for mobility. This debilitating assumption is rarely, if ever, challenged in a positivistic, mechanistic educational psychology. Such an assumption affects almost everything that goes on in such a regressive educational psychology. Even though contemporary economic production in the West—and increasingly in Western style economic systems in a globalized world—is grounded on unequal social divisions of race, class, and gender, educational psychologists have been reticent about using the term oppression.

Postformalists grounded in a critical multiculturalism assert, as they argue vehemently in the spirit of W. E. B. DuBois, the necessity of the struggle for equality and democracy in the economic sphere of society. As diverse world cultures have begun to slide toward the hyperreality of globalized markets, with their fast capitalism, U.S. neo-imperial policies, and assault of electronic information, their ability/willingness to distribute their resources more equitably has substantially diminished. Class and other forms of inequality and the maldistributed cultural capital that accompanies them are key concerns of a multiculturalized postformalism. This puts us directly in contact with the study of power and the ways it has operated historically and contemporaneously to legitimate social categories and divisions. In this context, postformalists analyze and encourage further analysis of how in everyday, mundane, lived culture and cognition these dynamics of power play themselves out.

In this seemingly banal level of human thinking and interaction the power of race, class, and gender asserts itself—often under the radar of consciousness. Indeed, it is at these unsuspected microsocial levels that the power of patriarchy, white supremacy, class elitism, heterosexism, and other power blocs accomplish their hurtful work. A critical multiculturalism appreciates both the hidden nature of these operations and the fact that most of the time they go unnoticed even by those who participate in them. The subtlety of this process is at times disconcerting, as the cryptic nature of many forms of racism, sexism, class bias, heterosexism, makes it difficult to convince individuals from the dominant culture of their reality. Such subtlety is matched by the nuanced but vital cognizance of the fact that there are as many differences within cultural groups as there are between them. Nevertheless, it is unacceptable that psychologists and educational psychologists have limited insight into the way these power dynamics work. These scholars must be leaders in understanding the ways that power shapes those domains traditionally associated with psychology and educational psychology.

In this context postformalists drawing upon their critical multicultural insights maintain that educational psychologists must be attuned to the ways that power shapes consciousness. Such a process involves the means by which ideological inscriptions are imprinted on subjectivity, the ways desire is mobilized by power forces for hegemonic outcomes, the means by which discursive powers shape thinking and behavior through both the presences and absences of different words and concepts, and the methods by which individuals assert their agency and self-direction in relation to such power plays. Central to the domain of educational psychology, critical multiculturalism vis-à-vis postformalism works to illustrate how individuals produce, revamp, and reproduce meanings in contexts constantly shaped and reshaped by power.

How can educational psychologists possibly study cognitive processes—not to mention teaching and learning—without any appreciation of these dynamics? This culturally informed meaning making activity always involves the ways power in the multitude of forms it takes helps to construct collective and individual experiences in ways that operate in the interests of white supremacy, patriarchy, class elitism, heterosexism, and other dominant forces. Here mechanistic educational psychologists and the pedagogies they help shape often work in complicity with dominant power blocs, as they serve as gatekeepers who transmit dominant values and protect the "common culture" from the "barbarians" at the gates of the empire.

Without an understanding of power and how it undermines the quest for justice, educational psychology becomes a form of disciplinary power—an apology for the status quo. As a politically transformative project, critical multiculturalism helps postformalists work with diverse constituencies who have not traditionally supported movements for social justice. This is why whiteness studies are so important in critical multiculturalism and postformalism. This is why class issues are so important in a transgressive educational psychology, where postformalists see themselves not merely as academic students of culture but as initiators of social movements. An educational psychology that is unable to lead a social, political, and educational transformation undermines the traditional critical notion that there is a moral emptiness to academic work that attempts to understand the world without concurrently attempting to change it.

THE MULTILOGICALITY OF CRITICAL MULTICULTURALISM: MOVING THE BRICOLAGE INTO EDUCATIONAL PSYCHOLOGY

As discussed in my introduction, postformalism calls on educational psychology to bring multiple perspectives to its work. This concept of multilogicality rests at the heart of critical multiculturalism and postformalism. I have expanded these notions in my description of the research bricolage. A complex science is grounded on this multilogicality. One of the reasons we use the term complex is that the more we understand about the world, the more complex it appears to be. In this recognition of complexity we begin to see multiple causations and the possibility of differing vantage points from which to view a phenomenon. It is extremely important to note at this juncture that the context from which one observes an entity shapes what he or she sees. The set of assumptions or the system of meaning making the observer consciously or unconsciously employs shapes the observation.

This assertion is not some esoteric, academic point—it shapes social analysis, political perspectives, curriculum development, teaching and learning, and the field of educational psychology. Acting upon this understanding, postformalists understand that scholarly observations hold more within them to be analyzed than first impressions sometime reveal. In this sense different frames of reference produce multiple interpretations and multiple realities. The mundane, the everyday, and the psychological dimension are multiplex and continuously unfolding—while this is taking place, human interpretation is simultaneously constructing and reconstructing the meaning of what we observe. A multilogical educational psychology promotes a spatial distancing from reality that allows an observer diverse frames of reference.

The distancing may range from the extremely distant like astronauts looking at the earth from the moon, to the extremely close like Georgia O'Keeffe viewing a flower. At the same time, a multilogical scholar values the intimacy of an emotional connectedness that allows empathetic passion to draw knower and known together. In the multiplex, complex postformal view of reality, Western linearity often gives way to simultaneity, as texts become a kaleidoscope of images filled with signs, symbols, and signifiers to be decoded and interpreted. William Carlos Williams illustrated an understanding of such complexity in the early twentieth century as he depicted multiple, simultaneous images and frames of reference in his poetry. Williams attempted to poetically interpret Marcel Duchamp's "Nude Descending a Staircase," with its simultaneous, overlapping representations serving as a model for what postformalists call a cubist cognition.

Teachers and scholars informed by critical multiculturalism's multilogicality understand these concepts. Such educators work to extend their students' cognitive abilities, as they create situations where students come to view the world and disciplinary knowledge from as many frames of reference as possible. In a sense the single photograph of Cartesian thinking is replaced by the multiple angles of the holographic photograph. Energized by this cubist cognition, teachers informed by postformalism and a critical multiculturalism come to understand that the models of teaching they have been taught, the definitions of inquiry with which they have been supplied, the angle from which they have been instructed to view intelligence, and the modes of learning that shape what they perceive to be sophisticated thinking all reflect a particular vantage point in the web of reality. They seek more than one perspective—they seek multilogical insights.

Like reality itself, schools and classrooms are complex matrices of interactions, codes, and signifiers in which both students and teachers are interlaced. Just as a complex and critical multiculturalism asserts that there is no single, privileged way to see the world, there is no one way of representing the world artistically, no one way of teaching science, no one way of writing history. Once teachers escape the entrapment of the positivist guardians of Western tradition and their monocultural, one-truth way of seeing, they come to value and thus pursue new frames of reference in regard to their students, classrooms, and workplaces. In this cognitivist cubist spirit, critical multiculturalist teachers begin to look at lessons from the perspectives of individuals from different race, class, gender, and sexual orientations. They study the perspectives their African American, Latino, white, poor, and wealthy students bring to their classrooms. They are dedicated to the search for new perspectives.

Drawing upon this postformal multilogicality in this cognitive and pedagogical pursuit, these educators, like liberation theologians in Latin America, make no apology for seeking the viewpoints, insights, and sensitivities of the marginalized. The way to see from a perspective differing from that of the positivist guardians involves exploring an institution such as Western education from the vantage point of those who have been marginalized by it. In such a process, subjugated knowledges once again emerge allowing teachers to gain the cognitive power of empathy—a power that enables them to take pictures of reality from different vantage points. The intersection of these diverse vantage points allows for a form of analysis that moves beyond the isolated, decontextualized, and fragmented analysis of positivist reductionism.

Cognitively empowered by these multiplex perspectives, complexity-sensitive, multilogical educators seek a multicultural dialogue between Eastern cultures and Western cultures, a conversation between the relatively wealthy Northern cultures and the impoverished Southern cultures and an intracultural interchange among a variety of subcultures. In this way forms of knowing, representing, and making meaning that have been excluded by the positivist West move us to new vantage points and unexplored planetary perspectives. Understandings derived from the perspective of the excluded or the "culturally different" allow for an appreciation of the nature of justice, the invisibility of the process of oppression, the power of difference and the insight to be gained from a recognition of divergent cultural uses of long hidden knowledges that highlight both our social construction as individuals and the limitations of monocultural ways of meaning making.

Taking advantage of these complex ways of seeing, a whole new world is opened to the field of educational psychology. As cognitive cubists, teachers, students, psychologists, and cultural analysts all come to understand that there are always multiple perspectives. No conversation is over, no discipline totally complete. The domain of art and aesthetics helps us appreciate this concept, as it exposes new dimensions of meaning, new forms of logic unrecognized by the sleepwalking dominant culture. As a cognitive wake-up call, art can challenge what Herbert Marcuse (1955) in *Eros and Civilization* called "the prevailing principle of reason" (p. 185). In this context we come to realize that art and other aesthetic production provide an alternate epistemology, a way of knowing that moves beyond declarative forms of knowledge. Here we see clearly the power of multilogicality and the bricolage: educational psychologists gain new insights into the traditional concerns of their academic domain by looking outside the frameworks of one discipline. It could be quantum physics, it could be history, or as in this case it could be art and aesthetics.

Indeed, literary texts, drama, music, dance, sculpture, and painting empower individuals to see, hear, and feel beyond the surface level of sight and sound. These aesthetic forms can alert educational psychologists to the one-dimensional profiles of the world promoted by reductionistic positivistic researchers. Herbert Marcuse (a central figure in the Frankfurt School of Critical Theory was acutely aware of this cognitive dimension of art and linked it to what he called a critical politics. Art assumes its critical emancipatory value, he wrote, when it is viewed in light of specific historical conditions. Thus, for Marcuse, aesthetic transcendence of repressive social and cultural reality is a deliberate political and cognitive act that identifies the object of art with the repressive social situation to be transcended. This transcendence, this going beyond, of course, is a central goal of postformalism in its politicization of educational psychology.

Following Marcuse's arguments and the sociopolitical concerns of complex aesthetics, does not mean the promotion of educational psychology—or any academic discourse—as propaganda for a particular point of view. This would be a misguided and disastrous interpretation of the ideas promoted here. Engaging in a multilogical critical multiculturalism and postformalism, does not mean following a blueprint for sociopolitical action—instead it implies the opposite. A critical educational psychology passionately seeks justice but is always attuned to new perspectives on what this might mean and how the well-intentioned pursuit of justice may unintentionally oppress particular groups and individuals—critical multiculturalists have watched this occur far too often. To reduce this possibility postformalism promotes a rigorous self-reflection and self-criticism.

Postformalism as it is conceptualized here simply cannot work without this commitment to self-reflection and self-criticism. Indeed, it is obsessively concerned with the ways our consciousness is constructed and our worldviews are formed and how these dynamics shape our interactions. If postformalism is unable to view its own flaws and mistakes, then it is a miserable failure and should be swept into the dustbin of historical folly.

Thus, these critical psychological discourses illuminate the problematic, as they construct new concepts, new modes of cognition, new angles from which to view the world. In this way they give birth to new meanings, as they break through the surface to explore the submerged social, political, and psychological relationships that shape events. When postformalism is at the top of its game and operating effectively, the pedagogy it supports is characterized by acts of defamiliarization. Moreover, an education grounded on a critical educational psychology seeks not only to defamiliarize the commonsense worlds of students but also to create situations where student experience can be used to demilitarize the world of schooling.

In this critical multicultural, postformal form of education, educators employ aesthetic concerns with the "now" to defamiliarize the postivist school's unfortunate tendency to functionalize the role of instruction. In this context postformalist educators join with students to seek pleasurable ways of remaking the institution in line with a respect for intelligence. Overcoming the educational tyranny of an exclusive bourgeoisie reliance on delayed gratification and the mistrust of pleasure that accompanies it, teachers operating in the multilogical zone of complexity promote cognitive abilities unbowed by the mystifying power of the given. Emerging from this playful haughtiness is the realization that postformalism can promote a form of teaching that requires interpretation and a form of thinking that seeks new experiences that facilitate interpretation. Such interpretation exposes the forces that suppress creativity, innovation, and new forms of intelligence. These are the very dynamics that lead us to new frontiers of human being, to what I have labeled a "critical ontology."

The power of the multilogicality of the bricolage is manifested. Cognitive cubism produces a multidimensional form of knowledge that is always open to new interpretations in its hermeneutical connection to larger social, cultural, political, and cognitive processes. Such a multilogical knowledge can never be final because it cannot control the differing contexts within which it will be encountered. In this absence of interpretive closure a critical educational psychology moves understanding away from reductionism into a more complex realm. This cognitive vis-à-vis hermeneutic dynamic reflects the power multiple ways of knowing and their ability to help teachers and students appreciate their own imaginations, creativities, and intelligences. When we rely on particular ways of knowing usually associated with modernist linearity and positivism, teachers operate in a manner that teaches students—particularly those who see the previously unseen—that they are not capable. The Einsteins of our world, the many geniuses who walk among us are quashed before they ever get started. This is a human tragedy.

The guardians of tradition in mechanistic educational psychology are uncomfortable with admitting outsiders into the community of the "cultured" or the fraternity of the "intelligent." This postformal, critical multiculturalist multiple-ways-of-knowing idea is dangerous, they argue, because such openness is the first step down the dangerous road to a loss of standards. The only cognitive and educational alternative to this subversion of standards, the guardians maintain, is an unyielding protection of official ways of seeing and the certified canon of science, history, and literature. In this context, those of us who point to the boundaries and limitations of Western logical thought and its tendency for domination, ethnocentric arrogance and brutality are often faced with the anger and revenge of the guardians. Our call in critical multiculturalism and the bricolage is to not only include previously marginalized knowledges and their ways of seeing in the canon but to bring these scientific, cultural, aesthetic, cognitive, political, and educational perspectives to the effort to rethink intelligence and even who we are as human beings has not been warmly received.

Despite the mainstream resistance to these concerns, critical multiculturalism and postformal educational psychology continue to promote modes of cognition that are: (1) capable of identifying ideological inscriptions in educational and cultural texts of all varieties; and (2) able and willing to challenge them. As a critical educational psychology breaks through parameters of expectation and reveals new ways of seeing and thinking, it performs a unique and valuable role in a democratic society. Once this process is closed off and limited to only what is "acceptable" to particular forms of dominant power, another thread is removed from the democratic tapestry; another perspective is erased from our multiple ways of seeing. The human state of being is reduced.

CHAPTER 101

Postformalism and Critical Ontology—Part 1: Difference, Indigenous Knowledge, and Cognition

JOE L. KINCHELOE

A key dimension of postformal thinking involves valuing and making use of the power of difference. In this context postformalists engage in a form of metaphoric cognition that involves looking at one entity in relation to other entities, in new contexts, in light of new knowledges. Such previously unencountered relationships open new insights to the individual, causing her to think in new ways. In many ways this is what Vygotsky's Zone of Proximal Development (ZPD) is about—it moves the learner to new forms of encounters via the different experiences and vantage points of a learning community. Those operating in the ZPD have experiences that are different from the individual moving into it, thus, providing the newcomer with unanticipated ways of seeing. These new relationships between different entities and different people are profoundly important in understanding cognition, the world around us, and even who we are as human beings.

As I have written elsewhere, Albert Einstein is extremely helpful in getting across the importance of difference and relationship. In his Special Theory of Relativity, for example, Einstein explained that gravity could be used as a case study of how the universe itself could be better understood as a relationship rather than as a collection of separate objects. This concept was missed by Sir Isaac Newton who argued that gravity was a thing, not an Einsteinian relationship. Gravity is not a substance—a wave or a particle—as physicists argued for 250 years after Newton's work on the subject. The genius of Einstein involved his ability to discern that gravity reflected the relationships between space, time, and mass. Indeed, this insight gave Einstein the power to modify the way we understand the universe and lead to a new world of physics that continues to expand. Postformalism employs this Einsteinian concept to think about cognition and educational psychology. Connecting Einsteinian physics with Umberto Maturana and Francisco Varela's Enactivist understanding of the way the mind emerges in response to a diversity of relationships between humans and the world, postformalism begins to make sense of the inseparability of cognition and identity.

This emergence in *relationship* changes the way we conceptualize *being* for both humans and for things-in-the-world. Thus, educational psychologists informed by postformalism begin to appreciate the fact that patterns of connection become more important than sets of fragmented parts. Acting like a metaphor, postformal cognition "sees" these relationships in ostensibly unrelated things, thus connecting patterns of relationship between diverse entities. In this cognitive domain humans construct relationships, in the process building bridges between themselves and their circumstances. On the basis of such relationships we migrate to new cognitive and ontological levels—that is, new ways of thinking and being. This chapter explores the ways teachers and learners can build their own ZPDs in relation to the concept of difference. In this context postformalists draw upon the power of subjugated knowledges—the knowledges of indigenous peoples in particular.

Mainstream teacher education and the mechanistic educational psychological tradition are not very interested in the power of difference and the relationships such power can construct. Concurrently, mainstream teacher education and mechanistic educational psychology have been uninterested in questions of ontology. Mainstream teacher education, for example, provides little insight into the forces that shape teacher identity and consciousness. Becoming educated, becoming a teacher-scholar-researcher necessitates personal transformation based on an understanding and critique of these forces. Here is where postformalists bring in their conception of critical ontology to the reconceptualization of educational psychology. Ontology is the branch of philosophy that studies what it means to be in the world, to be human. In an educational psychological context postformalists study what it means to *be* a teacher in relation to indigenous knowledges and ways of being.

As teachers from the dominant culture explore issues of indigeneity, they highlight both their differences with cultural others, and the social construction of their own subjectivities. In this context they come to understand themselves, the ways they develop curriculum, and their pedagogy in a global world. Such issues become even more important at a time where new forms of economic, political, and military colonialism are reshaping both colonizing and colonized societies. This chapter makes three basic points:

- Critical ontology is grounded on the epistemological and ontological power of difference.
- The study of indigeneity and indigenous ways of being highlights tacit Western assumptions about the nature and construction of selfhood and cognition.
- A notion of critical ontology emerges in these conceptual contexts that helps postformalists push the boundaries of Western selfhood in the twenty-first century as we concurrently gain new respect for the genius of indigenous epistemologies, ontologies, and modes of cognition.

WHAT IS CRITICAL ONTOLOGY?

In this context postformalists engage in the excitement of attaining new levels of consciousness, cognition and "ways of being." Individuals who gain such a critical ontological awareness understand how and why their political opinions, religious beliefs, gender role, racial positions, and sexual orientation have been shaped by dominant cultural perspectives. A critical ontological vision helps postformalists in the effort to gain new understandings and insights as to who we can become. Such a vision helps us move beyond our present state of being—our ontological selves—as we discern the forces that have made us that way. The line between knowledge production, learning, and being is blurred, as the epistemological, the cognitive, and the ontological converge around questions of identity. As we employ the ontological vision we ask questions about ethics, morality, politics, emotion, and gut feelings, seeking not precise steps to reshape our subjectivity but a framework of principles with which we can negotiate. Thus, we join the quest for new, expanded, more just and interconnected ways of thinking and being human.

An important dimension of a critical ontology involves freeing ourselves from the machine metaphors of Cartesianism and its mechanistic educational psychology. Such an ontological stance recognizes the reductionism of viewing the universe as a well-oiled machine and the human mind as a computer. Such colonialized ways of being subvert an appreciation of the amazing life force that inhabits both the universe and human beings. This machine cosmology has positioned human beings as living in a dead world, a lifeless universe. Ontologically, this Western Cartesianism has separated individuals from their inanimate surroundings, undermining any organic interconnection of the person to the cosmos. The life-giving complexity of the inseparability of human and world has been lost and social/cultural/pedagogical/psychological studies of people abstracted—removed from context. Such a removal has exerted disastrous ontological effects. Human beings, in a sense, lost their belongingness to both the world and to other people around them.

The importance of indigenous (Ladislaus Semali and Joe Kincheloe's (1999) *What Is Indigenous Knowledge?*) and other subjugated knowledges emerges in this ontological context. With the birth of modernity, the scientific revolution and the colonial policies they spawned, many pre-modern, indigenous ontologies were lost. Ridiculed by Europeans as primitive, the indigenous ways of being were often destroyed by the colonial conquerors of not only the military but the political, religious, and educational variety as well. While there is great diversity among premodern worldviews and ways of being, there do seem to be some discernible patterns that distinguish them from modernist perspectives. In addition to developing systems of meaning, cognition, and being that were connected to cosmological perspectives on the nature of creation, most premodern viewpoints saw nature and the world at large as living systems. Western, often Christian, observers condescendingly labeled such perspectives as pantheism or nature worship and positioned them as an enemy of monotheism. Not understanding the subtlety and nuance of such indigenous views of the world, Europeans subverted the sense of belonging that accompanied these enchanted understandings of nature. European Christomodernism transformed the individual from a connected participant in the drama of nature to a detached, objective, depersonalized observer.

The Western modernist individual emerged from the process alienated and disenchanted—the micro-individual was removed from the macrocosmos. Such a fragmentation resulted in the loss of cosmological significance and the beginning of a snowballing pattern of ontological imbalance. A critical ontology involves the process of reconnecting human beings on a variety of levels and in numerous ways to a living social and physical web of reality, to a living cosmos. Of course, in this process Westerners have much to learn from indigenous thinkers and educators. Teachers with a critical ontological vision help students connect to the civic web of the political domain, the biotic web of the natural world, the social web of human life, the cognitive web of diverse learning communities, and the epistemological web of knowledge production. In this manner, we all move to the realm of critical ontology where new ways of thinking and being and new ways of being *connected* reshape all people.

THE POSTFORMAL EMPLOYMENT OF THE POWER OF DIFFERENCE

The concept of difference is central to a critical ontology. Gregory Bateson uses the example of binoculars to illustrate this point. The image of the binocular—a singular and undivided picture—is a complex synthesis between images in both the left and right side of the brain. In this context a synergy is created where the sum of the images is greater than the separate parts. As a result of bringing the two different views together, resolution and contrast are enhanced. Even more important, new insight into depth is created. Thus, the relationship between the different parts constructs new dimensions of seeing. Employing such examples of synergies, critical ontologists maintain that juxtapositions of difference create a bonus of insight, of cognitive innovation. This concept becomes extremely important in any psychological, epistemological, social, pedagogical, or self-production activity.

Cartesian rationalism has consistently excluded subjugated/indigenous knowledges from validated databases in diverse disciplines. These local, unauthorized knowledges are central to the work of difference-grounded research. I have referred to this type of multiperspectival (multimethodological and multitheoretical) research as the bricolage. Too often in Western colonial and neocolonial history Europeans have viewed the knowledges and ways of seeing of the poor, the marginalized, and the conquered in a condescending and dismissive manner. Many of these perspectives, of course, were brimming with cosmological, epistemological, cognitive and ontological insight missing from Western perspectives.

Western scholars were often simply too ethnocentric and arrogant to recognize the genius of such subjugated/indigenous information. Critical ontologists unabashedly take a hard look at these perspectives—not in some naïve romantic manner but in a rigorous and critical orientation. They are aware that Western scientific thinking often promotes contempt for indigenous individuals who have learned about a topic such as farming from the wisdom of their ancestors and a lifetime of cultivating the land. Many of the subjugated knowledges critical ontologists employ come from postcolonial backgrounds. Such ways of seeing force such scholars and teachers to account for the ways colonial power has shaped their approaches to knowledge production while inscribing the process of self-production.

Starting research, cognitive studies, and pedagogy with a valuing of non-Western knowledges, critical ontologists can spiral through a variety of such discourses to weave a multilogical theoretical and empirical tapestry. They can even juxtapose them with Western ways of seeing. For example, using a Hindu-influenced ontology that delineates the existence of a non-objective, purposely constructed reality, a critical theory that traces the role of power in producing this construction, a Santiago cognitive theory that maintains we bring forth this constructed world via our action within and upon it, and a poststructuralist feminist theory that alerts us to the ways patriarchal and other structures shape our knowledge about this reality, postformalists gain a more profound understanding of what is happening when human beings encounter the world. The insights we gain and the knowledges we produce with these concepts in mind move us to new levels of both epistemological, cognitive, and ontological awareness. Such an awareness may be similar to what the Vajrayana tradition of Buddhism calls "crazy wisdom." Critical ontologists seek the multilogical orientation of crazy wisdom in their efforts to push the envelope of knowledge production, higher order thinking, and selfhood.

With these insights in mind postformal scholar-teachers can operate in a wide diversity of disciplines and use an infinite number of subjugated and indigenous forms of knowledge. Ethnomathematical knowledges can be used to extend understanding of and knowledge production about math and math pedagogy. Organic African American knowledges of grandmothers, beauticians, and preachers can provide profound insight into the nature of higher order cognition. Hip-hop musicians can help educators working to develop thicker and more insightful understandings of youth cultures and their implications for pedagogy. Ancient African epistemologies and ontologies can help shape the theoretical lenses one uses to study and teach about contemporary racism and class bias.

Feminist understandings are important as they open doors to previously excluded knowledges. Such knowledges often point out the problems with the universal pronouncements of Cartesianism. The presence of gender diversity in this context reveals the patriarchal inscriptions on what was presented as universal, always true, validated knowledge about some aspect of the world. Indeed, this psychological pronouncement about the highest form of moral reasoning may apply more to men than it does to women—and even then it may apply more to upper-middle-class men than to lower socioeconomic class men or more to Anglo men than to Asian and African men. With these feminist insights in mind, critical ontologists find it easier to view the ways the knowledges they produce reflect the cultural, historical, and gendered contexts they occupy. In this context universality is problematized. Indeed, the more we are aware of those different from us on a variety of levels, the harder it is to produce naive universal knowledges. In our heightened awareness, in our crazy wisdom, we produce more sensitive, more aware modes of information. Once the subjugated/indigenous door is open the possibilities are infinite.

POSTFORMAL KNOWLEDGE: THE BRICOLAGE, DIFFERENCE, AND SELF-AWARENESS IN RESEARCH

When researchers, for example, encounter difference in the nature of the other, they enter into symbiotic relationships where their identity is changed. Such researchers are no longer merely obtaining information, but are entering a space of transformation where previously excluded perspectives operate to change consciousness of both self and the world. Thus, research in a critical ontological context changes not only what one knows but also who one actually is. In this process the epistemological and ontological domains enter into a new relationship that produces dramatic changes. Returning to the beginning of this chapter, Lev Vygotsky was on the right track as he documented the importance of the context in which learning takes place—the zone of proximal development (ZPD). Difference in the sense we are using it here expands the notion of the ZPD into the domain of research, drawing upon the power of our interactions in helping shape the ways we make meaning. In the new synergized position, ontologically sensitive researchers construct new realities where they take on new and expanded roles.

Aware of the power of difference, these researchers develop a new consciousness of the self: (1) the manner in which it has been constructed; (2) its limitations; and (3) a sense of immanence concerning what it can become. Self-awareness is a metacognitive skill that has historically been more valued in Eastern traditions such as Buddhism, Taoism, and Yoga than in the West. Time and again we see the value of pluralism manifest itself in this discussion of difference and the bricolage. A pluralistic epistemology helps us understand the way we are situated in the web of reality and how this situatedness shapes what we see as researchers, as observers of the world. Such awareness reveals the limited nature of our observations of the world. Instead of researchers making final pronouncements on the way things are, postformalists begin to see themselves in a larger interdisciplinary and intercultural conversation. Critical ontologists attuned to this dynamic, focus their attention on better modes of listening and respecting diverse viewpoints. Such higher order listening moves them to new levels of self-consciousness.

Of course, difference does not work as an invisible hand that magically shapes new insights into self and world. Humans must exercise their complex hermeneutic (interpretive) abilities to forge these connections and interpret their meanings. In this context postformalists as critical ontologists confront difference and then decide where they stand in relation to it. They must discern what to make of what it has presented them. With this in mind these critical scholar-educators work hard to develop relationships with those different from themselves that operate to create new meanings in the interactions of identity and difference. In this interaction, knowledge producers grow smarter as they reject modernist Cartesian notions that cultural conflicts can be solved only by developing monological universal principles of epistemology and universal steps to the process of research. Too often, these scholars/cultural workers understand that these "universal" principles simply reflect colonial Western ways of viewing the world hiding in the disguise of universalism. Rigorous examination of the construction of self and society are closed off in such universalism. Indeed, it undermines the development of a critical self-consciousness.

In the face of a wide variety of different knowledges and ways of seeing the world, the cosmos human beings think they know collapses. In a counter-colonial move critical ontologists raise questions about any knowledges and ways of knowing that claim universal status. In this context they make use of this suspicion of universalism in combination with global, subjugated, and indigenous knowledges to understand how they have been positioned in the world. Almost all of us from Western backgrounds or non-Western colonized backgrounds have been implicated in some way in the web of universalism. The inevitable conflicts that arise from this implication do not have to be resolved immediately. At the base of these conflicts rest the future of global culture as well as the future of research, cognition, and pedagogy. Recognizing that these are generative issues that engage us in a productive process of analyzing self and world is in itself a powerful recognition. The value of both this recognition and the process of working through the complicated conceptual problems are treasured by critical ontologists. Indeed, they avoid any notion of finality in the resolution of such dilemmas.

POSTFORMAL INTERCONNECTIONS: INDIGENEITY AND THE CONSTRUCTION OF SELFHOOD

Always looking for multiple perspectives, insight in diverse places, the power of difference, postformalists as critical ontologists examine human interconnectedness via the lens of indigenous knowledges. Many systems of indigenous knowledge illustrate the *enaction* of interconnectedness and raise profound questions about the ways Western scholars have constructed knowledge, intelligence, scientific methods, and the scholarly disciplines. While there is great diversity in these indigenous knowledges, most assume that humans are part of the world of nature. Extending this holism, many indigenous scholars maintain that the production and acquisition of knowledge involves a process of interactions among the human body, the mind, and the spirit. R. Sambuli Mosha (2000) in *The Heartbeat of Indigenous Africa: A Study of the Chagga Educational System* writes that among the East African Chagga peoples knowledge that is passed along to others must further the development of morality, goodness, harmony, and spirituality. Indeed, he continues, in the Chagga worldview it is impossible to separate these domains. Such fragmentation simply does not make sense to the Chagga. Embedded in every Chagga child is a part of the divine dimension of reality, illustrating the interconnectedness of all dimensions of the cosmos. Thus, knowledge production and the construction of selfhood cannot take place outside this intricate web of relationships.

In Cartesian-Newtonian modes of colonial science the interrelationships cherished by the Chagga are not as *real* as their individual parts. For example, in mechanistic educational psychology consciousness is often reduced to neural and chemical dynamics. Researchers in this context often study nothing outside the narrow confines of brain chemistry from graduate school to retirement. The notion that the understanding of human consciousness might be enhanced by anthropological, theological, or philosophical investigations rarely, if ever, occurs to such researchers over the decades of their research.

Making use of indigenous knowledges and the theological insights of Buddhism in this domain, cognitive theorist Francisco Varela develops a dramatically different concept of consciousness. Understanding the indigenous notion that the individual cannot be understood outside the community of which she is a part, Varela posits that human consciousness *emerges* from the social and biological interactions of its various parts. This understanding, postformalists contend, will revolutionize the fields of cognitive science, educational psychology, and even pedagogy. When scholars grasp the multilogical, interrelated nature of the possibilities for dramatic changes in the ways scholars and educators operate begin to take place. Using the indigenous metaphor, knowledge *lives* in the cultures of indigenous peoples. As opposed to the disciplinary knowledges of Cartesian-Newtonianism, which are often stored in archives or laboratories, indigenous knowledges live in everyday cultural practices.

Critical ontologists ask hard questions of indigenous knowledges. They know that folk knowledges—like Western scientific knowledges—often help construct exploitation and oppression for diverse groups and individuals. With this caution and resistance to essentialism in mind, ontological scholars study the ways many indigenous peoples in Africa construct the interrelationships of their inner selves to the outer world. This indigenous tendency to avoid dualism that when unacknowledged undermines the balance of various relationships is profoundly important. For example, the dualism between humans and nature can wreck havoc in an indigenous social system. In many indigenous African conceptions humanness is viewed as a part of nature, not separate from it. Unlike scholars in the Cartesian-Newtonian disciplines, the world was too sacred for humans to study and dominate or conquer. Once humanness and the environment were viewed as separate entities, forces were unleashed that could destroy the delicate eco- and social systems that sustained the indigenous culture. Thus, to accept the dualism between humanness and nature in the minds of many African peoples was tantamount to committing mass suicide.

Another example of indigenous culture whose knowledges critical ontologists deem valuable is the Andean peoples of South America. Everyone and everything in traditional Andean culture is sentient, as, for example, the rivers and mountains have ears and eyes. Acting in the world in this cultural context is a dimension of being in relationship to the world. In one's actions within the physical environment, an Andean individual is in conversation with the mountains, rivers, trees, lakes, etc. This language of conversation replaces in Andean culture a Western traditional scientific language of knowing. A profound epistemological shift has taken place in this replacement. In Andean culture the concept of knower and known is irrelevant. Instead humans and physical entities engage in reciprocal relationships, carrying on conversations in the interests of both.

These conversations have been described as mutually nurturing events, acts that enhance the ontological evolution of all parties involved via their tenderness and empathy for the living needs of the other. Thus, the epistemology at work here involves more than simply knowing about something. It involves tuning oneself in to the other's mode of being—its ontological presence—and entering into a life generating relationship with it (Apffel-Marglin, 1995). Critical ontologists take from this an understanding of a new dimension of the inseparable relationship between knowing and being. Those working in the academic disciplines of Western societies must enter into ontological relationships with that which they are studying. Such relationships should be enumerated and analyzed. How am I changed by this relationship? How is the object of my study changed or potentially changed by the relationship?

Great change occurs as a result of the Andean peoples' conversation with nature. Nature's voice is heard through the position and brilliance of planets and stars; the speed, frequency, color, and smell of the wind; and the size and number of particular wild flowers to mention only a few. Such talk tells Andeans about the coming weather and various dimensions of cultivation and they act in response to such messages. Because of the overwhelming diversity of ecosystems and climates in the Andes mountains and valleys, these conversations are complex. Interpretations of meanings—like any hermeneutic acts—are anything but self-evident. Such conversations and the actions they catalyze allow the Andean peoples to produce an enormous variety of cultivated plant species that amaze plant geneticists from around the world.

The Andeans actually have a word for those places where the conversation between humans and the natural world take place. *Chacras* include the land where the Andeans cultivate their crops, the places where utensils are crafted, and the places where herds and flocks live and graze. According to the Andeans these are all places where all entities come together to discuss the regeneration of life. The concept of interrelationship is so important in the Andean culture that the people use the word, *ayllu*, to signify a kinship group that includes not only other human beings but animals, mountains, streams, rocks, and the spirits of a particular geographical place. Critical ontological scholars adapt these indigenous Andean concepts to the rethinking of the ways they study, as they identify the methodologies, epistemologies, ontologies, cultural systems, social theories, ad infinitum that they employ in their multilogical understanding of the research act. Those who research the social, psychological, and educational worlds hold a special responsibility to those concepts and the people they research to select critical and life affirming logics of inquiry. A critical hermeneutics demands that relationships at all levels be respected and engaged in ways that produce justice and new levels of understanding—in ways that regenerate life and, central to our ontological concerns, new ways of being.

Thus, postformalists as critical ontologists are able to make use of the power of difference in the context of subjugated/indigenous knowledges. The power of difference or "ontological mutualism" transcends Cartesianism's emphasis on the thing-in-itself. The tendency in Cartesian-Newtonian thinking is to erase mutualism's bonus of insight in the abstraction of the object of inquiry from the processes and contexts of which it is a part. In this activity it subverts difference. The power of these synergies exists not only in the cognitive, social, pedagogical, and epistemological domains but in the physical world as well. Natural phenomena, as Albert Einstein illustrated in physics and Humberto Mataurana and Francisco Varela laid out in biology and cognition, operate in states of interdependence. These ways of seeing have produced perspectives on the workings of the planet that profoundly differ from the views produced by Western science.

What has been fascinating to many is that these post-Einsteinian perspectives have in so many ways reflected the epistemologies and ontologies of ancient non-Western peoples in India, China, and Africa and indigenous peoples around the world. Thus, critical ontology's use of indigenous knowledge is not offered as some new form of postcolonial exploitation—as in pharmaceutical companies' rush into indigenous locales to harvest plants that indigenous peoples have known for millennia possess medicinal qualities. In this context such products are then marketed as culturally sensitive postcolonial forms of exotica. The hipness of such entrepreneurial diversity provides little benefits for the indigenous people watching the process—they are not the beneficiaries of the big profits. Instead, postformalism vis-à-vis critical ontology employs indigeneous peoples as teachers, as providers of wisdom. In their respect for such indigenous knowledges and indigenous peoples, critical ontologists use such indigenous teachings to create a world more respectful and hospitable to indigenous peoples' needs and ways of being.

REFERENCE

Apffel-Marglin, F. (1995). Development or decolonization in the Andes? *Interculture: International Journal of Intercultural and Transdisciplinary Research,* 28(1), 3–17.

CHAPTER 102

Postformalism and Critical Ontology—Part 2: The Relational Self and Enacted Cognition

JOE L. KINCHELOE

Making use of our concept of difference and the insights provided by indigenous knowledges, cognitive activities, and ways of being, we are ready to examine the relationship connecting the epistemological, the cognitive, and the ontological. In a critical ontology, the teaching and learning emerge as profoundly exciting enterprises because they are always conceptualized in terms of what we can become—both in an individual and a collective context. In our socio-ontological imagination, we can transcend the Enlightenment category of abstract individualism and move toward a more textured concept of the relational individual. While abstract individualism and a self-sufficient ontology seem almost *natural* in the Western modernist world, of course, such is not the case in many indigenous cultures and has not been the case even in Western societies in previous historical eras. In ancient Greece, for example, it is hard to find language that identified "the self" or "I"—such descriptions were not commonly used because the individual was viewed as a part of a collective who could not function independently of the larger social group. In the "commonsense" of contemporary Western society and its unexamined ontological assumptions this way of seeing self is hard to fathom.

ESCAPING THE WESTERN FRAGMENTED SELF

Enlightenment ontology discerns the natural state of the individual as solitary. The social order in this modernist Eurocentric context is grounded on a set of contractual transactions between isolated individual atoms. In other works I have referred to Clint Eastwood's "man with no name" cinematic character who didn't need a "damn thing from nobody" as the ideal Western male way of being—the ontological norm. Operating in this context, we clearly discern, for example, cognitive psychology's tradition of focusing on the autonomous development of the individual monad. In postformalism's critical ontology a human being simply can't exist outside the inscription of community with its processes of relationship, differentiation, interaction, and subjectivity. Indeed, in this critical ontology the relational embeddedness of self is so context dependent that psychologists, sociologists, and educators can never isolate a finalized completed "true self." Since the self is always in context and in process, no final delineation of a notion such as ability can be determined. Thus, we are released from the rugged cross of IQ and such hurtful and primitive colonial conceptions of "intelligence." In this context it is interesting to note that famed psychometricians Richard Herrnstein and Charles Murray (1994), in *The Bell Curve*, noted without any data that the average IQ of Africans is probably around seventy-five—epistemological/ontological neocolonialism in a transparent form.

One can quickly discern the political consequences of a Cartesian ontology. Human beings in Western liberal political thought become abstract bearers of particular civic rights. If individuals are relational, context-embedded beings, however, these abstract rights may be of little consequence. A critical ontology insists that individuals live in specific places with particular types of relationships. They operate or are placed in the web of reality at various points of race, class, gender, sexual, religious, physical ability, geographical place, and other continua. Where individuals find themselves in this complex web holds dramatic power consequences. Their location shapes their relationship to both dominant culture and Western colonialism and the psychological and curricular assumptions that accompanies them. In other words the intelligence mechanistic psychology deems these individuals to possess profoundly depends on this contextual, power-inscribed placement. A prime manifestation of ontological alienation involves a lack of recognition of the dramatic effect of these dynamics on everything that takes place in the psycho-educational cosmos.

In the context of postformalism's critical ontology the autonomous self with a fixed intellectual ability becomes an anachronism. As an effort to appreciate the power of human beings to affect their own destinies, to exercise human agency, and to change social conditions, critical ontologists study selfhood in light of the sociological, cultural studies, cultural psychological, and critical analytical work of the last few decades. Much of what dominant psychology and education consider free will and expressions of innate intelligence are simply manifestations of the effects of particular social, cultural, political, and economic forces. While we can make decisions on how we operate as human beings, we are never completely independent of these structuring forces. This is true no matter who we are—nobody can operate outside of society or free from cultural, linguistic, ideological influences.

It is important to note here that neo-positivist educational policy makers contend that their work takes place outside of the influence of these dynamics. They claim that their work avoids cultural values and morally inscribed issues and because of such diligence, they have presented us the truth about how students learn and how teachers should teach. In the critical ontological context developed here, such researchers must take a closer look at who they are and the structuring forces that have shaped their views of the world, mind, and self. Their inability to discern the effects of these forces reflects ontological alienation. Such alienation undermines their ability to imagine new and better ways of being human both for themselves and for the teachers and students their knowledges and policies oppress.

A postformal education informed by a complex ontology asks the question: how do we move beyond simply uncovering the sources of consciousness construction in our larger attempt to reconstruct the self in a critical manner? Critical teachers must search in as many locations as possible for alternate discourses, ways of thinking and being that expand the envelopes of possibility. In this context teachers explore literature, history, popular culture, and ways of forging community in subjugated/indigenous knowledges. Here teachers develop their own and their students' social and aesthetic imaginations. As postformalists we imagine what we might become by recovering and reinterpreting what we once were. The excitement of education as ontological quest is powerful.

CONSTRUCTING A CRITICAL ONTOLOGY:
A POSTFORMAL SELF

Employing an understanding of complexity theory, Maturana and Varela's Santiago Enactivism as the process of life, a postcolonial appreciation of indigeneity, critical theoretical foundations, the critique of Cartesianism, and poststructuralist feminist analysis, we can lay the conceptual foundations for a new mode of selfhood. Such a configuration cannot be comprehensively delineated here, but we can begin to build theoretical pathways to get around the Cartesian limitations on the ontological imagination. With Humberto Maturana and Francisco Valera's concept that living things constantly remake themselves in interaction with their environments, our notion of a new self or a critical ontology is grounded on the human ability to use new social contexts and experiences, exposure to new knowledges and ways of being to reformulate subjectivity. This reformulation of subjectivity is a central dimension of learning in a postformal context—the inseparability of ontology and cognition. In this context the concept of personal ability becomes a de-essentialized cognition of possibility. No essentialized bounded self can access the cognitive potential offered by epiphanies of difference or triggered by an "insignificant" insight.

As we begin to identify previously unperceived patterns in which the self is implicated, the possibility of cognitive change and personal growth is enhanced. As the barriers between mind and multiple contexts are erased, the chance that more expanded forms of "cognitive autopoiesis"— self-constructed modes of higher-order thinking—will emerge is increased. A more textured, a thicker sense of self-production and the nature of self and other is constructed in this process. As we examine the self and its relationship to others in cosmological, epistemological, linguistic, social, cultural, and political contexts, we gain a clearer sense of our purpose in the world especially in relation to justice, the indigenous-informed notion of interconnectedness, and even love. In these activities we move closer to the macro-processes of life and their micro-expressions in everyday life. We are developing the postformal self where cognition and identity are never seen as separate dynamics.

A key aspect of the life processes is the understanding of difference that comes from recognition of patterns of interconnectedness. Knowing that an individual from an upper-middle-class European background living in a Virginia suburb will be considered culturally bizarre by a group of tribespeople from the Amazon rainforest is a potentially profound learning experience in the domain of the personal. How is the suburbanite viewed as bizarre? What cultural practices are seen as so unusual? What mannerisms are humorous to the tribespeople? What worldviews are baffling to them? The answers to such questions may shock the suburbanite into reorienting her view of her own "normality." The interaction may induce her to ask questions of the way she is perceived by and the way she perceives others. Such a bracketing of the personal may be quite liberating. This interaction with the power of difference is another example of Maturana and Valera's structural coupling that creates a new relationship with other and with self. In Maturana and Varela's conceptualization a new inner world is created as a result of such coupling.

Such explorations on the ontological frontier hold profound curricular implications. As students pursue rigorous study of diverse global knowledges, they come to understand that the identities of their peer groups and families constitute only a few of countless historical and cultural ways to be human. As they study their self-production in wider biological, sociological, cultural studies, historical, theological, psychological, and counter-canonical contexts, they gain insights into their ways of being. As they engage the conflicts that induce diverse knowledge producers to operate in conflicting ways, students become more attuned to the ideological, discursive, and regulatory forces of power operating in all knowledges. This is not nihilism, as many defenders of the Eurocanon argue; this is the exciting learning process of exploring the world and the self and their relationship in all of the complexity such study requires.

The processual and relational notions of self structurally couple with the sociocultural context and can only be understood by studying them with these dynamics in mind. These characteristics of self hold profound implications politically, psychologically, and pedagogically. If our notion of the self emerges in its counter-colonial relationship with multiple dimensions of the world, it is by its nature a participatory entity. Such an interactive dynamic is always in process, and thus demands a reconceptualization of the concept of individualism and self-interest—a reconceptualism that leads to the postformal self. The needs of self and others in this context begin to merge, as the concept of self-reliance takes on new meanings. Notions of educational purpose, evaluation, and curriculum development are transformed when these new conceptions of the personal domain come into the picture. In the first decade of the twenty-first century we stand merely on the threshold of the possibilities this notion of selfhood harbors.

POSTFORMALISM AND ENACTIVISM: PSYCHO-ONTOLOGICAL POSSIBILITIES

A critical ontology understands that the effort to explain complex cognitive, biological, social, or pedagogical events by the reductionistic study of their components outside of the larger processes of which they are a part will not work. It will not move us to new levels of understanding or set the stage for new, unexplored modes of being human. The social, biological, cognitive, or the pedagogical domain is not an assortment of discrete objects that can be understood in isolation from one another. The fragmented pieces put forth in such studies do not constitute reality—even if commonsense tells Westerners they do. The deeper structures, the tacit forces, the processes that shape the physical world and the social world will be lost to such observers. As I argue in the introduction to *The Stigma of Genius: Einstein, Consciousness, and Education* (1999), Einstein's General Theory of Relativity could not have been produced without this ontological understanding of connectedness, process, and the limitations of studying only things-in-themselves.

For 250 years physicists had been searching for the basic building block of gravity—some contended it was a particle (a graviton), others argued it was a gravity wave. Einstein pointed out that it was neither, that it was not a *thing* at all. Gravity, he maintained, was a part of the structure of the universe that existed as a relationship connecting mass, space, and time. This insight, of course, changed the very nature of how we conceptualize the universe. It should have changed how we conceptualize epistemology, cognition, pedagogy, and ontology. Of course, it didn't— and that's what we are still working on. The emphasis on studying and teaching about the world as a compilation of fragmented things-in-themselves has returned with a vengeance, of course, in recent educational reforms and mandates for use of only positivistic forms of educational research.

In this context the work of Humberto Maturana is instructive. Maturana and Varela's Santiago Enactivism employ the same ontological concept of interconnectedness that Einstein's used in the General Theory of Relativity to explain life as a process, a system of interconnections. Indeed, they argue, that the process of cognition is the process of life. In Enactivism mind is not a thing-in-itself but a process—an activity where the interactions of a living organism with its environment constitute cognition. In this relationship, life itself and cognition are indelibly connected and reveal this interrelationship at diverse levels of living and what are still considered nonliving domains. Where mind ends and matter begins is difficult to discern, a situation that operates to overturn the long-standing and problematic Cartesian separation of the two entities. In Mataurana's and Varela's conception, mind and matter are merely parts of the same process—one cannot exist without the other. A critical ontology seeks to repair this rupture between mind and matter, self and world. In this reconnection we enter into a new phase of human history, new modes of cognition, and dramatic changes in educational psychology and pedagogy.

According to the Enactivists, perception and cognition also operate in contradiction to Cartesianism, as they construct a reality as opposed to reflecting an external one already in existence. The interactive or circular organization of the nervous system described by Mataurana is similar to the hermeneutic circle as it employs a conversation between diverse parts of a system to construct meaning. Autopoiesis as the process of self-production is the way living things operate. Self-construction emerges out of a set of relationships between simple parts. In the hermeneutic circle the relationships between parts "self-construct" previously unimagined meanings. Thus, in an ontological context meaning emerges not from the thing-in-itself but from its relationships to an infinite number of other things. In this complexity we understand from another angle that there is no final meaning of anything; meanings are always evolving in light of new relationships, new horizons. Thus, in a critical ontology our power as meaning makers and producers of new selfhoods is enhanced. Cognition is the process in which living systems organize the world around them into meaning. With this in mind critical ontology creates a new era of immanence—"what could be" has never implied so much.

Specifically, Mataurana and Varela argue that our identities do not come with us into the world in some neatly packaged unitary self. Since they "rise and subside" in a series of shifting relationships and patterns, the self can be described using the Buddhist notion that the self is empty of self-nature. Understanding this, Francisco Varela maintains, self-understanding and self-change become more possible than ever before. The self, therefore, is not a material entity but takes on more a virtual quality. Human beings have the experience of self, but no self—no central controlling mechanism—is to be found. Much is to be gained by an understanding of the virtual nature of the self. Such knowledge is an important dimension of a critical ontology. According to the Enactivists this knowledge helps us develop intelligent awareness—a profound understanding of the construction and the functioning of selfhood. Intelligent awareness is filled with wisdom but devoid of the egocentrism that undermines various notions of critical knowing. In such a context intelligent awareness cannot be separated from ethical insight. Without this ontological understanding many of pedagogies designed to empower will fan the flames of the egocentrism they attempt to overcome. If nothing else, a critical ontology cultivates humility without which wisdom is not possible.

ENACTIVISM AND THE POSTFORMAL SELF—RELATIONAL SELFHOOD

From Maturana and Varela's perspective learning takes place when a self-maintaining system develops a more effective relationship with the external features of the system. In this context Enactivism is highlighting the profound importance of *relationship* writ large as well as the centrality of the nature and quality of the relationships an organism makes with its environment. In a cognitive context, this is an extension of Vygotsky's notion of the zone of proximal development (ZPD) to the ontological realm—it is our assertion here that indigeneity should become a part of Westerners' ZPD. In the development of a critical ontology, we learn from these ideas that political empowerment vis-à-vis the cultivation of the intellect demand an understanding of the system of relationships that construct our selfhood. In the case of a critical form of pedagogy, these relationships always involve students' connections to cultural systems, language, economic concerns, religious belief, social status, and the power dynamics that constitute them. With the benefit of understanding the self-in-relationship teachers gain a new insight into what is happening in any learning situation. Living on the borderline between self and external system and self and other, learning never takes place outside of these relationships. Such an appreciation of the postformal self changes our orientation toward pedagogy.

Teachers who view classroom practice in the ontological framework of the postmodern self understand their role as creators of situations where students' experiences could intersect with information gleaned from the academic disciplines. They value the pragmatic dimensions of the classroom intersection of selfhood and cognition. In contrast, if knowledge and learning are viewed as simply mastering an external body of information independent of human beings, then the role of the teacher is to take this knowledge and insert it into the minds of students. Thus, in the separation of cognition, epistemology and ontology, evaluation procedures, for example, tend to emphasize the retention of isolated bits and pieces of data. Conceptual thinking is discouraged, as mechanistic schooling trivializes the complexity of learning. Students are evaluated on the lowest level of human cognition—the ability to memorize in a decontextualized context. Thus, if pedagogical practice is removed from the understandings provided by these epistemological, ontological, and cognitive dynamics, schooling will remain merely an unengaging hoop through which to jump on the road to adulthood.

As we now know, a critical ontology is intimately connected to a relational self. Humans are ultimately the constructs of relationships, not fragmented monads or abstract individuals. From Varela's perspective this notion of humans as constructs of relationships corresponds precisely to what he is labeling the virtual self. A larger pattern—in the case of humans, consciousness— arises from the interaction of local elements. This larger pattern seems to be driven by a central controlling mechanism that can never be located. Thus, we discern the origin of traditional psychology's dismissal of consciousness as irrelevant. This not only constituted throwing out the baby with the bath water but discarding the tub, the bathroom fixtures, and the plumbing as well. In this positivistic articulation the process of life and the basis of the cognitive act were deemed unimportant. A critical ontology is always interested in these processes because they open us to a previously occluded insight into the nature of selfhood, of human being. The autopoiesis, the self-making allows humans to perpetually reshape themselves in their new relationships and resulting new patterns of perception and behavior.

There is no way to predict the relationships individuals will make and the nature of the self-(re)construction that will ensue. Such uncertainty adds yet another element of complexity to the study of sociology, psychology, and pedagogy, as it simultaneously catalyzes the possibilities of human agency. It causes those enamored with critical ontology yet another reason to study the inadequacies of Cartesian science to account for the intricacies of the psychological domain. Physical objects *don't necessarily* change their structures via their interaction with other objects. A critical ontology understands that human beings do change their structures as a result of their interactions. Thus, the human mind moves light years beyond the lifeless mechanistic computer model of mind—a psychological way of seeing that reduces mental activity to information processing.

The human self-organization process—while profoundly more complex than the World Wide Web—is analogous to the way the Web arranges itself by random and not-so-random connections. The Web is an autopoietic organism that constructs itself in a hypertextual mode of operation. Unanticipated links create new concepts, ways of perceiving, and even ways of being among those that enter into this domain of epistemological emergence. Such an experience reminds one that a new cultural logic has developed that transcends the mechanical dimensions of the machine epistemologies and ontologies of the modernist industrial era. Consider the stunning implications that when numerous simple entities possessing simple characteristics are thrown together—whether it be Web sites on the Internet or individuals' relationships with aspects of their environments—amazing things occur. From such interactions emerge a larger whole that is not guided by a central controlling mechanism. Self-awareness of this process of creation may lead to unanticipated modes of learning and new concepts of human being.

Postformalist teachers and students have no choice; they must deal with these ontological issues. When they are considered within the context of our understanding of the power of difference and the specific benefits of indigeneity, a postcolonial pedagogy begins to take shape that is truly global in its scope, its concerns and its influences. Such a curriculum is transformative in ways that other "transformative" curricula have not been in its connection to a plethora of knowledges and ways of being. Employing interconnectedness with difference to push the boundaries of the Western alienated self, this postcolonial pedagogy sets off an autopoietic process energized by the interplay of multiple forms of difference—cultural, political, epistemological, cognitive, and, of course, ontological. It will be fascinating to watch where a critical ontology can take us in the coming years.

REFERENCES

Herrnstein, R. J., and Murray, C. (1994). *The Bell Curve: Intelligence and Class Structure in American Life.* New York: Free Press.

Kincheloe, J. L., Steinberg, S. R., and Tippins, D. (1999). *The Stigma of Genius: Einstein, Consciousness, and Education.* New York: Peter Lang.

CHAPTER 103

Educational Psychology in a New Paradigm: Learning a Democratic Way of Teaching

ROCHELLE BROCK AND
JOE L. KINCHELOE

Rochelle: I recently attended an event at a high school in the Bronx that celebrated the creative expression of its students. The event was called One Mike! and was put on by a group of students who were members of The Society for Independent Thought to showcase the poetic talent of its members. I sat in the audience surrounded by students (and their parents) who were considered by the system "throw-aways." Instead these students recited poetry and prose about love, death, hope, despair in voices filled with humor and anger, strength and sadness. They were aware of how they are perceived in society and they are aware of the obstacles (at least on a surface level) that confront them daily, yet there was a vibrancy that was infused in the event and in their words. I left the school feeling both hopeful for the future of these children, based on what I had just experienced, and incredibly sad because I knew what they were up against.

When I place my visit to the Bronx in the context of this article I of course can see the immediate connections between the students, their teachers, and the problematics with traditional educational psychology. These same students that displayed an abundance of talent and insight into the human condition would be deemed unintelligent by the school system and the psychometrics of education psychology. All the students were Black or Latino and most were from low-income families. These two factors in the minds of education psychologists presuppose the intellect and ultimate destiny of the students.

Joe: I can understand your sadness. As class inequality, especially along the lines of race and gender, continues to expand in the twenty-first century, students, of course, are the innocent victims caught in the trap of neoliberal economic policies and a pervading social unconsciousness. What is particularly amazing to me is that the very discussion of this growing class inequality and its impact on students seems somehow out of place in mainstream educational discourse. Educational leaders frequently tell me that calls to abolish welfare exact more severe punishment for crime, end social programs, destroy affirmative action, and have little to do with questions of education. "Let's keep politics out of education," they politely ask. My point is exactly the opposite of such educators—I want to make explicit what everyone wishes would just go away. My purpose in general is to expose the tacit political dynamics that exacerbate the class divisions between students. I am specifically interested in the ways that mainstream educational psychology often "certifies the damage" that class politics exacts on contemporary American students.

Rochelle: I always find it so ironic when people insist that education and the ways schools operate is not political. In order to understand the most important things about schooling—what is taught, who teaches, how it is taught—you have to address the political dimensions of schooling.

Joe: Something educational psychology is afraid to do. The term psychologization, has been used in recent years to denote the tendency within social, cultural, and educational work to depoliticize. Embedded in the concept is a moral and ethical relativism that subverts the attempt to connect teaching with questions of social justice. In mainstream educational psychology the insights gained over the past few decades concerning the political and cultural inscriptions of research have fallen on deaf ears. Without such an understanding, educational psychologists support an education that views the poor and nonwhite through the lenses of dominant Western European, male, upper-middle-class culture. As cultural actors, such psychologists look only for cognitive traits with which they are familiar. As a result, only a culturally specific set of indicators of aptitude is sought. In this way the abilities of students from cultures different than the psychologist are dismissed. In a political context, those who deviate from the socioeconomic and cultural norms of psychology fail to gain the power of psychological and educational validation so needed in an effort to achieve socioeconomic mobility and status in contemporary societies.

Rochelle: Historically, education has served as a convenient means of maintaining the status quo of those in power. Michael Apple (1999), posits that education in the United States fosters our belief in the concept of a meritocratic society. We become who we are based on our merits and not on the social, political, historical structures of society. And when we don't succeed it's our fault and not the societal structure that is constructed on inequality based on race, class, and gender differences. In this way, education mirrors the undemocratic and class-based character of economic life in the United States. The system of education in a capitalistic economy trains a class of people to be nonthinkers. Although the American Dream persists, the truth behind it proves to be a falsehood many times over. The American Dream is defined primarily by the economic market, property, and, power relationships. We are talking about power. Put simply, "they" will not let anything happen that is not in "their" best interest.

Just as insidious as the concept of The American Dream is the current administrations educational policy No Child Left Behind (NCLB). In a misguided attempt to improve public education this policy is perhaps one of the most detrimental to students and teachers. Based on education psychology, NCLB uses test, test, and more tests to prove a school is doing well or poorly. Those schools who pass are rewarded, and those failing are punished. But we of course know that the pass and fail rate of the various schools is importantly based on factors that NCLB doesn't take into account. So we are left with good teachers who in fear for their jobs teach to the test, schools that are given report cards for poor performance, NCLB requiring items that the funding is not available for and ultimately (as one anti-NCLB Web site calls itself) *No Child Left*, at least a certain type of child. The school that the students of One Mike! attended was one of the NCLB failing schools and is due to be closed in two years.

The American educational system has three functions. The first purpose of education is to provide information for students. This information cannot be neutral by its very nature, and for communities of color the information provided is more often inferior to and at odds with the information provided to the White community. The second goal is to control people and to pigeonhole individuals into their predetermined place in society. The final purpose or goal of Euro-American education is to instill Anglo-Saxon male values or cultural frames of reference.

The purpose of schooling whenever delineated by critical thinkers all have in common the knowledge that schools are not about creating a just society but more about maintaining the status quo—keeping power out of the hands of the poor and blacks and Latinos. Educational psychologists help schools fulfill this based on the paradigm under which they operate. Either a student fits into the accepted, culturally specific norm of White, male, upper-middle-class values or they are placed at the margins of acceptability. Education psychologists base their hierarchy of intelligence on cultural traits with which they are familiar—their own.

Joe: The discipline of educational psychology and the educational leaders it informs have had difficulty understanding that the poor and nonwhite students are not stupid. Often children from working class and lower-socioeconomic-class homes do not ascribe the same importance to the mental functions required by intelligence/achievement tests and academic work that middle- and upper-middle-class students do. In this context the difference between cultural disposition and intellectual ability is lost upon the field of educational psychology. Working class and poor students often see academic work as unreal, as a series of short-term tasks rather than something with a long-term justification. Thus, these students many times display little interest in school. This lack of motivation is often interpreted by teachers, of course, as inability or lack of intelligence. Poor performance on standardized tests scientifically confirms the "inferiority of the poor students."

Rochelle: Case in point. The stigma of being black according to Claude Steele (1992) is the endemic devaluation many face in American society and schools. The connection of stigma to school achievement among black Americans has been vastly underappreciated, asserts Steele. He further states that, "if blacks are made racially valuable in school, they can overcome even substantial obstacles" (p. 86). At the root of the black achievement problem is the failure of American schooling to meet this simple condition for black students. Doing well in school requires a belief that school achievement can be a promising basis of self-esteem, and that belief needs constant reaffirmation even for advantaged students. Education psychology is not informed by these racial understandings. Because it decontextualizes the lived realities of individual students and the impact of their racial, class, and gender groups, educational psychologist is blinded to the subjective nature of its own discipline. This single mindedness blocks educational psychology from realizing (and deeming that realization worthy) the social constructions of the lived reality of students.

Jacqueline Jordan Irvine, in *Black Students and School Failure: Policies, Practices, and Prescriptions*, posits that black students are subject to school failure because of their race, social class, and culture. According to Irvine, race is a "salient factor that contributes to unequal school treatment, participation, and distribution of rewards for all black students." She goes on to say, "black students regardless of social class and education, do not share with whites equal opportunities for jobs, housing, and political and economic power" (p. xxii). Her observations force me to ask how would the experiences of students be different if they lived in a society that constantly attempted to place them at the bottom?

Joe: Research on the educational status of low-status groups in other countries provides important insight into the psychological assessment and educational performance of marginalized students in American schools. In Sweden, Finnish people are viewed as inferior—the failure rate for Finnish children in Swedish schools is very high. When Finnish children immigrate to Australia, however, they do well—as well as Swedish immigrants. The same can be said for Korean children in Japanese schools versus Korean children in American schools. The results are numerous and generally follow the same pattern: racial, ethnic, and class groups who are viewed negatively or as inferiors in a nations dominant culture tend to perform poorly in that nation's schools. Such research helps dispose of the arguments that schools failure results from the cultural inferiority of the poor or the marginalized. It teaches us that power relations between groups (class, race, ethnic, gender, etc.) must be considered when various children's performance is studied. Without the benefits derived from such understandings brilliant and creative young people from marginalized backgrounds will continue to be relegated to the vast army of the inferior and untalented. Such an injustice is intolerable in America. There is something wrong with a discipline that cannot discern the impact of the social on the psychological, that claims neutrality and objectivity but fails to appreciate its own sociocultural embeddedness, and that consistently rewards the privileged for their privilege and punishes the marginalized for their marginalization.

Rochelle: Yes, so what we need is a system that understands the difference and therefore develops curriculum that helps students to appreciate the social, political, historical, and economic forces that shape their lives. Program designs that do not take note of the differences, and develop approaches that work to maximize the abilities of all ethnic groups, will not be effective. Currently, most education research seeks to minimize, decrease, or ignore differences between groups so that education can proceed more easily and economically. The reverberation is cultural incongruity between poor and minority students and the pedagogy of the school system. The obstacles that students encounter that facilitate academic underachievement are manifested in the classroom as a result of societal problems that have been a part of America since its inception. Reading the newspaper on any given day illuminates the obstacles that face blacks and other ethnic minorities. Unfair housing, unequal political representation, and high unemployment present the myriad obstacles that minority students must overcome. All too often in the public school setting, it is expected that poor and minority students cannot achieve; therefore not much is expected of them. For example, it is perfectly "okay" for a Black child to do "C" work. Can you visualize a school and teachers that expected and encouraged children to perform to their full potential?

Joe: Yes I can and that visualization leads me to ask how do we induce mainstream educational psychologists and teachers to understand the importance of these political aspects of cognition? Within the psychometric web of Cartesian-Newtonian (referring to the work of Rene Descartes and Isaac Newton of the seventeenth and eighteenth century) scientific assumptions, our arguments are dismissed as empirically unsupported. What exactly does such an accusation mean? A democratic psychology is unsupported in the sense that little experimentation has taken place to determine if sociolopolitical awareness actually improves cognition. The way this would be empirically measured would involve controlled observation of a classroom operated by a socially aware teacher and the administration of a research instrument designed to determine if students acquired more "certified data" in this context. Such verification of the "validity" of such teaching would have little to do with our concerns and purposes. In the first place, we do not believe that the measure of our success involves how much unproblematized data students might memorize. Secondly, the types of understandings we seek to generate do not lend themselves to quantitative measurements that ask "how much." Because of such paradigmatic mismatches, it is hard for critical educators to carry on conversations about the effort to democratize education with many mainstream educational psychologists.

Rochelle: These psychometric assumptions devastate the lives of increasing numbers of minority and poor students, leading them to question their own existence, their worth as they try to maneuver a world they have not been taught to understand. I again return to the students and One Mike! In addition to the monthly program the students also publish a creative journal every semester with entries from past and present students, parents, teachers, and members from the community. As I read through the 2004 issue I noticed the level of questioning in virtually all the pieces. Questioning self, society, unjust rules. Reading the various pieces I continuously wondered if my undergraduate students (mostly white, rural, and middle class) would be as critically cognizant and in tune with the world as these students. The answer is probably not yet. But by education psychology standards my undergraduate students would nevertheless be viewed as more intelligent.

Joe: When we rethink intelligence a schooling shaped by a sociopolitically contextualized educational psychology, self-reflection would become a priority with teachers and students, as critical educators attend to the impact of school on the shaping of the self. In such a context, learning would be considered an act of meaning-making that subverts the technicist view that thinking involves the mastering of a set of techniques. Education could no longer separate techniques from purpose, reducing teaching and learning to de-skilled acts of rule following and concern with methodological format. Schools guided by a democratized educational psychology would no longer privilege white male experience as the standard by which all other experiences are measured. Such realizations would point out a guiding concern with social justice and the ways unequal power relations at school destroy the promise of democratic life. Democratic teachers would no longer passively accept the pronouncements of standardized tests and curriculum makers without examining the social contexts in which their students live and the ways those contexts help shape their performance. Lessons would be reconceptualized in light of a critical notion of student understanding. Postformal educators would ask if their classroom experiences promote the highest level of understanding possible.

Rochelle: In such a world, education psychologists would understand the power of race and racism to affect what goes on in school and society that influences student performance. Education psychologists assume that we live in a just society but a postformal educational psychologist would question the concept of a just world. Moreover they would work to create curriculum that would provide the student with the knowledge to read the world, thereby creating a place of possibilities and belief in self.

Joe: At its worst, mainstream educational psychology reduces its practitioners to the role of test administrators who help devise academic plans that fit students' ability. The individualistic assumptions of this work move practitioners to accept unquestioningly the existence of a just society where young people, according to their scientific measured abilities, find an agreeable place and worthwhile function. Thus, the role of the educational psychologist is to adjust the child, regardless of his or her unmeasured (or unmeasurable by existing standards) abilities, to the society, no matter how unjust the system may be. Thus, the discipline and the practice it supports play an important role in maintaining the power inequities of the status quo. Those children from marginalized racial or class positions are socialized for passivity and acceptance of their scientifically pronounced "lack of ability."

Rochelle: The sad and scary part is that as long ago as 1933, Dr. Carter G. Woodson discussed what the miseducation of a child's mind could do to that child.

When you control a man's thinking you do not have to worry about his actions. You do not have to tell him not to stand here or go yonder. He will find his 'proper place' and will stay in it. You do not need to send him to the back door. He will go without being told. In fact, if there is no back door, he will cut one for his special benefit. His education makes it necessary (p. xi)

The phrase "best practices" that seeps through education literature is a form of teaching that forces students to find the backdoor. I have come to hate that phrase because I know it equates to those practices that have continuously worked to subvert the intellectual growth of students instead of attempting to connect teaching and learning to questions of social justice and student self-reflection.

Joe: The backdoor to life is possible because a form of politically passive thinking is (and has been) cultivated that views good students and teachers as obedient to mainstream educational, psychology-based ways of seeing. In such a context neither students nor teachers are encouraged to construct new cognitive abilities when faced with ambiguity. Piaget labeled this process accommodation, the reshaping of cognitive structures to accommodate unique aspects of what is being perceived in new contexts. In other words, through our knowledge of a variety of comparable contexts we begin to understand their similarities and differences, we learn from our comparison of the different contexts.

Rochelle: That word makes me uneasy. When I think of accommodation I think of an action that removes agency from the individual. You know, "I'll accommodate to your way of being, seeing, or experiencing the world."

Joe: I agree with you but politically conscious teachers push Piaget one more sociocognitive step to produce a critical emancipatory notion of accommodation. Understanding the socially constructed nature of our comprehension of reality, critical accommodation involves the attempt to disembed ourselves from the pictures of the world that have been painted by power. For example, a teacher's construction of intelligence would typically be molded by a powerful scientific discourse that equated intelligence with scores on intelligence tests. The teacher would critically accommodate the concept as she or he began to examine children who had been labeled by the scientific discourse as unintelligent but upon second look exhibited characteristics that in an unconventional way seemed sophisticated. The teacher would then critically accommodate (or integrate) this recognition of exception into a definition of intelligence that challenged the discourse. Thus empowered to move beyond the confines of the socially constructed ways of seeking intelligence, the teacher could discover unique forms of intelligence among his or her students—students who under the domination of the scientific discourse of intelligence testing would have been overlooked and relegated to the junk heap of the school.

Rochelle: Okay I can hang with you using the critical notion of accommodation. Instead of accommodation taking away agency it affords agency. Being critical is the key and it is that criticality that would allow the teacher to not simply accept the labeling of poor and minority children unquestioningly but to instead reconstruct their knowledge of who that child is and what that child brings to the table. But what I constantly hear from those who accept traditional educational psychology like a religion is that it is an objective science. For example, they believe that standardized tests simply measure intelligence and if the child possesses intelligence then they will do well on the test. They refuse to accept that educational psychology is a situated cultural/political practice—whether it wants to be or not—that addresses the ideology of learning. Whenever learning and knowledge are conceived the nature of the conception affects individuals differently: it validates the cognitive process of some and invalidates others.

Imagine an educational psychology that exists within a different paradigm. One that accepts subjectivity as its calling. And the subjectivity becomes the vehicle that allows an understanding of the political nature of schooling.

Joe: It is difficult to imagine such a paradigm since we both know that dominant educational psychology is uncomfortable with moving to a different way of thinking and understanding and that many practitioners consider critical discourse a defacement of the field, a disruption to its orderly proceedings. Thinking constructed as a political activity in this context is marked by a hint of scandal or at least a lack of middle/upper-middle class "good taste." Despite such uncomfortable representations critical teachers push their political agenda, confronting the dominant discourse with its erasure of irrationality, emotion, power, paradigms, and morality in the learning process. With this point delineated, such teachers construct the role of a politically conscious educational psychology in terms of its effort to understand the subjective ways learners experience political issues. The focus on this domain delineates a unique and critical role for a reconceptualized educational psychology in macro-transformational efforts.

Rochelle: Not just how learners experience political issues but importantly what they do with the information. Anything short of thought leading to action ultimately means that talk of a move toward social justice is moot. Once the political dynamics of education reaches the level of revolutionary consciousness what happens in the person? What is the relationship between school performance and a student's or a teacher's political consciousness and resulting moral sensibility? How do issues of power shape the learning process?

Joe: Such questions would encourage research involving the subjective experience of students deemed unintelligent and relegated to lower ability tracks. The practical meaning of the effort to contextualize children is easily understood in this example. A central feature of this process involves the study and reappraisal of everyday knowledge that is distributed throughout the society. Indeed, as a discipline educational psychology must explore the previously dismissed margins in order to identify the intelligence and creativity that exist in the lives of the people who reside there. To search for intelligence where one has previously found only deficiency is a transformative act that holds radical political consequences. The refusal to recognize such cognitive dynamics is testimony to the dysfunctionality of educational psychology. This dysfunctional impulse also expresses itself in ways that devalue indigenous knowledge or forms of intelligence that are produced outside of school. Learning in this mainstream configuration is narrowly constructed as merely the acquisition of unexamined knowledge that takes place inside the school.

Critical educators argue that intelligence is not something that manifests itself only on standardized tests and in academic classrooms. If progressive educators and educational psychologists can move their colleagues to study intelligence in ordinary lived situations, they will have initiated an important step in the larger effort to democratize our conception of intelligence. As we begin to gain clearer understandings of the cognitive sophistication of everyday life, we will not only broaden our definition of intelligence but we will be better able as educators to heed Vygotsky's enjoinder to "call out" what our marginalized students already know. In the calling-out process critical teachers would bracket student abilities, bring them to the student's consciousness, induce students to think about how to enhance the processes and engage them in thought experiments and activities designed to facilitate the transfer of the skills into new domains.

What type of thinking might emerge when we democratize intelligence for social justice? Utilizing recent advances in social and educational theory that understand the way our consciousness, our subjectivity, is shaped by the world around us, such a perspective grants us a new conception of what "being smart" might entail. This postformal view of higher-order thinking induces psychologists and educators to recognize the politicization of cognition in a manner that allows them to desocialize themselves and others from mainstream psychology's and school-based pronouncements of who is intelligent and who is not. Postformalism is concerned with questions of justice, democracy, meaning, self-awareness, and the nature and function of social context.

Rochelle: The type of thinking would know no bounds. Students and teachers together could and should create a pedagogy that works to produce a change in their community, their lives, and the life of others. Being able to legitimately place self in a historical and political context allows, no demands, you work to transform self and the world.

Joe: The point is the recognition that the postformal vision is not only about revealing the humanely constructed nature of all talk about cognition (postformal talk included), but also about creating new forms of human being and imagining better ways of life for our young people. Reconceptualizing the abilities of students involves the political struggle to reshape educational psychology in the service of progressive values. As it lurks in the shadows of pseudo-objectivity, mainstream educational psychology denies its political complicity in oppressing the marginalized. In contrast, postformalism embraces its own politics and imagines what the world would become. As Aostre Johnson puts it in her chapter in Kincheloe's, Steinberg's, and Villaverde's *Rethinking Intelligence*, cognitive formalism undermines the expression of human multidimensionality by excluding spiritual dimensions of being.

Rochelle: Spirituality in teaching is essential. A teacher must attend to the spirit of the child. King (1994) speaks of the "clarity of soul" which when missing allows pain to fester in that empty space. Education should be the means toward poor and minority students reestablishing their connection with self and the world. Moreover, education should be the key to a student unlocking the mysteries of their existence and provide the road map to creating their own knowledge.

Education should not only afford students an understanding of the sociopolitical forces that oppress, but also insure that the new knowledge is internalized with enough strength to uproot the old.

A vitalness of humanity is essential to the education of any oppressed students. King (1994) gives a definition of human vitalness as:

> aliveness of the human spirit expressed with honest vigor. . .being awake; looking; seeing, tasting, and engaging in nonoppressive uses of the power of one's autonomous soul; participating in self's human rights and responsively demonstrating the Afrohumanity of caring, closeness, creating, and calling for truth (p. 271).

She crafts her language with such love and care for transformative thought and existence and at the same time it is solid language, grounded in a cultural theory which determines the trajectory of our existence and our transformation. The healthy survival of students is dependent on the transformative, human vitality education should provide.

Joe: The new forms of democratic living that postformalism attempts to make possible are indelibly linked to an alternative rationality. Contrary to the claims of some of our critics in mainstream educational psychology, postformalism does not seek to embrace irrationalism or to reject the entire enterprise of empirical research. We borrow the phrase, alternative rationality, from Stanley Arnowitz, whose critique of mainstream science helps shape our vision of postformalism. In this schemata new rationalities employ forms of analysis sensitive to signs and symbols, the power of context in relation to thinking, the role of emotion and feeling in cognitive activity, and the value of the psychoanalytical process as it taps into the recesses of (un)consciousness.

Rochelle: This alternative rationality is exactly what I experienced as I watched the students at One Mike! That concept relates to the name and purpose of the student organization that sponsored the event—The Society for Independent Thought. Rather than succumbing to society's depiction of them the students were creating a different reality, operating within a new paradigm.

The vehicle for this was their teacher, Winthrope Holder, who started the program in 2001 when he first arrived at the school. Now this man is the embodiment of the democratic, postformal teacher we have been discussing. He sees and acts on the humanness of his students. Although he understands the ideological forces that shape the lives of his students he works to make the students aware of, understand, and change those forces. Holder creates an environment that is safe for the students. He helps them feel comfortable enough to push the boundaries of their learning and thinking. In order to take them from where they are to where they can go he uses democratic teaching to both expose the social construction of their identities and to ensure that they gain control over that construction. Ultimately, he achieved the connection between teaching and social justice, creating a new and better way to think about "best practices."

Joe: Do certain forms of thinking undermine the quest for justice? Do certain forms of research cause observers to view as problematic ways of seeing as if they involved no issues of power and privilege? Educational psychology has simply never encouraged a serious conversation about the reasons students engage in certain behavior, about the purpose of high-order thinking, or about the social role of schooling in a democratic process. For the most part the discipline has never considered the implications that Paulo Friere's notion of conscientization (the consciousness of self) holds for the work of practitioners. What happens in the realm of cognition when individuals began to gain a new consciousness via the process of (a) transforming themselves through changing their realities, (b) grasping an awareness of the mechanisms of oppression, and (c) reclaiming their historical memory in order to gain an awareness of their social construction, their social identity?

The effort to rethink student's abilities extends Arnowitz's powerful alternatives by asking ethical questions of cognition and action. Such inquiries induce educational and cognitive psychologist to study issues of purpose, meaning, and ultimate worth. Until educators and psychologist appreciate a new way of thinking about cognition schools will continue to certify the damage that marginalized children have to endure in the late twenty-first century.

Rochelle: I need to believe that there are more teachers in the world like Winthrope holder who inspires the student of One Mike! I also need to believe that there are a multitude of students who are benefiting from such teachers. When we stop believing in a brighter future and an educational system that provides endless possibilities for students rather than limiting their chances, we give up and allow "them"—the purveyors of psychological "truths" about European/White supremacy—to win.

REFERENCES

Apple, M. (1990). Rhetorical reforms: Markets, standard, and inequality. *Current Issue in Comparative Education*, 1(2), 4–17.

King, J. E. (1994). Being the Soul-freeing Substance: A Legacy of Hope and Humanity. In M. J. Shujaa (Ed.), *Too Much Schooling Too Little Education: A Paradox of Black Life in White Societies*, pp. 269–294. Trenton [New] Jersey: Africa Free World Press.

Steele, C. M. (1992, April) Race and the Schooling of Black America. *The Atlantic Monthly* 68–78.

Woodson, C.G. (1933). *The Miseducation of the Negro*. Nashville TN: Winston-Derek Publishers.

CHAPTER 104

Alternative Realities in Educational Psychology: Postformalism as a Compelling Force in Opposition to Developmental Theories

ERIK L. MALEWSKI

This chapter explores postformal theory and its impact on the discourses of educational psychology as both a theoretical paradigm and school practice. To begin, postformalism challenges dominant developmental, formal conceptions of cognition and redirects educational psychology away from a focus on rules and generalities toward pathways leading to alternative forms of teaching, research, and assessment. Unlike the search for intellectual truth that undergirds formalism, there is no easily produced or simply defined method for describing postformal educational psychology. In quite the other direction there are, it seems, many dimensions to postformalism. Along the first dimension, the mind and the character of knowledge are reconceptualized. There are investigations into the origins of ideas, recognition of the links between the mind and life forces, and appreciation for imagining what is possible. Along the second dimension, conventional cultural categories are brought into question. This involves reflection on the implicit patterns and structures that draw seemingly disparate elements into relation, appreciation of non-linear holism that eschews cause and effect, and investigation into implicit patterns and structures in ways that draw seemingly disparate elements into relation. Along the third dimension, interstices are reconfigured as potential spaces of understanding. This involves the examination of interspaces as unique beyond the connections they provide, investigation of third spaces that exist between particularities and generalities, elevation of problem detection over the ability to locate existing solutions, and attention to the ways power relations shape representations of intellect. In response to these dimensions and the possibility that some scholars contend that postformalism is less a definitive set of rules or principles than a disposition—a mood or attitude toward intelligence. I agree with this analysis and would add that postformal educational psychology emphasizes the journey toward understanding over a sense of arrival or closure on the topic.

At this point, the reader might come to sense that any attempts to define postformal educational psychology are difficult and, some might even say, inappropriate. I tend to take the middle ground, asserting that it is possible to characterize and explore many of the key features of postformal theories and their implications for educational psychology while also recognizing postformal I tend to take the middle ground, asserting that it is possible to characterize and explore many of the key features of postformal theories and their implications for educational psychology while also recognizing postformalism defers closure in an attempt to avoid asymmetrical structures.

Here insights are crested upon the vanishing point of a receding horizon, always within sight yet never fully known. At this juncture in history, a time when we bear witness to attempts to formalize most aspects of education, my sense is that we can no longer offer graduate education without attending to the major changes in cognitive discourses, including teaching, research, and assessment. More specific, the time has passed when we can make sense of public education without acknowledging and interrogating the rift that has developed between how educational psychology is thought about and how it is practiced in educational settings. The theory practice divide that has brought attention to the politics of intellect and the negative repercussions of an overinvestment in formalism, a move that more recently moved many educators to ask what happened to the connection between happiness and the pursuit of further understanding.

My point is postformal theories must be explored if for no other reason than for the creation of rigorous, nuanced, and critical insights into the ways intellect functions in the present as well as historically. The aim of this chapter is to offer tentative description of what postformalism has to offer educational psychology as well as its implications for educational practice. In the chaos and uncertainty of our current world, the common response involving an increased reliance upon formalism might be ill-conceived. As an alternative, a postformal approach to educational psychology offers fresh perspectives on intelligence, descriptions of a multitude of ways of knowing that, if engaged critically, might offer further understandings of our most pressing social, political, and economic issues.

Postformalism, as a disposition, can be detected in many elements of what might be termed a personal-sociocultural outlook—the exposition of thought that has laid bare the assumptions of Cartesian logic that structures the traditions of educational psychology and how an alternative disposition—one that eschews structure while retaining direction, gives credence to our imaginary worlds and tacit knowledge not easily accessed through empirical means. Some would suggest that the critical perspectives that are key to understanding postformalism began in the 1960s movements that emphasized multilogicality, multiculturalism, and diverse forms of intelligence in addition to paradox, complexity and chaos theory, ultimately opening up spaces for those voices under arrest. The emphasis on criticality broke open customs and traditions as at least, in part, socially constructed phenomena. Just like a fictionalized text, critical approaches to cognition illustrated how theories of intelligence and their counterparts, the ignorance we cannot bear to imagine has anything of value to offer, function according to the arbitrary rules of a language game that had its origins in culture. Lyotard in his 1984 book *The Postmodern Condition: A Report on Knowledge* attributed conventional ways of knowing that commonly exceed examination to metanarratives, theories that attempt to provide a universal, all-encompassing single narrative "plots" regarding the ways people think, schools are structured, people learn, curriculum is assessed, teachers practice, corporations become involved, and government intervenes. Before further exploring the insights postformalism has to offer, a feat we will engage further throughout the rest of this chapter, it is first important to look at the notion of criticality in more detail.

More recent approaches to educational psychology utilize textual analysis, multilogicality, and the study of interrelationships between intelligence and ignorance as theoretical approaches to challenging unjust symbolic and material valuations. As a result, postformal educational psychology does not choose as a starting point the establishment of the definitive properties of a scholarly discipline, but instead advances a movement that defies easy categorization, using strands of thought from cultural studies, narrative inquiry, critical pedagogy, feminist theory, insurgent black intellectual thought, and queer theory, among others, to produce and circulate theories of intelligence that will aid in the pursuit of social, economic, political, and economic equality. Postformal educational psychology teaching practices, research methods, and corresponding assessment are critical of monological approaches to curriculum and cognition, encouraging appreciation for nuanced overlays that more closely resemble the layers of an onion, a process where peeling back each concealed truth only discloses beneath it a more revealing and less understood way of thinking—critical methods capable of accounting for and bringing appreciation to anomaly, idiosyncrasy, and eclecticism. This attention to difference as a central organizing concept of intellect and cognition is key. Postformal educational psychology aims to unearth the contradictions, oversights, and limitations found within dominant educational discourses and exposes them for the knowledge and realities they subjugate. Once exposed, the particularities of overdetermined ideologies are drawn into broader relations that help better understand hegemonic articulations and totalizing narratives that operate at the level of establishing intellectual truth, the very realities that produce as their social effects officially recognized forms of knowledge as well as ways of knowing deemed not worth knowing about, subjugated knowledge forms relegated to the peripheries and occasionally acknowledged as signifiers of ignorance or, more common, not acknowledged at all. The dimensions of criticality key to postformal educational psychology involve theoretical axes that include but are not limited to

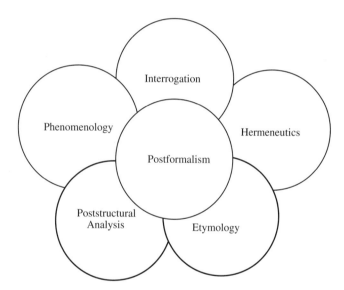

Etymology: The historical study of the origins of knowledge and intellect that involves critical explorations of our own customs and traditions. Through etymology the notion of textual analysis is expanded beyond the written word to allow for the application of critical reading practices to a myriad of social contexts.

Hermeneutics: The interpretive process that entails understanding intellect as a text examined through reconstructing the world in which intellect was conceived and then couching it in that world.

Interrogation: The process of decoding and exploring the unintended meanings of various texts. By moving beyond explicit meaning, interrogation involves reading between the lines of a text using a reconceptualized definition of text that for a teacher might be a classroom or for an administrator a budget.

Poststructural Analysis: A philosophical outlook that attends to the difficulty in knowing any text or expression, a perspective on intelligence originating out of the realization that placing authority in any one text or group of texts is a problem.

Phenomenology: A philosophical movement dedicated to the description of the structures of experience at the moment of awareness. A perspective that aims to capture heightened preconscious understandings without reliance upon reductionism, generalization, or categorization common to empiricism.

Working from these five dimensions, what might be found in postformal theory is an unending attempt to lay bare the contradictions, paradoxes, anomalies, and subjectivities that inform the texts and artifacts that provide intelligence with the opportunity for convention. What becomes fascinating regarding the implications of postformalism is that no theory of cognition, no textual representation of intelligence, holds complete or absolute truth within it. Working against the grain of formalism, postformalism asserts that intelligence cannot be reduced to an IQ test nor can it be appropriately characterized as a thing, a static substance. While many scholars, such as famous educational psychologists Arthur Jensen, Charles Murray, and the late Richard Herrnstein, have attempted to reduce intelligence to empirical assessment—as if intellect is static and knowledge easily captured—postformalism asserts that knowledge is never so much an issue of capturing a single iteration and labeling it intelligence, as human capacities cannot be consistently reduced to instrumental assessment or even known ahead of time. Postformal thinkers use the idea of form rather than the idea of thing in conceptualizing intelligence. Forms are structures whose fundamental function is to change and, as such, have dynamic, fluid properties. Things are structures whose fundamental function is to maintain their stability. They have the properties of simple, linear, causal models seen in formal operations used by educational psychologists such as Jensen, Inouye, Murray, and Herrnstein. Postformalism highlights form as a way to revolutionize educational psychology.

In postformal educational psychology, the value of temporally crystallized structures is reduced, and the perspectives revealed by the revaluation are used as interpretive strategies for revealing the ways in which society, nature, and the self are always undergoing continuous transformation. Postformalism uses criticality as a device for illustrating the ways intelligence exceeds the significations of its boundaries with the passing of each moment. Curriculum committees made up of teachers and administrators work through numerous history textbooks that offer a myriad of different interpretations of historical events. Galileo was sentenced to what amounted to house arrest for breaching the conditions laid down by the Inquisition of 1616, a sentence that was the result of the publication of *Dialogue*, a book that supported the Copernican theory that the earth revolved around the sun. Now this idea is often taught as an unequivocal fact. Einstein failed an entrance examination that would have allowed him to pursue electrical engineering at the Swiss Federal Institute of Technology only to return later in life to become a physics teacher. We now cherish the ideas of a man who revolutionized physics with his theory of relativity. Government officials enter into heated debates over which assessment tools will most accurately measure intelligence, often coming to a standstill and handing over such evaluation to state or local government.

Postformalism recognizes that historically events are not so much witnessed as created, as can be attested to more recently in the different responses to the attack on the World Trade Center. To the present day, evolution and creation narratives are heavily debated topics in relation to school curriculum, culminating more recently in the August 1999 decision by the Kansas Board of Education to remove evolution, as well as the Big Bang theory, and any mention of cumulative changes in the earth or the age of the earth, from state science standards. Even within various communities, there are major schisms as people use various conflicting and divergent lenses to interpret the current state of the world and decisions regarding what knowledge is worthy enough to pass on to the next generation are a reflection of a myriad of tacit forces that bring into being moments of curricular understanding.

Various historical artifacts and individuals have undergone scrutiny, censorship, or celebration according to the zeitgeist. Rap music, for example, was derided in the late 1970s as little more than "street speak" and "beats stolen from music stars" only to become a multimillion-dollar industry by the beginning of the twenty-first century. Simply stated, there will never be a single standard against which to measure intelligence nor a way to bracket out the effects of religion, spirituality, history, aesthetics, music, art, kinesics, and sexual identities on the ways we know, live, interpret, and style the world. Postformalism suggests that attempts to create spaces of cultural neutrality through objectivity (think of, for example, the claims of creators of high stakes tests that they reveal what students' know, presumably outside of culture) can never be actualized when teaching, research, and assessment as themselves studied as cultural practices. In 1990 a Florida court ruled the rap album "As Nasty as They Wanna Be" by Two Live Crew obscene and, as a result, anyone caught selling or performing songs was subject to arrest and prosecution. By 2004, such lyrics were not deemed unsettling as the measure of decorum had greatly changed and rap, hip hop, and gangsta rap can be found on the music dial in every major city in Florida. As these examples illustrate, intelligence might more closely resemble the idea of a form than something of substance.

Similarly, there is little consistency of knowledge or clarity of importance regarding what might constitute signs of intelligence or discrete facts important enough to test. Woodrow Wilson is often credited with women's suffrage when it might be more appropriate to highlight that he was unsympathetic to the cause at first. Only after public pressure and hunger strikes by those in the movement did Wilson decide that opposition to women's suffrage was politically unwise. Few recognize Helen Keller as more than an unruly and difficult hearing-impaired girl who eventually learned to read, write, and speak. Equally important to understanding her life but rarely mentioned was that Helen Keller described herself as a radical socialist. She was a member of the socialist party in 1909 and emphasized that it was her own interests, not her schooling at Radcliffe, that spurred her political interests. After attempting to simplify the alphabet for the blind she began to recognize that she was addressing the symptoms of a problem rather than work toward its prevention. Utilizing postformal notions of problem detection, she distinguished that blindness was distributed across society disproportionately, based largely on class differences. By connecting ostensibly different realities she became aware of the sociocultural realities that made blindness more common in men of lower socioeconomic standing who often worked in factories and lacked adequate health care and in poor women who turned toward prostitution for additional income and, as a result, contracted syphilis. It was this higher-order thinking that allowed her to see the origins of blindness, an insight that is rarely if ever taught in formal, depoliticized classrooms.

To take the field of educational psychology seriously we must be able to move beyond formalism, understanding the subtle interactions of particularities and generalizations and the various connections between mind, social context, and power relations that shape the knowledge that is, in the current era, found worthy. To employ postformalism within educational psychology requires historicizing past figures, the understanding that both knowledge and intellect, as they are conventionally understood, are shaped by the forces of their production. Knowledge often thought of as transhistorical more appropriately bears the marks of its creation, less a reflection of a pure experience, a sole truth, or a scientific discovery than the confluence of economic, political, and social forces that shape knowledge deemed bearable. For postformal educational psychology, metanarratives that concur it is possible to fully assess intelligence through IQ testing or draw conclusions regarding the role historical figures have played in shaping present social, economic, and political practices is not only dangerous but also presumptuous and, through the lack of attention to subjugation, unjust. Postformal educational psychology fosters the role of dissenting voices developing alternative descriptions of intelligence, elevating voices of opposition to unearth the ways in which intelligence functions as a social convention that works borderlands into existence.

Postformalism recognizes that formalism, with its emphasis on principles and rules, is an outgrowth of Enlightenment rationality and can be evidenced in domains of thought from developmental psychology to Saussurian linguistics and Newtonian physics. As the previous example illustrates, postformal educational psychology does not assert that intelligence is absolutely relative and therefore beyond description. Rather, postformal educational psychology contends that there are many truths that are produced and circulated based on factors as varied as social group identifications, lived histories, and the particularities of place. Unlike misguided attacks on postformalism, the aim of postformal educational psychology is to bring to light the limitations of developmental formalism and the effects an emphasis on universalized, unalterable truths regarding intelligence for all people in all categorical domains has on those who fall outside predetermined boundaries. While there are many more dimensions to postformal educational psychology, this brief introduction works as an overview of its moods and dispositions, what some scholars might agree are its key features at this occasion in time.

CHARACTERIZING THE POSTFORMAL

At this juncture in history it is safe to assert that we have ushered in new realities characterized by compression of time and space, simulation over realism, and the loss of authority associated historically with truths founded upon tradition and custom. There is no easy way to characterize these changes, possibly because we are in the midst of the shifts and redirections associated with the accelerated rate at which change has occurred. While it is clear that formalism has continued to have an impact on educational practices, and some would surmise, and rightly so, that as its influence has increased with the rise of state and national standards, there has been the development of a decidedly new urge in educational psychology to account for alternative ways of knowing. Unlike some who have characterized postformalism as the replacement for formalism, the characterization offered here provides a more nuanced and detailed portrait of how intelligence operates, formal and postformal impulses existing concurrently in occasional moments that are complementary and, at other moments, in conflict and dissonance.

Recognizing that preformal ways of knowing with their attention to mysticism and spiritual life failed to explain away dissonance, chaos, and the mysteries of mental illness, formalism became a way to overlay patterns, tenets, and rules on the bedlam of human thought. Over several iterations taking generations, the mapping of principles provided a set of assumptions or foundations for this urge to regulate, as Cartesian science aimed to understand the complexities of cognition through reductive techniques used to fragment thought into its most simple elements before engaging in analysis. Through this process of scientific categorization, what was pointed out in a 1977 translation of Foucault's work *Discipline and Punish* as the technologies of power and the attempt of dominant cultures to exhibit increasing control over society, ways of knowing became coded in relation to a series of assumptions regarding high-level cognition and the properties of recognizable intellect or intellect that would be recognized. Along with this orientation toward human thought came a socioeconomic feature that tied developmentalism to the formation of social hierarchies and the tenets of marketplace ideologies. Looked at from another angle, the practice of reducing phenomena to their simplest parts and then marking recognizable patterns did little to help in the study of the complexities and idiosyncrasies of human thought and worked instead to bring educational psychology into alignment with the requirements of capitalism and an unquestioned beliefs in 1) science and technology as pathways toward human progress, 2) instrumental reason as a method for overcoming emotion and mysticism, and 3) fragmentation and decontextualization as the best approach to ordering society so that it might be more easily regulated and controlled. Formalism led to an assembly line mentality regarding ways of knowing, bringing intelligence to operate as a standard against which human ability could be easily quantified and ranked in a never-ending search to mark winners and losers.

Postformalism, as a response to formalism, uses a language of critique to question the principles of developmental paradigms and, through the nurturing of critical consciousness, provides new ways to conceptualize intelligence. Postformalism works to unearth subjugated knowledge, exposing the ways various assumptions regarding human cognition, including the pursuit of objectivity and neutrality, shield educational psychology from more critical interrogations. Through postformalism, ways of knowing previously thought of as based in ignorance cross within the bounds of intelligibility, working to give evidence to historically subjugate forms of knowledge. The way intelligence operates under convention is rendered suspect as previously excluded voices offer until that time unheard questions regarding the agendas served through instrumental understandings of cognition. When the metanarratives of the field are ruptured, intellect no longer exists in an originary state but instead comes to be seen as a form of knowing structured by the unintelligible: the ways of knowing we cannot bear to know or the ways of knowing to which claims of ignorance result in the substantiation of a right to recognition, working the borderlands into irrelevance so that the highest forms of cognition can be upheld as recognizable.

Postformal educational psychology seeks new ways of knowing that transcend empirically verifiable facts, monologic, and the use of cause and effect arguments to operationalize intelligence in reductive and over determined ways. When educational psychology moves beyond reductive techniques that equate intelligence with IQ testing and the results of high stakes testing with knowledge acquisition, we can begin to address cognition critically as the generative process of building critical consciousness, weaving together a context for realities founded upon hope, possibility, and radical transformation: participatory democratic systems of meaning are central to conceptualizing intelligence as situational, the effects of social relations and everyday practices in and out of schools that either extend or limit the capacity for self-direction and understanding the conditions of one's own existence. With postformal emphasis not just on description but also on invoking a language of possibility, intelligence evolves from a highly individualized abstract mental aptitude to the practice of attaching meaning to and then altering the social contexts in which the mind has traditionally resided, dismantling hegemonic articulations that thwart the creation of symbolically and materially just communities that place difference at the core of viable, sustainable social relations and relations of intellect. Understanding how worldviews, self-conceptions, and ways of knowing that are valued have come to be constructed, postformalism provides educational psychology with a theoretical toolbox that is quite capable of facilitating the transformation of how we understand knowing in public education.

Postformalism, then, assists in understanding the changing nature of how we think, know, and interact in the world, providing a language of possibility that moves beyond the boundaries of instrumental rationality to value new realities that seem to be cropping up all around us in a new world order where images of war overlap seamlessly with images found in videogames and love affairs begin in virtual worlds where each person ceases to exist in a physical sense, born again into an alternate reality. Postformalism describes a new era in human psychology that helps to reconceptualize education as it takes place in schools and other cultural sites. It invokes the realization that those who continue to invest wholeheartedly in formalism will, in the end, be found naïve. Educators who have yet to acknowledge the impact of postformalism fail to realize they can no longer offer narratives from an omnipotent perspective, as each human being resides in a particular location in the web of reality and, as a result of these competing realities that are sometimes overlapping and just as often incommensurate, must reveal their own subjectivity, the identifications that constitute their particular social and historical vantage point. Intelligence no longer involves a single rationality, with the birth of postformal thinking, but infinite ways of reasoning based on the intersections of numerous social positions and the willingness to engage in self-examination. Postformalism grounds educational psychology in the particularities of place taking seriously Pinar's description of Currere, the Latin root of the word "curriculum," involving the examination of the nature of the individual experience of the public.

Postformalism offers educational psychology the possibility of providing redress for the myriad of social ills that have plagued formal, developmental theories and the recent recognition that the very forms of intelligence privileged under formalism, thought to be the remedy for individual and social pathologies, have been complicit in many of our recent tragedies including the Holocaust, racial discrimination, genocide, commodification, social elitism, narcissism, indentured servitude, and corporate welfare. Postformalism offers an alternative to the frame of mind that brought us the Phillip Morris Czech Report, the overly formal, procedural document that requested a reduction in excise taxes from the Czech government in response to its findings that "smoking can lead to a reduced life span of smokers" and therefore reduce the money paid out in government pensions and health care subsidies. It is postformalism that might offer educational psychology ways to deconstruct the intellectual sensibilities that have allowed for these tragedies as well as the anti-essentialism required for tentative descriptions of alternative visions. A postformal vision of educational psychology attuned to alternate forms of teaching, research, and assessment can bring about changes in symbolic and material valuations necessary for the actualization of equality.

TERMS FOR READERS

Formalism—The term refers to the empirical developmental operations of human thought that can be evidenced in patterns, rules, principles, and generalizations. Formalism assumes instrumental development where particular task performances are necessary to the development of more complex, higher-order task performances.

Hegemonic Articulations—This phrase refers to tentative linkage of social, political, and economic forces in ways that exacerbate individual and social group inequities by engendering the naturalization of oppression through nonphysical means. Hegemonic articulations involve allegiances of dominant cultures in what result in the subjugation of particular cultural styles and intellects.

Monologic—This term refers to the dominance of a single lens of perception and analysis. Monologic engages in reductive techniques that often mistake a single orientation toward cognition as the only way of knowing and understanding the world. Commonly an instrumental logic that emphasizes rules, procedures, and patterns, this approach to reason in its search for continuity fails to grasp the importance of abnormalities, idiosyncrasies, and eccentricities.

Multilogicality—This term describes the interplay of many competing, overlapping, and incommensurable ways of knowing that illustrate the complexity of perception and analysis. Multilogicality aims for the exploration of numerous axes of reason that hold differing values in society to illustrate the myriad ways human beings reason. Through attending to more than one form of knowing, multilogicality illuminates the ways in which particular forms of reason, such as bodily and emotional intelligence, have been historically subjugated.

Postformalism—The term belies easy categorization but can be safely stated that postformalism attends to alternate ways of conceptualizing cognition and human understanding. Postformalism acts as a response to formalism's search for definitive sets of rules and principles of cognitive operation. As a reaction, postformalism unearths the idiosyncrasies and abnormalities subjugated by the domination of developmental, formalist logic.

Textual Analysis—This phrase refers to inquiry into the ways in which formal texts (books, magazines, journals) and informal texts (conversations, physical spaces, social interactions, human creations) are given significance through reading and interpretation. Textual analysis can involve a myriad of dimensions but often includes entry into the deeper structures of meaning and the illustration of relationships between ostensibly different realities. Inquiry can include, for example, utilization of readership theory to analyze the significance of school space for shaping perceptions of participatory democratic practice.

Totalizing Narratives—This phrase refers to dominance of a particular storyline in a community or culture and the ways in which its sheer press or force gives it over to social convention or everyday practices so common that they are given little thought. As a result of their force, these stories allude to mundane aspects of human life or plot lines that often end with statements such as, "well, that's just the way life is." Through their saturation in production and circulation, these story lines regularly drown out alternative narratives that might bring attention to their socially constructed character. The American Dream narrative, for example, has so much power in U.S. American society that it become difficult to envision other ways of organizing social life and family structures.

Transhistorical—This term references the social group affiliations or heuristic devices that as a category are commonly described outside of the constraints of time, circumstance, and context. These axes of affiliation provide the possibility for grounding frameworks of analysis but in the process of setting boundaries the character of the category itself is often assumed to operate throughout history unchanged. The category of women, for example, helps situate gender and feminist studies while it might be difficult to argue that there are unchanging or essential elements to this category that exist unchanged across time and space.

SUGGESTED READING

Kincheloe, J. L. (1998). Pinar's currere and identity in hyperreality: Grounding the post-formal notion of intrapersonal intelligence. In W. Pinar (Ed.), *Curriculum: Toward New Identities* (pp. 129–142). New York: Garland Press.

Kincheloe, J. L., Steinberg, S., and Hinchey, P. (1999). *The Post-Formal Reader: Cognition and Education.* New York: Falmer Press.

Kincheloe, J. L., Steinberg, S. R., and Villaverde, L. E. (1999). *Rethinking Intelligence: Confronting Psychological Assumptions About Teaching and Learning.* New York: Routledge.

CHAPTER 105

Educational Psychology on the Move: Visual Representations of the Old and New Paradigms

FRANCES HELYAR

No pleasure is comparable to the standing upon the vantage-ground of truth.
—Sir Francis Bacon

The truth is not simply what you think it is; it is also the circumstances in which it is said, and to whom, why, and how it is said.
—Vaclav Havel

These opening years of the twenty-first century are, perhaps more than ever before in human history, a time of rapid change. In a world of hyperreality and globalization, the Western conception of what is normal and what is deemed true alters with increasing regularity. The authors whose writings are collected in this volume suggest that the time is right for a major conceptual shift in the field of educational psychology. Only with such a shift can we move beyond the old, restrictive paradigms toward more inclusive, expansive models. Assuming this is the case, the question becomes if not this, then what? And once identified, how can a newly defined concept best be explained? The answer to the first question, I believe, is to rearticulate the conceptualization of ed psych epistemology that relies on Cartesian–Newtonian–Baconian (CNB) understandings, and is characterized by a collection of simplistic binarisms, toward a more critical complex epistemology that I choose to describe as post-CNB. By adopting the post-CNB descriptor, I want to avoid the semantic difficulties inherent in any interpretation that limits itself to poststructuralism, postformalism, postmodernism, or any number of other "isms." Each of these terms means different things to different theorists, and too often disagreements result from conflicting definitions. I choose to describe post-CNB epistemology by focusing on what it is not. While I may use one name, however, it is important to remember that a post-CNB epistemology of ed psych is not monological and should not be construed as such. I will offer my definition of CNB epistemology, and then contrast it with a post-CNB framework. In doing so, I will describe the various ways in which the latter is multilogical, and quite distinct from CNB epistemology. The answer to the second question, how to explain this newly conceptualized educational psychology, is difficult, but I believe a series of diagrams helps to indicate the transformation from simple, static, and fixed knowledges to complex ways of knowing.

Figure 105.1
Dualisms of Cartesian–Newtonian–Baconian epistemology

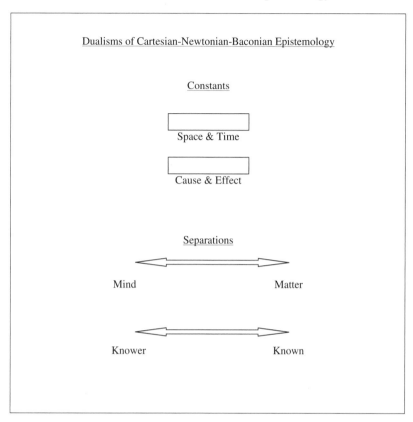

PICTURE THIS

The language of metaphor is often useful in describing paradigmatic change, and ordinarily I would use a metaphor to describe the difference between a CNB epistemology and a post-CNB model. None is forthcoming, however. Remembering the pedagogical lessons of my youth, when words won't work, I turn to pictures. I sketch several representations of a CNB epistemology of ed psych, the first (Figure 105.1) showing Sir Isaac Newton's constant dualisms of space and time, and cause and effect, and Réné Descartes' separate dualisms of mind and matter, knower and known. The constant dualism of space and time represents the assignment of universality to many of the findings of traditional ed psych; if it's true here and now, it's true everywhere and always. Context doesn't matter. The results of Piaget's study of a small group of boys in a Swiss school, for example, were universalized to apply to all children, everywhere. All learning is assumed to fit within the hierarchical confines of Bloom's taxonomy. The Cartesian constant dualism of cause and effect refers to the attribution of causality, that a particular cause will always have the same effect. Again, context is not a consideration in this paradigm, nor is interpretation. This dualism has as its most prominent example the "mind as computer" model. Human minds are conceptualized as computers that always work in a predictable way; the same input always results in the same output, without fail (Bruner, 1996). Predictability is an important requirement of research findings, because predictability makes possible the assignment of universality. Neither intuition nor imagination is acknowledged because each introduces too great a variable into the

Figure 105.2
Valued binarisms

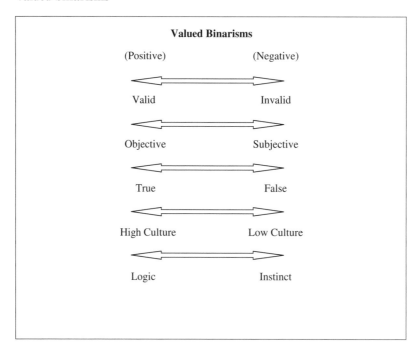

Valued Binarisms

(Positive)   (Negative)

Valid   Invalid

Objective   Subjective

True   False

High Culture   Low Culture

Logic   Instinct

process. Science, reasoned Sir Francis Bacon, can be used to harness nature, and reason should have dominance over imagination. Complex phenomena can be broken down into smaller parts and reassembled to adhere to laws of causation.

In a CNB epistemology, the dualisms of mind and matter, knower and known are completely separate. The traditional research methodologies of educational psychology, among other sciences, are held as sacred, and there is no connection between research method and research technique (Kincheloe, 2001). The identity of the researcher, the life experiences, preoccupations, and biases are assumed to have no impact on what is selected for study and how the study is undertaken. The researcher pursues an inquiry objectively, and the nature of the questions asked is seen to have no impact on the research findings.

CNB epistemology posits a series of valued binarisms, including valid versus invalid, objective versus subjective, true versus false, high culture versus low culture, and logic versus instinct, with the former of each pair positive and the latter negative (Figure 105.2). The result is a group of simple, two-dimensional images.

Of course, complexity may be inferred in the way these various dualisms and binarisms coexist simultaneously, but it is a limited complexity.

Scientific study in ed psych values findings that represent validity according to a prescribed set of norms. Invalid findings are discounted and discarded. For example, classroom studies of students are regarded as problematic because of the number of variables inherent in a real-life situation; the validity of such studies can be called into question, regardless of the fact that the classroom setting more closely reflects the actual life experience of students than does the laboratory. The child learning to divide is expected to complete the task using a particular approach according to a particular algorithm favored by the teacher. When parents or a tutor attempt to help the child but use a different algorithm, confusion arises, because in the context of the classroom and for the child to achieve success, one method is valid and any other is not. In a science classroom, the scientific method with its set pattern including hypothesis, observations, and conclusion is deemed the only valid method of inquiry. If the method is not followed, it's not science.

A CNB model of ed psych assumes that a certain narrowly defined objectivity is possible, lays out rules for achieving it, and devalues any findings that fall short, including those in which the identity or experience of the researcher "intrudes" upon the study. Truth and falsity are related to time and space; that which is true is ever thus, and that which is false is always so. The problem with the true/false binarism is immediately and frustratingly evident to adults who attempt to answer public opinion surveys. By reducing the possible answers to yes or no, true or false, the designers of the survey remove all nuance and complexity in a given issue. The child attempting to answer questions on an intelligence test is faced with a similar experience. Questions that reduce truth and value to mere binarisms conflict with the complexity of lived experience. No doubt educational psychologists who are parents value the presence of imagination and joy in their children's lives. But where in the mechanism of ed psych is it possible to measure imagination and joy? At what temperature does an imagination freeze? (Kincheloe, 2003).

In another valued binarism, high culture assumes that only art of a certain specific genealogy executed and displayed or performed in a narrowly defined way has value; if it doesn't fit the definition, it isn't art. This dichotomy can also refer to the culture of research. The work of educational psychologists of certain academic backgrounds or associated with certain schools is assumed to have greater value than the work of those whose institutions are not as widely recognized. Similarly, logic is valued over instinct. The results of empirical studies are accepted and valued for the logic of their findings, and illogical findings are rejected, never mind the huge role that instinct has always played in human exploration and discovery. In spite of the cult of scientific method, much scientific progress is the result of so-called "thinking outside the box." What is deemed logical may simply be an expression of that which is known at any given time or place. Einstein's general theory of relativity, for example, threw the world of physics on its head, but did not follow the conventions of knowledge in the discipline, as they existed in 1905 (Kincheloe, Steinberg, and Tippens, 1999).

NEW, COMPLEX PARADIGMS

With these simple diagrams in place to represent CNB epistemology, the challenge then becomes how to represent the complex epistemology of the post-CNB framework. I recall a doodle I used to draw in the margins of my notebooks as a student (when I should have been thinking deep thoughts, or did these doodles serve to elicit deep thoughts?). I would place as many dots as I desired in a circle, and connect the dots, each to the other, until I saw a geometric design reminiscent of the drawings one could create using the old Spirograph toy of the 1960s. With some investigation, I discover that this is a K-n graph, in which n represents the number of dots forming the boundaries of the circle. Further investigation on the Internet reveals the Hoffman–Singleton graph (Figure 105.3), which most closely resembles a sophisticated version of my notebook doodles. In this conceptualization, each dot, which when connected to all the other dots forms the boundaries of the graph, represents a part of what is deemed the knowledge of educational psychology, and the lines of the graph represent the relatedness of all parts of knowledge with each other. In other words, this graph resembles the web of reality and each of us lays claim to a picture that is uniquely our own. One dot might represent phenomenology, another hermeneutics, another ethnography, yet another history, and so on. The potential size of the graph is infinite, and is determined only by the knower. Connections on the graph do not share

Figure 105.3
Post-Cartesian–Newtonian–Baconian epistemology of complexity (Hoffman-Singleton graph). Retrieved from the Internet at http://mathworld.wolfram.com/Hoffman-SingletonGraph.html

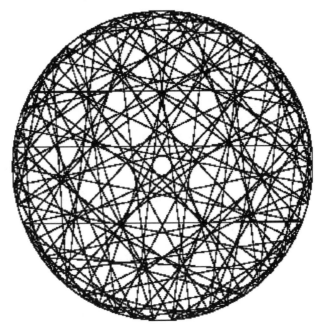

the primary focus at all times; at any given point some lines are recessive and some are dominant, depending on the focus of the knower's attention.

This conceptualization is far from perfect. While the *K-n* graph hints at the complexity of a post-CNB epistemology of ed psych and the relationships between all parts therein, it is overly tidy, symmetrical, and contained. A truer representation would picture changing lines of differing lengths that would be difficult to contain within the page. Rather than a two-dimensional static model, it would have three dimensions—height, width, and depth—and would be in constant motion, changing size and shape from moment to moment. The points on the graph include every element of the CNB paradigm of Figures 105.1 and 105.2, and many, many more ad infinitum. The important contrast to the CNB paradigm is that here, every point on the graph is connected to every other, and the representation for one person is never the same as that for another. It is also important to note that post-CNB epistemology does not reject out of hand the teaching of the Enlightenment; rather, it

analyzes social, philosophical, and educational forms previously shielded by the authority of modernist science. It does not attempt to throw out Western science but to understand its limitations and the underside of its application. It is a global perspective, since it admits to the conversation previously forbidden evidence derived from questions asked by previously excluded voices. (*Getting Beyond The Facts* 95)

In other words, post-CNB epistemology does not attempt to ignore the positive or beneficial effects of the Enlightenment. It involves a more complex, inclusive, and socially just conceptualization of pedagogy than is possible within the confines of CNB thought.

Let's return to the example of the child learning to divide. In order to determine how a child accomplishes the task of learning to divide double-digit numbers with single digits, for example, the researcher looks at a variety of different factors. If the *K-n* diagram of Figure 105.3 represents the research, the points on the graph are representative of the different interpretive lenses the researcher places on the phenomenon. The investigation may begin with biography. What is the child's previous experience with division? The child who has experienced success in the past will approach the task differently than the child who has struggled. What instruction outside the classroom does the child receive? A child who receives tutorial help may have additional insights into division that breed success, or may simply be confused because of contradictory instructions. What is the family attitude toward mathematics? The child of parents who view division as a daunting challenge has a different perspective than the child of mathematicians. Does the child speak sufficient English to understand instructions? Language is an integral part of mathematics, and facility with language affects acquisition. Other questions may be ethnographic in nature. Did the child fight with a friend before class? Is this the day before a long weekend? The ability to concentrate has a profound impact on attention to a learning task. A phenomenological approach raises different questions. What experience with division does the child have in everyday life? What is the lived experience of the child during the lesson? What is the lived experience of the teacher?

This leads to an important contextual point: questions about the teacher might be considered irrelevant in the CNB paradigm, but they are key in a post-CNB epistemology. What is the classroom teacher's attitude toward mathematics? The teacher who is a trained mathematician has an approach different than the nonspecialist, and may have the ability to use a variety of approaches. What tools are used in the lessons? A wealthy school may have the resources to provide manipulatives and visual aids to supplement instruction or due to small class size, may afford the teacher greater amounts of time to work with students on an individual basis. What does the teacher believe are the child's capabilities? Pedagogical decisions based on a teacher's expectations can have an enormous impact on classroom learning. The broader context is also important. What is the prevailing societal attitude toward mathematics? A society that values mathematical ability and achievement influences classroom instruction by providing funding, and honoring individuals with demonstrated talent, whether they are students or teachers. These questions and many, many more can affect the student's ability to learn a mathematics task that is apparently simple. Of course, it would be impossible to address all questions in order to come up with the definitive answer to the question about a child's learning. But what is most important is not the answer, it is the questions, and the complexity of the process of attempting to discover the answer leads to a sense of humility for the researcher. By acknowledging that any answers may be dependent upon context, the researcher avoids the sweeping generalizations that have served in the past to harm, not help, those being researched.

CONCLUSION

Clearly, the tendency exists to reduce epistemology to an easily digestible form, whether by adherents to Cartesian–Newtonian–Baconian thought or by those who reject CNB entirely. Even in describing the tendency, I delineate a tension between one side and another! Thus, by my own example, binarisms exert a powerful pressure on the conceptualization of knowledge. It is best, then, to keep in mind the dynamic qualities of the *K-n* graph of Figure 105.3. Is it possible to avoid binarisms? It takes a concerted effort, and perhaps the question "What binarisms are evident in what I just described?" becomes a useful question for the student of epistemology. The question serves as one of the checks and balances enabling the creation of an epistemology that moves more often than not toward dynamism instead of stoicism, expansion instead of contraction, and inclusion instead of exclusion. The motion is understood to take place on a continuum so that the ideal is never achieved, but always remains in sight. And how does all of this influence educational psychology? Keep in mind the contrast between Figures 105.1 and 105.2 and the greater complexity of Figure 105.3. An epistemology that acknowledges multilogicality can become a tool that aids in a study of teaching and learning for the twenty-first century.

REFERENCES

Bruner, J. (1996). *The Culture of Education*. Cambridge: Harvard University Press.

Kincheloe, J. L. (2001). *Getting Beyond the Facts: Teaching Social Studies/Social Sciences in the Twenty-first Century* (2nd ed.). New York: Peter Lang.

Kincheloe, J. L. (2003). *Teachers as Researchers: Qualitative Inquiry as a Path to Empowerment* (2nd ed.). New York: Routledge Falmer.

Kincheloe, J. L., Steinberg S. R., and Tippens, D. J. (1999). *The Stigma of Genius: Einstein Consciousness and Education*. New York: Peter Lang.

CHAPTER 106

Toward a Postformal Model of History Education

FRANCES HELYAR

INTRODUCTION

For over a hundred years, historians, educators, and indeed the general public have struggled with definitions of the purpose, form, and content of history education. The questions have been many: Should history education serve to promote nationalism and patriotism? Should the goal be to create responsible citizens? To what extent should the practice of the history student in an elementary or secondary reflect the practice of the professional historian? How much access to primary and secondary historical sources is appropriate? Whose history should be told, and whose should be left out? Should children be learning history, or are social studies the better approach?

These are complicated questions, and different times and places produce different answers. What is generally consistent, however, is the infrequency with which students of history or student teachers are included in the discussion. Their minds are instead imagined as empty vessels into which a fully formed, well-defined (for the moment) history can be poured. Too often, history education as it is practiced even in the twenty-first century follows the positivist model, producing an understanding of the past that reduces the complexity of human experience to a simple cause and effect without complication. The linear nature of textbook narration reinforces this simplicity, and the study of history remains a dry-as-dust examination of undisputable facts and figures. The canon of acceptable knowledge appears monolithic and unchanging. While teaching to the test, history educators are unable to elicit in their students a sense of the relations between historical events, and the patterns that emerge, disappear, and reemerge. The wonder, the surprise, the sheer unexpectedness of human existence is lost in translation.

It doesn't need to be so. History education that has as its foundation a critical historiography can take the same source materials and elicit a deep understanding, on both a cognitive and an affective level, not just of the past but of how the past is constructed and perceived, how that construction and perception can be altered, and to what effect. As students examine their own knowledge and its origins, and then compare their knowledge to that of their peers, the textbook authors and others, they begin to develop the ability to think hermeneutically. This postformal approach serves the students not just in history class, but it becomes a life skill to enable them to approach critically new situations, both in and out of school. In this way, students move beyond the positivistic process of assimilation whereby they shape an event to fit their cognitive structure, toward a process in which they restructure their cognition to fit an event. This accommodation allows them to anticipate different situations and thereby formulate strategies that will produce emancipatory outcomes as a result of new encounters. Students become explorers of the implicate order, a deeper structure of reality (Kincheloe, 1999).

HISTORY TEXTBOOKS

It has long been acknowledged that the tools of history teaching should include more than one textbook. Over a hundred years ago, teachers were entreated to bring multiple sources, primary and secondary, into the classroom. A century has passed, however, yet the complaint still persists that teachers rely on too few sources, with the history textbook always at the forefront. The textbook may have been revised to include different racial, ethnic, gender and other perspectives, but it remains a cultural artifact, reflective of the era in which it was produced and at the mercy of the particular ideologies of the publishers and the prescribing jurisdictions. Methods textbooks for preservice teachers are equally reflective of particular pedagogical trends but most fail to elicit anything more than a shallow understanding of the notion of historiography and criticality. At the same time, the public discourse refers sentimentally, and sometimes angrily, to a so-called golden age of history education that never existed.

In the late nineteenth to early twentieth century, high school history textbooks were hardcover books no bigger than the size of today's trade paperbacks. They contained some maps and illustrations, but for the most part the text was dense, with the density often relieved within chapters by numbered sections or paragraphs. This textual separation was designed to make the content material easier for the student reader to grasp. Single male authors who were usually university professors of history wrote these tomes with an authoritarian voice. In many nineteenth-century classrooms, textbooks were the antidote to the ill-trained teacher who had no understanding of history (FitzGerald, 1979). The text often included a message from the author about the nature of history, and during this era, it was all about progress. "The study of history was the study of the progress of man [*sic*] in the Baconian sense, with the pinnacle of achievement explicitly identified as white European civilization" (Swinton, 1883). Of course, the particular example of that pinnacle depended on the national origin of the author; in British texts, the British Empire provided the model with which all others were compared, while American authors preferred the American touchstone. Primitive societies were described as inferior, and while mentioned, were dispatched with due haste. In subsequent editions, some authors altered their writing styles slightly to adhere to the characteristics of a story (Myers, 1906/1921). Textbooks were, and still are, big business, and authors and publishers then as today regularly made changes to their books to fit the needs and desires of the committees that approved their use in schools.

As the twentieth century continued, however, history textbooks changed in some significant ways. They became larger in size and the font size of the text was similarly expanded. Illustrations and maps became more numerous, photographs and color were added, and chapters were more likely to be followed by study aids such as questions about content, map-reading activities, and references for further study. The questions were fact-based, and the answers contained within the pages of the texts. These books were written not by lone authors but by teams, which necessitated the removal of authors' signed messages in favor of unsigned forewords or prefaces. The focus on the progress of civilization remained, however, and Western civilization continued to be the gold standard. Science led the way with an unquestioning acceptance of scientific discovery as unambiguously positive. The narrative was chronological and linear, presenting a clean, uncomplicated view of history. Smith, Muzzey, and Lloyd's 1946 *World History: The Struggle for Civilization*, for example, includes a middle section on "The Growth of Nationalism."

The section concentrates on Europe and European colonial power, including a passage titled "How Africa Came to Belong to the Europeans," with additional passages about Russia, Japan, and China. The section ends with a science-focused chapter titled "Rapid Progress of the Nineteenth Century," including passages about "The Magic of Modern Chemistry" and "Knowledge Brought Within the Reach of All."

There were exceptions to this typical textbook along the way. Harold Rugg's popular series of social studies texts, published under the group title "Man and His Changing Society," were widely read by American school children until a concerted campaign by business interests and patriotic groups resulted in their effective banishment from prescribed book lists by the early 1940s (Zimmerman, 2002). The main complaint against the texts seems to have been their critique of America in a social, cultural, and economic context. America as an example of the ideal nation was under attack, and that kind of criticism was deemed unseemly and inappropriate for the country's children. The texts went from being perennial bestsellers for nearly a decade to disappearing entirely, all within the space of about five years.

The appearance of textbooks in use in twenty-first century schools is not much different from those of the mid–twentieth century. The dimensions are more or less the same, and the text is still arranged in columns, with topics separated by headings. Information is organized chronologically and accompanied by illustrations, maps, charts, photographs, and other visuals. Chapter titles range from those echoing the notion of progress from earlier textbooks, using words like *launching*, *triumph*, *upsurge*, *rise*, *shaping* and *creating*, and those which indicate struggle, including *duel*, *friction*, *ferment*, *controversy*, and *ordeal* (see Bailey and Kennedy, 1987).

The biggest changes in textbook content during the last half of the twentieth century concern race and gender. The civil rights movement and feminism of the 1950s, 60s, and 70s had a direct impact on history textbooks so that no longer do they tell an exclusively white, European male story. Photographs, excerpts from primary source documents and other artifacts create a more inclusive portrait of the past. The change is not uncontroversial, however. The nature of history textbook publishing and the economies of textbook size mean that any time one part of history is included, it necessitates the removal of another. By definition, then, there is no such thing as a perfect textbook, and textbook controversies arise with a regularity that would be comical if the consequences to history education were not so severe.

Throughout the history of history textbooks, a distinction can be made between those books prepared for school children and those intended for a general adult audience. For instance, a glance at the *New York Times* nonfiction bestseller list at any time yields a number of histories and historical biographies. No matter the author's perspective, the book for adults will include the author's name, probably a biographical paragraph and perhaps even a photograph. In addition, the volume will include bibliographical references. In contrast, only in the late twentieth century have history textbooks written for children begun to contain biographical material about the authors. At the same time, bibliographical material that was included in textbooks in the late nineteenth century has been missing for most of the twentieth. No wonder students accept what they read as the undisputed truth; they are provided few clues to the source of the material. They are simply hearing the voice of authority.

The point, of course, is that students of history do not often compare their textbooks to popular histories. They do not look at old history textbooks (I was once fortunate enough to intercede at a school when a collection of elementary school textbooks was being relegated to the trash. I now own enough copies of that textbook to enable group textbook analysis). They do not think of their textbooks as having been written by a human being, someone's mother, father, daughter, or son. A positivistic history course does not lay bare the intricacies of textbook approval and production, of the machinations of the publishing industry, or the labored discussion at the school administration level that precede the arrival of an approved textbook in the classroom. Instead of analyzing why a point of history is included for study, that point of history is simply memorized for the test. Student knowledge is limited to the lowest of cognitive levels.

How would a postformal history lesson make use of textbooks? It would include a critical historiography that not only examines what is there, but what is not there. It goes beyond the assumptions of a single perspective to embrace a multiplicity of vantage points from which to view a particular history. It gets beyond the facts. For instance, students begin with a collection of textbooks from various eras. These books may be examined with a number of questions in mind. Within a broad context, those questions may include the following:

- When was this book published? What was going on in the world at the time?
- What are the chapter headings of this textbook? What do this textbook's authors consider to be important?
- What kinds of words are used in the chapter headings to make them more interesting?
- What names occur in the index? How often do they occur?
- Are there supplemental activities in the text? What form do they take?
- How do the above examined features compare to what is found in other textbooks?

Looking more specifically at the content of the textbooks, the following questions could be asked:

- Choosing a particular historical event, how does this textbook describe that event?
- What descriptive verbs, adjectives, nouns, and adverbs are used?
- Which historical figures are highlighted in this account?
- How do the authors feel about this historical event?
- How do the above details compare with the way the same historical event is depicted in other textbooks?

Students then use the answers to the above questions to frame their understanding of textbooks. This process removes the mystique of the authoritative author and brings to the fore perspective, bias, and knowledge production (see student reflections on this kind of approach to textbooks at the Urban Academy Web site, http://www.urbanacademy.org/diverse/studentreflect.html). The process may also be extended with the addition of popular historical nonfiction, film, and television to the mix. By critically comparing presentations of the past, students begin to recognize and make judgments about editorial choices and the multitude of forces that affect textbook production and the production of other historical media.

METHODS TEXTBOOKS

This type of critical historiography should begin with teacher education. Like history textbooks, methods textbooks are reflective of the era in which they were produced. To use one text as an example, William Mace's 1897 *Method in History* describes the organizing principle of history as the growth of institutional life. Mace's perspective is highly Eurocentric and reductionistic. His chapter headings include "Essential Elements of History," "Processes Involved in Organizing History," and "Organization of the Periods of American History." He splits "The Elementary Phases of History Teaching" into two sections, "The Sense Phase of History" and the "The Representative Phase of History," and he introduces the former saying, "No one can intelligently determine what the method of history work should be without first discovering the logical relations in the subject-matter itself. The subject in its scientific form stands as the goal toward which every lesson must point, no matter where the material is found along the line between these two points" (see Mace, p. 255).

While Mace's methods text is overwhelmingly positivistic, it is not without useful information for the student teacher. For instance, he offers a simple method of determining which "facts" should be included in a test. Using, among others, the example of the arrival of the Pilgrims to Plymouth Rock aboard the Mayflower in December 1620, he asks if it would have made any difference had the ship been called the Speedwell. Would the destiny of America have been different had there been one hundred or one hundred and two souls aboard instead of one hundred two? The answer in each case is no, and so Mace concludes that these are pieces of information students of history need not retain. Instead, they should learn about the political, religious, and social ideas animating the Pilgrims, because these ideas had consequence for the development of the nation.

The student teacher who reads an old methods textbook such as Mace's, while perhaps recognizing a few pedagogical gems within, cannot help but remark upon the archaic sentence structure and presentation and, more important, the vastly different approach to the study of history recommended in 1897. By examining such documents historiographically, the student can trace the changes that occur in texts over a long period. This examination influences the way the student approaches the contemporary methods textbooks because it provides a context and reveals the situatedness of any prescribed methodology.

In contrast to Mace's hundred-year-old text, Jack Zevin's *Social Studies for the Twenty-First Century: Methods and Materials for Teaching in Middle and Secondary Schools* (1992) opens with a "Personal Prologue," which addresses the reader directly. Throughout the text, Zevin continues this approach, saying on p. 67 for instance, "You may find yourself in a situation in which the text defines both the curriculum and your teaching plan." Not only is the writing style considerably different from the older text, but also in an echo of the comparison between history textbooks new and old, the dimensions of Zevin's book are greater, and the text is broken up with photographs, charts, and special activities. Most interestingly, where history textbooks tend to omit bibliographical material, Zevin's text contains full references. Where the old and new methods texts resemble each other is in their organization. Zevin's text is divided into five parts, each of which has its counterpart in Mace's text: a definition of the field; a contextual description; strategies for instruction; curriculum information; and a final, wrap-up section. In addition, although Zevin's text tries to represent the range of opinions surrounding the field of social studies, he still reduces the field into three interrelated dimensions—the didactic, the reflective, and the affective.

How would a postformal teacher-educator make use of these texts? An historiographical approach in which many of the same questions asked of history textbooks is appropriately applied to a range of methods texts. Students may examine the context of the historical era in which each text was produced, and delineate the language used in the chapter headings as well as in the body of the text. By comparing methods textbooks from different eras, student teachers begin to acknowledge that pedagogy is not static, but instead is a product of its time and is ever changing. As they recognize changing approaches to teacher education, they begin to question the assumptions implicit in each text. Among the questions they may ask about each text,

- What approach to pedagogy does this author take?
- How does this author's approach compare to others'?
- How does this author's approach compare to my own?
- What about this discipline does this author value the most?
- What does this author not value?
- What claims does this author make?
- Do I believe this author's claims?

In answering these questions, the student teacher develops a personal approach informed by a historical understanding of the discipline. On a cognitive level, the student teacher has a deeper understanding and is better able to articulate what she is teaching and why she is teaching it.

PEDAGOGY

The pedagogy of history education has undergone profound changes over the past hundred years, although in some ways assertions of the past have their counterparts today. In 1912 the American Historical Association's Committee of Five issued *Study of History in Secondary Schools*, in which the most important factor in the classroom was deemed to be not the curriculum or the method or the textbook, but the teacher. The Committee paints a cautionary picture of the kind of mind-numbing history class that has served as the stereotype for nearly one hundred years, in which the pupil works her way page by page through the textbook with a teacher who is in no danger of telling untruths if the students ask no questions. History education as the study of a series of facts was as unacceptable in the early twentieth century as it is in the postformal classroom:

If history teaching results only in the memorizing of a modicum of bare facts in the order in which they are given in a text there is not much to be said in favor of the retention of the subject as an important part of the curriculum. This does not mean that pupils should not be accurate, painstaking, and thorough; it means that in addition to learning, and learning *well*, a reasonable amount of history from the text, the pupil should gain something more: he should learn how to use books and how to read them; he should be led to think about historical facts and to see through the pages of the book the life with which history deals; he may even be brought to see the relation between evidence and historical statement in simple cases where material is close at hand; he should in some measure get the historical state of mind. (pp. 39–40)

The goal of history education is the same, only the methodology has changed. But it is the positivist classroom, with students deep in preparation for the standardized test, that bears a closer resemblance to the negative example of a history classroom in 1912, than does the postformal model. No doubt it will be possible in the future to compare standardized tests of the early twenty-first century with their associated history textbooks and see, just as happened in the early years of the twentieth century, students underlining sections of the text that comprise the answers for the test questions. This marginalia begs the question: what have the students learned, and how has it served them in their lives?

As hierarchical and taxonomical organization became the dominant feature of curriculum design in the twentieth century, the pedagogy of history education became bogged down. Part of the problem was the curriculum designers' inability to harmonize the grand goals of the documents with the instructions for implementation. The stated goal of the curriculum may have been that students achieve equally everything from comprehension to synthesis and analysis of the material covered, but an examination of the language used within the curriculum document itself revealed an unequal balance of expectations. No wonder teachers found themselves frustrated in their attempt to fulfill goals that were unattainable. At the same time, the hierarchical nature of the expectations imposes a value judgment on knowledge that may have little or nothing to do with what the students know, or what they learn.

Whereas the positivist pedagogy of history education envisions the students' minds as vessels to be filled with facts, the postformal model acknowledges that students begin their study with a worldview, with a preexisting notion of history. The teacher's first job is to enable them to articulate that view. Not only do students investigate *what* they know of history, more important, they look at *how* they know history. The following questions prove useful in undertaking this investigation:

- What history books have you read? (school textbooks or popular histories)
- What public monuments are familiar to you?
- What media representations of history have you seen or heard? (films like Alexander, Troy, or Saving Private Ryan, programs on television networks such as The History Channel or Biography, television mini-series, etc.)
- How have historical events affected you or your family or your friends? (immigration, migration, refugee experience, military service, etc.)

The postformal teacher uses the answers to these questions to shape the study of history. It is not enough to set a course of study before classes begin and plow through a series of lesson plans leading up to the test. The critical teacher, aware of both the cognitive and affective aspects of history education, is sensitive to the fact that different students experience the study of history in unique ways. For example, in a thematic study of immigration and migration, the teacher must be cognizant of the fact that the theme will have a different meaning to the child who is an immigrant himself than for the child whose family has lived in the same location for generations. It is foolhardy and a waste of precious intellectual resource for the teacher not to acknowledge the personal experience of the student, to fail to welcome the sharing of that experience in the classroom. This is not to say that the child should become essentialized, that the immigrant child should become the center of every conversation about immigration, or that the student with a long history in the school district should have no contribution to make other than that relating to her family's longevity. Student knowledge, however, can effectively inform a study of immigration patterns and experience, and bring the study of history into sharp relief with a study of the present and the lived lives of the student population.

The postformal study of history has a particular role in acknowledging the affective as part of the classroom experience. As students examine historical documents and learn about the events and forces that have impacted on the lives of people in the past, it is highly likely that they will experience an emotional reaction. Rather than brushing aside the emotion, the critical teacher acknowledges it, interrogates it and accepts it as an integral part of historiography. In addition, student intuition is similarly recognized, acknowledged, and encouraged. The professional historian, who as one who wonders about history, does not make use of intuition, is a historian who misses much in her study of the past. Students should be no less vigilant in recognizing the affective as an accepted component of the serious historiographer's tools of the trade.

Another important postformal tool is the concept of metaphorical cognition (Kincheloe, 1999). Students should be encouraged to represent their understanding of history in the form of a metaphor. Depending upon their age and cognitive level, the metaphor may be sophisticated or not. The activity is not a discrete one, however. Rather, it serves as an ongoing process in which students revisit previous thoughts and reformulate their metaphors in light of recent learning. As they do so, they interrogate the reasons for the changes in their thinking. This activity can be incorporated into a journaling process in order to trace the development of their historical understanding. Thus they recognize in a very personal way the constructed, fluid, and changing nature of knowledge, and experience the possibilities for deep thinking inherent in the discovery of patterns and connections.

Positivist education places a heavy emphasis on the activity of problem solving, both for students and teachers. It is true that the problem solving process can be useful, and can help to break away from a worldview that sees history or education as neat, linear processes, for instance in the case where a solution to a problem is not possible. But within the context of many disciplines, and in particular history education, such a focus can seem nonsensical, especially to students. Why should they attempt to solve problems that arose in the distant past, and for which solutions have likely already been found? The resulting crisis in motivation provides only one impediment to deep learning; other impediments may include the sometimes-forced connections imposed between the past and the present, the low-level thinking required to solve the problem, or simply the top–down hierarchy of dealing with problems as defined by others. For teachers, the act of problem solving must begin with an acceptance of the way the world is, not as it could be. This is a limiting view which renders the teacher blind to conditions in the classroom and the school that may serve to impede student success; it is antithetical to the goals of emancipation and social justice that are the cornerstone of postformal education.

The postformal counterpart of problem solving is problem detection (Kincheloe, 2001). This process begins not with a set of predetermined problems, but with observation. For example, teachers examine their curricula, and students examine their textbooks. Both may notice that American history is viewed as a story of progress, and that America is identified, in the words of the national anthem, as "the land of the free." This observation leads to a definition of freedom, and an examination of the concept in the context of American history. The problem is detected: how is it possible to reconcile that identity with the institution of slavery, with the fight for civil and women's rights, with the country's labor history, treatment of ethnic minorities, immigration policies, and so on. The inevitable next step is an examination of freedom as it relates to current events, as students discover where the word is used in political and social discourse, how varying definitions of freedom affect public policy, and what are the consequences in America and throughout the world. This hermeneutic process allows them to interpret this and subsequent situations. When students become experts at problem detection, they develop simultaneously an expertise in historical thinking. The potential for creative investigation and deep understanding is huge, yielding results immeasurable in a standardized test.

CONCLUSION

History education has been surrounded by controversy since its inception. There never was a golden age. The discipline has always been lacking in someone's estimation: Students don't know enough, they know too much about this and too little about that, they don't know who, they don't know where, when, how, or why. Sometimes the criticism is motivated by a sense of injustice; sometimes it arises in response to a perceived threat to traditionally dominant interests. The only constant is its persistence. Surely the twenty-first century is the time, after so much has been said by so many, to create a new paradigm of history education that is inclusive, equitable, and socially just. Surely now is the time to turn to a rigorous pedagogy that stimulates deep involvement both cognitively and affectively. Acceptance of this new paradigm is not a matter of throwing the baby out with the bathwater; instead it invites a closer look at the baby, the bathwater, the tub, the soap—asking questions, seeing relationships, developing understanding. Educators thus move beyond the model of their own educational backgrounds and become pioneers of the new millennium, forging into the truly undiscovered territory of postformalism. By taking this approach, concentrating heavily on historiography to unearth tacit assumptions of the present and the past, educators and students can abandon memorization of the mere facts inherent in traditional education, to learn the processes and patterns of the dance of human history. Thus they come to understand in a meaningful way their own position in the web of reality. They develop the ability to detect problems, to apply hermeneutics to their experience, and to deconstruct a variety of texts, both literal and figurative. In doing so, they open to themselves a new world of possible interpretations of yesterday, today and tomorrow, hearts open with humility and wonder.

REFERENCES

Bailey, T., and Kennedy, D. M. (1987). *The American Pageant: A History of the Republic.* Boston, MA: Houghton Mifflin.

FitzGerald, F. (1979). *America Revised: History Schoolbooks in the Twentieth Century.* New York: Little, Brown, and Company.

Kincheloe, J. L. (1999). *The Post-Formal Reader: Cognition and Education*, eds. S. Steinberg, J. Kincheloe, and P. Hinchey. New York: Falmer Press.

———. (2001). *Getting Beyond the Facts.* New York: Peter Lang.

Myers, P. V. N. (1906/1921). *A General History for Colleges and High Schools.* Kilia MT: Kessinger Publishing.

Swinton, W. (1883). *Outlines of the World's History: Ancient, Medieval and Modern.* New York: Ivison, Blakeman, Taylor.

Zimmerman, J. (2002). *Whose America? Culture Wars in the Public Schools.* Cambridge, MA: Harvard University Press.

CHAPTER 107

Postformalism and a Literacy of Power: Elitism and the Ideology of the Gifted

JOE L. KINCHELOE

One of the most important ideological tools designed to maintain existing power relationships involves the use of mainstream educational psychology and psychometrics to validate the "intelligence" of the privileged and the "deficiency" of the socially and politically marginalized. Drawing upon the discursive critique of the fragmentation of the discipline of modern psychology and the need for sociohistorical contextualization of the study of giftedness and intellectual ability, a critical psychology understands that human sociality is a fundamental aspect of the self. Criticality induces us to appreciate that the self is never complete, always in process of shaping and being shaped by the sociocultural, symbolic, and ideological realms. In this context a critical psychoanalysis replaces the term *self* with its implication of autonomy and unity with the term *subject* with its connotation of the self's production by its interaction with the world around it.

In this context, therefore, the development of mental functions must account for a wide variety of factors, including contextual analysis, the conscious and unconscious production of subjectivity, the subtle dynamics of interpersonal interaction, and an individual or a group's position in the web of reality. Simply put, contrary to the pronouncements of proponents of gifted and talented education for the elite, the mind extends beyond the skin. Intelligence, memory, and thinking are not the simple possessions of individuals—they are always social and political processes. With these understandings the primitive nature of psychometric IQ testing is exposed with its measurement of cultural familiarity with the discourse of Western schooling and linguistic socialization.

Thus, a critical theoretical encounter with educational psychology involves a critique of the authority of psychological knowledge and the paradigm in which it is produced. The mainstream psychological paradigm, for example, has ignored the stories, experiences, and life world of culturally and politically marginalized groups. A critical reassessment of psychology and its elitist assumptions induces the field to confront the Eurocentrism of the discipline and the ways such a dynamic shapes psychological knowledge. It challenges mainstream psychology's monocultural value system that reflects the standpoint of a positivist epistemology that reflects the senses over interpretive, more hermeneutical forms of knowledge. Such epistemological orientations impede scholars from critically reading the sociopsychological world in ways that connect psychological processes to their larger contexts in ways that provide meaning to ostensibly isolated and abstracted phenomena.

Such a dynamic results in a psychology guilty of individuation. Mainstream psychologists have often reused to employ the sociological strategy of studying individuals in relation to their various group identifications, choosing instead to highlight individualism. The critical theoretical critique of Cartesian–Newtonian science rejected this individuation and the theory of the autonomous rational subject that supports it. Residing at the epicenter of the positivist universe, this possessive egocentric individual has corrupted particular scientific ways of seeing to the point that manifestations of difference are excluded. Operating in this epistemological and ontological galaxy, cognitive psychology validates this individualization impulse as it positions the individual as the nonproblematic unit of scientific analysis. In this context learning becomes a simple process of absorbing the given while pedagogy is a matter of transmission and assimilation. Such a perspective establishes strict boundaries between the inside and outside of the mind—students in this epistemology and its attendant learning theory take in information from outside themselves. The mindset builds fences between ourselves and other people, borders between our mutual emotional needs—indeed, fragmented knowledge fragments the community.

THE POSTFORMAL MISSION: EXPOSING POWER IN PSYCHOLOGY'S NATURALIZATION OF INEQUALITY

Mechanistic educational psychology—and, of course the other branches of psychology—has used its positivistic methodology to "naturalize" cognitive superiority and inferiority. As educational psychology presents statistical relationships as natural laws, Spearman's g as natural, transhistorical, transcultural, and stable, and IQ scores as the true measure of intelligence, the discipline covers up the human construction of such notions with social, political, and economic assumptions. When psychometricians, for example, contend that IQ is "normally distributed," they have implicitly assumed that IQ scores really do signify cognitive superiority, this "intelligence" exists inside the mind as a material entity, and the material mental entity has been proportionately passed out to human beings by nature itself.

The cognitively gifted in this context have been granted validation by beneficent nature itself—the ultimate act of naturalization. Curiously absent in this conversation about cognition, however, is the realization that standardized intelligence tests are devised and revised until they produce a normal distribution, a bell curve. Claims of natural cognitive laws ring hollow in such a constructed, if not contrived, positivistic context. Indeed, mechanistic psychology's use of terms such as natural laws and human nature make it look like the mind has no connect to the social, cultural, or political domain. The ability of power to produce knowledge that supports its own interests is irrelevant in this rarefied, naturalistic context.

As we struggle with our postformal reconceptualization of educational psychology, we are profoundly struck by the political dynamics of this interrelationship between mind and culture. The political (power-related) dimensions of the social realm confront us with the role of power in the shaping of consciousness. Our critical constructivist emphasis on the fiction of the preexistent, innate self forces us to face some complex issues. Many critical analysts argue that if we deny the existence of an innate, presocial self then concepts such as ideology lose their meaning. The argument such critical analysts are making in this context is that the ideology of the power wielders distorts the socially pure self.

The concept of ideology can play a profoundly valuable role in understanding both the micro-social production of the individual subject and the macro-social perpetuation of the status quo. If we view ideology as simply one dynamic in a larger sociopolitical constellation of influences, notions of the production of "false consciousness" do not have to be employed with their implication of a corresponding "authentic consciousness"—that is, a presocial, fixed self. In this conceptual context we can refute the reductionistic nature of modernist psychology's disposition to naturalization. At this point we can begin to analyze the ways that ideological power complements disciplinary power's shaping of subjectivity. Subjectivity and power are inseparable concepts.

In this encyclopedic context this reference to ideological and disciplinary power provides a good opportunity to delineate just what these concepts denote. Such knowledge, it seems to me, are key understandings in a critical educational psychology, in postformalism.

Ideological Power: The Basic Characteristics

- Hierarchical power relations are constructed and maintained by diverse ideological expressions that mobilize meaning.
- Ideology is part of a larger process involving the maintenance of asymmetrical power relations—it is not a body of political beliefs.
- Ideology is not a misrepresentation of what is real in society.
- Ideology plays a role in constructing reality—it is found in the interplay of meaning and symbols that make up the lived world of the individual.
- Ideological meaning is always contingent on the process by which a dominant group is able to frame the interests of a competing worldview.
- Ideology as a semiotic phenomenon is located at the level of the social—it uses signs and signifiers to serve the interests of dominant power.
- Ideology is an interpretive framework through which the world is understood in a way that operates to sustain relations of domination.
- Ideology often exists in the realm of the preinterpreted—words, concepts, expressions, symbolic constructions all gain part of their meaning in this domain.
- Ideological refraction refers to the process by which the relationship between a sign and its referent is transformed. Such refraction creates a particular relationship that predisposes individuals to an interpretation of an event that serves the interests of dominant power.
- Ideology does its work in secret—it never says "I am ideology."
- Ideology struggles to hide social antagonisms and conflicts—an ideological historical account of the U.S. past, for example, hides particular class and race problems.
- So-called reflexive legitimation (very important in educational psychology and pedagogy) induces the oppressed to accept their low place in the social hierarchy, their own "inferiority."
- Ideology is not a monolithic, unidirectional entity imposed on individuals by a secret cohort of power wielders—it is far more complex and nuanced.
- A hyperreal ideology is found in a variety of social locations, places previously thought to be outside the domain of ideological struggle—for example, ideology in the contemporary electronic world often operates at the level of affects and emotion as well as at the rational level.
- The world can only be viewed through ideologically shaped lenses—no objective, pristine view is available.
- A critical complex understanding of ideology understands its operations at the macro, meso, and micro levels of the social—it also understands both the production and the reception of ideological power.
- The postformal understanding of ideology demands attention to the ways ideology represents the world and the symbolic processes that are used to shape these representations.

Hegemonic Power: The Basic Characteristics

- Views dominant power formations as shifting terrain of consensus, struggle, and compromise rather than a one-dimensional ideology imposed from above.

- Hegemonic power blocs exercise power by winning the consent of the governed—not via force.
- Hegemonic consent is never completely established, as it is always contested by various groups with different agendas.
- Hegemony involves the transmission/reception process that takes place around particular preconceptions, notion, and beliefs (ideologies) that help shape the worldview of particular social groups.
- The process of hegemony involves the social construction of reality through particular ideological institutions, practices, and discourses.
- Hegemony is a much more subtle process of incorporating individuals into patterns of belief, feeling, and behavior than the older notion of propaganda. Propaganda assumes citizens are malleable victims who easily fall prey to indoctrination.
- Consent is garnered by power blocs by turning their own beliefs and ways of seeing into "common sense."
- In winning consent, the power bloc must be prepared to accept a degree of compromise with those who give their consent. While the power bloc doesn't give up essential interests, it does cooperate with and respect some of the interests of other groups. A good example of this over the last thirty years has been the traditional Republican Party's acceptance of fundamentalist Christian politics and ways of seeing the world in order to win their consent to trickle down economics and regressive tax policies.
- Hegemony takes on very different forms in light of differing social conditions.
- Hegemonic consent is always fragile and precarious and is always being contested. Because the material and political disparity between the power bloc and the hegemonized is always known, hegemony is threatened by people's awareness of and anger about this inequality.
- Hegemony and ideology are inseparable. Ideologies are the tools used to win consent.
- Obviously, hegemony is not the only mode of domination in a society—other forms of domination coexist with hegemony.

Disciplinary Power: The Basic Characteristics

- Disciplinary power "disciplines" or regulates human beings via the use of the human sciences.
- The human sciences have created a society of normalization through specialized discourses deployed at socially specific sites—hospitals, schools, prisons, and asylums.
- Disciplinary power is nonegalitarian and asymmetrical and uses management and surveillance as technologies of control.
- Disciplinary power includes social systems whose rules, practices, and procedures exert an impact on the ways people, institutions, and social life operate.
- Disciplinary power works within human sciences (psychology, education, social work, psychiatry, medicine, etc.) that purport to be caring and humane. In this context—like power in general—disciplinary power is often masked.
- Important theorists of disciplinary power: Michele Foucault theorized a disciplinary power that produces "truth" and "knowledge" about human beings; Mikhail Bakhtin focused on the indiscipline (life force) that dominant power needs to control by disciplinary means; Michel DeCerteau emphasized human beings' creative agency to resist disciplinary power.
- In the context of disciplinary power theory, power relations are both conditions and effects of the production of truth about humans.
- Disciplinary power extracts data from and about human beings by "qualified experts" and "licensed professionals" who possess and apply the knowledge gained.
- Disciplinary power involves the power of science. The sciences arose in institutional settings structured by hierarchical relations of power. As a form of disciplinary power, science can be used *against* people.

- Disciplinary power, as Michel Foucault maintained, produces "regimes of truth" that involve privileging certain types of discourse, sanctioning certain ways of distinguishing true from false statements (positivism, for example), underwriting certain techniques at arriving at truth, and according a certain status to those who competently employ them.
- Disciplinary power understands that power and knowledge directly imply one another—there is no power relation without the constitution of a body of knowledge.
- The art of management is studied in the context of disciplinary power—management science promotes a regime of knowledge and power. The power to manage life necessitates the knowledge of life's processes
- When disciplinary power is exerted, there is an attempt to position people as receivers of information not producers—right-wing school curriculum manifests this dynamic.
- Disciplinary power as science disguises its dominating ability with the language of objectivity. Thus, it naturalizes power.

Central to postformalism is a sophisticated literacy of power. Such an understanding is essential in understanding mechanistic psychology's attempts to naturalize the mind. A postformal educational psychology is focused on the analysis of the way macro-social processes construct identity. In this context postformalists appreciate the Freudian assertion that reality is not pregiven but is fashioned by human beings, that the unconscious is not a biologically bounded black box but just as much a social construction as any other aspect of the psyche. Such understandings are grounded on a social, cultural, political appreciation of the influence of dominant power and power blocs. Drawing upon the work of John Fiske on power blocs, we gain a far more complex view of how power works.

Power Blocs: The Basic Characteristics

- Power blocs are alliances of social interest around specific issues that arise in particular conditions.
- A power bloc is better identified by what it does than what it is—it is not simply a social class, for example.
- A power bloc operates not as a conspiracy but from the recognition of mutual interests—for example, threats to family values, heterosexual dominance.
- Imperializing (dominant macro-) power and localizing (weak, resistant, micro-) power come into conflict at zones of interaction.
- A power bloc is an exercise of power to which certain social formations have privileged access—primarily racial (white supremacy), class (moneyed elite), gender (patriarchy), sexual (heterosexual dominance), religious (Christianity), and several other groups constitute power blocs.
- Social formations that are subordinated along some axes of social difference can align themselves with a power bloc on others. Some have referred to this as the contradictory and ambiguous positioning of individuals in the web of power relations. For example, men subordinated by class or race can and do exert imperializing power along the axes of gender and sexuality. One can observe this phenomenon with economically poor white men in recent U.S. elections.

Of course, what we're dealing with here is the intersection of educational psychology with critical theory and its concern with power and oppression. Such critical scholarship refuses to accept the reductionism common to mechanistic psychology that reduces complex sociopsychological processes to separate syndromes or stages on the basis of a single criterion. This reductionism views psychological truth as a knowledge of discrete and stabilized stages and categories—for example, she's operating at a concrete level of cognition or he is dull normal. Typically a reductionistic, mechanistic educational psychology is constructed on an epistemology that is unable to deal with complexity, diverse cultural contexts, transitional states, or entities in process. In a critical postformal educational psychology, for example, IQ is not a genetically fixed phenomenon but a rather insignificant signpost in an ever-changing, socially contingent process.

Such a reductionistic educational psychology, thus, is blinded to the possibility of growth or breakthroughs that can occur with a modification of sociocultural, historical, or political context. It is blinded to the possibility of a pedagogy that refuses to give in to the determinism of psychological classifications. A postformal educational psychology is a discourse of hope that is optimistic about the ability of humans operating on their own recognizance. Understanding these power dynamics, postformalists believe, is a first step on a longer trek toward human potential. We have to become experts into the way ideology and disciplinary power *construct* human incompetence.

MARGINALIZATION BY PSYCHOLOGIZATION

The failure of educational psychologists to operate with a literacy of power, to understand the social structuring of the self, leads to a variety of problems, especially for those who are in less-powerful, marginalized positions. Without such contextualization individuals from dominant cultural backgrounds are often unable to understand that the behaviors of socioeconomic subordinates may reflect the structural pressures under which they have to operate. In addition, men and women from the mainstream often believe that socioeconomic success is the result of individual merit and that social hierarchies and bell curves represent the natural dispersion of biological cognitive aptitude. Quite conveniently for the more privileged members of society, such individualized belief structures serve to hide the benefits bestowed by dominant-group membership. The same type of elitist concealment by individualization has also taken place in Western cognitive science. Such a tacit process allows gifted education to promote the chimera that giftedness is exclusively an individual not a socially constructed phenomenon.

The mind, mainstream cognitive scientists have contended, is the "software program" that can be studied in sociohistorical isolation by fragmenting it and analyzing the parts—a quick and clean form of analysis that avoids the complication of "messy" sociohistorical contextualization. Such messiness involves touchy issues such as social values or politics and the intersection of the biological (individual) with the collective. Thus, individualized psychology studies the machine (mind) but not the uses to which it is put in the social cosmos of ideological conflict and political activity. Psychologists and teachers like specialists in all fields are often educated as technicians who must pursue a critical and contextualized view of the world through their own efforts outside of their professional education.

These decontextualization processes tend to psychologize the study of cognition or the formation of subjectivity in that analyses of such phenomena are undertaken only as psychological processes, not psychological, sociological, political, economic, and other processes as well. Jean Piaget decontextualized his study of children, often removing questions of cultural context from his observations and analyses. Did children in non-European cultures develop in the same way? In other historical times? In diverse class contexts? Child development in Piaget's work was not examined in these contexts. In the attempt to understand human political behavior, modernist political scientists often neglected to view political beliefs and actions in the context of desire and other emotions, focusing instead on rational dynamics.

Such abstraction/decontextualization undermined the larger effort to make sense of such activity. Students of education often approach schooling as an institution that exists outside the cultural, linguistic, or political economic context. Indeed, the very organization of schooling in America is grounded around the modernist belief that knowledge can be decontextualized. Only in this decontextualized domain can intelligence testing be viewed as an objective, uncontaminated instrument of measurement. Moreover, only in this domain can giftedness and gifted and talented education be viewed as simply a phenomenon of individual cognitive ability. To maintain the psychological, educational, social, and political economic status quo, contextual insights must be removed from efforts to understand cognitive and pedagogical processes.

THE HIERARCHIES OF MIND

Employing a variety of sociopsychological modes of inquiry, critical students of the mind gain new angles from which to make sense of cognition and intelligence. Lacanian psychoanalysis's emphasis, for instance, on the ways social institutions shape individual subjectivity is essential knowledge for educational psychologists seeking to trace the subtle ways schooling inscribes student consciousness. Vygotskian cognitivism alerts these same psychologists to the ways social relationships and cultural context are not only influential in cognitive development but are the sources of the mind. When the understandings of psychometricians do not include such cultural appreciations, these specialists in measurement/assessment will perceive no problem with standardized texts being prepared by people from only one culture. What's the problem, they may ask, intelligence is intelligence, giftedness is giftedness, no matter where it's found.

Because psychology is an important aspect of the social and political world, the discipline has responsibilities to such a cosmos. The sociocultural dynamics that shape psychological functions do not alert us simply to methodological features of scholarly conversation—from a critical perspective they focus our attention on the human damage that results from the cultural blindness of professionals in psychological positions. When cultural difference is confused with, for example, mental deficiency or pathological behavior, serious ethical questions arise. Concurrently, when social privilege is confused with giftedness, great injustice can be justified.

If we accept Lacan's view of the positivist notion of an inner "authentic" self as a fiction and that there is no biological schema that presets behavior in advance, then we will find it difficult to accept Piagetian developmentalism. A critical educational psychology interrogates the foundations on which developmental psychology is grounded, positing that there are (1) no predetermined stages to human development existing independently of an individual's personal history or social group(s) affiliation and (2) no genetically programmed stages of intellectual maturation. Cognitive science's and education's taxonomies are merely heuristic, tools for facilitating understanding—not descriptions, as many assume, of an absolute independent reality. Indeed, postformal psychology finds nothing wrong with Piaget's efforts to discern patterns in child maturation. William Perry's attempt to identify levels of commonality in adult modes of thinking, or Freud's isolation of syndromes and disorders. There is no difficulty with such academic work as long as the theorists and their faithful followers don't take the insights as the truth. Piaget, Perry, and Freud's work are mere constructs, conceived in particular times and places about individuals carrying particular cultural and historical baggage.

Lev Vygotsky alerted us to these problems of reification and universalization of cognitive theorizing. Arguing for the need for social contextualization, Vygotsky turned his attention to the ways cognitive development occurred rather than pursuing stage theory. Development is much more complex, constantly changing as it unfolds. Indeed, a postformal cognitive psychology views cognitive growth as a dynamic hermeneutic, a process of culturally inscribed meaning making and knowledge production that continues throughout one's entire life. Such a reconceptualization holds dramatic implications for education and entities such as talented and gifted programs, as it rejects traditional developmentalist notions that education should guide students through their natural phases of development. Instruction, Vygotsky maintained, does not follow children's "cognitive unfoldment" to some genetically programmed developmental plateau.

In this pedagogical context postformal psychology understands the damage that cognitive science's notions of developmental appropriateness inflict on the economically and culturally marginalized. Riddled with ethnocentric and class-biased conception of where children should be along the developmental spectrum at any particular age, mechanistic educational psychology's discourse of developmental appropriateness makes no allowance for the ravages of poverty, racism, or other forms of disadvantage in children's lives. In the name of ordering the experiences of students who are "developmentally arrested" compensatory programs overstructure marginalized students' school routines to the point that meaningful self-initiated play and other activities are eliminated. In the name of providing special challenging education for the gifted and talented, elitist pedagogy makes sure that privileged students gain the maximum benefits of school resources and high expectations. Thus, cognitive psychology through its labeling and pedagogical prescriptions actually creates and perpetuates an educational caste system—a hierarchy blessed by the imprimatur of science and thus immune from serious questioning.

In schooling shaped by a sociopolitically contextualized educational psychology, self-reflection would become a priority with teachers and students. In such a critical educational psychology, postformalist educators attend to the impact of school on the shaping of the self. In such a context learning would be viewed as an act of meaning making that subverts the mechanistic view that thinking involves the mastering of a set of techniques. Education could no longer separate techniques from purpose, reducing teaching and learning to deskilled acts of rule following and concerned with the methodological format. Schools guided by a democratized educational psychology would no longer privilege white male experience as the standard by which all other experiences are measured.

Such realizations would point out a guiding concern with social justice and the ways unequal power relations at school destroy the promise of democratic life. Democratic teachers would no longer passively accept the pronouncements of standardized tests and curriculum makers without examining the social contexts in which their children live and the ways these contexts help construct their academic performance. Lessons would be reconceptualized in light of a critical notion of student understanding. Postformalists would ask if their classroom experiences promote the highest level of understanding possible. Such insights would undermine the elitism promoted by mechanistic educational psychology. Educational psychologists would understand that elitism is a socially constructed, power-related phenomenon, justified by the social privileges derived around issues of race, class, gender, sexuality, and religion. Again, a literacy of power is central to moving to a more critical interpretivist form of educational psychological practice. Such a psychology would see these issues of elitism and hierarchies in a new light, a new discursive framework—discursive power.

Discursive Power: The Basic Characteristics

- Too rarely do we analyze the deep social assumptions and power relations embedded in everyday language—language inscribed by the power bloc.

- Creations of particular discursive forms mobilize meanings that often sustain domination.

- Traditional linguistics was comfortable with the assumption that language neutrally conveys a description of reality. A more complex linguistics understands the power-inscribed nature of language.

- Critical linguistics sees language as the substance of social action, not simply the reflection of it.

- A discourse is defined as a set of tacit rules that regulates what can and cannot be said, who can speak with the blessings of authority and who must listen, and whose social constructions are scientific and valid and whose are unlearned and unimportant.

- Consider the power relations in the existing mechanisms for producing and distributing scientific knowledge about teaching. In this discourse teachers are deprived of power, as they are effectively eliminated from the active process of uncovering and disseminating knowledge. They are delegated instead to the passive role of knowledge consumers of the predigested products of educational science.

- Discursive practices are present in technical processes, institutions, and modes of behavior and in their forms of transmission and representation. Discourses shape how we operate in the world as human agents, construct our (un)consciousness, and what we consider true.
- Knowledge is interdependent with discourse, in that it acquires its meaning through the context provided by rules of discursive practice.
- In research and knowledge production, discourses validate particular research strategies, narrative formats, and modes of representation.
- In the domain of research methodologies, for example, consider the discourse of traditional ethnography. Such a discourse was quick to exclude nonlinear narratives and surrealistic forms of representation. Like nineteenth-century gatekeepers of the Parisian art world who rejected impressionistic representations of reality, ethnographic guardians dismissed literary forms that fell outside the boundaries of the dominant discourse.
- All language is multiaccentual, meaning that it can be both spoken and heard, written and read in ways that reflect different relationships to social groups and power formations. When language is used in an imperializing manner, meaning, as a form of social regulation, this multiaccentual dynamic is repressed. Power wielders attempt to establish one *correct* meaning among listeners or readers in an effort to implant a particular ideological message into their consciousness.
- Such a linguistic act is an example of what is labeled discursive closure—a language game that represses alternate ways of seeing, as it establishes a textual orthodoxy. In this context discursive practices define what is normal and deviant, what is a *proper* way of representing reality and what is not.
- Indeed, this process of definition, inclusion, and exclusion connects discourse to modes of social ordering and of regulation of knowledge production. For example, mainstream research discourses avoid representations of the concept of oppression when examining questions of justice or injustice. Often terms such as discrimination or prejudice are used to represent race, class, and gender injustice—the concept of oppression being a much more inclusive and damning concept is inappropriate in a discourse complicit with the dominant power bloc. Thus, discursive closure is effected; the status quo is protected.
- The relationship between discourse and power, Michel Foucault argued, is always contradictory. While discourse applies power, it also makes it visible. Discourse may carry the meanings of the power bloc, but it also exposes them to challenge.
- Discourse analysis disputes psychology's traditional assumption that people possess stable properties such as attitudes and beliefs. Instead, language is viewed as an arena where identity is continuously renegotiated.

A POLITICAL EDUCATIONAL PSYCHOLOGY

Even among many critical of educational psychology these power dynamics, these political dimensions, are missed. As I documented in the introduction to this encyclopedia, this political dynamic is erased in the mechanistic articulation of the discipline. Macro-sociopolitical concerns and the impact they exert on human experience in general and learning in particular are not a part of the discourse of the discipline. Until the relationship between existing social structures and power configurations and the questions of educational psychology are addressed, the work of professional practitioners will mystify and oppress more often than it will clarify and liberate.

In such a depoliticized, power-illiterate context mechanistic educational psychology reduces its practitioners to the role of test administrators who help devise academic plans that fit students' abilities. The individualistic, contextually stripped assumptions of this work move practitioners to accept unquestioningly the existence of a just society where children, according to their scientifically measurable abilities, find an agreeable place and worthwhile function—leadership roles for the elite and the rule following domains for the marginalized. Thus, the role of the educational psychologist is to *adjust* the student, regardless of his or her unmeasured—or unmeasurable by the instruments typically used in the field—abilities, to the society, no matter how unjust the system may be.

Here again we see how mechanistic educational psychology and the practice it supports play an important role in maintaining the power inequities of the status quo. Those children from marginalized racial or class positions are socialized for passivity and acceptance of their scientifically pronounced "lack of ability." Thus, a form of politically passive thinking is cultivated that views good students and teachers as obedient to mechanisitic educational, psychology-based ways of seeing. In such a context neither students nor teachers are encouraged to construct new cognitive abilities when faced with ambiguity. Mechanistic educational psychology has generally ignored the sociopolitical issues of the day as it pursues its work in "neutral" isolation.

The irony of its claims of hands-off objectivity in relation to the sociopolitical realm is not lost on critical educators who have tracked the discipline's profound impact in this domain. These postformalists jump into the political fray with its overt call to reform mechanistic educational psychology with a transgressive psychology and pedagogy. Educational psychology is a situated cultural/political practice—whether it wants to be or not—that addresses the ideology of teaching and learning. Whenever teaching, learning, and knowledge are conceived, the nature of the conception affects individuals differently: again, it validates the privileged and invalidates the marginalized. Postformalists are members of a monkey-wrench gang dedicated to subverting this power-driven process.

Many mechanistic educational psychologists are so uncomfortable with such a political psychology that they consider the postformal discourse a defacement of the field, a disruption to its orderly proceedings. When Shirley Steinberg and I were first involved in developing postformalism in the early 1990s, several of our colleagues from the mechanistic domain of the field became very upset when we received positive publicity about our work. During one of my classes, a colleague from this domain of educational psychology came into my class and literally screamed that I was "destroying the field" and to stop what I was doing. I told her that we could talk about our differences later and asked if she would allow me to finish teaching my class. She refused to stop talking and after several minutes of listening to her angry soliloquy, I finally had to dismiss my class. I have to admit the incident provided a powerful lesson for my students on the differences in paradigms within disciplines and the heat such differences could generate.

Cognition viewed as a political activity in this context is marked by a hint of scandal or at least a lack of middle/upper-middle class "good taste." Despite such uncomfortable representations, critical teachers push their political agenda, confronting the dominant discourse with its erasure of irrationality, emotion, power, paradigms, and morality in the teaching and learning process. Thus, elitist practices are allowed to remain in place, unchallenged by the very professionals who such understand how they came to be supported by shifting power blocs in the larger social order. Postformalists in this context come to play a special role, as they ask hard questions about cognitive and psychological issues.

• How do some of the most important issues of teaching and learning come to be erased?
• How do political issues play out at the level of consciousness?
• How is the learning process shaped by power?
• What is the relationship between school performance and a student's or a teacher's political consciousness and resulting moral sensibility?

Such questions would encourage research involving the subjective experiences of children deemed unintelligent and relegated to lower-ability tracks. I frequently visit with students classified as "slow" or "incapable" by mechanistic educational psychology who can make up creative games that can be played in the confines of an urban neighborhood; who build vehicles out of abandoned car and bicycle parts; who write their own music and choreograph their own dances; who write brilliant "spoken word" poetry; who have collected junk from the neighborhood, fixed it up, and sold it at garage sales; and who have used paint found in the bottom of discarded paint cans to produce sophisticated portraits of themselves and their communities. Critical psychologists and educators recognize the genius of such children early in their school experience. Assuring them of their abilities and engaging them in activities designed to utilize such talents, democratic teachers create situations for these kids that replace their need to employ their talents in illegal, dangerous, and socially damaging activities. The understanding of the politics of cognition that informs such teaching strategies helps rethink educational psychology in ways that profoundly change individual lives.

CHAPTER 108

Research in Educational Psychology: Incorporating the Bricolage in Educational Psychology—Part 1

JOE L. KINCHELOE

It does not seem a conceptual stretch to argue that there is a synergy that emerges in the use of different methodological and interpretive perspectives in the analysis of an artifact. Historians, for example, who are conversant with the insights of hermeneutics, will produce richer interpretations of the historical processes they encounter in their research. In the interdisciplinarity of the bricolage the historian takes concepts from hermeneutics and combines them with historiographical methods. What is produced is something new, a new form of hermeneutical historiography or historical hermeneutics. Whatever its name, the methodology could not have been predicted by examining historiography and hermeneutics separately, outside of the context of the historical processes under examination. The possibilities offered by such interdisciplinary synergies are limitless. This is a central concept in the postformalist reconceptualization of educational psychology—the power of multiple perspectives, of multilogicality, can reshape the discipline of educational psychology.

For example, an ethnographic researcher who is conversant with social theory and its recent history is better equipped to transcend certain forms of formulaic ethnography than are reduced by the so-called observational constraint on the methodology. Using the x-ray vision of contemporary social-theoretically informed strategies of discourse analysis, *poststructural psychoanalysis*, and ideology-critique, the ethnographer gains the ability to see beyond the literalness of the observed. In this maneuver the ethnographer-as-bricoleur moves to a deeper level of data analysis as he or she sees "what's not there" in physical presence, what is not discernible by the ethnographic eye. Synergized by the interaction of ethnography and the social theoretical discourses the resulting bricolage provides a new angle of analysis, a multidimensional perspective on a social, cultural, educational, or psychological phenomenon.

Carefully exploring the relationships connecting the object of inquiry to the contexts in which it exists, the postformal researcher constructs the most useful bricolage his or her wide knowledge of research strategies can provide. The strict disciplinarian of mechanistic educational psychology operating in a reductionistic framework chained to the prearranged procedures of a monological way of seeing is less likely to produce frame-shattering research than the synergized bricoleur. The process at work in the bricolage involves learning from difference—the value of multilogicality. Researchers employing multiple research methods are often not chained to the same assumptions as individuals operating within a particular discipline. As they study the methods of diverse disciplines, they are forced to compare not only methods but also differing epistemologies and social theoretical assumptions. Such diversity frames research orientations as particular socially constructed perspectives—not sacrosanct pathways to the truth. All methods are subject to questioning and analysis, especially in light of so many other strategies designed for similar purposes.

GETTING STARTED: THE POWER OF THE BRICOLAGE

This postformal defamiliarization process highlights the power of the confrontation with difference to expand the researcher's interpretive horizons. Bricolage doesn't simply *tolerate* difference but *cultivates* it as a spark to researcher creativity. Here rests a central contribution of the interdisciplinarity of the bricolage: as researchers draw together divergent forms of research, they gain the unique insight of multiple perspectives. Thus, a complex understanding of research and knowledge production prepares bricoleurs to address the complexities of the social, cultural, psychological, and educational domains. Sensitive to complexity, bricoleurs use multiple methods to uncover new insights, expand and modify old principles, and reexamine accepted interpretations in unanticipated contexts. Using any methods necessary to gain new perspectives on objects of inquiry, bricoleurs employ the principle of difference not only in research methods but in cross-cultural analysis as well. In this domain, bricoleurs explore the different perspectives of the socially privileged and the marginalized in relation to formations of race, class, gender, and sexuality.

The interdisciplinarity of bricolage is sensitive to multivocality and the consciousness of difference it produces in a variety of contexts. Described by Norman Denzin and Yvonna Lincoln (2000) in their *Handbook of Qualitative Research* as "multi-competent, skilled at using interviews, observation, personal documents," the bricoleur explores the use of ethnography, historiography, genre studies, psychoanalysis, rhetorical analysis, discourse analysis, content analysis, ad infinitum. The addition of historiography, for example, to the bricoleur's tool kit profoundly expands his or her interpretive facility. As bricoleurs historically contextualize their ethnographies, discourse analysis, and semiotic studies, they tap into the power of etymology. Etymological insight—a central feature of postformalism—involves an understanding of the origins of the construction of social, cultural, psychological, political, economic, and educational artifacts and the ways they shape our subjectivities. Indeed, our conception of self, world, and our positionalities as researchers can only become complex and critical when we appreciate the historical aspect of its formation. With this one addition educational psychologists dramatically sophisticate the quality and depth of their knowledge work.

Utilizing these multiple perspectives, the bricolage offers an alternate path in regressive times. Such an alternative path opens up new forms of knowledge production and researcher positionality (one's location in the sociocultural, political, psychological web of reality) that are grounded on more egalitarian relationships with individuals being researched. Bricoleurs in their valuing of diverse forms of knowledge, especially those knowledges that have been subjugated, come to value the abilities and the insights of those who they research. It is in such egalitarian forms of researcher–researched relationships that new forms of researcher self-awareness is developed–a self-awareness necessary in the bricoleur's attempt to understand the way positionality shapes the nature of the knowledge produced in the research process.

The French word *bricoleur* describes a handyman or handywoman who makes use of the tools available to complete a task. Some connotations of the term involve trickery and cunning and remind me of the chicanery of Hermes, in particular his ambiguity concerning the messages of the gods. If hermeneutics came to connote the ambiguity and slipperiness of textual meaning, then bricolage can also imply the fictive and imaginative elements of the presentation of all formal research. Indeed, as cultural studies of Western science have indicated, all scientific inquiry is jerryrigged to a degree; science, as we all know by now, is not nearly as clean, simple, and procedural as scientists would have us believe. Maybe this is an admission many in the social and psychological sciences would wish to keep in the closet.

In the first decade of the twenty-first century bricolage is typically understood to involve the process of employing these methodological strategies as they are needed in the unfolding context of the research situation. While this interdisciplinary feature is central to any notion of the bricolage, I propose educational psychologists go beyond this dynamic. Pushing to a new conceptual terrain, such an eclectic process raises numerous issues that researchers must deal with in order to maintain theoretical coherence and epistemological innovation. Such multidisciplinarity demands a new level of research self-consciousness and awareness of the numerous contexts in which any researcher is operating. As one labors to expose the various social, cultural, and political structures that covertly shape our own and other scholars' research narratives, the bricolage highlights the relationship between a researcher's ways of seeing and the social location of his or her personal history. Appreciating research as a power-driven act, the educational psychological researcher-as-bricoleur abandons the quest for some naïve concept of realism, focusing instead on the clarification of his or her position in the web of reality and the social locations of other researchers and the ways they shape the production and interpretation of knowledge.

In this context bricoleurs move into the domain of complexity. The bricolage exists out of respect for the complexity of the lived world. Indeed, it is grounded on an epistemology of complexity. Allow me to interrupt this analysis of the use of the bricolage in educational psychology with a brief delineation of an epistemology of complexity.

Characteristics of an Epistemology of Complexity

- Knowledge is never simply given—it is socially constructed. If educational psychologists accept this premise then an important part of their work has to involve understanding the nature and consequences of such construction. If psychological data does not just exist "out there" waiting to be discovered but is produced by human beings operating with particular blinders and in specific contexts, then postformal educational psychologists must understand the nature of this process.

- Human consciousness/subjectivity is also a social construction. Humans are more complex than mechanistic psychologists ever thought. We are not abstract, simply individualistic entities; we are connected on a variety of levels to our environments in ways that shape and mold us. This is why Vygotsky's concept of the ZPD is so important in the history of educational psychology.

- In the social construction of selfhood, power plays an extremely important role. This is why critical theory is central to the postformal reconceptualization of educational psychology. Psychological inquiry and the knowledge it produces is never neutral but constructed in specific ways that privilege particular logics and voices while ignoring and even silencing others. Thus, the culture of psychology privileges particular practices and certain methods of discerning truth. As Michel Foucault argued, truth is not relative (i.e., all worldviews embraced by different researchers, cultures, and individuals are of equal worth), but is relational (constructions considered true are contingent upon the power relations and historical context in which they are formulated and acted upon). Dominant hegemonic power-driven research orientations preclude researchers from pointing out forms of domination—such orientations obstruct attempts to encourage critical social change for the betterment of the individuals, groups, and communities being studied. An understanding of the power hierarchical relationships between researcher and researched alerts postformalists to the ways psychological research produces knowledge that regulates and shapes the consciousness of its producers and consumers. We are *in part* what power wants us to be. Importantly, we also have the power to resist such attempts to construct us.

- Focus on the nature and production of human consciousness even though it is difficult to measure in an empirical manner. For postformalists operating on the basis of this critical complex epistemology, consciousness is a central focus of educational psychology. The mechanistic psychological tradition has never been comfortable with the notion of consciousness—some mechanists even denied its existence because of its resistance to positivist measurement. Such problems with measurability remind postformalists of the necessity of the multiple methodologies of the bricolage in educational psychology.

- The importance of logic and emotion/affect/feeling in both knowledge production and the learning process—the centrality of the cognitive dimension of empathy. The Italian social theorist Antonio Gramsci well understood this epistemological concept, when he wrote from Mussolini's prisons in the late 1920s and 1930s. The intellectuals' error, he wrote, consists of believing that one can know without "feeling and being impassioned." Postformalists learn from Gramsci and argue that a central role of educational psychologists should involve the effort to connect logic and emotion in order for them to "feel" the elementary passions of the people. Such an emotional connection would allow the educational psychologist to facilitate the struggle of men and women to locate their lived world in history. Finding themselves in history they would be empowered by a consciousness shaped by a critical informed view of the ways that macro-structural forces interact with individual lives. One cannot *make* history without this passion, without this connection of feeling and knowing, since, without it, the relationship between individuals and educational psychologists is reduced to a hierarchical formality. In such hierarchy the logic of positivism and bureaucracy prevails and the social construction of individual needs is deemed irrelevant.

- The knower and the known are inseparable—thus, the questions researchers ask shape what they come to know. In mechanistic educational psychology the notion of knower–known inseparability has not been the dominant position in research and practice. Educational psychologists need to understand that the Myth of Archimedes, the belief in an objective body of knowledge unconnected to the mind of the knower, has helped formulate how the discipline operates. Such an assumption tacitly constructs not only what counts as valid knowledge but, via the power of research, it formulates what we "know" about mind and intelligence. The myth assumes that the human perceiver occupies no space in the known world. Since the psychologists operate outside of history, they objectively know the mind, intelligence, teaching, leaning, etc. In this epistemological context what they know about, say, intelligence becomes the truth. It is not simply the view of one knower operating in a particular place and time about a very complex phenomenon.

- Our view of psychological and educational phenomena in a complex epistemology is shaped by the perspectives of those individuals who have suffered as a result of existing social, cultural, political, economic, and epistemological conditions. The voices of the marginalized have been pathologized and excluded in mechanistic educational psychology. Such a move has profoundly shaped the nature and effects of the discipline over its history. Postformalists begin their explorations of educational psychology with the perspectives of the marginalized, they search for insights in unexplored perspectives of non-Western peoples. Understandings derived from the perspective of the excluded or the "culturally different" allow for new insights into diverse definitions of intelligence, the nature of justice, the nature of the mind, the invisibility of the process of oppression, and the difference that highlights our social construction as individuals. In this spirit postformal educational psychologists begin to look at their work from the perspectives of their Asian, African, Latino, and indigenous colleagues around the world. Such cognitive cross-fertilization often reveals the tacit assumptions that impede innovations. Here we see the epistemological foundation of the power of difference.

- The significance of multiple realities constructed in part by our location in the web of reality. A positivist epistemology claims to provide "the one true portrait" of reality. Using common sense, postformalists understand that people living in different times and places with differing amounts of social capital will see the world in quite diverse ways. The social study of science indicates that the social context in which scientists of any stripe operate will profoundly shape the knowledge they produce. Postformalists place great value on the multiple perspectives about mind, intelligence, teaching, learning, the production of identity, etc. provided in these diverse contexts. The domain of educational psychology is nothing if not complex. In this context the idea of relying on one privileged way of viewing psychological and educational phenomena seems to postformalists quite myopic. The epistemological roots of the bricolage sink deep into the importance of multiple perspectives and multiple realities.

- Aware of these multiple realities, educational psychologists come to appreciate where they are located in the complex web of reality—thus, they become humble scholars aware of the blinders of their place and time. As we come to appreciate this particular epistemological point, we gain a self-knowledge that alerts us to both our strengths and weaknesses as scholars and practitioners. Where we stand or are placed in the web of reality makes a difference on how we see the world around us and our role in it. Epistemologically savvy educational psychologists can no longer rely on some universal, sacrosanct body of professional knowledge that tells them how to conduct their professional lives. Operating in their particular locale in the web of reality, these informed psychologists understand the partiality and historically and socially specific nature of their knowledge. Thus, epistemologically aware educational psychologists are fallibists who are able to laugh at, learn from, and adjust their practice to their own fallibility. In this way they become humble scholars liberated from the arrogance of positivist certainty.

- Appreciating their location in the complex web of reality, postformal educational psychologists are better prepared to produce humble and useful knowledge. Here educational psychologists begin to act on their understanding that psychological knowledge like all information is contingent on the context in which it was produced. Positivistic psychological knowledge is typically a fragmented body of knowledge that dismisses the context in which it, itself, was produced as well as the contexts that shape the psychological processes in question. Such knowledge, postformalists understand, is better suited for storage in a file cabinet in a knowledge warehouse. The types of epistemologically complex knowledges in which postformalists are interested are kinetic forms of information. Such knowledges seeks to connect with human beings in action, they seek to find relationships with diverse experiences. In this framework, these posformal knowledges seek to inform professional practice and the process of living.

- The value of producing useful knowledge for professional practice—developing a critical epistemology of practice. Postformal useful knowledge helps educational psychologists construct new conceptual frameworks for approaching new professional experiences. Such knowledge—as John Dewey helps us understand—is interested in the future reference of such information. Useful knowledge helps us to understand present situations and guides us in our formulation of what should be done to improve them. This takes us directly to the important topic referred to as the epistemology of practice. In the 1980s, questions began to emerge in a variety of fields about how one learns to engage in the practice of a profession. Profound questions were raised about the role of professional knowledge and how it is used in the process of educating practitioners in a variety of domains. Teacher educators, for example, have learned from researchers studying situated cognition and reflective practice that practitioner ways of knowing are unique, quite different from the technical ways of knowing traditionally associated with professional expertise. Indeed, professional expertise is an uncertain enterprise as it confronts constantly changing, unique, and unstable conditions in social situations, cultural interchange, sci-tech contexts, and, of course, in the practice of educational psychology. The expert practitioners studied by sociocognitivists and scholars of reflective practice relinquished the certainty that attends to positivist professional expertise conceived as the repetitive administration of techniques to similar types of problems. Advocates of rigorous complex modes of professional practice insist that practitioners can develop higher-order forms of cognition and action, in the process becoming researchers of practice who explore the intricacies of professional purpose and its relation to everyday life. Grounding their insights on this epistemological notion of useful knowledge, postformalists are fascinated with what exactly higher-order forms of cognition and action might look like in relation to the process of engaging in the practice of educational psychology.

- Coming to understand the nature of complexity, in the process overcoming positivist reductionism. Unlike positivism an epistemology of complexity understands that thinking cannot be conceived as mere problem solving. Problems, as complexity theory informs us, do not unambiguously present themselves. Positivist epistemology does not allow educational psychologists to explore the origins of a problem, the assumptions that move us to define some situations as problems and others as not problems, or the source of authority that guides us in our formulation of criteria for judging which problems merit our thinking and analysis. This is where our complex epistemological consciousness helps us understand the complexity of the work of educational psychology. Employing this epistemological tool, postformalists begin to uncover the hidden ways ideology, discourse, and other forms of power shape the questions that ground the practice of educational psychology. In this context, postformalists are prepared to rethink the very foundations of the discipline.

- Knowledge is always in process—it is always a part of larger processes. As I have alluded to throughout my contributions to this encyclopedia a central dimension of a positivist epistemology involves its fragmentation of the world into separate and discrete parts. In a complex epistemology, processes become more important than separate entities. Thus, phenomena in the world are always in process, they have a past and a future. Any knowledge about such phenomena that claims to represent the truth about them is suffering from an epistemological naivete—what we know about them today may change tomorrow as they enter a new phase of the process of which they are a part. An entity's interaction with another entity may illustrate a larger process previously missed by scientists. This is exactly what has happened in educational psychology, as the discipline's positivist focus on the brain occluded insight into the social processes of which the mind was a part. Outside of an understanding of these processes, the field's fragmented data about the brain was at best mundane and at worst misleading.

- The necessity of interpretation in the production of knowledge—the power of hermeneutics. A complex epistemology grounds postformalism's concern with the meaning of knowledge that is produced about the psychological and educational domains. Positivism is dismissive of hermeneutics because empirical data speak for themselves. Hermeneutics takes issues with such an assertion, maintaining that all knowledge is an interpretation. Indeed, all knowledge involves many levels of interpretation. Critical postformal educational psychologists employing the research bricolage act on their understanding of these many levels of interpretation in all research and knowledge production. They are aware that the consciousness and the interpretive frames they and other educational psychologists bring to their tasks are historically situated, ever changing, ever evolving in relation to the cultural and ideological climate. The way Americans see the world and interpret world events, for example, has been quite different in the years following 9-11 than before the attacks took place. And, of course, not all American interpretations in this context have been shaped in the same way. There is nothing simple about the social construction of interpretive lenses: consciousness construction is contradictory and the result of the collision of a variety of differing ideological forces. Thus, the study of interpretation and the forces that shape it are central to a postformal psychology—there is, however, nothing simple about such analysis.

- Gaining awareness that the frontier of knowledge is located at the points where personal experience intersects with secondary information. Mechanistic educational psychology has accepted the positivist assertion that knowledge is a simple reflection of the world "out there" and as such is independent of human construction. Not only do the personal experiences of human beings shape knowledge to begin with, but also the knowledge different individuals encounter shapes them and induces them to reinterpret their lives and their professional practice. Postformal educational psychologists use their personal experiences to examine the disciplinary knowledge they encounter. How does this knowledge help us reconsider our prior experiences and their effect on our subjectivity, our view of ourselves as educational psychologists, our understanding of the goals of our profession? Secondary disciplinary knowledge, thus, always interacts with what we already know and have experienced.

- Insight into the importance of the ontological domain—constructing new forms of human being. This epistemological concept grounds much of the work of postformalism. As critical educational psychologists gain insight into their status as historical, cultural, and social beings, they begin to understand why they have embraced a particular view of the psychological domain. They understand the etymology of their own consciousness and their construction of themselves as psychological practitioners. In this context, postformalists understand not only who they are but are empowered to think about who they and their clients might become. As they question the shibboleths of positivism and the mechanistic educational psychology it supports, postformalists draw upon the bricolage of multiple perspectives to develop new definitions of useful knowledge, caring practice, intelligence, academic success, and professional expertise. In such actions they imagine new ways of being educational psychologists who are emancipatory, just, democratic, humble, and practical. The postformalist reconceptualization of educational psychology—especially in this ontological context—is one of great possibility and hope.

Understanding this epistemology of complexity we are better equipped to understand postformalism and its employment of the bricolage. One dimension of this complexity can be illustrated by the relationship between research and the domain of social theory. All observations of the world are shaped either consciously or unconsciously by social theory—such theory provides the framework that highlights or erases what might be observed. Theory in a modernist empiricist mode is a way of understanding that operates without variation in every context. Since theory is a cultural and linguistic artifact, its interpretation of the object of its observation is inseparable from the historical dynamics that have shaped it. The task of the bricoleur is to attack this complexity, uncovering the invisible artifacts of power, and document the nature of its influence on not only their own but on scholarship and knowledge production in general. In this process, bricoleurs act upon the concept that theory is not an explanation of nature—it is more an explanation of our relation to nature. In the twenty-first-century neocolonial era this task becomes even more important.

TERMS FOR READERS

Poststructural psychoanalysis—Psychoanalysis offers hope to postformalists concerned with social justice and the related attempt to rethink cognition and intelligence as it expands the possibility of human potential. The postformalist vision of psychoanalysis is a poststructuralist psychoanalysis—poststructuralist in the sense that it reveals the problems embedded in the sciences emerging from positivism and the universal structures it constructs. As poststructualist psychoanalysis makes use of the subversive aspects of the psychoanalytical tradition, it presents a view of humans quite different than the modernist psychological portrait. In the process, it challenges the modernist erasure of feeling, valuing, and caring in contemporary Western societies and attempts to rethink such features in light of power and its construction of consciousness.

CHAPTER 109

Research in Educational Psychology: The Bricolage and Educational Psychological Research Methods—Part 2

JOE L. KINCHELOE

In its hard labors in the domain of complexity the bricolage views research methods actively rather than passively, meaning that postformalists actively construct our research methods from the tools at hand rather than passively receiving the "correct," transcultural universally applicable methodologies. Avoiding modes of reasoning that come from certified processes of logical analysis, bricoleurs also steer clear of preexisting guidelines and checklists developed outside the specific demands of the inquiry at hand. In its embrace of complexity, the bricolage constructs a far more active role for humans both in shaping reality and in creating the research processes and narratives that represent it. Such an active agency rejects deterministic views of social reality that assume the effects of particular dominant social, political, economic, and educational processes. At the same time and in the same conceptual context this belief in active human agency refuses standardized modes of knowledge production from particular power blocs.

In many ways there is a form of instrumental reason, of rational irrationality in the use of passive, external, monological, monocultural research methods. In the active bricolage, we bring our understanding of the research context together with our previous experience with research methods. Using these knowledges we *tinker* with our research methods in field-based and interpretive contexts. This tinkering is a high-level cognitive process involving construction and reconstruction, contextual diagnosis, negotiation, and readjustment. Researchers' interaction with the objects of their inquiries, bricoleurs understand, are always complicated, mercurial, unpredictable and, of course, complex. Such conditions negate the practice of planning research strategies in advance. In lieu of such rationalization of the process bricoleurs enter into the research act as methodological negotiators. Always respecting the demands of the task at hand, the bricolage, as conceptualized here, resists its placement in concrete as it promotes its elasticity.

Research method in the bricolage is a concept that receives more respect than in more rationalistic articulations of the term. The rationalistic, colonialist articulation of method subverts the deconstruction of wide varieties of unanalyzed cultural assumptions embedded in passive methods. Bricoleurs in their appreciation of the complexity of the research process view research method as involving far more than procedure. In this mode of analysis bricoleurs come to understand research method as also a technology of justification, meaning a way of defending what we assert we know and the process by which we know it. Thus, the education of psychological researchers demands that everyone take a step back from the process of learning research methods. Such a step back allows us a conceptual distance that produces a critical consciousness. Such a consciousness refuses the passive acceptance of externally imposed research methods that tacitly certify modes justifying universal knowledges that are decontextualized and reductionistic.

In this context it is important to note that the use of the term, bricolage, in relation to multimethod, multilogical interdisciplinary research is relatively new—emerging in the mid-1990s. Norm Denzin and Yvonna Lincoln, central figures in the development and sophistication of qualitative research in the social sciences, were the first to use the term in this specific context. In the domain of qualitative research and qualitative theory numerous scholars are beginning to use the term and employ the concept. In December 2001, *Qualitative Inquiry* published a special issue on the bricolage in which I took Denzin and Lincoln's delineation of the concept and detailed possibilities of what it might become. Lincoln, William Pinar, and Peter McLaren responded to my essay, offering their own vision of the bricolage. In addition to those directly involved with developing and enacting the bricolage, there are numerous researchers in psychology and interdisciplinary fields such as cultural studies, education, and ethnic studies who have already embraced multiperspectival inquiry. Denzin and Lincoln (2000) in their *Handbook of Qualitative Research* describe it as a methodological diaspora where humanists migrated to the social sciences and social scientists to the humanities. Ethnographic methodologists snuggled up with textual analysts; in this context the miscegenation of the empirical and the interpretive produced the bricoleur love child.

UNDERMINING POSITIVIST METHODOLOGIES: TRANSCENDING NAÏVE REALISM AND REDUCTIONISM

There's impudent dimension to the bricolage that says "who said research has to be done this way?" Such impudence is based on a cynicism toward the notion that monological, ordered methods get us to the "right place" in educational psychological research. Postformalists use the methods that are best suited to answering our questions about a particular phenomenon. For the bricoleur to use the means at hand he or she must first be aware of them. Such awareness demands that the bricoleur devote time for rigorous study of what approaches to research are out there and to how they might be applied in relation to other methods. Do not be deceived, this is no easy task that can be accomplished in a doctoral program or a post-doctoral fellowship (Thomas, 1998). Becoming a bricoleur, who is knowledgeable of multiple research methodologies and their uses, is a lifetime endeavor. Such multilogicality will change educational psychology forever.

Indeed, the bricoleur is aware of deep social structures and the complex ways they play out in everyday life, the importance of social, cultural, and historical analysis, the ways discursive practices influence both what goes on in the research process and the consciousness of the researcher, the complex dimensions of what we mean when we talk about "understanding." In this context the bricoleur becomes a sailor on troubled waters, navigating a course that traces the journey between the scientific and the moral, the relationship between the quantitative and the qualitative, and the nature of social, cultural, educational, and psychological insight. All of these travels help bricoleurs overcome the limitations of monological reductionism, the Empire's developmentalism while taking into account the new vistas opened by the multilogical and the pluralistic. Such victories provide entrée into the diverse community of inquirers—an inclusive group that comes from academia and beyond. Such individuals critique, support, and inform each other by drawing upon the diversity of their cultural backgrounds and concerns. In this process they expose and discuss one another's assumptions, the contexts that have shaped them, and their strengths and limitations in the exploration(s) at hand. The participants in this community come from a wide range of race, class, gender, sexual, ethnic, and religious groups and enter into their deliberations with humility and solidarity.

Norm Denzin and Yvonna Lincoln's work on the bricolage has profoundly influenced numerous researchers from a plethora of disciplines. Concerned with the limitations of monological approaches to knowledge production, we all subscribe to the "practical reason" of the bricolage that operates in concrete settings to connect theory, technique, and experiential knowledges. Here the theoretical domain is connected to the lived world and new forms of cognition and research are *enacted*. This improvisational enactment of the bricolage, buoyed by the insights of Francisco Varela and Humberto Mataurana's Santiago Theory of Enactivism, moves research to a new level. This is the place where the multiple inputs and forces facing the researcher in the immediacy of her work are acknowledged and embraced. The bricoleur in educational psychology does not allow these complexities to be dismissed by the excluding, reducing impulses of monological methodology coming from particular power blocs. Such a refusal is in itself an act of subversion.

The subversive bricolage accepts that human experience is marked by uncertainties and that order is not always easily established. "Order in the court" has little authority when the monological judge is resting in *his* quarters. Indeed, the rationalistic and reductionistic quest for order refuses in its arrogance to listen to cacophony of lived experience, the coexistence of diverse meanings and interpretations in a socially, culturally, economically, and ideologically diverse world. The concept of understanding in the complex world viewed by bricoleurs is unpredictable. Much to the consternation of many there exists no final, transhistorical, transcultural, and non-ideological meaning that bricoleurs strive to achieve. As bricoleurs create rather than find meaning in enacted reality, they explore alternate meanings offered by others in similar circumstances. If this wasn't enough, they work to account for historical, social, and cultural contingencies that always operate to undermine the universal pronouncement of the meaning of a particular phenomenon. When researchers fail to discern the unique ways that historical, social, and cultural context make for special circumstances, they often provide a reductionistic form of knowledge that impoverishes our understanding of everything connected to it—the process of research included.

The monological, monocultural quest for order so desired by many social, political, educational, and psychological researchers is grounded on the positivist epistemological belief that all phenomena should be broken down into their constitute parts to facilitate inquiry. The analysis of the psychological world in this context becomes fragmented and disconnected. Everything is studied separately for the purpose of rigor. The goal of integrating knowledges from diverse domains and understanding the interconnections shaping, for example, the biological and the cognitive, is irrelevant in the paradigm of order and fragmentation. The meaning that comes from interrelationship is lost, and questions concerning the purpose of research and its insight into the human condition are put aside in an orgy of correlation and triangulated description. Information is sterilized and insight into what may be worth exploring is abandoned. Ways of making use of particular knowledges are viewed as irrelevant, and creative engagement with conceptual insights is characterized as frivolous. Empirical knowledge in the quest for order is an end in itself. Once it has been validated it needs no further investigation or interpretation. While empirical research is obviously necessary, its process of production constitutes only one step of a larger and more rigorous process of inquiry. The bricolage subverts the finality of the empirical act.

Bricoleurs make the point that empirical research, all research for that matter, is inscribed at every level by human beings. The assumptions and purposes of the researcher always find their way into a research act, and they always make a difference in what knowledge is produced. Even in the most prescribed forms of empirical quantitative inquiry the researcher's ideological and cultural preferences and assumptions shape the outcome of the research. Do I choose factor analysis or regression analysis to study the relationship of a student's IQ score to college success? The path I choose profoundly affects what I find. What about the skills included on the IQ? Are they simply neutral phenomena free from inscriptions of culture and power? How I answer such a question shapes how my psychological research proceeds.

Such inscriptions and the complexity they produce remind bricoleurs in educational psychology of the multiple processes in play when knowledge is produced and validation is considered. They understand that the research process is subjective and that instead of repressing this subjectivity they attempt to understand its role in shaping inquiry. All these elements come together to help bricoleurs think about their principles of selection of one or another research perspective. Such decisions can be made more thoughtfully when a researcher understands the preferences and assumptions inscribed on all modes of inquiry and all individuals who engage in research. Thus, an important aspect of the work of the bricoleur involves coming to understand the social construction of self, the influence of selfhood on perception, and the influence of perception on the nature of inquiry.

BUT THERE'S NOTHING THERE: THE BRICOLAGE AND EXPLORATION OF ABSENCE

In their embrace of diverse methods, different cultural knowledges, and subjugated ways of seeing as well as their transcendence of reductionism, bricoleurs seek to identify what is absent in particular situations—a task ignored by monological, objectivist modes of research. In this context bricoleurs seek to cultivate a higher form of researcher creativity that leads them, like poets, to produce concepts and insights about the social world that previously did not exist. This rigor in the absence can be expressed in numerous ways, including the bricoleur's ability:

* to imagine things that never were,
* to see the world as it could be,
* to develop alternatives to oppressive existing conditions,
* to discern what is lacking in a way that promotes the will to act,
* to understand that there is far more to the world than what we can see.

As always bricoleurs are struggling to transcend the traditional observational constraint on social and psychological researchers, as they develop new ways and methods of exposing social, cultural, political, educational, and psychological forces not at first glance discernible. Pursuing rigor in the absence, bricoleurs document venues of meaning that transcend the words of interviewees or observations of particular behavior.

Of course, a central feature of this rigorous effort to identify what is absent involves excavating what has been lost in the naivete of monological disciplinarity and Western rational developmentalism. As postformal educational psychologists engaging in the boundary work of the interdisciplinary bricolage explore what has been dismissed, deleted, and covered up, they bring to the surface the ideological devices that have erased the lived worlds, modes of cognition, and political perspectives of those living at the margins of power. As sociopsychological researchers employ the methodological, theoretical, interpretive, political, and narrative dimensions of the bricolage, they make a variety of previously repressed features of the educational and psychological worlds visible. Because they are describing dimensions of the socio-cultural, political, economic, pedagogical, and psychological cosmos that have never previously existed, postformal bricoleurs are engaging in what might be termed the fictive (or constructivist) element of research.

The use of the term, fictive, should not to be conflated with "unreal" in this context. Scientific inventors engage in a similar process when they have created design documents for the electric light, the rocket, the computer, or virtual reality. In these examples individuals used a fictive imagination to produce something that did not yet exist. The postformal bricoleur does the same thing in a different ontological and epistemological domain. Both the inventor and the bricoleur are future orientated, as they explore the realm of possibility, a kinetic epistemology of the possible. In the process the sophistication of knowledge work moves to a new cognitive level; the notion of rigor transmigrates to a new dimension. As in a 1950s sci-fi movie, bricoleurs in educational psychology enter the 4-D—the fourth dimension of research.

In this way bricoleurs create a space for reassessing the nature of the knowledge that has been created about the sociopsychological cosmos and the modes of research that have created it. In an era of information saturation and hegemony, this space for reassessing knowledge production and research methods becomes a necessity for democratic survival, the foundation of a pro-democracy movement, and new ways of thinking and being. Overwhelmed by corporate-produced data, befuddled by the complex of the social issues that face us, and inundated with stupidifying forms of political manipulation, individuals without access to the lenses of the bricolage often don't know how to deal with these debilitating conditions. As the bricolage provides us new insights into the chaos of the contemporary, educational psychological researchers become better equipped to imagine where we might go and what path we might take to get there through the jungle of hegemonic information surrounding us. The bricolage is no panacea, but it does allow us new vantage points to survey the epistemological wilderness and the socio-cognitive possibilities hidden in its underbrush.

NEW MODES OF RESEARCH IN EDUCATIONAL PSYCHOLOGY: MULTILOGICALITY

Thus, the bricolage in educational psychology is concerned not only with multiple methods of inquiry but with diverse theoretical and philosophical notions of the various elements encountered in the psychological research act. Bricoleurs understand that the ways these dynamics are addressed—whether overtly or tacitly—exerts profound influence on the nature of the knowledge produced by researchers. Thus, these aspects of research possess important live world political consequences, as they shape the ways we come to view the social cosmos and operate within it. In this context Douglas Kellner (1995) writes in his book, *Media Culture*, about the notion of a "multiperspectival cultural studies." Kellner's concept is very helpful, as it draws upon a numerous textual and critical strategies to interpret, criticize, and deconstruct the social and cultural artifacts under observation. In postformalism, of course, we move these social and cultural perspectives into the psychological realm.

Employing Frederich Nietzsche's notion of perspectivism to ground his version of a multi-methodological research strategy, Kellner maintains that any single research perspective is laden with assumptions, blindnesses, and limitations. To avoid one-sided reductionism, he maintains that researchers must learn a variety of ways of seeing and interpreting in the pursuit of knowledge. The more perspectival variety a researcher employs, Kellner concludes, the more dimensions and consequences of a text will be illuminated. Kellner's multiperspectivism resonates with Denzin and Lincoln's bricolage and its concept of "blurred genres." To better interpret, criticize, and deconstruct Denzin and Lincoln (2000) in their *Handbook of Qualitative Research* call for bricoleurs to employ "hermeneutics, structuralism, semiotics, phenomenology, cultural studies, and feminism" (p. 3). Embedded in Kellner, Denzin, and Lincoln's calls is the foundation for a new rigor—certainly in research but with implications for educational psychology and pedagogy.

Thus, in the early twenty-first century disciplinary demarcations no longer shape in the manner they once did in the way many scholars look at the world. Indeed, disciplinary boundaries have less and less to do with the way scholars group themselves and build intellectual communities.

Furthermore, what we refer to as the traditional disciplines in the first decade of the twenty-first century are anything but fixed, uniform, and monolithic structures. It is not uncommon for contemporary scholars in a particular discipline to report that they find more commonalities with individuals in different fields of study than they do with colleagues in their own disciplines. We occupy a scholarly world with faded disciplinary boundary lines. Thus, the point need not be made that bricolage should take place—it already has and is continuing in many domains. The point here, of course, is that it needs to take place in educational psychology. The research work needed in this context involves opening an elastic conversation about the ways such a bricolage can be rigorously conceptualized and enacted. Such cultivation should not take place in pursuit of some form of proceduralization but an effort to better understand the value of multiple perspectives and multilogicality, and to realize their profound possibilities.

DOING IT: PUTTING THE BRICOLAGE INTO ACTION

In my work with Kathleen Berry (*Rigour and Complexity in Educational Research: Conceptualizing the Bricolage, 2004*) on employing the bricolage, we suggest that beginning bricoleurs develop a Point of Entry Text (POET) written of course from the perspective of one or more fields of study and from particular theoretical frames of reference. While there are many possible ways of employing the bricolage, we suggest that researchers take their POET and *thread* it through a variety of conceptual maps including, for example:

* Discourses of social theory—for example, critical theory, poststructuralism, postcolonialism, complexity theory, ecological theory, constructivism.
* Research genres and methodologies—quantitative analysis, ethnography, phenomenology, psychoanalysis, historiography, semiotics, textual analysis, hermeneutics, discourse analysis.
* Cultural/social positionalities—racial (Afrocentric analysis, Chicano studies, Native American studies, indigenous studies, identity politics), class (materialist studies), gender (feminist theory, studies of alternate masculinities), sexuality (queer theory), ability, and religious (liberation theology, Islamic studies, Judaic studies).
* Disciplinary/interdisciplinary departmentalizations of knowledge: history, philosophy sociology, anthropology, political science, economics, geography, psychology, literary criticism, aesthetics, cultural studies, American studies.
* Philosophical domains—epistemology, ontology, axiology, teleology, cosmology.
* Power modes—hegemony, ideology, regulatory, discursive, disciplinary, coercive.
* Knowledge sources—oral, print, photographs, Internet, visual, works of art, cartoons, popular culture, media, historical documents, daily life, book, journals.

And there are many more categories such as these that can be enumerated.

In this context bricoleurs thread their POET through what they consider relevant conceptual maps. If my POET is an analysis of the ways contemporary racism affects cognition and school performance, then each time I engage the conceptual map I encounter knowledges that complicate my original thesis. The POET has been subjected to multiple readings, conflicting discourses, perspectives from diverse positionalities, different epistemologies, diverse modes of power, differing research methodologies, and a plethora of previously unconsidered knowledge sources. As the POET travels through these different domains, it circles back to its starting point. Each time it threads through the map the process looks more and more like a feedback loop. The bricolage process demands that this threading be repeated numerous times. The POET's interaction with the conceptual maps creates a state of turbulence, a disequilibrium that reflects a healthy feature of complexity and autopoiesis. Indeed, such turbulence sets up the possibility for discerning relationships and processes that open new conceptual vistas for the researcher in educational psychology. In this context conditions are created for analytical and interpretive spontaneity, random associations that yield profound insights, and novelty.

The bricoleur's feedback looping process is disconcerting in its freedom from step-by-step linearity. Whereas more objectivist forms of empirical research attempt to reduce variables, the bricolage works to increase them. The feedback looping process can work to disrupt the researcher's train of thought and move them in an unanticipated direction. Monological knowledge is subverted, as the feedback looping process juxtaposes numerous perspectives and knowledge forms. Such juxtapositioning confronts the researcher with contradictions, unexpected relationships and unities, zones of interpretive possibility, disjunctions and fissures, and previously unseen processes at work. Every time the POET threads itself back through the concept maps its original composition changes. What emerges after a few loops may surprise the bricoleur in its uniqueness and unanticipated qualities. The POET's confrontation with these diverse knowledges and vantage points move the researcher to a higher and more complex level of understanding. This level of understanding is characterized by unexpected turns, re-traveled paths, reconceptualized assertions, bifurcation points, and encounters with equilibrium/near equilibrium in relation to agitation and disconcerting revelations. The bricoleur needs to develop a comfort with ambiguity.

Employing our POET on the cognitive and educational impact of contemporary racism it may be helpful to thread it through the conceptual maps previously listed. As we examine the topic from diverse theoretical perspectives we come to ask new questions of our POET. In a critical theoretical perspective, for example, we ask questions about power theory. Does our text possess a sophisticated view of racial power, the power of white supremacy and other dimensions of dominant culture that shape the nature of racism and its effects in the twenty-first century? In a postcolonial sense does contemporary racism connect to issues of European/American colonialism and its long history of exploitation of nonwhite peoples? Is there insight to be gained by contextualizing the Civil Rights Movement and the reaction to it within larger global issues of the colonial rebellion emerging in the middle decades of the twentieth century? How in a mechanistic text like Richard Herrnstein and Charles Murray's *The Bell Curve, 1994* does this racism work to shape the discipline of educational psychology? Could use of constructivism in this context focus the bricoleur's attention on the social, cultural, and political economic forces that shape racial consciousness of educational psychologists in the twenty-first century? Constructivism's focus on the production of consciousness/subjectivity could help raise unasked questions about white racism, the ways it is produced in the contemporary *Zeitgeist*, and the process of its mutation into new forms and articulations in a variety of domains, including, of course, the field of educational psychology itself.

Looping our POET through diverse research genres and methodologies, the bricoleur asks what perspectives psychologists might gain through the use of different primary research strategies. Is there need for an ethnographic study of the way racism shapes the cognitive orientations and the school life of African American and Latino students? Is ethnography data essential in the effort to understand these dynamics? Is the question so complex that ethnographic insights need to be supplemented by phenomenological and even psychoanalytical inquiries? Is there a dimension to such effects that moves expression of them to the phenomenological realm of affect, emotion, and registers of feeling? Employing such phenomenological research the bricoleur in educational psychology may open a new realm of insight into both the nature of contemporary racism and the study of cognition. Historiographical analysis in this research project in particular may be necessary for the researcher to gain the needed understanding of how racism exhibits itself at the micro-individual level. Might the use of semiotics with its study of cultural signs and signifiers contribute to an understanding of the ways contemporary racism is encoded in various cultural texts? Indeed, it may be semiotic analysis that exposes the subtlety of new forms of racism and the ways they are implanted in unconscious ways in popular social images. Using discursive analysis bricoleurs can make sure their POET is informed by discourses of contemporary "race talk." This process of looping the original text through other research genres can continue (or not) through even more methodologies.

Running the POET through the category of diverse social/cultural positionalities, bricoleurs in educational psychology review their work from the perspectives of racial, class, gender, sexual, religious, ability, religious, and other groups for both the existential viewpoints they bring to observations and the theoretical orientations members of these groups have developed. In the case of our POET's focus on impact of racism on cognition and school performance, class and gender perspectives provide new levels of insight and complexity to our study. Such perspectives undermine essentialist pronouncements that fail to understand the different relations of racism to individuals of color occupying differing rungs of the class ladder. When race intersects class (or gender, sexuality, religion, etc.) issues of racism may play out in quite different and often contradictory ways. With these understandings in mind bricoleurs in ethnic studies are better equipped to turn out thicker and more complex research studies. In this context our study is profoundly modified. Our feedback loop through social/cultural positionalities has informed us that racism manifests itself and affects particular individuals of color in multiple ways depending on its relationship to class, gender, and other positional factors.

A loop through diverse disciplinary frameworks opens our POET to more perspectives and possibilities. When previous insights are juxtaposed with, say, cultural studies and its emphasis on the discourses of popular cultural knowledges, important sources of previously unexplored information are brought to the bricoleur's attention. The study of contemporary movies, TV shows, video games, Internet Web sites, popular music, etc. allows the bricoleur in educational psychology to explore what could be described as the "social and psychological dreams" of U. S. society in the twenty-first century. Within these unguarded sociopsychological dreams of popular culture the researcher can begin to ask questions about new forms of racial representation, racial fears of the dominant culture, and the nature and meaning of the commodification and exoticization of "racial others." In this context the bricoleur finds unlimited resources to compare with data mined from other domains. What do these new knowledges tell us about the ways contemporary racism is constructed and disseminated? How do these media shape racial messages in ways that affect the identities of students of color? Does racism in an electronic era (hyperreality) encounter unprecedented forces that fashion it new and hard-to-discern ways—ways that complicate our understanding of its psychological/cognitive effects?

Analyzing our POET in relation to the philosophical domains allows bricoleurs to embrace a form of philosophical research often missing from research in educational psychology. Such insights remind bricoleurs of the complexity of the research act in educational psychology and the need to avoid monological forms of epistemology. Such monological forms of knowledge are often based on the assumption that knowledge reflects objective reality. In this context the researcher understands that no objective, disinterested understanding of contemporary racism and its effects is possible. The interpretations we make about contemporary racism and its effects are interpretations, the researcher's constructions. In this context post-formalists understand the role that our diverse frames of reference—our multilogicality—have played in shaping these interpretations. Are we satisfied with this process? Do we sense that we have negated isolating and decontextualizing tendencies in epistemologically monological and mechanistic research and that in this process we have worked with multiple forms of knowledge to deepen our insight into contemporary racism and its cognitive effects? How has this exposure to epistemological difference changed the nature of our understanding of these dynamics?

A central benefit of the bricolage's threading through the philosophical, specifically the epistemological domain for educational psychology, involves the way the process works to bring previously excluded people and categories of people into the research process. "Exclude these uneducated peons," the blind monks of reductionism exclaim. Multilogical epistemological analysis reminds educational psychologists that their research is one aspect of a larger political process involved with apportioning power and resources. Bricoleurs know that racially, ethnically, and class marginalized peoples have influence in such a process. Once research is viewed as a humanly constructed process and not a transcultural and transhistorical universal enterprise, diverse and conflicting perspectives can be viewed as profound resources.

Threading our POET through the modes of power can provide compelling new insights into the power of contemporary racism. When researchers of contemporary racism pass their analysis through the filter of ideology, they begin to see the ways particular forms of Eurocentrism and white supremacy operate in the contemporary society. Ideology is grounded on the notion that particular ways of seeing the world may work to sustain existing power relations in the cognitive domain. In a bow to complexity these same ways of seeing may undermine dominant power relations in another context. A complex definition of ideology dismisses traditional viewpoints that define ideology as a coherent system of beliefs. Instead, bricoleurs move to a more complex, process-oriented, culturally sensitive perspective that views ideology in its dominant articulation as part of a larger process of protecting unequal power relations and maintaining domination. Specifically, a dominant cultural form of ideology involves sustaining these power asymmetries through the process of making meaning, producing a common sense that justifies prevailing systems of domination. Such a view of ideology corrects historical definitions of ideology as a monolithic, unidirectional entity that was imposed on individuals by a secret cohort of ruling class tsars. In concrete psychological terms ideology shapes what we call intelligence and school success.

Understanding domination in the context of concurrent struggles among different classes, racial, and gender groups and sectors of capital, students of ideology analyze the ways such competition engages differing visions, interests, and agendas in a variety of social and psychological locales. Individuals use ideology to help them organize their lived experiences, to make sense of their predicaments. In this context, bricoleurs studying contemporary racism in relation to ideology begin to discern an encoded ideology of white supremacy inscribed throughout the social, cultural, and psychological landscape. Such a hidden ideology often operates to naturalize the unequal relationships.

Indeed, ideology constructs racial and ethnic interactions in a way that erases the historical processes that have helped mould the present social order and extant racial dynamics within it. As bricoleurs in educational psychology trace this ideology of white supremacy they often discern that it induces many peoples that the world could exist only in the way that it does today. "Its just a natural fact—white people are cognitively superior to Africans and Latinos. Such ideological awareness moves our understanding of the uniqueness of contemporary racism and its cognitive and educational effects to a new level of sophistication. As educational psychologists we are empowered to act in anti-racist ways previously unimagined.

The last domain through which we will thread our POET in this example (there are many more) involves the category of knowledge sources. While there are many we will focus here on works of art, the aesthetic realm. Exploring, for example, artistic and aesthetic styles that fall outside the confines of the Euro-canon, the bricoleur discerns a whole new domain where the uniqueness of contemporary racism can be analyzed. In numerous art shows illustrating, say, African or African American art (Rose and Kincheloe, 2003) guardians of the Euro-canon worked diligently to contain perceived threats to prevailing aesthetic standards and definitions of quality. The aesthetic orientations of such artists moved the priests of high art to equate difference with deficiency—a racist tendency that can be found in various social locales including, of course, cognition and education. Indeed, the art of the racial other in this context is seen through the constructed lenses of the canon. That which is artistically transgressive is "tamed" and rendered harmless by including it as a primitive stage of canonical development.

Representatives of the dominant culture in this social domain claim the right to establish the universal characteristics of "good art." Bricoleurs in this example work to demystify these hidden cultural and ideological dimensions of high art. And what may be key to the study of contemporary racism and its psychological and educational effects, in this demystification process bricoleurs expose not only what is excluded but also the ideological precepts shaping the *inclusion* of the other. How can we talk about racism in the art world, many might complain in this context—the contemporary canon includes the work of more Africans, African Americans, Latin Americans, and indigenous peoples than ever before. The aesthetic commitments required for inclusion, however, are profoundly revealing to the educational psychologist studying the effects of contemporary racism. The insight researchers develop into the terms of multiracial and multiethnic inclusion in the world of high art may help them discern similar patterns in the cognitive domain.

Of course, these are merely a few of the domains bricoleurs in educational psychology can use to inform their multilogical research. Bricoleurs have to make decisions about which domains to engage as they pursue new insights and exploit the conceptual power provided by the interaction of different perspectives. Understanding a phenomenon such as the effects of contemporary racism is enhanced by exposure to these multiple categories of diversity. After the bricolage researchers in educational psychology can never view the concept of diversity in the same light. Always devoted to importance of diversity, educational psychologists in this reconceptualized context move diversity into a new conceptual terrain. On this new landscape they begin to discern the insidious ways that racism has all along worked to shape the defining assumptions of their field of study.

REFERENCE

Rose, K., and Kincheloe, J. L. (2003). *Art, Culture, and Education: Artful Teaching in a Fractured Landscape*. New York: Peter Lang.

Thomas, G. (1998). *The Myth of Rational Research. British Eductional Research Journal*, 24, 2.

CHAPTER 110

The Spiritual Nature of Postformal Thought: Reading as Praxis

SHARON G. SOLLOWAY AND
NANCY J. BROOKS

The influence of educational psychology's behaviorist models has been heavy handed in shaping the policies that construct classrooms and educational experiences. In spite of years of challenge by humanist and constructivist models, behaviorist structures and practices persist, crippling students by vigilantly separating mind and body and ruthlessly denouncing spirituality as irrelevant in learning. The end result is most often students who rarely see education as an exploration of the awe and wonder in life, but regard it as simply something you do to get a grade.

Spirituality, as we define it here, is both a way of perceiving and a way of acting. As a way of perceiving, it opens our eyes to the "moreness" of our lives. We are always "more" in the sense that we possess the possibility of reaching beyond our present state—of transcending who and what we currently are. And we are always "more" in the sense that we do not dwell in the world alone; we cannot be *human* beings without others. It is this second aspect that leads us to the action of spirituality—becoming aware of our oneness with others and the world, then acting on this perception. In other words, when education is conducted in sync with our spirituality, children grow to be empathic, compassionate adults. Unfortunately, most schooling ignores the spiritual nature of human beings, and the Technorational reigns supreme as both students and knowledge are sorted and slotted in the most efficient manner. The school's spiritual mission as a work of transcending the status quo is forgotten or ignored.

The history of educational reform since the publication of *A Nation at Risk* in 1983 might be more rightly described as simply a ratcheting up of the same technorational methods that emerged early in the twentieth century in the heyday of social darwinism. While these methods have waxed and waned throughout the last hundred years, the youngest members of our society were somewhat sheltered from them. If there has been one place where the education of the whole-child has been respected, it has been in the early childhood environment. However, with the latest round of federal legislation, this is changing. It appears that the same spiritually deficient methods that have been used to categorize and normalize older students are to be foisted upon the youngest members of our society and upon their teachers. In this chapter, we call attention to changes that are emerging in the knowledge base of the field of early childhood education, discuss the implications of those changes, and present postformal thought as a heuristic for making meaning of them.

READING AS PRAXIS

While it was obvious early on that recent federal legislation would significantly impact education at all levels, the enormity of the implications for early childhood education is only now becoming evident. Subtle but substantial shifts are occurring in the official knowledge base of the field, represented in part by changes in textbooks for preservice teachers. As these changes have become evident, our concerns have grown, leading us to document the revisions of one particular textbook series. Our selection of this particular text was based on its success in the field,[1] and our observation of its evolution over the last six years.

As teachers who acknowledge the spiritual nature of education, we believe our task is not to affirm prevailing forces but to question critically what appears to be the "necessary" and to challenge what appears to be the "logical." As repositories of expert knowledge, our selected textbooks represent the official knowledge that is sanctioned by prevailing forces. That is, in a very real sense these texts are the result of power struggles over exactly what is "knowledge." The forces that prevail in the struggle win the right to decide what is included in the texts (the "presences" of the text) and what is left out (the "absences"), thereby determining what is "true," what is not, what is important, and what may be ignored. Accordingly, significant social meaning is constructed by official knowledge. We wonder—in this case, what social meanings are being produced for the many preservice teachers who study this particular text? What absences in the text will limit possibilities for them by being that which it is impossible for them to even think? What presences will become for them the "logical" and "necessary"?

As we approached this project, therefore, we looked for a theoretical framework that held the potential for illuminating evidences of power struggles within the text, a process that would allow us to see through and beyond the self-evident and to perceive present social meanings that might otherwise be missed. In other words, we sought for a framework that would make our reading of these texts a type of praxis. We settled upon postformal thought as a framework compatible with our concern for transcending the status quo, especially toward the ends of social justice, human emancipation, and increased opportunity for personal agency. With its concern for emancipation via ideological disembedding, postformal thought offers the possibility of a critique that may be analogous to "spiritual warfare" and that, we believe, enables our notion of reading as praxis.

No one particular method of postformal critique exists. Our approach to the textual analysis was to begin with a general overview of the editions, examining which concepts had been chosen by the author/editors to be foregrounded by placing them in the table of contents and preface. Noted changes were further explored through the index and a general read through of the books. Our understanding of discursive (or "rhetorical") strategies in each edition was guided by the four features of postformal thinking, as explained by Kincheloe and Steinberg in their 1993 groundbreaking article in the *Harvard Educational Review*. For this project we understand each feature as follows:

1) Etymology—a consideration of the possible forces producing the culture that validates the knowledge of each edition.

2) Pattern—a consideration of the assumptions that underlie the conceptualization/implementation of presences and absences within the three editions. This feature provides a perspective for understanding the connecting patterns and relationships that undergird the lived world of such positions.

3) Process—a consideration of the presences and absences across the three editions in order to consider not only what it is possible for early childhood professions to do, but how (or if) it is possible for them to challenge the necessary, the logical, and the taken for granted authority (of people or ideas).

4) Contextualization—a consideration of the embeddedness of the presences and absences across the three editions in political, social, and cultural positions.

We see these four features as configuring a web of "reality" through which we may map and understand the implications of our findings.

BACKGROUND—THE NEW PARADIGM

The first of our texts appeared in 1998. For those who survived the decade of the nineties (in a professional sense) it is remembered as a time of increasing governmental regulation of education at all levels. Technologies of standardization and surveillance tightened their grip on the local schoolhouse. In the aftermath of *A Nation at Risk* in 1983, the world of education entered full-throttle into the new paradigm of outcomes-based education: Everything can be measured and everything will be; a place for everyone and everyone in her place as determined by standardized assessment instruments. We believe it is important to remember here that most traditional preservice teachers remember *no other paradigm* of education.

As a part of the first wave of top-down reform efforts, the federal government had authorized funds for the creation of national standards. This movement died due to controversies over content and fears over the loss of the tradition of local control. Those same fears, however, did little to curb the growth of regulation at the state level. States jumped on the band wagon to stem the "rising tide of mediocrity" in schools through the creation of core curricula and high stake exams that held students accountable for learning by withholding promotion and/or diplomas.

As the failure of the earliest wave of educational reform began to be apparent, twin forces of increasing governmental regulation and the efforts of higher education agencies conspired to conceive and bring forth an incestuous new phenomenon christened the "professionalization" of the teaching field.[2] This movement involved setting a higher bar for who could be a teacher, determined by a bevy of new tests, including both entry and exit exams. At one point in the nineties, preservice teachers in some states had to perform satisfactorily on as many as four exams to receive state certification. Following the medical model, certification was also delayed until the candidate had completed an internship, overseen typically by local teachers, administrators, and higher education representatives operating within the framework of state legal requirements.

All this was legitimized by a new set of directives concocted by the nation's political/business establishment and signed by America's first education president, the elder Bush, in 1991. The first directive of *America 2000* was "All children will start school ready to learn." This goal, which was no doubt set with the best of intentions, set the stage for increased surveillance of young children, making it possible for them to be increasingly observed and monitored to determine their developmental levels and the needed experiences that could lead to more advanced forms of readiness. With the election of Clinton the list of goals morphed into "Goals 2000" and grew to total of eight directives. Number eight declared, "Every school and home will engage in partnerships that will increase parental involvement and participation in promoting the social, emotional, and academic growth of children." This goal, combined with the first goal and with the original Head Start requirement of parental involvement (also set with the best of intentions) effectively set the stage for greater surveillance of the family of the preschool child.

As the nineties closed, the preface to the eighth edition of our text crowed, "We are in the golden age of early childhood education" (Morrison, 2001, p. vii).

MAPPING THE TEXT

In our analysis of these three texts we found that what was remarkable was not so much the number of changes across the editions, but how far apart the seventh and ninth editions were on certain key issues and the subtlety with which this move was made across a rather wide ideological chasm. We will not attempt to cover in this chapter all the changes we noted, but will focus instead on the two most directly related to our concern for human emancipation and a sense of personal agency (for both teachers and students). Those issues, not surprisingly, relate to the increasing emphasis on accountability and control and the identity this requires the fledgling early childhood professional to assume.

One clear and immediate indication of change in this area is seen in the tables of contents. Assessment becomes increasingly emphasized—moving from only a couple of subheadings over short sections in the seventh edition to a full chapter near the end of the book in the eighth edition, to being a chapter in Part I in the ninth edition (following a chapter reconfigured to feature "public policy"). Such space allotment and placement indicate valuation. Naturally, as one topic moves up the value scale, something else must move down. In this case, that appears to be the notion of child-centered education and related topics. We find this especially disturbing since early childhood education has, in many regards, been the last bastion of a concern for educating the whole person in our schools.

As of the seventh edition, child-centered education is "alive and well" in the primary grades (Morrison, 1998, p. 261). It is recommended for preschoolers, with a gentle warning to "strive to provide a balance between academics and all areas of development" (p. 216). A lengthy section on Open Education describes it as child-centered education:

Adults do not do all the talking, decision making, organizing, and planning when it is children who need to develop these skills. Open education seeks to return the emphasis to the child, where it rightfully belongs. Open education teachers respect students and believe children are capable of assuming responsibility for their own learning. Teachers consider themselves primarily teachers of *children*, not of subject matter . . . (1998, p. 87; emphasis in original)

In addition, child-centered education is featured prominently in the seventh edition in a Chapter 1 section entitled "The Return of Child-Centered Education" (p. 55). The same section appears in the eighth edition (2001, p. 95), although it is downgraded from Chapter 1 to Chapter 3 ("The Past and the Present: Prologue to the Future"). Significantly, this section disappears in the ninth edition and the term "child-centered" begins to morph into a concept more compatible with the age of accountability. Readers are told it is "a widely used term misunderstood by many" (p. 104). Indeed, Chapter 1 implies the need for a redefinition of the term as it ends with a section entitled "A new meaning of child-centered education"

Everything we discuss in this book is based on the child being the center of the teaching and learning processes. Unfortunately, not all teachers have practiced child-centered approaches, nor have they made children's learning a high priority. This is changing. Included in the child-centered approach are the ideas that children can learn at high levels of achievement; that children are eager to learn; and that they are capable of learning more than many people thought they could. So a new concept of child-centeredness embraces the whole child in all dimensions: social, emotional, physical, linguistic, and cognitive. (2004, p. 24)

A comparison of these two descriptions of child-centered education shows an unfortunate trend away from a pedagogy that is compatible with human emancipation. Success becomes synonymous with "achievement," instead of with an increasing capacity for personal agency.

In spite of the ninth edition's satisfaction that the new child-centeredness embraces the whole child, we are concerned with the apparent move to value only that which is in line with current school reform goals of achievement on standardized tests for the purpose of bulking up the nation's twenty-first-century workforce. Although the holistic approach in editions seven and eight is considered valuable for the fact that it met a wide range of needs for children and their families, including health, the ninth edition emphasizes, "When children are healthy, they achieve better" (2004, p. 34). Achievement, of course, refers to a cognitive response to artificial stimuli that does little to nurture the child's sense of awe and wonder at existence or nuanced relationships to self and the world on a web of interdependency.

The space that is created by dropping some of the emphasis on child-centeredness, whole language, open education, etc., in the seventh edition, allows for more than just increased coverage of assessment. Several new pages on School to Work appear in the eighth edition ("School to Career" in the ninth). Preservice early childhood teachers read about kindergartners who research jobs, salaries, and required skills and hear how schools like Western Dubuque Community Elementary emphasize the world of work for their youngest constituents:

For the past three years, counselors have developed career portfolios on each child to build a record of the activities completed. All first graders used the new portfolios and the national Career Guidelines to track career awareness. Third graders visited area businesses and then created newspaper ads . . . (2004, p. 359)

We wonder what happens to the soul when exposed so young to life goals embodied as a series of steps to your place in society's economic machine.

As we consider these strategies that draw our youngest learners into the governmentality of educational reforms, we think of the failure of the accountability-driven system to reduce inequities in academic achievement. In spite of such failure, educational reformers continue to support the very techniques that have generated the inequalities in the first place: higher standards (which stigmatize average performance), increased surveillance (which, through tougher codes of conduct, further restricts opportunities to learn self-agency), and more explicit punishment and reward systems.

As the discourse of early childhood education more and more adopts this same ideology of standardization and accountability, we run the risk of subjecting children at ever younger ages to a system that stigmatizes them. It increasingly robs them of the opportunity to understand living as a nuanced journey of awe and wonder punctuated with both joy and sorrow. We worry that such texts too closely suggest a curriculum and classroom practice that demands for both teacher and young students unnecessary conformity and the inherence of a neglect of difference. In spite of that danger the textbooks examined here continue to increasingly define the necessary for early childhood professionals as observing, testing, and normalizing. This change in discourse is not pointed out to preservice teachers after the seventh edition. In addition, the soon-to-be professionals are seldom challenged to critique any position. Indeed at one point they, as readers, are told that in spite of the controversy over testing children as young as preschoolers, they "will probably be involved in discussions that help assume that this process of evaluation is developmentally appropriate" (2004, p. 218).

IMPLICATIONS

What do the discursive strategies noted above mean for students in early childhood teacher education programs? How does the presentation of official knowledge across the three editions shape what it is possible for them to think about the education of young children? How is their understanding of themselves as early childhood educators affected? How are their beliefs constrained regarding their own personal sense of agency for advancing a concern for social justice and the honoring of multiple perspectives in order to challenge the status quo? Unfortunately, it appears that current preservice teachers are being molded into agents of the status quo, who are taught implicitly not to think critically about their work or their world.

This analysis provides an illustration of the value of postformal thought as a heuristic for reading as praxis in the early childhood teacher education classroom. The use of current political language, the privileging of its values (as seen, for example, in space allotment and placement of text), and the absence of alternative perspectives are problematic for future teachers in early childhood classrooms. The education of young children is being framed more and more as academic preparation for externally designed assessments. To be an early childhood teacher is to unquestioningly implement public policy rather than model teaching and learning as an ongoing inquiry into one's place in the interconnectedness of life. The lack of encouragement for critical reading of multiple social, historical, political, and cultural positions inhibits preservice teachers from developing an awareness of a need to challenge dominant ideologies. They remain unaware of the way their unexamined compliance with authority contributes to the production of their identities and ability to function in the world. Furthermore, the invisibility of their oppressions produces teachers with a diminished capacity for personal agency in regard to recognizing and effecting social justice for all their students. Our analysis points to the urgency for more postformalist classrooms where the teaching is comprised of human acts that assist students in forming ethical frameworks, emotional balance, and spirituality to guide their lives.

SPIRITUAL NATURE OF POSTFORMAL THOUGHT

Using postformal thought to move reading into a praxis of seeing other possible realities, opens awareness to the way dominant educational discourses can limit human possibilities and of the way an openness to multiple perspectives can cultivate an appreciation for the interconnectedness of life. This praxis offers opportunities for developing spiritual relationships on a web of compassion; as children recognize their relatedness to others, as they collaborate to reach common goals, sharing resources and knowledge, they grow to be empathic, compassionate adults.

Compassion in this sense becomes a radical form of criticism. It is not a compassion whose empathy stops with the intellectual and heart-felt acknowledgment of the oppression of the other. Rather, compassion as a radical form of criticism moves acknowledgment into positive action to overturn the oppression. This is compassion that does not rest upon, but acts out the implications of the interconnectedness experienced. We see this kind of spirituality in Virginia Durr, who provided the financial backing for Rosa Parks' two-week stay at the Highlander Folk School in Monteagle, Tennessee, just months before Mrs. Parks refused to give up her seat on the bus in December 1955. This is a spirituality that is a way of perceiving *and* a way of acting.

CONCLUSION

The erosion of the landscape of early childhood education by the forces of traditional educational psychology ideologies that preclude the possibility of thinking beyond their boundaries is sinister in its subtlety. Postformal thought as a way of reading early childhood textbooks offers not a new grand narrative, but a heuristic that might act as a "force" in the sense where force breaks up that which would constrain and breaks open new visions/readings, revealing oppressions and injustices and igniting acts of solution. In addition, it may provoke the sort of shift in consciousness that effects cultural transformation. Postformal thought, when applied as a reading praxis, facilitates the erasure of socially constructed boundaries and the liberation of oppressed peoples.

When spirituality is recognized as that experience which opens our awareness and frees us to *slow experience down*, we can see in between the lines, so to speak. And what we find there is what was not possible to see or think within the confines of the judgment that language requires when reading is practice, not praxis. Postformal thinking moves thought to those spaces between the lines to reveal the need for asking what unacknowledged assumptions invisibly inhere there. It reconceptualizes traditional educational psychology ideologies, creating space for spirituality to be understood as a critical part of an education which is "... not to make you fit into the social pattern; on the contrary, it is to help you to understand completely, deeply, fully, and thereby break away from the social pattern..." (Krishnamurti, 1964/1970, p. 95). Deep awareness of the power of culture to establish unquestioned hierarchies offers the opportunity to see differently. The spirituality of postformal thought lies in the living out of answers to the question: Who benefits when postformal thought as a way of being in the world orients the reader to a praxis in the in-between-spaces where we meet the other as an enfoldment of ourselves?

TERMS FOR READERS

Discourse—the medium by which ideas are exchanged; a field's discourse is a system of knowledge or a "language map" by which the truth of statements related to that field can be determined.

Governmentality—A centralization and increase of government power, which produces reality through "rituals of truth." Governmentality also includes a growing body of knowledge that presents itself as "scientific," and which contributes to the power of governmentality.

Normalize—To mold people into "normal" as opposed to "abnormal" forms, and the process by which a culture encourages each individual to regulate and achieve his or her own conformity with the established rules. This is achieved through governmentality.

Praxis—Cycle of reflection and action of individuals upon their world to transform it.

Surveillance—As used here, this term means more than simply "observation." It refers to part of the technique by which individuals are continuously observed, categorized, and disciplined, so that they are normalized, so that they docilely fit into the machinery of society's needs.

Technorational—An approach to education which values efficiency and effectiveness above all else.

NOTES

1. Evidenced by the fact that it is now in its ninth edition. We wish to emphasize here that our purpose is not to debase the work of any other early childhood educators. These texts serve merely as an example of the construction and function of discourse in the field.

2. Gail Cannella, a well-known scholar of early childhood education, points out that professionalism is a double-edged sword that (1) could lead to strengthening of position and increased respect, but (2) has more often resulted in increased domination by those in power.

FURTHER READING

Cannella, G. (1999). Postformal Thought As Critique, Reconceptualization, and Possibility for Teacher Education Reform. In J. L. Kincheloe, S. R. Steinberg, and L. E. Villaverde (Eds.), *Rethinking Intelligence: Confronting Psychological Assumptions About Teaching and Learning*, pp. 145–163. New York: Routledge.

Huebner, D. E. (1985/1999). Spirituality and Knowing. In V. Hillis (Ed.), *The Lure of the Transcendent: Collected Essays by Dwayne E. Heubner*, pp. 340–352. Mahwah, NJ: Lawrence Erlbaum Associates. (Original work published 1985).

Kincheloe, J. L., and Steinberg, S. R. (1993). A Tentative Description of Postformal Thinking: The Critical Confrontation with Cognitive Theory. *Harvard Educational Review,* 63(3), 296–320.

Krishnamurti, J. (1964/1970). *Think on These Things.* New York: Harper Perennial, HarperCollins.

Moffett, J. (1994). *The Universal Schoolhouse: Spiritual Awakening Through Education.* San Francisco: Jossey-Bass.

Morrison, G. S. (1998). *Early Childhood Education Today* (7th ed.). Upper Saddle River, NJ: Prentice-Hall, Inc.

———. (2001). *Early Childhood Education Today* (8th ed.). Upper Saddle River, NJ: Prentice-Hall, Inc.

———. (2004). *Early Childhood Education Today* (9th ed.). Upper Saddle River, NJ: Pearson Education.

Index

About the Contributors

MARY FRANCES AGNELLO teaches at Our Lady of the Lake University working in teacher education, foundations, and educational leadership. Her most recently published work included studies of teacher beliefs about culture and literacy, multicultural issues in higher education, and student critical thinking. Her book, *A Postmodern Literacy Policy Analysis* (2001), addresses literacy policy and the social discourses about literacy surrounding their implementation from 1970 to 1995.

J. E. AKHURST is a senior lecturer at York St. John University in York, United Kingdom. She was formerly a senior lecturer in educational psychology in KwaZulu-Natal, South Africa, and worked extensively with trainee and in-service teachers, school counselors, and school psychologists. Her research interests now focus on the teaching of psychology and student development in higher education, career psychology, and adolescent mental health and well-being.

ROMY M. ALLEN is a well-known educator and advocate of children in North Carolina. She is on the Anti-Bias Task Force of Forsyth County, the NCDCA district coordinator, the preschool liasion for the Children's Theater Board, and a partner in the Forsyth Early Childhood Partnership Education Committee. A Central Region mentor for the Partnership for Inclusion, Allen is a state assessor for the North Carolina Rated License Project at University of North Carolina, Greensboro.

ADRIANA AUBERT is consulter at UNED, the National Distance Education University in Spain. She is member of the Center of Research CREA at the University of Barcelona, where she is responsible for the project of schools' transformation "Learning Communities." She is coauthor of the book *Dialogar y Transformar. Pedagogía crítica del siglo XXI.*

RACHEL BAILEY JONES is currently in the final stages of work toward a doctorate in Educational Leadership and Cultural Foundations at the University of North Carolina, Greensboro. She is an artist and art educator, with special interest in the postmodern creation of art in the transnational space of the twenty-first century. Her current research is into the visual representation of Muslim women in the post-9/11 United States, and the use of contemporary art as a pedagogical tool for a more multifaceted understanding of difference.

KATHLEEN S. BERRY has written books, many chapters and articles regarding the implications of contemporary theories, such as poststructuralism and postcolonialism, on educational practices. Recently she received the Allan P. Stuart Award for Excellence in Teaching at University of New Brunswick, Canada, where she is a professor of education in critical studies, drama, and literacies.

JEANETTE BOPRY is currently an assistant professor of instructional sciences at the National Institute for Education in Singapore. She edits *Teaching & Learning: The Journal of Natural Inquiry and Reflective Practice,* and is associate editor of *Cybernetics and Human Knowing.*

LUIS BOTELLA is professor of psychotherapy at the Department of Psychology (Ramon Llull University, Barcelona, Spain) where he also directs the master's course in clinical psychology and psychotherapy. He is a member of the Editorial Board of the *Journal of Constructivist Psychology,* the *International Journal of Psychotherapy,* the *European Journal of Psychotherapy, Counselling, and Health* and the *Revista de Psicoterapia.* His publications and research interests include postmodern thought, constructivism and social constructionism, psychotherapy (process and outcome research), psychotherapy integration, Personal Construct Theory, narrative psychology and psychotherapy, cognitive complexity, identity, and Eastern spirituality (Taoism and Zen Buddhism). He coordinates the Psychotherapy Service at his University.

ROCHELLE BROCK is a graduate of UC Berkeley and Pennsylvania State University. She is currently taking a leave from academia to concentrate on writing and research. Completing her doctorate in curriculum and instruction in 1999 Dr. Brock began an academic career as assistant professor in curriculum studies at Purdue University, teaching undergraduate preservice teacher courses in Multicultural Education, and graduate courses, which analyze the complexities in the education of African Americans, Native Americans, and Latinos. Dr. Brock is also an education consultant, most recently working with the Center for the Education of Students Placed at Risk (CRESPAR) as Co-Principal Investigator of the Elementary School Project: Asset-Based Education. She is the author of *Sista Talk: The Personal and the Pedagogical* (2005).

NANCY J. BROOKS is an assistant professor in the Department of Educational Studies at Ball State University, where she teaches graduate and undergraduate courses in curriculum and the foundations of education. Her current teaching and research interests focus on critical hermeneutics and on the relationship between contemporary curriculum theory and classroom practice.

STEPHEN BROOKFIELD began his teaching career in 1970 in England. He has taught in Canada, Australia and the United States, teaching in a variety of college settings. He has written and edited nine books on adult learning, teaching, and critical thinking, three of which have won the World Award for Literature in Adult Education (in 1986, 1989, and 1996). He also won the 1986 Imogene Okes Award for Outstanding Research in Adult Education. He now holds the title of Distinguished Professor at the University of St. Thomas in Minneapolis, Minnesota.

DEBORAH S. BROWN is currently a professor of educational psychology at West Chester University. She has recently coauthored the text *Educational Pstchology: A Practioner-Researcher Model Teaching.* Dr. Brown has authored or coauthored over thirty research articles; her research areas include teacher planning, action research, middle school practice, and teachers' writing of case dilemmas. She has also supervised secondary student teachers and has taught at both the middle and high school levels.

ANNE BROWNSTEIN is a doctoral student in the Urban Education Program at the CUNY Graduate Center in New York.

ERICA BURMAN is professor of psychology and Women's Studies at the Manchester Metropolitan University, where she codirects the Discourse Unit and the Women's Studies Research Centre. She is the author of *Deconstructing Developmental Psychology* (1994), coauthor of *Challenging Women: psychology's exclusions, feminist possibilities* (1995) and *Psychology Discourse Practice: From regulation to resistance* (1996), editor of Feminists and Psychological Practice (1990) and *Deconstructing Feminist Psychology* (1998), and coeditor of *Discourse Analytic Research* (1993) *Culture, Power and Difference* (998).

MONTSERRAT CASTELLÓ is professor of educational psychology at the Department of Psychology at Ramon Llull University, Barcelona, Spain where she also directs the doctoral programs in Psychology and Education. She coordinates at the same University the postgraduate and long-life learning courses in Psychology and Education. She is a member of the editorial board of Cultura y educacion and Infancia y aprendizaje. She is an active member of the European Research of Learning and Instruction (EARLI) and she belongs to the Specials Interests Groups in writing and higher education. She is member of the EARLI Spanish Committee, the Spanish SIG-Writing and the interuniversity seminar of learning strategies (SINTE).

DANIEL E. CHAPMAN is completing his dissertation under the guidance of Dr. Leila Villaverde at the University of North Carolina at Greensboro. His diverse background includes teaching middle school in urban and rural settings, directing several documentaries and other educational media, working with home school students, and teaching creative writing at a drug rehabilitation facility. His interests include Media Literacy, Media Studies, Critical Theory, and Literacy Education.

BRENDA CHEREDNICHENKO is currently the head of the School of Education at Victoria University, Australia. The School has preservice and postgraduate programs in primary, secondary, and early childhood Education, Training and Youth Studies. Brenda's research interests are in collaborative practitioner research in educational reform, the teaching of thinking and philosophical inquiry, equity, and social justice in learning and teaching, democratic learning and socio-philosophy and education. Her books and articles are widely used.

PETER CHIN is an associate professor in the Faculty of Education at Queen's University in Kingston, Ontario, Canada. His research interests can be found in science education with particular focus on science teaching and learning in school and workplace environments. The inclusion of students with exceptionalities and at-risk students is emphasized.

LISE BIRD CLAIBORNE is the director of postgraduate studies and Senior Lecturer in the School of Education, Victoria University, Wellington, New Zealand. She has researched and taught in the area of critical educational psychology for many years, and is coauthor of the widely used textbook *Human Development in Aotearoa* (2003).

KEVIN CLAPANO received his BS in psychology from the Ateneo de Manila University in 1992 and his MS in experimental psychology with a focus on Health Psychology in 1995 from Saint Joseph's University. He is currently pursuing his doctoral degree in education at Saint Joseph's University with a focus on interdisciplinary educational leadership.

THOMAS R. CONWAY is currently the Social Studies Chairperson and Summer School Coordinator at Philadelphia Electrical and Technology Charter High School. Conway is an adjunct professor of religion at La Salle University and is pursuing his doctoral degree in Educational Leadership at Saint Joseph's University.

ALISON COOK-SATHER, Director of the Bryn Mawr/Haverford Education Program and associate professor of education, teaches core courses for students seeking state certification to teach at the secondary level. Recent publications include "Education as Translation: Students Transforming Notions of Narrative and Self" (*College Composition and Communication*, 55, 1, 91–114, 2003); "Movements of Mind: The Matrix, Metaphors, and Re-Imagining Education" (*Teachers College Record*, 105, 6, 946–977, 2003), and "Authorizing Students' Perspectives: Toward Trust, Dialogue, and Change in Education" (*Educational Researcher*, 31, 4, 3–14, 2002).

RUTHANN CRAWFORD-FISHER is a doctoral student in educational leadership at Saint Joseph's University. She is a consultant for the Pennsylvania Service Learning Alliance and the Pennsylvania Department of Education. Her research interests are in alternative education, service learning, at risk youths, and school to career programs.

BRENT DAVIS is Canada Research Chair in Mathematics Education and the Ecology of Learning at the University of Alberta. He has published three books, the most recent of which is *Inventions of Teaching: A Genealogy* (2004). His refereed articles have appeared in journals that include *Harvard Educational Review*, *Educational Theory*, *Qualitative Studies in Education*, *Journal of Curriculum Studies*, *Teaching Education*, and *American Journal of Psychology*. He is founding coeditor of *Complicity: An International Journal of Complexity and Education*

STANLEY DOYLE-WOOD is a doctoral candidate in the Department of Sociology and Equity Studies in Education at the Ontario Institute for Studies in Education. Areas of research, writing, and pedagogy involve: Integrated AntiRacism Praxis in Relation to Community, Family and Early Years Development/Experience: Programming Literacy Teaching Techniques for Undergraduate Student Teachers Within an Anti-Oppression Framework.

GEORGE J. SEFA DEI is professor and chair of the Department of Sociology and Equity Studies in Education at the Ontario Institute for Studies in Education. He served as first Director of the Centre for Integrative Anti-Racism Studies at OISE/UT. Publications include: *Anti-Racism Education: Theory and Practice* (1996): *Hardships and Survival in Rural West Africa* (1992): *Reconstructing 'Drop-out': A Critical Ethnography of the Dynamics of Black Students' Disengagement from School*, with Josephine Mazzuca, Elizabeth McIsaac, and Jasmine Zine (1997): *Indigenous Knowledges in Global Contexts: Multiple Readings of our World*, with Budd Hall and Dorothy Goldin Rosenberg (2000): *Schooling in Africa : The Case of Ghana* (2004): *Playing the Race Card: Exposing White Power and Privilege*, coauthored with Leeno Karumanchery and Nisha Karumanchery-Link.

DELIA D. DOUGLAS was born in Britain and raised in Canada. Douglas completed her doctoral work in the Sociology department at the University of California Santa Cruz. At present she lives and writes in Vancouver, British Columbia.

JULIA ELLIS is a professor in elementary education at the University of Alberta. She completed her doctoral and master's programs in educational psychology at the University of British Columbia. Prior to her position at the University of Alberta she held appointments in educational psychology departments at the University of Lethbridge and the University of Toronto. Author of many books and articles, she is currently completing *The Creative Problem Solving Primer*.

CHRIS EMDIN is a doctoral candidate in the Urban Education Program at the CUNY Graduate Center in New York. He is a science teacher in the New York City Schools.

BENJAMIN ENOMA is a doctoral candidate in the Urban Education Program at the CUNY Graduate Center in New York.

ELLEN ESSICK is a faculty member in the Department of Public Health Education at the University of North Carolina, Greensboro where she teaches elementary school, health methods, human sexuality, and emotional health. Her research interests include eating disorder, feminist theory, gender studies, pedagogy and HIV/AIDS.

SCOT D. EVANS holds a master's degree in counseling and is a student in the Doctoral Program in Community Research and Action at Peabody College. His interests are in youth civic engagement and organizational transformation.

TODD FELTMAN is a doctoral student in the Urban Education Program at the CUNY Graduate Center. He is an elementary classroom teacher in the New York City Schools.

TARA FENWICK is associate professor of adult education in the Department. of Educational Policy Studies at the University of Alberta. Her research focuses on learning through work, with particular interest in the knowledge, desires, and subjectivities produced in networks of activity in the contested terrains of contemporary organizations. Most recently she published *Learning Through Experience: Troubling Assumptions and Intersecting Questions* (2003).

KERRY FINE is a doctoral student at Teachers College of Columbia University in New York.

LEE GABAY is a doctoral candidate in the Urban Education Program at the CUNY Graduate Center. He is a classroom teacher in the New York City Schools.

MARK J. GARRISON is assistant professor of education at D'Youville College, in Buffalo, New York. His book, *The Political Origins of Failure: Education, Standards and the Assessment of Social Value* is with SUNY Press. He also has forthcoming material on the social context of the use of educational technology.

SUSAN GEROFSKY uses linguistics, genre studies, and arts-based research to look critically at education, particularly mathematics education. Her book, *A Man Left Albuquerque Heading East: Word Problems as Genre in Mathematics Education* is with Peter Lang Publishing. She teaches at an alternative high school, Ideal School, and Simon Fraser University in Vancouver, Canada.

CATHY B. GLENN is a doctoral candidate in the Department of Speech Communication at Southern Illinois University, Carbondale. Her general research focus is philosophy of communication with particular emphases on process thought, personalism, and pragmatism where they intersect critical/culturalist theory and method. She has published work on topics related to critical rhetoric and pedagogy, Whiteheadian process philosophy, temporality and ethics, cultural politics, and communication activism.

NICOLE GREEN is a Doctoral student in the Department of Elementary Education at the University of Alberta, Edmonton, Canada. She has a bachelor of education (Early Childhood) from the Queensland University of Technology, Brisbane, Australia, and a master of education (Early Childhood) from the University of Alberta. She has enjoyed teaching and learning with students in Kindergarten to Grade Six in both regular Elementary Schools and at a School of Distance Education. Her current research focuses on home educating families' experiences of Distance Education in Queensland, Australia.

KECIA HAYES received her PhD from the CUNY Graduate Center where she was a MAGNET Scholar. She coauthored a chapter in *19 Urban Questions: Teaching in the City* by Shirley

Steinberg and Joe Kincheloe (Eds.). Kecia also coedited three texts including: *The Praeger Handbook of Urban Education, Metropedagogy: Power, Justice, and the Urban Classroom, and City Kids: Understanding, Appreciating, and Teaching Them.* Her research examines how social policies and practices impact the educational experiences of children and families of color in urban communities, with particular focus on disconnected and court-involved youth.

FRANCES HELYAR is completing her doctorate in education at McGill University in Montreal. A former teacher, CBC broadcaster, and voice of New Brunswick Bell, Helyar is interested in education via history, historiography, and archiving.

VALERIE HILL-JACKSON is a clinical assistant professor at Texas A&M University. She has also served as public school educator, not-for-profit consultant, and university program director. Hill-Jackson's research is in the fields of critical race theory, community education, and urban education. In addition, Hill-Jackson is an AERA/Spencer and Geraldine R. Dodge fellow.

RAYMOND A. HORN Jr., is an associate professor of education, Director of the Interdisciplinary Doctor of Education Program for Educational Leaders, and Director of Educational Leadership and Professional Studies at Saint Joseph's University in Philadelphia, Pennsylvania. He is the coeditor of the journal, *The Scholar-Practitioner Quarterly.* His books include: *Teacher Talk: A Post-formal Inquiry into Educational Change, Understanding Educational Reform: A Reference Handbook, and Standards Primer*; as well as the coauthored book, *American Standards: Quality Education in a Complex World-The Texas Case.* In addition, he has published numerous journal articles involving educational leadership, critical pedagogy, teacher education, systems theory, and scholar–practitioner leadership.

DAVID HUNG is an associate professor at the National Institute of Education, Nanyang Technological University (Singapore). He is also Head of the Learning Sciences and Technologies Academic Group and the associate dean for the learning sciences. His research interests include situated cognition, social constructivism, and issues related to identity and communities of practice.

NANCY L. HUTCHINSON is professor and coordinator of Graduate Studies and Research in the Faculty of Education at Queen's University in Kingston, Ontario, Canada. She conducts research on workplace learning and on a range of issues related to the education and inclusion of individuals with disabilities. She received her doctorate in instructional psychology at Simon Fraser University in 1987.

KAREN E. JENLINK is a professor and dean of the School of Education at Saint Edward's University in Austin, Texas. Dr. Jenlink is author of numerous scholarly publications in teacher education. Her research interests are in teacher preparation in urban settings, teacher leadership and professional identity, and professional development.

PATRICK M. JENLINK is a professor of doctoral studies in the Department of Secondary Education and Educational Leadership and Director of the Educational Research Center at Stephen F. Austin State University. He is also a research fellow of the International Systems Institute in Carmel, California. He has edited books and authored or coauthored numerous chapters. Currently he serves as editor of *Teacher Education and Practice* and coeditor of *Scholar-Practitioner Quarterly.* He is also editing four book projects.

RACHEL BAILEY JONES is currently in the final stages of work toward a doctorate in Educational Leadership and Cultural Foundations at the University of North Carolina, Greensboro. She is an artist and art educator, with special interest in the postmodern creation of art in the transnational space of the twenty-first century. Her current research is into the visual represen-tation of Muslim women in the post-9/11 United States, and the use of contemporary art as a pedagogical tool for a more multifaceted understanding of difference.

PAM JOYCE received her doctorate from the Urban Education Program at the CUNY Graduate Center. She teaches high school English in Montclair, New Jersey. She is the author of an upcoming book from Peter Lang Publishing.

YATTA KANU is associate professor in the Department of Curriculum, Teaching and Learning, Faculty of Education, University of Manitoba in Winnipeg, Canada. Her areas of research in-terest are curriculum, culture and student learning, inclusive education, curriculum reform, and international education.

LYNDA KENNEDY is a doctoral student in the Urban Education Program at the CUNY Graduate Center. She has worked extensively in museum education.

JOE L. KINCHELOE is the Canada Research Chair at the McGill University Faculty of Education. He is the author of numerous books and articles about pedagogy, education and social justice, racism, class bias, and sexism, issues of cognition and cultural context, and educational reform. His books include: *Teachers as Researchers, Classroom Teaching: An Introduction, Getting Beyond the Facts: Teaching Social Studies/Social Sciences in the Twenty-first Century, The Sign of the Burger: McDonald's and the Culture of Power, City Kids: Understanding Them, Appreciating Them, and Teaching Them, and Changing Multiculturalism* (with Shirley Steinberg). His coedited works include *The Urban Education Encyclopedia, White Reign: Deploying Whiteness in America* (with Shirley Steinberg et al.) and the Gustavus Myers Human Rights award winner: *Measured Lies: The Bell Curve Examined* (with Shirley Steinberg and Aaron D. Gresson).

KATHRYN KINNUCAN-WELSCH is associate professor and coordinator of graduate programs in the Department of Teacher Education, University of Dayton. She has served as facilitator and researcher of numerous professional development initiatives in Georgia, Michigan, and Ohio. Her research interests include professional development of teachers, literacy, and qualitative research methodology.

THIAM SENG KOH is an associate professor at the National Institute of Education, Nanyang Technological University. He is a faculty member of the Natural Sciences and Science Education Academic Group. His research interests include communities of practice, the use of ICT in science education and policy studies on the integration of ICT into the curriculum.

B. LARA LEE is a doctoral candidate in Educational Leadership and Cultural Foundations at the University of North Carolina, Greensboro. She has taught for seven years as an Adjunct Professor and more recently as a Graduate Teaching Assistant in her doctorate program. Her research interests are in Communication and Cultural Studies. She has lectured and participated in conference organization and workshops nationally and internationally to examine gender-gap issues grounded in communicational, educational and social inequities. Her aspiration, and lifelong mission, is the promotion of social justice and equity through education.

XIAOMING LIU is an assistant professor of Reading at the Pennsylvania State University – Harrisburg. She teaches both undergraduate and graduate literacy courses. Her research interests include authentic/alternative literacy assessment and literacy portfolios in particular; English language learners' language acquisition, literacy development, home-school connections, and identity issues; and content area literacy.

CHEE–KIT LOOI is Head of the Learning Sciences Lab and an associate professor in the National Institute of Education. He has published widely in the field of educational technology. His current research includes technology-enabled mathematics learning, and computer-supported collaborative learning. He obtained his doctorate from the University of Edinburgh.

ERIK L. MALEWSKI is an assistant professor of curriculum studies at Purdue University. He is interested in scholarship on critical theory, postformalism, and cultural studies as they relate to reconceptualizing curriculum and the social contexts of education. In particular, he is focused on understanding educational organizations as curricula, critically informed notions of standards and assessment, and the ways symbolic and material inequities connect to our implicit understandings of teaching and learning and intelligence in public education.

RUTHANN MAYES-ELMA completed her doctorate in education at Miami of Ohio University. She is presently a classroom teacher in Mason, Ohio. Her areas of research include gender studies and urban education. She is the author of the book, *Females and Harry Potter: Not All that Empowering.*

JAMES MOONEY is a doctoral student in educational leadership at Saint Joseph's University. His research interests include early intervention, education of low-socioeconomic students in urban areas, and social justice. Mr. Mooney received his MEd from Lehigh University, as well as a BA in theatre with a minor in writing.

MARLA MORRIS is an assistant professor at Georgia Southern University. She is Editor of *JCT/ The Journal of Curriculum Theorizing.* She is author of *Curriculum and the Holocaust: Competing Sites of Memory and Representation* (2001). Marla has edited several readers including *Difficult Memories: Talk in a (Post) Holocaust Era* (2002), and *How We Work* (1999) with William F. Pinar and Mary Aswell Doll. She has authored numerous articles in curriculum studies. Her main interest is the intersection between psychoanalysis and education.

DONAL E. MULCAHY is a doctoral student in the Urban Education Program at the CUNY Graduate Center in New York City. He is a teacher in the New York City Schools.

HUGH MUNBY accepted a position at Queen's University, Kingston, in 1971 and is currently Professor Emeritus. He has an extensive record of research and publication in science education, curriculum theory, and teacher knowledge. In 1998, his interest in learning from and in experience led to the creation of a research program in cooperative education and workplace learning with Nancy Hutchinson and Peter Chin at Queen's University.

CYNTHIA CHEW NATIONS worked in Texas public schools for thirty years as a teacher, a teacher mentor, an assistant principal, a principal, and as the director of mathematics and science instruction in the Urban Systemic Program. During her career, she has focused on school reform efforts that lead to distributed leadership in learning organizations, improving the quality of classroom instruction, and recognizing the diversity of all learners. She is currently a visiting full-time professor at New Mexico State University.

KATE E. O'HARA is a doctoral student in the Urban Education Program at the CUNY Graduate Center in New York City. She is a teacher in the New York City Schools.

DORIS PAEZ Director of the Metropolitan Studies Institute at the University of South Carolina Upstate, also runs her own psychological consulting business. Paez specializes in the fields of psychology and education for children with special needs, particularly those of Hispanic, African American and Native American descent. As a doctoral level licensed and certified school psychologist, she is widely recognized at the national, state, and local levels for her work on educational and mental health issues for culturally and linguistically diverse students.

KATHRYN PEGLER is a reading specialist at The Haverford School. She previously taught first grade in the School District of Haverford Township. She is currently enrolled in a doctoral program in Educational Leadership at St. Joseph's University in Philadelphia.

JANE PIIRTO is the author of thirteen books including textbooks, an award-winning novel, poetry chapbooks, and a book in Finnish. She is Trustees' Professor at Ashland University, Ashland, Ohio. She has won Individual Artists Fellowships in both poetry and fiction from the Ohio Arts Council, and consults and speaks nationally and internationally in the area of talent development education and creativity.

RICHARD S. PRAWAT is a professor of educational psychology and teacher education and chair of the Department of Counseling, Educational Psychology, and Special Education at Michigan State University. His current interest is in the teaching and learning of subject matter from a "realist constructivist" perspective.

ISAAC PRILLELTENSKY is professor of human and organizational evelopment at Peabody College of Vanderbilt University. He is the author or coeditor of five books dealing with values, wellness, power, and mental health practice.

MOLLY QUINN is associate professor at Teachers College, where she teaches courses in the foundations of education, children's literature, and the arts. The author of *Going Out, Not Knowing Whither: Education, the Upward Journey, and the Faith of Reason* (2001), much of her work engages spiritual and philosophical criticism toward embracing a vision of education that cultivates beauty, compassion, and social action.

SANDRA RACIONERO teaches sociology of education at the Universitat de Barcelona, and she is a researcher at CREA, where she is member of the coordinating team of the project Learning Communities. Her background is in educational psychology and sociology, and currently her research interests are about dialogic learning, and the creation of meaning in the learning process among at-risk students, as an avenue to overcome schooling failure.

DANIEL RHODES is a PhD student in Cultural Studies at the UNC-Greensboro. His research interests include Ecopsychology, Philosophy and Religion as well as Anarchism. He received his MSW from UNC-Chapel Hill in 1996 and has been working as a psychotherapist for the past ten years.

PATRICIA A. RIGBY earned a doctorate in educational leadership at Saint Joseph's University and is currently an Assistant Principal for Academic Affairs at Archbishop John Carroll High School in Radnor, Pennsylvania. Her research interests include teacher mentoring, spirituality in teacher induction and practice, democratic education, and theology as curriculum text.

DONYELL L. ROSEBORO received her doctorate from the University of North Carolina, Greensboro. She is an assistant professor at the University of Southern Illinois.

SABRINA N. ROSS is a doctoral candidate in Cultural Foundations in the department of Educational Leadership and Cultural Foundations at the University of North Carolina at Greensboro. Her dissertation explores relationships between specific cultural discourses and libratory education. Her research interests include critical pedagogy, African American studies, and social justice projects.

WOLFF-MICHAEL ROTH is Lansdowne professor of applied cognitive science at the University of Victoria. His cross-disciplinary research is concerned with knowing and learning science and mathematics across the life span. He has published over 200 peer-refereed articles and chapters and eleven books on teaching and learning.

DIANA RYAN is currently an assistant professor at Roosevelt University in Chicago, Illinois. She has been an International Systems Institute Research Fellow since 1993, and is a contributing editor to *Teaching & Learning: The Journal of Natural Inquiry and Reflective Practice*.

DANA SALTER is a doctoral student at McGill University in the Department of Integrated Studies in Education. Her research involves youth and gaming.

ADRIENNE SANSOM has just completed her doctorate in Education and Cultural Foundations at the University of North Carolina at Greensboro, where her focus has been on examining dance education as an approach to critical pedagogy. She is a senior lecturer in dance and drama education with the School for Visual and Creative Arts in Education, Faculty of Education, at The University of Auckland, Te Kura Akoranga o Tamaki Makaurau, in Aotearoa, New Zealand.

RUPAM SARAN recently received her doctorate from the Urban Education Program at the CUNY Graduate Center. Her area of research centers around South Asians and education in the United States.

ANGELINA VOLPE SCHALK has her master's in elementary and special education. Angel is completing her doctoral studies in educational leadership at Saint Joseph's University, and one area of research is role of teacher play in creating educational equity and opportunity for students. She currently teaches at an inclusive elementary school in Glenside, Pennsylvania.

WARREN SCHEIDEMAN is an assistant professor in the School of New Learning at DePaul University in Chicago. He is the Summit Director and teaches literacy courses.

LOIS SHAWVER is a clinical psychologist with a philosophy background who publishes on postmodernism as it relates to therapy. She is a contributing editor for the *American Journal of Psychoanalysis* and for the *New Therapist*, an external faculty member for the Virtual Faculty in New Zealand and with VIISA in Germany. She is, however, most known for her hosting of a popular online community for therapists who are interested in postmodernism and for associated online publications.

DOUGLAS J. SIMPSON is a professor and holder of the Helen DeVitt Jones Chair in Teacher Education, Texas Tech University. His academic background includes school psychology, educational theory, and curriculum philosophy. He is the author or coauthor of *John Dewey Primer* (Lang), *John Dewey and the Art of Teaching* (Sage), and *Educational Reform: A Deweyan Perspective* (Garland).

MARTA SOLER is Ramon y Cajal Researcher at the University of Barcelona, and member of the Center of Research CREA at the same university. She has a doctorate of education at Harvard, with a dissertation on dialogic reading. Among her highlighted publications is her book with John Searle *Lenguaje y ciencias sociales* and her chapter to the book *The Dialogic Self by M.C. Bertau*.

SHARON G. SOLLOWAY is an associate professor in the Department of Early Childhood and Elementary Education at Bloomsburg University, where she teaches graduate and undergraduate courses in literacy, early childhood education, and elementary curriculum. Her current research interests focus on the efficacy of mindfulness for classroom practice and social justice in the classroom.

MICHELLE STACK is an assistant professor in educational studies at UBC. Her University of Toronto/OISE doctoral research focused on the role of the media in constructing Peggy Claude-Pierre, the founder of the Montreux Center for the Treatment of Eating Disorders in British Columbia, Canada, as a miracle-worker for children and youth with anorexia nervosa.

IAN STEINBERG is completing his doctorate in communication at the School of Journalism, Columbia University. Steinberg's research interests include the political economy of information and knowledge production. Specifically, he is interested in the roles knowledge and information play in creating, maintaining, and challenging systems of social stratification. His current research is focused on the library as a place and agent of social change. He is the managing editor of *SOULS: A Critical Journal of Black Politics, Culture, and Society.*

SHIRLEY R. STEINBERG is an associate professor at the McGill University Faculty of Education. She is the author and editor of numerous books and articles and coedits several book series. The founding editor of *Taboo: The Journal of Culture and Education*, Steinberg has recently finished editing *Teen Life in Europe*, and with Priya Parmar and Birgit Richard *The Encyclopedia of Contemporary Youth Culture*. She is the editor of *Multi/Intercultural Conversations: A Reader.* With Joe Kincheloe she has edited *Kinderculture: The Corporate Construction of Childhood* and *The Miseducation of the West: How Schools and the Media Distort Our Understanding of the Islamic World.* She is coauthor of *Changing Multiculturalism: New Times, New Curriculum, and Contextualizing Teaching* (with Joe Kincheloe). Her areas of expertise and research are in critical media literacy, social drama, and youth studies.

DENNIS SUMARA is professor and head of the Department of Curriculum Studies at the University of British Columbia. Prior to his appointment at UBC in 2006, he held positions at the University of Alberta, York University, and Simon Fraser University. During the 1980s he was a classroom teacher in rural southern Alberta, specializing in middle school language arts instruction. His book, *Why Reading Literature in School Still Matters: Imagination, Interpretation, Insight* (2002) was a recipient of the National Reading Council's 2003 Ed Fry Book Award. His refereed articles have appeared in journals that include *Harvard Educational Review, Educational Theory, Qualitative Studies in Education, Journal of Curriculum Studies, Teaching Education,* and *Journal of Literacy Research.*

RICH TAPPER is an educational psychologist and learning specialist with nearly 20 years of experience as a professional teacher and seminar leader. He has worked in a variety of urban and suburban public and private schools and universities. His current research involves the application of dialogue and mindfulness to contemporary education and educational psychology.

EDWARD TAYLOR is an associate professor in adult education at Penn State Capitol College in Harrisburg, Pennsylvania. He has conducted research and written extensively on transformative learning theory. He is the author of *Transformative Learning: A Critical Review* (1998). In addition, Ed has published in *Adult Education Quarterly, The Canadian Journal of the Study of Adult Education, International Journal of Life long Education,* and *Studies in the Education of Adults.*

P. L. THOMAS is an assistant professor at Furman University in Education. The author of numerous books and articles, his area of research centers around the teaching of writing. His latest book, coauthored with Joe Kincheloe, *Reading, Writing, and Thinking: The Postformal Basics* is published with SENSE Publishers.

ELIZABETH J. TISDELL is associate professor of adult education at Penn State, Harrisburg. She received her doctorate in adult education from the University of Georgia in 1992. She is the author of *Exploring Spirituality and Culture in Adult and Higher Ed, Creating Inclusive Adult Learning Environments: Insights from Multicultural Education and Feminist Pedagogy"* and numerous book chapters and journal articles dealing with diversity and equity issues, the interconnection of spirituality and culture and their role in transformative education, and feminist pedagogy in adult and higher education.

KENNETH TOBIN is presidential professor of urban education at the Graduate Center of City University of New York. Prior to commencing a career as a teacher educator, Ken taught high school science and mathematics in Australia and was involved in curriculum design. His research interests are focused on the teaching and learning of science in urban schools, which involve mainly African American students living in conditions of poverty. A parallel program of research focuses on coteaching as a way of learning to teach in urban high schools. Recently Ken edited a *Handbook* about *Teaching and Learning Science*, coedited *Doing Educational Research* with Joe Kincheloe, and coedited *Improving Urban Science Education* with Rowhea Elmesky and Gale Seiler.

ERIC D. TORRES is a Peruvian Educator and Lawyer, with a specialization in Political Science. He currently teaches Spanish Language and Literature at Pinecrest High School, Southern Pines, North Carolina; and is a Franklin/Houston Scholar and PhD Candidate in the Educational Leadership and Cultural Foundations Program at the University of North Carolina at Greensboro. He is doing research on how national security policies affect education.

JOELLE TUTELA is a doctoral student at the CUNY Graduate Center in the Urban Education Program. She is a high school social studies teacher in Montclair, New Jersey.

ROSA VALLS is professor in the Department of Theory and History of Education in the Faculty of Pedagogy at the University of Barcelona. She is also a researcher of CREA (Centre of Research in Theories and Practices that Overcome Social Inequalities). Her main area of research is: social pedagogy, learning communities, and critical theory. She has recently coauthored *Comunidades de Aprendizaje. Transformar la educación* [*Learning Communities. Transforming education*] (2002), published with the editorial Graó.

LEILA E. VILLAVERDE is an associate professor in cultural foundations in the department of educational leadership and cultural foundations, the university of North Carolina at Greensboro. She is the coeditor of *Dismantling White Privilege; and Rethinking Intelligence* and *Rethinking Intelligence*. She also lectures on feminist theory, curriculum studies, critical pedagogy, and aesthetics.

DANNY WALSH is a doctoral student at the CUNY Graduate Center in the Urban Education Program. He is a teacher in the New York City Schools.

JOHN WEAVER is associate professor of curriculum studies at Georgia Southern University. He is the author of numerous books and articles on popular culture, critical curriculum, and youth culture. He is the author of *The Popular Culture Primer*.

ED WELCHEL is an associate professor of education at Wofford College in Spartanburg, South Carolina. He taught social studies, particularly Advanced Placement United States History, for twenty-three years in the public schools of South Carolina. In addition to his duties at Wofford College, Dr. Welchel serves as a social studies consultant to several secondary schools in the Spartanburg area. He is currently working on a book concerning the work of Howard Zinn for Paul Thomas's series, *Confronting the Text, Confronting the World: Bringing Writers into the Classroom*, to be published by Peter Lang Publishing.

PATRICIA A. WHANG, associate professor of psychological foundations at California State University Monterey Bay, critical educator, and dharma student is committed to awakening, becoming, and the asking of hard questions. May her children continue to inspire the will and reason for her commitments.